ULYSSES JENKINS

2

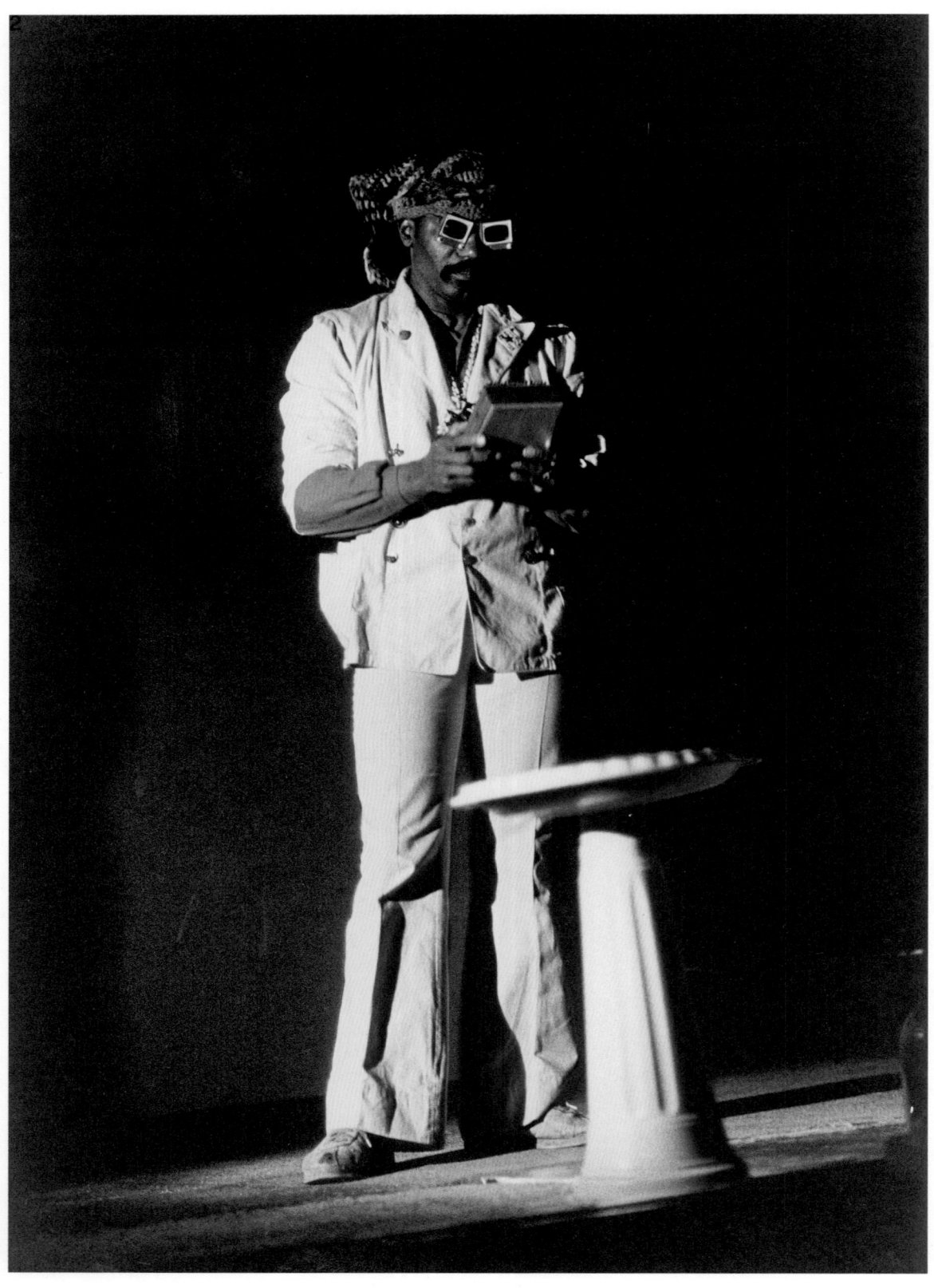

Ulysses Jenkins, *Peace and Anwar Sadat*, 1981. Performance for *Thanks but No Thanks* at the Church in Ocean Park. Courtesy of the artist. Photo: Basia.

ULYSSES JENKINS

WITHOUT YOUR INTERPRETATION

EDITED BY
ERIN CHRISTOVALE & MEG ONLI

INSTITUTE OF CONTEMPORARY ART,
UNIVERSITY OF PENNSYLVANIA / HAMMER MUSEUM

REFLECTIONS

GREG DE CUIR JR., MICHAEL BOYCE GILLESPIE, CHRISSIE ILES, AND ALESSANDRA RAENGO
TRANSMISSIONS: A ROUNDTABLE CONVERSATION
PAGE 239

LIV PORTE CHRONOLOGY
PAGE 265

EXHIBITIONS, SCREENINGS, PERFORMANCES, MURALS, AND COMMUNITY PROJECTS
PAGE 273

DISCOGRAPHY AND VIDEOGRAPHY
PAGE 278

SELECTED BIBLIOGRAPHY
PAGE 281

CONTRIBUTORS
PAGE 283

Ulysses Jenkins: Without Your Interpretation is the most comprehensive retrospective of the Los Angeles–based video and performance artist, bringing together nearly five decades of work. An innovator and beloved member of a cohort of artists who shaped the contemporary artistic landscape in Los Angeles and beyond, Ulysses Jenkins set a precedent for generations to come. From his earliest explorations into art making as a painter to his embrace of video and performance art, Jenkins has paved a unique creative path rooted in powerful collaborations, multidisciplinary collectives, and new frameworks for video, media, and the origins of digital work. Throughout his career, Jenkins has offered pointed critiques of popular media's depictions of Blackness, centered the act of solidarity within multiculturalism, and challenged political views that uphold Western imperialism. Incorporating poetry, movement, and music within his work, he has maintained a practice that is marked by early 1980s conceptualism and the origins of video as a democratic and malleable format.

Jenkins has made enormous contributions to the field of video art and to an ever-evolving Los Angeles community. His work was featured prominently in ICA's 2018 exhibition *Broadcasting: EAI at ICA*, an in-depth look at the origins and legacy of Electronic Arts Intermix, and in the Hammer's groundbreaking 2011 exhibition *Now Dig This! Art & Black Los Angeles, 1960–1980*. But a retrospective for the artist is long overdue, and it is largely through his generous collaboration, enthusiasm, and guidance that ICA and the Hammer have been able to realize a project of this magnitude.

Ulysses Jenkins: Without Your Interpretation continues ICA's and the Hammer's deep commitment to supporting artists whose work and trajectories are often lost to art historical circles and placed on the margins. Like others who have been the focus of monographic exhibitions at our respective institutions, such as Charles Gaines, Barbara Kasten, Rodney McMillian, Lari Pittman, and Cauleen Smith, Jenkins defines a practice that is rooted in both a local context—Los Angeles—and a format—video—that shifted the landscape of media-based art making.

Curators Erin Christovale and Meg Onli have been uncompromising in their efforts on behalf of this endeavor, and we are grateful to them for taking up the challenge of bringing Jenkins's powerful and expansive career to the fore. It has been a pleasure to watch the development of their creative partnership and deep commitment to Jenkins, which exemplifies true collaboration between artist and curators. The project also benefited from the adroit contributions of curatorial assistant Ikechúkwú Onyewuenyi, including a text authored for this publication.

The insightful essays for this publication situate Jenkins's practice in ways that are personal, historical, and educational, building a critical framework within which to view his work. In addition to the curatorial texts, significant contributions were provided by artists Aria Dean, David Hammons and The Charles White Archives, Maren Hassinger, Kerry James Marshall, Senga Nengudi, Cauleen Smith, and May Sun; professors Michael Boyce Gillespie and Alessandra Raengo; curators Greg de Cuir Jr. and Chrissie Iles; and art historian and curator Kellie Jones. We are grateful for the rich array of voices and perspectives they offer.

Special acknowledgment goes to Electronic Arts Intermix for generously lending the majority of Jenkins's video works. We also extend our thanks to Maren Hassinger, The Collection of Kerry James Marshall, Senga Nengudi, and May Sun for lending works to this exhibition.

We gratefully acknowledge The Pew Center for Arts & Heritage for their generous support of this project, as well as Pamela J. Joyner and Alfred J. Giuffrida, and Lyndon J. Barrois and Janine Sherman Barrois. Funding for curatorial research has been provided by The Andy Warhol Foundation for the Visual Arts and the Robert Rauschenberg Foundation. The republication of Jenkins's *Doggerel Life: Stories of a Los Angeles Griot* is made possible by the J. Paul Getty Trust.

Finally, we express our heartfelt thanks to Ulysses Jenkins for his commitment to this project and for entrusting his work with us. This exhibition has afforded ICA and the Hammer the opportunity to center the full sweep of his unparalleled and inspiring oeuvre within a greater art historical context for future scholarship.

Ann Philbin, Director, Hammer Museum

Zoë Ryan, Daniel W. Dietrich, II Director, Institute of Contemporary Art, University of Pennsylvania

Throughout his career, Ulysses Jenkins has consistently examined the detrimental impacts that racial stereotypes—particularly those broadcast through television and film—have had on people of marginalized identities. In an early treatment for his video *Inconsequential Doggereal* (1981) he writes, "We need only to ask ourselves a question: 'What about our repressed media unconscious?'" Over the past fifty years, he has wrestled with that question, among others, creating work that has engaged cutting-edge technology to transmit alternative depictions of life from the West Coast. Organized in close collaboration with the artist, *Ulysses Jenkins: Without Your Interpretation* presents the first major retrospective of his groundbreaking practice.

For the presentation at the ICA, we thank Daniel W. Dietrich, II Director Zoë Ryan, who has zealously supported the project from her arrival, and her predecessor, Amy Sadao, who said yes to this exhibition without hesitation. Daniel and Brett Sundheim Chief Curator Anthony Elms, with support by former curatorial administrative coordinator Caitlin Palmer, has been instrumental in thinking through this complex exhibition. A special shout-out to Dorothy and Stephen R. Weber (CHE'60) Curator Alex Klein, who first brought Jenkins's work to the ICA through the 2018 exhibition *Broadcasting: EAI at ICA*. The promotion of this exhibition was ably handled by director of marketing & communications Jill Katz, with digital content editor Ali Mohsen. Director of development Bruno Nouril, with associate director of development Taja Jones, assistant director of development & alumni relations Christina Yu, and development administrative coordinator Michele Pierson, provided crucial support from the project's early research phase. Thoughtful public programming came through the collaborative efforts of DAJ Director of Public Engagement James E. Britt Jr., with audio/visual coordinator Derek Rigby, program coordinator Natalie Sandstrom, and visitor services coordinator Elizabeth Chong. Administration support was overseen by director of administration Shannon Freitas, with administrative coordinator Jes Kaminski and executive assistant to the director Lauren Downing. The exhibition's installation was overseen by Marc J. Leder Director of Curatorial Affairs Robert Chaney, chief preparator & building administrator Paul Swenbeck, and registrar Kate Abercrombie. Love to officer Linda Harris for being a fantastic ambassador for the show.

For the presentation at the Hammer, we thank director Ann Philbin for her dedication in bringing this ambitious exhibition to fruition; deputy director of curatorial affairs Cynthia Burlingham and chief curator Connie Butler for their support throughout the project; and curatorial assistant Ikechúkwú Onyewuenyi for his administrative support and essay in the publication. We are beholden to director of exhibitions and publications Melanie Crader for her keen eye and guidance. Director of registration and collections management Portland McCormick, registrar Linda Yun, registrarial assistant Emma Rudman, and former registrar Jean-Ha Park coordinated the handling and care of works in the exhibition, and manager of exhibition design and production Adam Peña, alongside chief preparator Jason Pugh, helped us realize the installation. We are grateful to chief development officer Veridiana Pontes, associate director, former manager of development Hannah Howe, manager of individual giving Jessica Vrazilek, and grant writer Sara Friedman for their critical efforts in raising the necessary funds to support the exhibition. Related programming was thoughtfully created by director of public programs Claudia Bestor and her programming team. We also are indebted to the communications team, led by chief communications director Scott Tennent, with support from senior manager of public relations Nancy Lee and senior designer Tara Morris.

In 2012 the two of us, separately, came across Jenkins's work through the landmark exhibition *Now Dig This! Art & Black Los Angeles, 1960–1980*, curated by the inimitable Dr. Kellie Jones. That exhibition ushered in new scholarship and numerous shows in its wake, including this one. The utmost love, respect, and gratitude to Dr. Jones for her brilliance and generosity throughout the years and for her contribution to this publication. The beautiful book that you hold in your hands and the exhibition's identity were thoughtfully designed by ELLA: River Jukes Hudson, Stephen Serrato, and Carina Huynh. Our deepest respect to you all, as you dug deep to get into the trippy world that Jenkins has created. Within these pages are voices representing the rich community that Ulysses Jenkins has cultivated throughout his life. Our heartfelt appreciation to David Hammons and The Charles White Archives, Maren Hassinger, Dr. Jones, Kerry James Marshall, Senga Nengudi, and May Sun for the lifelong friendships and perspectives you captured in your reflections. Much gratitude to Cauleen Smith for an insightful reflection on Jenkins's impact on a younger generation of artists, and to Aria Dean for her rigorous essay, which introduced Jenkins's work to new audiences; we are so appreciative of her permission to reprint this text. Until now, there had not been a robust conversation about Jenkins's work in relationship to the history of video and cinema, and we are proud of the thoughtful roundtable conversation that Greg de Cuir Jr., Michael Boyce Gillespie, Chrissie Iles, and Alessandra Raengo realized together. Liv Porte diligently researched the extensive chronology that provides a cultural context to the works that are highlighted. We owe our sincerest appreciation for the excellent editorial work of Michelle Piranio, who was with us every step of the way. Tony Manzella of Echelon went above and beyond on the color corrections for this book—many thanks, Tony!

This exhibition and catalogue have been greatly enhanced by the labor and love of some of the artist's closest friends and colleagues. We extend our deepest gratitude to Peter Kirby, a long-term collaborator of Jenkins's who greatly assisted in the video digitization that is on view. Rosanna Albertini provided great insight into the artist's writing through her editing of his memoir *Doggerel Life*. Electronic Arts Intermix has long supported Jenkins's work, and we thank Rebecca Cleman and Karl McCool for their assistance. Nancy Buchanan answered our many queries about the Los Angeles art scene that Jenkins was a part of. Our colleagues at the Getty Research Institute LeRonn Brooks, Rebecca Peabody, and Glenn Phillips have been keen supporters at every turn. We received substantial curatorial support from a very talented crew of historians and curators. Our gratitude to Mariana Fernandez, Mara Hassan, Christal Perez, and CJ Salapare for all their contributions to this project.

Finally, our profound love and admiration goes to Ulysses Jenkins. We entered this project as longtime admirers of his pathbreaking practice without knowing the true depths and expanse of his oeuvre. His generosity and spirit are encoded in every work that he has made, and he approached this project with the same enthusiasm and openness. Though he is already an influence on numerous generations of artists, we hope this catalogue and exhibition will expand the reach of his legacy for years to come. Thank you, Ulysses, for letting us into your life.

Erin Christovale, Associate Curator, Hammer Museum

Meg Onli, Andrea B. Laporte Associate Curator, Institute of Contemporary Art, University of Pennsylvania

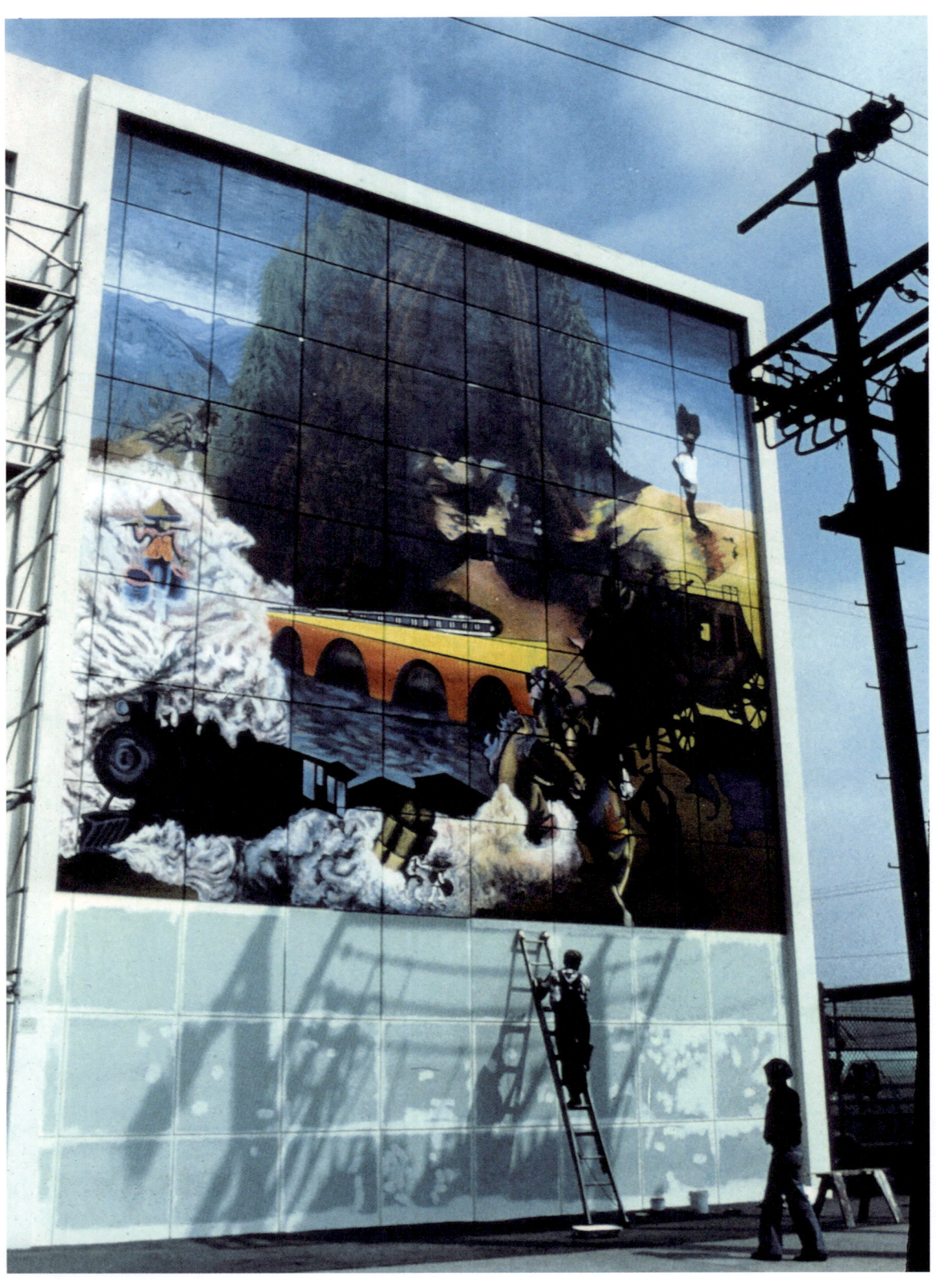

Ulysses Jenkins, *Transportation Brought Art to the People*, 1976. Mural at 3500 South Hope Street, Los Angeles, CA 90007. Commissioned by California Department of Motor Vehicles, Los Angeles Citywide Mural Program. Courtesy of the artist.

ERIN CHRISTOVALE

A
MULTICULTURAL
GRIOT

The artist Charles White famously argued that his everyday depictions of Black people were in fact universal in that they embody the deep range and core of the human condition: "I like to think that my work has a universality to it. I deal with love, hope, courage, freedom, dignity—the full gamut of human spirit."[1] In the same fashion, Ulysses Jenkins has strategically utilized the notion of multiculturalism within his practice as a means to highlight, honor, and align people of color and a variety of cultures that have historically been oppressed or nearly erased by white supremacy. Situating multiculturalism through the lens of Blackness and offering an approach rooted in collaboration, throughout his oeuvre Jenkins has opposed the apparatuses and systems of power that often regulate and muddy productive and innovative cultural exchange.

Jenkins's investment in multiculturalism stems from a deeply personal place of being a by-product of the Great Migration (his parents descend from Texas and Louisiana) and being born and raised in the cultural epicenter that is Los Angeles. Growing up, his formative years in education were shaped within the Los Angeles Unified School District (LAUSD); he attended Hamilton High School, which, at that time, was unofficially integrated but still predominantly white. Jenkins graduated from high school in 1964, the same year the Civil Rights Act was enacted, though LAUSD would not officially desegregate schools until 1976. In her 2017 book *South of Pico: African American Artists in Los Angeles in the 1960s and 1970s*, the art historian Kellie Jones outlines this tumultuous era of both integration and "white flight" throughout the city:

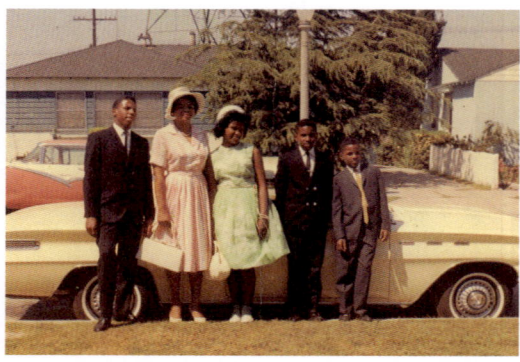

Fig. 1: Family portrait in Ulysses Jenkins's childhood neighborhood, 1962. Courtesy of the artist.

Los Angeles public schools emerged in a multicultural environment, serving Asian, Latino, African American, Native American, and white pupils. In the nineteenth century, however, California law allowed the separation of whites once there were ten or more students of color. This practice continued into the next century, with liberal transfer policies that allowed white students to leave their racially mixed district schools for those where whites were in the majority. . . . By the 1970s, Los Angeles was one of the battlegrounds in the ongoing struggle for desegregation and educational equity, reinforcing the view that education continued to be an important emblem of citizenship.[2]

Jenkins recounts this time during his childhood, growing up near Culver City on the edge of the various Hollywood studios and the larger entertainment industry while dealing with the racial implications of the time. In his memoir *Doggerel Life: Stories of a Los Angeles Griot*, he notes, "When I was a kid, the whole area around

1   Jeffrey Elliot, "Charles White: Portrait of an Artist," *Negro History Bulletin* 41, no. 3 (May–June 1978): 825.

2   Kellie Jones, *South of Pico: African American Artists in Los Angeles in the 1960s and 1970s* (Durham: Duke University Press, 2017), 12.

La Cienega and Jefferson was just open fields and they used to shoot Westerns near the vacant lots. We were the third Black family that moved in on the block (fig. 1). For the most part, the other people were Caucasian. It was sort of a welcome to the integration movement and getting to know other people from different backgrounds. That's the way that I grew up. To a certain degree, it ends up being reflected in my work."[3]

After deciding to attend college in the South and receiving his BA in fine arts (drawing and painting) in 1969 from Southern University in Baton Rouge, one of the largest

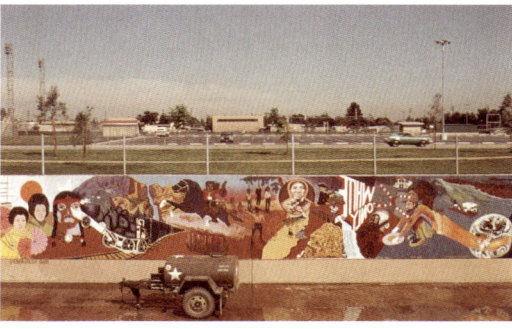

Fig. 2: *The Great Wall of Los Angeles*, 1978. Conceived by Judy Baca with SPARC. Located on the west wall of the Tujunga Wash flood control channel, Los Angeles. Courtesy of the artist.

historically Black colleges in Louisiana, Jenkins returned to Los Angeles to continue his artistic career with a focus on painting. He was inspired to take on muralism after building large-scale painted sets for skits and performances created by youth during his time as a probation officer through the Los Angeles Probation Department at Central Juvenile Hall. Other influences he would cite were the murals of East Los Angeles and alternative and anti-mural interventions performed by Asco, the Chicanx art collective; Jenkins would later go on to work with several members of the collective, including Harry Gamboa, Juan Garza, Daniel Joseph Martinez, and Patssi Valdez.[4] Shortly after his time as a probation officer, Jenkins moved to Venice and initiated and participated in mural projects across the city, including the historic *Great Wall of Los Angeles* (fig. 2), which was spearheaded by the artist Judy Baca through the Social and Public Art Resource Center (SPARC). Located in the Tujunga Wash flood control channel, the half-mile-long mural focuses on the history of California and highlights the often underrepresented figures of color who have shaped the cultural and sociopolitical landscape of the state. Recalling the several-year endeavor that was initiated in the summer of 1976, Baca described her vision for the mural: "When I first saw the wall, I envisioned a long narrative of another history of California; one which included ethnic peoples, women and minorities who were so invisible in conventional textbook accounts. The discovery of the history of California's multi-cultured peoples was a revelation to me as well as to the members of my teams.... Working toward the achievement of a difficult common goal shifted our understanding of each other and most importantly of ourselves."[5] Made with the collective efforts of artists and youth groups from various parts of the city, Jenkins's section of the mural, titled "1848 Bandaide," portrays a revisionist history of the Gold Rush era, centering figures such as Joaquín Murrieta, a legendary Mexican American outlaw who, in Jenkins's depiction, represents the dispossessed Native and Mexican communities who were violently forced off of their land. He also depicts historical Black figures such as Biddy Mason, a woman born into slavery who famously petitioned her right to freedom upon arriving

3   Ulysses Jenkins, *Doggerel Life: Stories of a Los Angeles Griot* (Los Angeles: Oreste, 2018), 10.
4   Jenkins in conversation with the author, May 2021. Martinez and Garza were members of Asco only briefly. Valdez was the makeup artist for Jenkins's *Without Your Interpretation* (1984), and Jenkins was the executive producer on two episodes of the public access television show *Theatré Twenty Two* in which Gamboa and Garza starred. Jenkins has collaborated with Martinez many times over the years, most notably in his performance *Talking Hut* (1992).
5   Erika Doss, "Raising Community Consciousness with Public Art: Contrasting Projects by Judy Baca and Andrew Leicester," *American Art* 6, no. 1 (1992): 71.

in California. She eventually founded the First African Methodist Episcopal Church in Los Angeles and became a real estate mogul in the late 1800s.

Jenkins also worked with the Brockman Gallery, helmed by the brothers Alonzo and Dale Davis, and was hired as a project manager to work with Black and Brown youth in areas such as Gardena, Inglewood, and Lawndale to generate several murals on local storefronts and city agencies. He was later invited to contribute to the sprawling Crenshaw Wall mural, a visual landmark in the historically Black neighborhood of Leimert Park that was initiated in 1974. Jenkins's contribution to the mural was titled *The Azz Izz* (1976) and featured the legendary jazz musicians Billy and Carolyn Harris, who ran a popular jazz club in Venice under the same name. Finally, Jenkins embarked upon his own large-scale mural, *Transportation Brought Art to the People* (1976), a monumental vision of the various cultural influences that have shaped California, flanked by the roaring presence of a high-speed train and the majestic stillness of a redwood tree, which doubles as two brown hands in prayer. This mural, which still holds court alongside the US 101 freeway on what was then the Department of Motor Vehicles building on Hope Street, depicts Chinese, Black, Mexican, and Native figures in cultural garb, highlighting their presence and contributions to the emergence of the transcontinental railroad, a major railway system that ultimately allowed for mass migration and trade between the East and West Coasts. These figures represent the multitude of invisible laboring bodies who ultimately did the backbreaking work to make this pivotal means of transportation possible, once again rubbing against the history of erasure and instating the advent of multiculturalism as the driver of California's excellence.

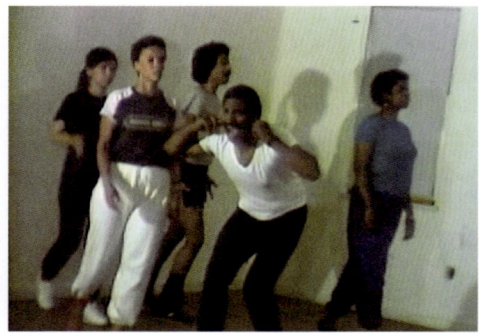

Fig. 3: Ulysses Jenkins, *Art Moves* (video still), 1983. Color, sound, 22:19 min. Courtesy of the artist and Electronic Arts Intermix.

After his stint in muralism, Jenkins eventually studied video and performance at Otis Art Institute (now Otis College of Art and Design) in the now-defunct Intermedia Department and was taught by such luminaries as Chris Burden, Carl Cheng, Betye Saar, and Charles White. Upon graduating he submitted his performance-turned-video work *Two-Zone Transfer* (1979) to the NEA and received an Individual Artist Fellowship Grant for video in 1980. A few years later, using some of the funds from a second NEA grant, Jenkins created Othervisions Studio, an "artistic outlet for multi-cultural expression" in Los Angeles.[6] The "other" aspect of the studio's philosophy was rooted in alternative and experimental forms of art making but was also a response to the lack of representation and support for artists of color from major art institutions and galleries in the city. Jenkins initiated Othervisions as a conceptual incubator in which fellow artists could workshop and collaborate on new ideas and projects. He utilized the space as both a working studio and a communal center for performance, live music, dance, and other creative endeavors. Among those who frequented Othervisions were artists Maren Hassinger, Senga Nengudi, and May Sun, as well as Rudy Perez, a noted innovator in postmodern dance who offered a series of movement workshops in the space called "Art Moves" (fig. 3). During this time, these artists produced several seminal performances that Jenkins participated in or documented through video. *Voices* (1984), which premiered at the Women's

Building in Los Angeles, was a performance written and directed by Hassinger that dealt with the
precarity of nature in an ever-evolving technological society. The piece consisted of individual voices
that represented survival, intolerance, nature (performed by Jenkins), message, and aging, and the
performers were conducted like members of an
orchestra into an interplay of monologues and a
rousing crescendo of concerns. Sun produced *The
Great Wall or How Red Is My China?* (fig. 4), a multimedia performance that debuted in 1986 at Los
Angeles Contemporary Exhibitions (LACE). *The
Great Wall* was in part a response to the mixed
feelings of a younger generation of Chinese Ameri-

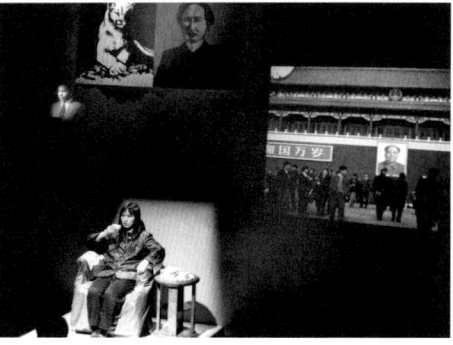

Fig. 4: May Sun, *The Great Wall or How Red Is My
China?*, 1986. Los Angeles Contemporary Exhibitions,
Los Angeles. Courtesy of the artist.

cans with regard to the Chinese Communist Party led by Mao Zedong. Sun, who deliv-
ered a riveting and comical monologue about the turbulent history, reflected upon
her own familial connections to the party, centering her two aunts who joined while
attending Yenching University in Beijing. Jenkins played the acclaimed singer and
actor Paul Robeson, who was a noted ally of Mao and who famously sang "Chee Lai!"
(or, "March of the Volunteers") in Mandarin, which eventually became the national
anthem for the party.

    Aside from participating in and facilitating other artists' projects, Jenkins pro-
duced several works during the formation of Othervisions Studio. Inspired by teaching
alongside Allan Kaprow during a brief stint as an assistant professor of video production at the University of California, San Diego, Jenkins integrated the concept of
Happenings into his work, orchestrating multilayered, large-scale performances and
bridging together artists from various cultural backgrounds and practices. *Dream City*
(1981) was a performance that took place over the course of nearly twenty-four hours
at the dancer Rachel Rosenthal's studio, culminating in a midnight celebration of his
thirty-fifth birthday.[7] *Dream City* showcased a variety of artists and performers who,
over the course of the day, were invited to take the stage and embark upon improvisational or premeditated performances. Jenkins would intermittently intervene
between acts, presenting himself as a griot, enacting various rituals and dreamscapes
throughout the durational performance. As Nengudi later reflected, "Maren, Ulysses,
and I were in the space for 24 hours. So, what happened is artists like Nobuko Miyamoto and various others would come in to perform, but we were the constants. It was
important that when all this stuff was happening with the institutions, we as people
of color were working together: Japanese, Chinese, Latino, and African American. We
were actually working together, and that was really exciting, sharing our cultures."[8]

    Jenkins was also deeply invested in the plight and ongoing struggle of Indig-
enous peoples. In an artist statement written in 1995, he proclaimed, "The invisible made visible <u>American Apartheid</u>: A practice made apparent by the reduction of
Native American heritage by business to mascot and symbol for consumption by the

6   Othervisions mission statement, circa 1995. Artist's
archive, Los Angeles.
7   The performance was later turned into Jenkins's
video *Dream City* (1983).
8   Allie Tepper, "Individual Collective: A Conversation
with Senga Nengudi," in *Side by Side: Collaborative Artistic*

Practices in the United States, 1960s–1980s, ed. Gwyneth
Shanks and Allie Tepper, Vol. 3 of the *Living Collections
Catalogue* (Minneapolis: Walker Art Center, 2020), https://
walkerart.org/collections/publications/side-by-side
/individual-collective-a-conversation-with-senga-nengudi.

colonizing culture. Politicians debate reconciliation amongst the races yet rarely do they mention in these discussions anything about Native peoples unless it concerns denying assistance, manipulating into storing nuclear waste on reservations, spilling of oil in sacred fishing areas and denying the right to fish and hunt."[9] Jenkins centered the ongoing erasure and violence inflicted upon Indigenous peoples in various performances and video works, including *Columbus Day: A Doggereal* (1980), *Bay Window* (1991), and *Being Witness: Haida* (1992). *Columbus Day: A Doggereal*, performed at LACE on Columbus Day (now reclaimed as Indigenous Peoples' Day), came to fruition only a few short years after the height of activism by the American Indian Movement and spoke to the ongoing genocide of Native Americans. The performance piece Jenkins created took place within a multimedia environment that featured a vintage lawn mower encircled by a barrier of soil and propped atop a palm tree trunk. Unbeknownst to the audience, Jenkins had placed a dead squirrel inside the trunk, which eventually filled the gallery with an inescapable stench of rotting flesh. While the squirrel's decomposing carcass represented the Indigenous peoples who had lost their lives to colonial violence, the lawn mower symbolized the brute gestures of imperialism, unmercifully mowing down anything in its path.

Shortly after moving to the Bay Area, Jenkins attended the annual Unthanksgiving Day or the Indigenous People's Sunrise Ceremony that is held on Alcatraz to commemorate the 1969 protest in which members from the Red Power movement occupied the island. During this time he also produced *Bay Window*, a performance event that took place at the Exploratorium in San Francisco, where he was part of the museum's artist research program. Jenkins utilized the videophone, an early teleconferencing technology that could transmit video and audio signals to multiple users who could see and interact with each other in real time. *Bay Window* centered environmental justice and the reclamation of land, and included performance, poetry, and music in front of a live audience. Uniting several artists and Indigenous groups up and down the West Coast with a technology that would precede the likes of Zoom or FaceTime, *Bay Window* comprises a multitude of happenings, including documentation of the Coast Miwok people at Point Reyes during their annual Acorn Festival; spoken word by L. Frank Manriquez (Tongva/Ajachmem), based in Santa Monica; and a conversation with Reg Davidson and Jim Hart, two prominent Native carvers from Haida Gwaii, off the coast of British Columbia. The following year, while in residence at the Headlands Center for the Arts, Jenkins produced *Being Witness: Haida,* a cinema verité–style documentary in which he followed and interviewed Davidson and Hart. The video opens with the omnipresent voice of Davidson overlaid with a still image of meandering clouds and a bright blue sky: "We spent the last five hundred years listening to Europeans on their ways of life and doing things and what they've done to the Earth. Now it's their turn to listen to us, the way we looked after it before they came and did what they did." Jenkins documents the two men's individual processes of carving a totem pole and a sea canoe, highlighting the sacred rituals and generational practices that have shaped their work, culminating in a public reception and ceremony surrounding the objects.

The utilization of multiculturalism as a national ideal and collective marker has received ongoing criticism within political and scholarly circles alike, and the

9   Ulysses Jenkins, artist statement, 1995. Artist's archive, Los Angeles.

question of who benefits from this identity has been complicated by its fraught history of being instrumentalized by governing bodies and cultural agencies time and again. The use of the term in the 1990s, flanked by the aftermath of the Reaganomics era and the onset of the culture wars, marked it as a failed project in an attempt to elicit a picture of the nation as a unified front as opposed to the reality of a fractured and complex society marked by cultural differences and helmed by Western imperialism. The interdisciplinary scholar Lisa Lowe, in *Immigrant Acts: On Asian American Cultural Politics*, writes, "If the nation proposes American culture as the key site for the resolution of inequalities and stratifications that cannot be resolved on the political terrain of representative democracy, then that culture performs that reconciliation by naturalizing a universality that exempts the 'non-American' from its history of development or admits the 'non-American' only through a 'multiculturalism' that aestheticizes ethnic differences as if they could be separated from history."[10] What does it mean, though, when the term is utilized, practiced, and documented through a Black radical imaginary? How does this imaginary propose a universalism that differs from a faux universalism typically handed down to people of color in an attempt to quell the injustices and oppression that are inflicted upon them? How can the term be reclaimed or appropriated for liberatory use, as a way to truly unite and build solidarity among communities and cultures marked by their own individual histories?

These are the questions that center Jenkins's practice and his ongoing pursuit of laying bare the sociopolitical issues of our time and creating space and platforms for a vibrant community of California artists who have survived on the margins, only to be accepted by the institution decades later, if that. In *Doggerel Life* Jenkins writes of his beloved comrades:

> Their worthiness was not always considered significant, kept under the shadow of an uncharted matrix for artists of color in the face of the pretentiousness asserted and reflected by insensitive, mainstream depictions of multiculturalism, at the time due to the honorarium attached to commissioned, multicultural opportunists. We played and paid no attention to our cultural differentials as a divarication; rather myself and my associates continued to greatly benefit. The acceptance of multiculturalism professes the true cultural importance of our shared reality. Premises of multiculturalism will sustain and nurture the evolution of our society, to develop new genres of artistic expression based upon the visions of all sectors of our society. This has been our benefit to behold and mine to pronounce.[11]

Jenkins would later go on to create works such as *The Video Griots Trilogy* (1989–91), a three-part exploration of the African diaspora that considers the interconnectedness of Native and African American histories and the origins and cultural influences of East African communities, and *Bequest* (2002), a direct response to the xenophobia experienced by Middle Eastern women post-9/11. Jenkins's ongoing desire to explore, connect, and provide education around the various cultures and backgrounds that have shaped him speaks to a multicultural griot whose practice is rooted in collaboration, collectivity, and the possibility of an emancipatory future.

10   Lisa Lowe, *Immigrant Acts: On Asian American Cultural Politics* (Durham: Duke University Press, 1996), 9.   11   Jenkins, *Doggerel Life*, 148–49.

THE NATURE OF DOGGEREL

MY WORK CAN BE BEST DESCRIBED AS ''INTER-MEDIA''. AN ART FORM WHICH USES
AND MANIPULATES ALL AVAILABLE MEDIUMS TO EXPRESS THE DESIRED ARTISTIC EXPRESSION;
EVEN THOUGH THE   MAJOR AREA OF CONCERN HAS BECOME A CONCEPTUAL AXIOM. AXIOLOGY
THEREFORE DETERMINES THE CONTEXTUAL USE OF WHICH PROCESS WILL EXAMPLIFY THE ARTIST
CREATIVITY. MY WORK, ALSO, IS A DIDACTICAL MULIT-LAYERED CONTENT: EXPERIMENTAL,
DOCUMENTARY AND NARRARIVE, YET MY STRUCTURE IS DOGGEREL; IT IS CONTEMPLATION.

THE WEAVING OF A SYMBOLOGY WHICH UTILIZES THE RITUAL FORMAT FROM THE EAST
AFRICAN SOCIETY (NUBIAN), THAT OF SOCIAL CRISIS AND SURVIVAL. WHERE THE ISSUES ARE
PRESENTED TO THE COMMUNITY AT LARGE (THE TOWN HALL) FOR EXAMINATION AND UNDERSTANDING.
MY CONCEPTUAL CONCERNS ARE INTRICATELY CREATED WITHIN THE TECHNICAL FORMS OF THE VIDEO
PROCESS AND THE ASSOCIATED DISCIPLINES OF PERFROMANCE ART.

I HAVE COMPOSED AN EVOLVING SEQUENCE OF RITUALS, WHICH ARE IN CONSTANT STATE
OF METAMORPHOSIS. THE RITUALS ARE CONCERNED WITH SOCIAL CRISIS AND SURVIVAL, WHICH
UTLILIZE OUR SOCIETIES TECHNOLOGIES AS AN INTRICATE PART OF THE MANIFESTATION OF THE
HARDWARE VERSUS SOFTWARE CONSCIOUSNESS; MAKE REFERENCES THAT ARE INDIGENOUSLY :
''AFRO-AMERICAN UNIVERSALITY''. SO, MY WORK CAN BE CONSIDERED ALSO AS A TRANSLATION
IN CROSS-CULTUAL EXPERIENCES AND COMMUNICATIONS.

THIS CREATIVE AND UNIQUE DIALOGUE : MY DOGGEREAL : WHERE METAPHORS EXPAND
AND ASK QUESTIONS OF THEMSELVES AND OURSELVES; AS WELL AS, THE WORLD IN WHICH WE LIVE.
I CONSIDER THE GENRE THAT I MOST REPRESENT IS A VISUAL ARTIST/VIDEO-PERFORMANCE ARTIST.

YOURS TRULY,

ULYSSES S. JENKINS JR.

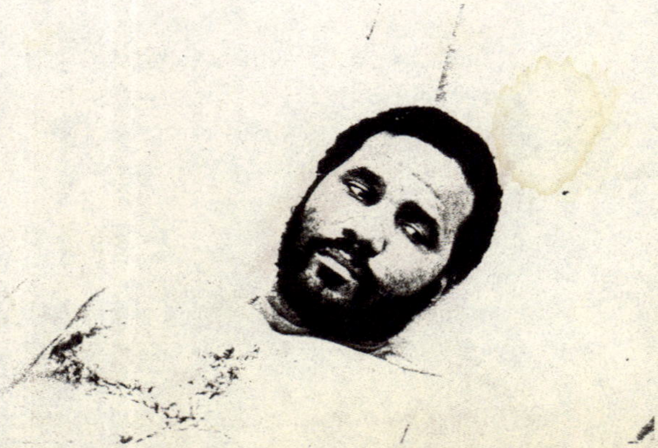

Ulysses Jenkins, "The Nature of Doggerel," 1985, artist's writing.

MEG ONLI

DOGGEREAL LIFE

"When the film *Superman* came out, I was reading in the calendar section an interview with [Marlon] Brando about what it was like playing Superman's father and he said he really liked those doggerel moments. And I said, 'doggerel moments? What the fuck is he talking about?'"
— Ulysses Jenkins[1]

Ulysses Jenkins and I have had a running joke since we first met in 2018, which I still do not fully understand and yet, for years now, have avoided asking for any clarification. It happened over lunch at a small cafeteria on the campus of the University of California, Irvine, where Jenkins has taught since 1993. We were meeting because Erin Christovale had put us in touch, and unbeknownst to him, I was there to begin conversations about organizing a retrospective of his work. I was convinced, and I guess we convinced him, that Erin and I were well suited to undertake this show—we're both Black, we're both from Los Angeles, we both work with video. More crucially, we saw that the work he was making in the early 1980s and 1990s anticipated that of many of the emerging artists we were working with today. For me, Jenkins's art was weird, wild, and ahead of its time. He was an overlooked figure whose practice required and deserved deeper examination, from his use of videophone technology that could connect him across geographical boundaries—a precursor to the technology we use today for Zoom and Face Time—to his dedication to working with a diverse collective of collaborators. I told him all of this over lunch. As he accepted the accolades that I was bestowing upon him, he pivoted—not uncommon for the artist, who, even though he is the star of many of his works, is at times surprisingly shy—and asked me, being that I lived in Philadelphia, if I liked Sun Ra. Certainly I did. He proceeded to tell me about the first time he saw Sun Ra and his Arkestra perform at the Club Lingerie in Los Angeles. It was in 1985, with David Hammons, and prior to the show Jenkins had taken acid while watching Terry Gilliam's *Time Bandits*.[2] While the Arkestra performed, Sun Ra pulled Jenkins onstage and invited him to dance and perform. The story there gets a bit blurry, as acid trips tend to, but he ended with what seemed like a punch line to a joke that hadn't been told: "If you ever take acid, keep your pants on!" That was the final thing he said to me that day as we departed, and it became a quasi-running joke the first year we got to know each other. Advice from an elder passed on to another generation.

In recalling this first encounter with Ulysses Jenkins, I was reminded of the final scenes in his video *Inconsequential Doggereal* (1981). The video is a barrage of visual stimuli, but at the end Jenkins is the central focus. He's cast himself as the griot,[3] and we find our traveling poet walking in a foggy field in San Diego, dressed in white chinos and what looks to be a maroon Members Only jacket. He is casually tossing a football over his head and catching it, until he comes to a stop and poses with one

1   Jenkins in conversation with the author, January 1, 2021.
2   In 1985 Hammons would design a stage (in collaboration with Angela Valerio and Jerry Barr) for the performance program "Art on the Beach" in Manhattan's Battery Park City. The porch of his "bottle cap shack," titled *Delta*

Spirit, functioned as a stage that would host the blues singer Willie Mae Wright, along with Sun Ra & the Solar Arkestra.
3   A member of a class of traveling poets, musicians, and storytellers who maintain a tradition of oral history in parts of West Africa.

hand on his hip while the other cradles the football. The swirling strings and horns of William Kraft's orchestral composition *Contextures: Riots-Decade '60* (1967–68) provide the scene's soundtrack.[4] As the orchestra reaches the crescendo, all of Jenkins's clothing vanishes, leaving him completely naked, with the football still at his hip (fig. 1). Although this might be alarming to some, the griot is unfazed, proceeding to pick dandelions and blowing on the flowers to scatter their seeds. The work ends with Jenkins placing a flower behind his ear and walking toward the camera before a quick cut of the moon takes the viewer to the end credits.

Inconsequential Doggereal is one in a series of early works—along with the performances *Columbus Day: A Doggereal* (1980) and *Adams Be Doggereal* (1981)—that exemplify Jenkins's interest in metaphor and ritual and that employ the strategy of "doggerelism."[5] As the epigraph above illuminates, Jenkins came across the term *doggerel* through popular media, and it piqued his interest. With origins dating to the fifteenth century, the word describes a type of verse that is "loosely styled and irregular in measure especially for burlesque or comic effect" or verse "marked by triviality or inferiority."[6] When he first encountered the word in 1978, Jenkins understood the arrhythmic nature

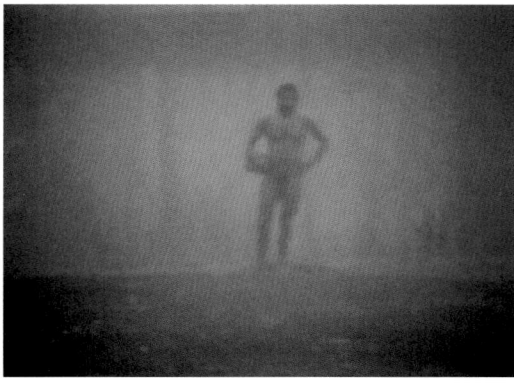

Fig. 1: Ulysses Jenkins, *Inconsequential Doggereal* (video still), 1981. Video transferred to DVD, color, sound, 15:19 min. Courtesy of the artist and Electronic Arts Intermix.

and "bad comedy" seen in doggerel to be reflective of the lives of Black Americans. Because of this, he adapted the spelling to be "doggereal" in order to emphasize the lived reality of the oppressed.[7] By 1990, when he wrote his memoir *Doggerel Life: Stories of a Los Angeles Griot*, Jenkins would explicitly use the word as a methodology for his practice and would come to think of the term as a kind of ethos of the artist communities (particularly Studio Z and Othervisions) in which he practiced. In *Doggerel Life* he writes:

> I saw "doggerel" ... as an expression encouraging humble possibilities. This loose and poor style seemed adaptable as mocking adoration, a humorous adornment for a group of artists and their activities spurned by the mainstream "avant-garde." When our group's function began its evolution as art-world like entropic entities, this period of multi-cultural expressions made itself evident ... and the High became Low as the Last became First.[8]

4   This goes beyond the scope of this essay, but while researching *Inconsequential Doggereal* I could not help but notice the common theme of death that is around this work, but not directly of the work. Jenkins has mentioned that he was thinking about the murder of John Lennon while making this video. (Ulysses Jenkins, *Doggerel Life: Stories of a Los Angeles Griot* [Los Angeles: Oreste, 2018], 87.) I might argue that it is the first major video made after the death of Jenkins's mentor Charles White. Finally, Kraft's *Contextures: Riots-Decade '60* premiered on the day of Martin Luther King Jr.'s assassination and would forever be linked to that event, so much so that a portrait of King was on the cover of the album.

5   Jenkins relates doggerelism to the traditions of Dadaism and Surrealism.

6   *Merriam-Webster's Collegiate Dictionary*, s.v. "doggerel," accessed May 8, 2021, https://unabridged.merriam-webster.com/collegiate/doggerel.

7   *Adams Be Doggereal* and *Columbus Day: A Doggereal* are sometimes spelled with *Doggerel*. Jenkins would switch his spelling to "Doggerel" for clarity for the viewer.

8   Jenkins, *Doggerel Life*, 6.

For Jenkins, his group of collaborators moved along their own irregular path outside of the mainstream (read: white and New York–centric) art world, making art at the edge of the Pacific Ocean. Doubly marginalized both as people of color and as artists creating outside of a marketplace that could define or limit their work, the "humble possibilities" that Jenkins writes of would come to have major impacts on the broader culture. Within his own practice, Jenkins's deep explorations of doggerel would lead him to produce a seminal work within his oeuvre, whose dizzying editing techniques and disappearing wardrobe would set the tone for his practice moving forward.

In a small way, *Inconsequential Doggereal* was made in response to advice given to Jenkins by the groundbreaking video artist Nam June Paik.[9] While a visiting lecturer at the University of California, Los Angeles, Jenkins met Paik and showed him a tape of his work *Two-Zone Transfer* (1979). Paik saw promise in the video, which depicts a fever dream with thick hazy visuals of a quasi-minstrel show turned church service turned James Brown concert. He encouraged the then young artist to try and capture his audience's attention within the first seconds of the work.[10] Emboldened by Paik's advice and a new teaching gig at the University of California, San Diego, Jenkins set out to create a new video that not only would allow him to teach video editing techniques but also, more important, would serve as a visualization of his notion of doggerel.

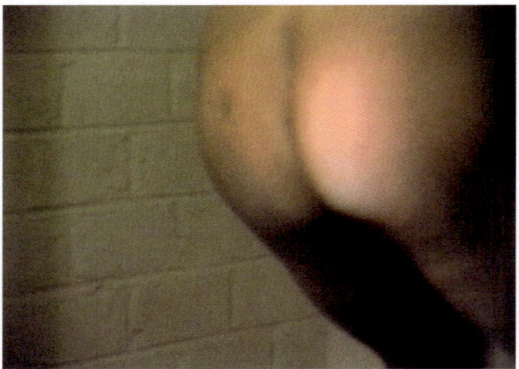

Fig. 2: Ulysses Jenkins, *Inconsequential Doggereal* (video still), 1981. Video transferred to DVD, color, sound, 15:19 min. Courtesy of the artist and Electronic Arts Intermix.

Inconsequential Doggereal opens with what seems to be found audio and some video of a program on the big bang theory, chopped and screwed. We then see Jenkins shirtless, drinking what seems to be an uncomfortably hot cup of liquid.[11] He grimaces in pain as he swallows—a metaphor for the cup of life. Before we can process these events, a lawn mower is shown on-screen as Jenkins lies down in front of it. The lawn mower (one appeared in *Columbus Day: A Doggereal* as well) symbolizes Western imperialism's way of mowing down Black, Indigenous, and people of color around the world. Jenkins's performance in *Inconsequential Doggereal* exudes a kind of resignation toward the impending violence of the lawn mower. We even see him gesture to its operator that he is ready to be pulverized by the machine's blades. But before he meets his fate, the video jumps to Jenkins naked, wagging his ashy ass at the camera (fig. 2). It's the kind of taunting scene one encounters at the end of a Looney Tunes sketch when the Road Runner has outwitted Wile E. Coyote, yet again.

This opening sequence is reminiscent of Jenkins's video *Mass of Images* (1978), which deals with similar themes of the media's role in constructing devastating stereotypes of Black Americans in film and television.[12] Melvin Van Peebles's 1971 film *Sweet Sweetback's Baadasssss Song*—which is often considered the first major Blaxploitation

9   Jenkins in conversation with the author, January 1, 2021.
10   Jenkins, *Doggerel Life*, 70.

11   I use the phrase "seems to be" often when describing the events of this video, as Jenkins's editing strategy intentionally disrupts the viewer's ability to fully capture what is happening in each scene.

film—had an influence on Jenkins, who was interested in creating images of Black life that contrasted with those depicted in mainstream media. In *Mass of Images* Jenkins repeats: "You're just a mass of images you've gotten to know / from years and years of TV shows. / The hurting thing; the hidden pain / was written and bitten into your veins / I don't and I won't relate / and I think for some it's too late!" *Mass of Images* follows a linear narrative, depicting Jenkins's "id" (as emblazoned on his T-shirt) wearing sunglasses on top of a clear plastic bowl that covers his face. He is in a wheelchair, holding a sledgehammer, and moves throughout an installation of television sets while stills from D. W. Griffith's *Birth of a Nation* and images of Al Jolson in *The Jazz Singer*, the minstrel performer Burt Williams, and numerous stereotyped characters from film and television appear on the screen. As the id continues to repeat the line "You're just a mass of images you've gotten to know. . .," the video builds to a climax that we expect to end with Jenkins smashing the televisions with the sledgehammer. Instead, he turns his attention toward the camera—and us, the viewers—and as he brings the sledgehammer close, the video cuts to hand-drawn credits. In both *Mass of Images* and *Inconsequential Doggereal*, Jenkins is pointed in his critique of the media, while slyly noting that its grasp is inescapable. Neglecting to wield his sledgehammer in one video, he shakes his ass in the other, a symbol that we, the viewer, can "kiss his Black ass."[13]

If *Mass of Images* dealt with the blatantly racist images we have all consumed, *Inconsequential Doggereal* engages with the images buried within the unconscious. In a treatment for the work written in 1982, Jenkins proclaims, "We need only to ask ourselves a question; 'What about our repressed media unconscious?,' which has always been collecting or concealing images, construed from everyday LIFE."[14] For Jenkins, the repressed media images we have ingested are filled with symbols and directives guiding our relationships with friends and lovers. All of these images are collaged throughout *Inconsequential Doggereal*, building up layers and carrying some symbols throughout the video. In particular, a football is seen in most of the scenes shot by Jenkins, serving as a stand-in for care or an object of great affection. When passed from one lover to the other, it takes on an absurdist effect of a dream attempting to process the day's events but conflating them instead, leaving the dreamer to parse out meaning from seemingly meaningless moments.

Structurally, the work is the first video in which Jenkins attempted to exercise his notions of doggerel formally. He has described the video, with its bifurcation of narratives, as a "kinetic structural connection between narrative and fictional concepts."[15] The visuals of that intersection produce the video equivalent of vertigo. *Inconsequential Doggereal* takes the viewer through a nonlinear journey of the visual detritus found on television at that time—news segments, animated graphics, and commercials—and recontextualizes them with several stories shot by Jenkins. The aim of the project was to inundate the viewer with all the symbolism and metaphors that we take in daily through our consumption of television programs—and, for a contemporary audience, through our computers, phones, and tablets. Composed of dozens of disruptions, the fifteen-minute video has the pacing of a person who has

12   The poet Anaïs Duplan offers a great reading on Jenkins's work—particularly *Inconsequential Doggereal* and *Mass of Images*—as well as that of Black video artists Tony Cokes and Lawrence Andrews, in their essay "Communication after Refusal: The Turn to Love and Polyvocality," in *Blackspace: On*

the Poetics of an Afrofuture (Boston: Black Ocean, 2020), 11–22.
13   Jenkins in conversation with the author, May 20, 2021.
14   *Inconsequential Doggereal* treatment, June 21, 1982. Artist's archive, Los Angeles.
15   Jenkins, *Doggerel Life*, 89.

just received their learner's permit. Footage sputters forward before reversing, coming to a stop, reversing again and again, before moving forward, now backward, and then cutting to something entirely unrelated. It's not unlike channel surfing, but what sets this work apart is its unorthodox rhythm, which is punctuated by a soundtrack that was created by editing the forward and backward sound effects to emphasize the motion.

Jenkins's encounter with the term *doggerel* was while he was a student at Otis Art Institute (now Otis College of Art and Design). During that time, he studied with the performance artist Chris Burden, who had just completed his series *The TV Commercials* (1973–77), which introduced the artist to a wider Los Angeles public. The four commercials—*TV Ad: Through the Night Softly; Poem for L.A.; Chris Burden Promo;* and *Full Financial Disclosure* (fig. 3), all paid for and produced by the artist—were interventions into what Burden has described as "the omnipotent stranglehold of the airwaves that broadcast television had."[16] Burden's intention was to disrupt the regularly scheduled programming by running one of his commercials, in which his performance varied from rolling on the floor on broken glass to reading poetry he saw written across the Los Angeles streets. I mention Burden's work with television, of which Jenkins was aware, as a means of contrasting Jenkins's approach to a very similar topic.[17] For Burden, the acts of purchasing the commercial spot and co-opting the platform are central to the concept of *The TV Commercials*. For these works, the medium is the message and the viewers at home are an unwitting audience.

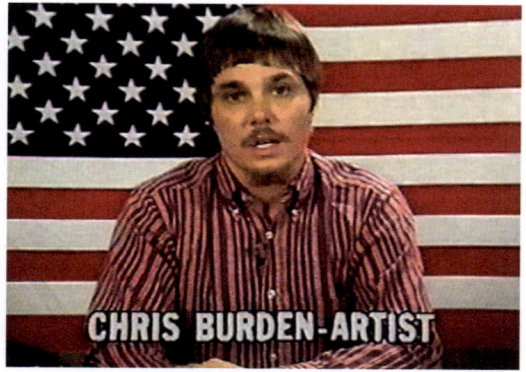

Fig. 3: Chris Burden, *Full Financial Disclosure*, 1977. © 2021 Chris Burden / licensed by The Chris Burden Estate and Artists Rights Society (ARS), New York. Courtesy of Electronic Arts Intermix (EAI), New York.

Jenkins's *Inconsequential Doggereal*, by contrast, was created for the purpose of a video-ritual, the result of which is akin to a purge or an exorcism of the imagery and messaging we consume, process, and, on a subconscious level, store in our minds. Its length and experimental nature made it "unfit" for mainstream television even though these techniques would soon be picked up in music videos. Of the video-ritual Jenkins wrote, "Re-appropriation became clearer for me, not only reclaiming a conceptual process—not unlike what Picasso had done—but also reinventing metaphors out of the medium's message commercials, the communication dogma of our time."[18] The work's creation came only a year after Jenkins's graduation from Otis, and one can read the influence of numerous professors on the work, not just that of Burden.[19] The artist Betye Saar has explored rituals throughout her entire career, authoring numerous poems addressing the notion of rituals and creating spiritual altars. In 1980, as Jenkins was working on *Inconsequential Doggereal*, Saar opened an exhibition titled *Rituals* at the Studio

16   Chris Burden, "The TV Commercials," Electronic Arts Intermix, https://www.eai.org/titles/the-tv-commercials-1973-1977.
17   In 1986 Jenkins joined South Bay Cablevision, where he would produce public access television for viewers in Gardena, California. Most notable of the works that remain from this time is *Theatré Twenty Two*, a collaboration with Harry Gamboa and Juan Garza of the Chicano artist collective Asco. Also of note is his *#9* series, which featured the bands Fat and Fucked Up, Primal Synthesis, and The Last Minstrel Show from Below the Underground. Jenkins would later leave the station when complaints came in that he was centering too many artists from Los Angeles.
18   Jenkins, *Doggerel Life*, 70.

Museum in Harlem. Ever an influence, ritual would be an aspect of almost all of Jenkins's work, throughout his career, typically as a means of connecting his performing as the griot to an audience. He was attracted to performing rituals as a way to decenter Western forms of engagement and to center those from the diaspora. Jenkins's use of technology as a form of ritual—something we take for granted every day—would allow him to connect with people across the imperialist construction of borders.

Behind Jenkins's performances and videos is a lifelong writing practice.[20] Almost every work—including unrealized projects—has a treatment, and for some works his archive also includes storyboards, choreography notes, stage design, and lyrics. In the case of *Inconsequential Doggereal*, there is both a treatment and a signed and dated text, "The Nature of Doggerel" (page 18), which includes an image of Jenkins shirtless and looking forlorn—most likely shot while *Inconsequential Doggereal* was being filmed. "The Nature of Doggerel" was written in 1985—years after he made his series of Doggereal works. What I find particularly revealing about this text is that Jenkins is still attempting to express his ideas about doggerelism to a wider audience. If *Inconsequential Doggereal* was a demonstration of his doggerel technique, "The Nature of Doggerel" allowed him a moment to reflect on the broader influence of the strategy within his practice. Most likely this text was part of a grant application, but as it stands alone now in Jenkins's archive, the text acts as a manifesto of his affinity for the doggerel. Even at this early stage of his career, Jenkins conveys the multitude of forms that his practice uses—experimental, documentary, and narrative—and he understands these works as an "evolving sequence of rituals, which are in [a] constant state of metamorphosis . . . where metaphors expand and ask questions of themselves and ourselves; as well as, the world in which we live."[21]

Recently, I called Jenkins to discuss some discrepancies I was noticing while compiling a videography of his work. The accuracy of dates has never been an interest or a strong suit of mine, and I thought at the time that this was the case with him as well (I would come to find that this was not an inaccurate assumption). In undertaking this exhibition with Erin, I came to realize that *Ulysses Jenkins: Without Your Interpretation* would have to set a semi-official record of the history of his work. Or at a minimum we should at least know when works of his were completed. I asked him why *Remnants of the Watts Festival* was shot in 1972 and 1973 but compiled in 1980; why *Dream City* was performed in 1981 but the video is dated 1983; and why *Cake Walk: A Performance by Houston Conwill* (fig. 4) was documented in 1983 but completed in 1989.[22] "It was all about access," he would tell me over the phone. "You gotta remember that we didn't have the editing software that you all have today, and as Black video artists we had way less access than the white artists at the time. Anytime you see a gap

19   Jenkins was also highly influenced by his former professors Charles White—subject of the video *Momentous Occasions: The Spirit of Charles White* (1977/1982)—Gary Lloyd, and Ilene Segalove. Media scholar Gene Youngblood's theory of expanded cinema, which is a definitive book for experimental moving-image work of the time, is also reflected in so much of *Inconsequential Doggereal*.
20   Jenkins's earliest writings date back to 1977, for a script-writing course at Santa Monica College. The script he wrote, "In Order to Better Understand: Excuse Me; In Order to

Better Understand Our Troubled World," reveals an affinity for doggerel writing even before Jenkins came across the term.
21   Ulysses Jenkins, "The Nature of Doggerel" (artist's writing, 1985).
22   *Cake Walk: A Performance by Houston Conwill* would be completed with support from the National Endowment for the Arts Fellowship, the California Arts Council, and the Long Beach Museum of Art's Video Access Program, which provided editing equipment at the museum's site.

in the years, you can assume that I didn't have
the proper equipment to finish that work.
Peter Kirby would change all of that for me
and that is why I still work closely with him.
It wasn't until I met him that I could get my
work done in a timely fashion." [23] I had always
understood doggerelism to be a methodology
that Jenkins ascribes to in order to center
experimentation and alternative narrative
structures in his work. I could see where an
irregular rhythm and comedic form would
appeal to an artist as musically inclined and
cheeky as he is. Now, however, I was seeing
the lived reality of him being a Black video
artist at the dawn of the medium's use in contemporary art.

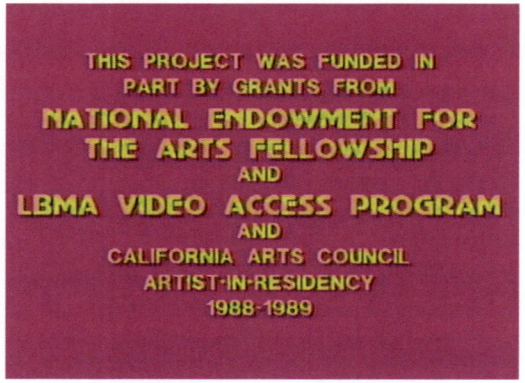

Fig. 4: Ulysses Jenkins, *Cake Walk: A Performance by Houston
Conwill* (video still), 1983/1989. Video transferred to DVD,
color, sound, 26:26 min. Courtesy of the artist and Electronic
Arts Intermix.

I have worked extensively with the concept of Colored People's Time (CPT).[24]
The Black vernacular phrase is partly political performance to trouble capitalism's
enforcement of productivity, efficiency, and timeliness while also being an inside joke
among kinfolk. CPT allows Black people to move at a temporality determined by our
own internal rhythms and not by the clock. CPT laughs in the face of white supremacy. I have always understood CPT, which originated on plantations in antebellum
America, to also speak to the plethora of delays that we as Black people experience
with regard to reparations, justice, and access to the wealth and support that white
Americans have. Doggerelism functions in a similar manner, acting both as a noun
and as a temporal space.

After Jenkins and I spoke about the variations in dates and the temporal dis-
sonance of his works, I turned to one final question I had around the accuracy of a
performance's description. Curating is sometimes about connecting an artist's practice to larger historical movements or conceptual ideas. But it is also asking mundane
questions that provide clarity around a work of art. I had noticed a discrepancy in the
duration of the performance *Dream City* (1981). This performance, which started on
September 18 (Senga Nengudi's birthday) and continued until Jenkins's birthday on
the 19th, is often cited as a twenty-four-hour performance. However, in the treatment
for *Dream City* he mentioned the duration as being eighteen hours. Which was it? We
calculated the timing of the performance, beginning at 6 am and continuing until
about 3 am the following morning, so about twenty-one hours. "That's in doggerel
hours," he said with laughter. "Is that your final answer?" I quipped. To which he
responded, "Yeah, I suppose," with a pause. "My whole life's trip is doggerel."

23   Jenkins in conversation with the author, May 12, 2021.
Director and editor Peter Kirby has run Media Art Services,
which provides research and production of media compo-
nents for museums, galleries, and artists, since 1989. He
was an integral collaborator in making *Ulysses Jenkins:*
Without Your Interpretation happen.
24   For more on CPT, see Meg Onli and Amber Rose
Johnson, eds., *Colored People Time* (Philadelphia: Institute
of Contemporary Art, University of Pennsylvania, 2020).

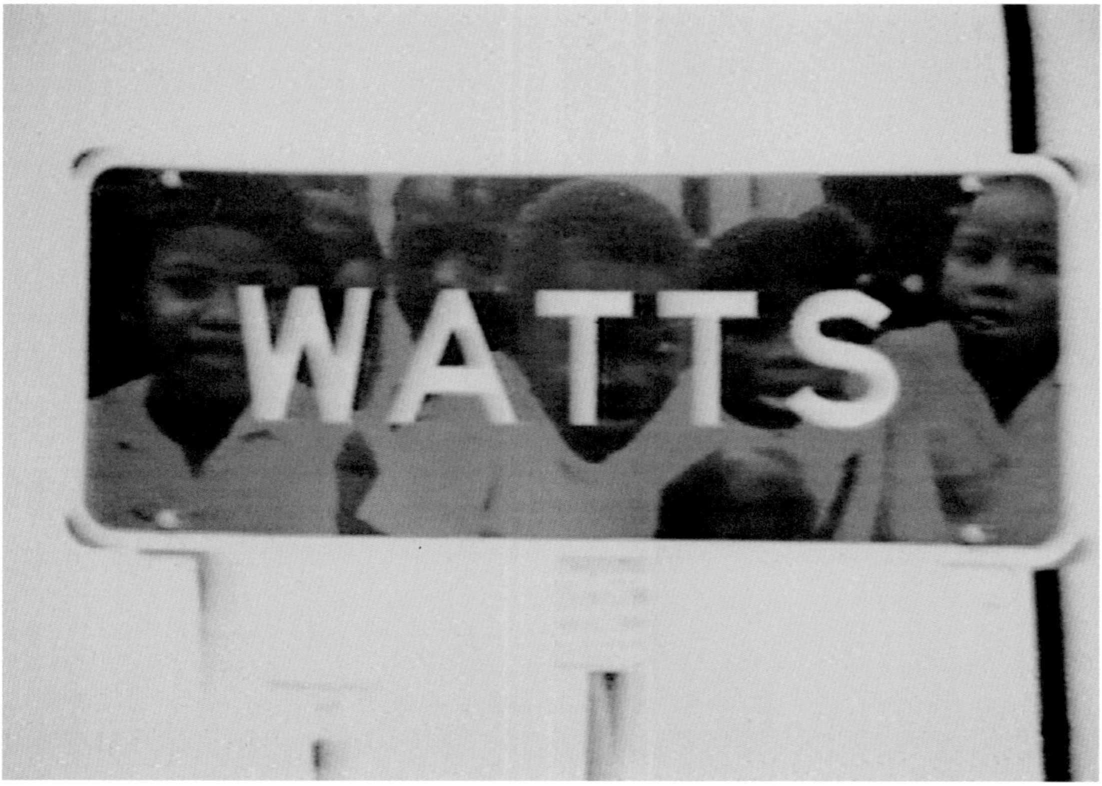

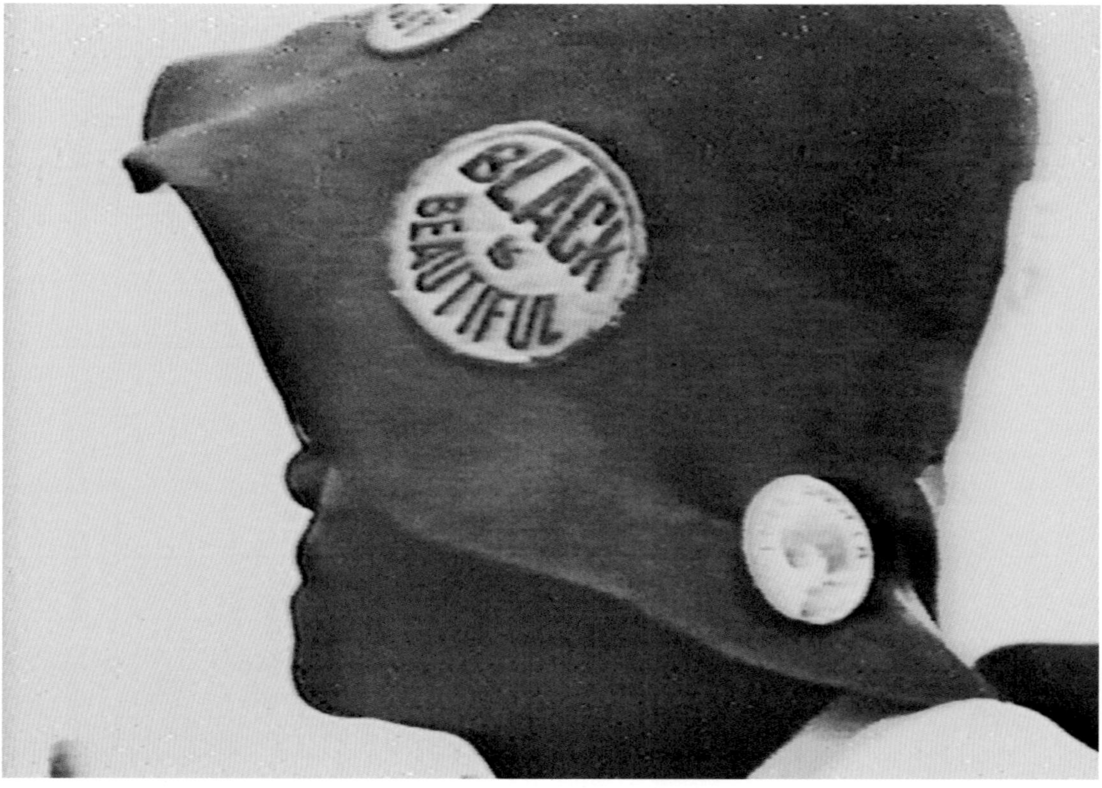

Ulysses Jenkins, *Remnants of the Watts Festival* (video stills), 1972–73, compiled 1980. Video transferred to DVD, black and white, sound, 55:44 min. Courtesy of the artist and Electronic Arts Intermix.

IKECHÚKWÚ ONYEWUENYI

AFTER
THE PRISM

THE MANY RETURNS OF
ULYSSES JENKINS

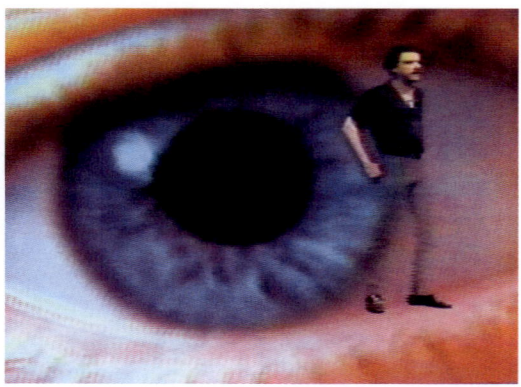

Fig. 1: Ulysses Jenkins, *Televiews and Cable Radio* (video still), 1981. Video transferred to DVD, color, sound, 11:18 min. Courtesy of the artist and Electronic Arts Intermix.

Ulysses Jenkins knows what's going on. He is a griot or, at least, known as one in Los Angeles lore. And in that sense, Jenkins knows there's more to see even as he sees (fig. 1). This way of seeing, in Fanonian parlance, suggests Jenkins exists "triply," occupying places and spaces that necessitate him to move toward and among others even when they would rather avoid him.[1] Wandering about in this way as a polyvalent being comes with foresight, which is another way of saying Jenkins, in a nod to Frantz Fanon, again, roams with an onus that he's "responsible . . . for [his] body, for [his] race, [and] for [his] ancestors."[2] If we move with this prismatic view of Black-ness, then it's worth sitting with the navigable limits and possibilities of Jenkins's oeuvre within the history of video art and television broadcasting. Over the years, I've wondered: What is Jenkins's compass? And *how* does he navigate the Manichean division of race that always already structures interpretations of his allegorical video and performance work? Multiculturalism—yes, that promising yet thorny political philosophy that edifies as much as it divides. Yet Jenkins's embrace of the multicultural wasn't a disavowal of Blackness. He built his artistic practice around the 1970s fervor for multicultural policies such that we might regard the singularity of Blackness as a cynosure with a capacious reach—one affording space for the iridescent amalgam of cultural affiliations, identities, and struggles. I'm drawn to this kaleidoscopic way of thinking about Jenkins, for it shines a light on the way Blackness, according to Denise Ferreira da Silva, "fractures the glassy walls of *universality*" when it comes to under-standing multiculturalism.[3] Shining this light onto Jenkins, we see the artist angles not toward achieving a melting-pot universality, but one that never fully resolves itself. That Jenkins envisions his myth making through a "fractured narrative" sug-gests that the "glassy prism" he locates in his 1981 performance *Adams Be Doggereal* might be the compass guiding his maneuverings as a griot.[4]

Jenkins's prismatic genre of storytelling converges with the "indeterminate pos-ture" emerging in Black performance practices coming out of Los Angeles since the '70s. For the art historian Kellie Jones, this posture was, in part, invested in "the visual image of others" or making encounters for others to visualize themselves.[5] Given this universalist care for others, I would say that while Jenkins "walked away" from undo-ing the "image problem" assailing Black representation, like any griot, he kept circling back. Embracing this ambulatory return for the benefit of others situates Jenkins's myth making with Michel Foucault's thoughts on the "reflexive prism."[6] Foucault

1   Frantz Fanon, *Black Skins, White Masks*, trans. Charles Lam Markmann (London: Pluto Press, 2008), 84.

2   Fanon, *Black Skins*, 84.

3   Denise Ferreira da Silva, "1 (life) ÷ 0 (blackness) = ∞ − ∞ or ∞ / ∞: On Matter Beyond the Equation of Value," *e-flux Journal*, no. 79 (February 2017), https://www.e-flux.com/journal/79/94686/1-life-0-blackness-or-on-matter-beyond-the-equation-of-value.

4   "Ulysses Jenkins," in *California Video: Artists and*

Histories, ed. Glenn Phillips (Los Angeles: Getty Research Institute and J. Paul Getty Museum, 2008), 112.

5   Kellie Jones, *South of Pico: African American Artists in Los Angeles in the 1960s and 1970s* (Durham: Duke University Press, 2017), 187.

6   Michel Foucault, *Security, Territory, Population: Lectures at the Collège de France, 1977–78*, ed. Michel Senellart, trans. Graham Burchell (London: Palgrave Macmillan, 2009), 276.

regarded the prism as a relational act that recognizes a scattered sensibility of governance, all while conceivably demanding of the steward of the state—or the griot—what Foucault deemed "an active, concerted, and reflected practice."[7] Extrapolating this to the griot, Foucault's idea of "conducting conduct" is akin to a subversive storyteller who revisits concerns, time and again, with the goal of cultivating discursive images rich with indirection.[8] Jenkins similarly moves with a certain circuitousness. He deems his pictorial visions within his video work as vacillating from "small integers to fractions," with this visual calculus engendering "fragmental areas of unconnected knowledge" from which

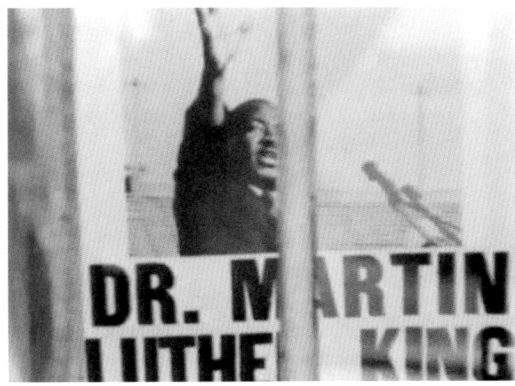

Fig. 2: Ulysses Jenkins, *Remnants of the Watts Festival* (video still), 1972–73, compiled 1980. Video transferred to DVD, black and white, sound, 55:44 min. Courtesy of the artist and Electronic Arts Intermix.

Jenkins envisioned his role as a griot—the connector of the unconnected—as paramount in "inform[ing] all cultures and the vital relative education of our future."[9] What we can deduce from this is that Jenkins's reflected practice as a griot decidedly harnesses the "felicity of the population" and not the sovereign state.[10]

I'm intrigued, then, with *how* Jenkins, through the prism, interrogates the refracting knowledge of Blackness as a way to fabricate and imagine a fractal kind of imagery that provides a glimmer toward a future, utopic or otherwise. A little-known instance of such futuring dates back to the past—1984. Jenkins was on the receiving end of an email from Darrell Jónsson, an experimental filmmaker living, at the time, in Reykjavík, Iceland. Quizzed by Jónsson on the "future possibilities for the distribution of alternative expressions in electronic media," Jenkins responded:

> It will take one who has the guts to put out what we know as video art in its real context without having to have an entertainment entity involved with it, because that is basically the criteria by which the business community is relating to it. If it don't [*sic*] have an entertainment value to it, it makes your audience think too much; they think people won't buy it. So that means philosophically thinking beyond just titillating your senses, and mostly your sexual senses.[11]

This response comes after Jenkins had already walked away from resolving the stereotyping of Black folks in American cinema and television. Yet his choice of words lands as rather impassioned—as though his bodily movements are still very much invested. Jenkins's embodied argument—the gut, the sentient, the libidinal—takes on a different resonance if we understand the Black radicalism in America that aired on network and public access television during the late 1960s and 1970s. At the germinal stages of the Black rebellion for human rights, television was a fount of political education and activism; Black leaders (fig. 2) turned to televised messages as a way to disseminate not

7   Foucault, *Security, Territory, Population*, 277.
8   This idea of "indirection" is key within Foucault's thoughts on resistance to state power. See Michel Foucault, "Sexual Choice, Sexual Act," in *Ethics: Subjectivity and Truth* (New York: New Press, 1997), 145; Foucault, *Security,*

Territory, Population, xxii.
9   Ulysses Jenkins, "Artist Statement," n.d.
10   Foucault, *Security, Territory, Population*, 277.
11   Darrell Jónsson, "Zone Transfers in Dream City" (unpublished interview, 1984), typescript.

just their rhetoric but the inhumane reality of America that had no desire to improve racial inequality and social unrest.[12] As the media scholar Devorah Heitner notes in *Black Power TV*, the paradoxical "desire to contain Black bodies and the desire to air Black voices" encapsulated the irony of television as an agreeable, passive platform for Black discontent.[13] Because even as televised boycotts and street demonstrations kept a segment of the Black population *contained* at home, the witnessing of nonviolent marches, sit-ins, and pray-ins turning bloody was simultaneously readying and radicalizing Black people for the violent "Reagan regime," as Jenkins puts it, that would devastate Black life.[14] There's a frank temerity to Jenkins's words, which revisit the logic of "television activism" during the 1960s and '70s that considered televisual control as "a resource ... worth fighting for."[15] For Jenkins, how we *fight* for that resource is at issue.

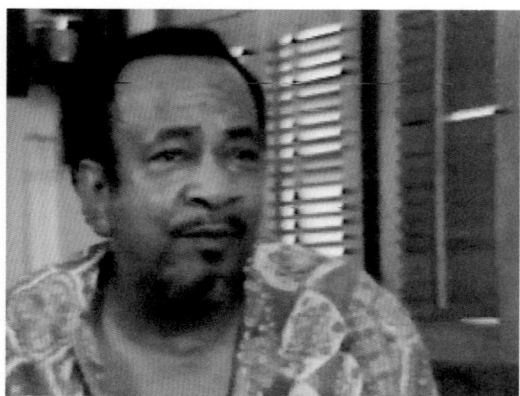

Fig 3: Cecil Ferguson responding to questions in Ulysses Jenkins, *Remnants of the Watts Festival* (video still), 1972–73, compiled 1980. Video transferred to DVD, black and white, sound, 55:44 min. Courtesy of the artist and Electronic Arts Intermix.

Jenkins knows this fight all too well. When he began making videos in the early 1970s with the Portapaks (portable video recording units), his initial output focused on everyday happenings and cultural events in and around Venice, California. This communal emphasis had no industry end in the sense that Jenkins's documentary practice wasn't invested in his videos appearing on broadcast television. Part of this had to do with access. But a large part had to do with what the video artist and writer Chris Meigh-Andrews observed as the sensibility among artists of that time to take up "position[s] critical of broadcast television" and seek "alternative strategies for production and distribution."[16] Jenkins shot a variety of projects for Video Venice News and continued this New Journalism approach to filmmaking when he began his studies at Otis Art Institute in 1977. No known footage exists from his Otis Video News days. But *Remnants of the Watts Festival* (1972–73, compiled 1980), the one surviving documentary from the Venice Video News era, shined an alternative light source on the image problem affecting Black Americans within television and cinema. Adopting the lens of participatory and performative documentary, *Remnants* finds Jenkins in dialogue, on multiple occasions, with the Black Arts Council cofounder Cecil Ferguson articulating how an influx of corporate funding shifted the control of the Watts Summer Festival away from the community (fig. 3). That pivot brought greater police presence at the festival, with Ferguson revealing that the Sons of Watts Improvement Association, a local government-funded self-help group, were no longer overseeing security during festivities. This show of state-sanctioned force coupled with extra-state actors (corporate, philanthropic, and private benefactors) further promulgated disinguuous narratives in the news that white festivalgoers were placing themselves in harm's way

12   Devorah Heitner, *Black Power TV* (Durham: Duke University Press, 2013), 8.
13   Heitner, *Black Power TV*, 11.
14   Ulysses Jenkins, *Doggerel Life: Stories of a Los Angeles Griot* (Los Angeles: Oreste, 2018), 110.
15   Jenkins, *Doggerel Life*, 110.
16   Chris Meigh-Andrews, *A History of Video Art* (New York: Bloomsbury, 2014), 172.

by venturing into Watts. Jenkins recalls news
outlets warning people not to "go to the festival, especially if you're not black. You'll be
mugged. You'll be jumped." [17] To negate these
negative accounts about the festival, Jenkins
employs in *Remnants* what the film scholar
Linda Williams termed "strategies of fictional
construction" through the likes of height-
ened subjectivity, reflexivity, and essayism
that question "the pernicious scapegoating
fictions" behind the prevailing perception of
Watts as violent.[18] Because, while Blackness is
the prism Jenkins crafts his narratives from,
he notes how stereotypes in the media go
"beyond the obvious thing about complexion.
We're talking about class. We're talking about
social positions. . . . But it all gets categorized
in a way that's called race problems." [19]

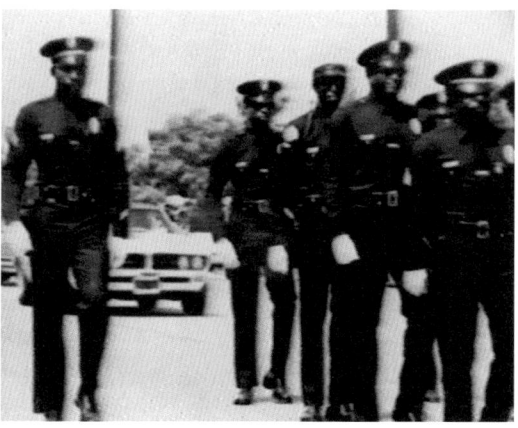

Fig. 4: Ulysses Jenkins, *Remnants of the Watts Festival* (video
still), 1972–73, compiled 1980. Video transferred to DVD,
black and white, sound, 55:44 min. Courtesy of the artist and
Electronic Arts Intermix.

The flow of corporate investment impinged on the festival exercising the human
right of Black gathering, merriment, and cultural defiance. While some organizers saw
the festival as offering up "rituals of status elevation," others also wanted the festivities to celebrate "rituals of status reversal" that defied white authority.[20] In fact, as
the historian Bruce M. Tyler notes, Black community leader and festival organizer
Maulana Ron Karenga considered the Watts Summer Festival to be "a cultural revolution before the violent revolution." [21] Considering the Los Angeles Police Department
(LAPD) never approved of the festival since it commemorated the Watts uprisings
(or supported what the police deemed civil disobedience), Karenga's desire for violence likely reignited what the scholar Molefi Kete Asante saw as the dialectic framework dominating the "content of television during the insurrections of the 1960s"
that pitted "black human rights [against] white property rights." [22] With the specter
of violence looming, corporations sought to safeguard their investments, above and
beyond Black cultural pride, and duly turned to the LAPD (fig. 4), who have, from time
immemorial and with contempt for Black humanity, protected the property interests
of the white privileged class.

This corporate about-face—or the commercial marketing of culture—reifies
Jenkins's wariness of entertainment encroaching on what was, at the time, the avant-
garde practice of video art. Like any true griot, Jenkins did not let up on his critique
of sustainable models for video art and broadcasting. In his 1990 memoir, *Doggerel
Life: Stories of a Los Angeles Griot*, he admits, on two occasions, to an unease with
LA Public Access (formerly Theta Cable Station, Los Angeles's first cable and public

17   Sally Jo Fifer, "What Are You Going to Do After You
Drink Up the Oceans? A Conversation with Ulysses Jenkins,"
Video Networks (Bay Area Video Coalition) 16, no. 4 (August
1992).
18   Linda Williams, "Mirrors without Memories: Truth,
History, and the New Documentary," *Film Quarterly* 46, no.
3 (Spring 1993): 20.
19   Fifer, "A Conversation with Ulysses Jenkins."
20   Victor W. Turner, *The Ritual Process: Structure and*

Anti-Structure (Chicago, 1969), 167, quoted in Bruce M. Tyler,
"The Rise and Decline of the Watts Summer Festival, 1965 to
1986," *American Studies* 31, no. 2 (Fall 1990): 63.
21   Tyler, "Rise and Decline of the Watts Summer Festival," 63.
22   Molefi Kete Asante, "Television and Black Consciousness," in *Channeling Blackness: Studies on Television and
Race in America*, ed. Darnell M. Hunt (New York: Oxford University Press, 2005), 62.

access channel). Jenkins regarded this media group as manipulative, noting that the people he dealt with there "had an exploitative relationship with people of color and women, in order to obtain more money for themselves."[23] Moreover, he found the media entity unwilling to teach him video editing, while "people from the academic community [were] getting direct access" so as to bolster the television station's "credentials for funders."[24] Paradoxically, *access* to learning editing came when Jenkins began his studies at Otis in 1977. This set in motion the creation of *Remnants of the Watts Festival*—footage he had been sitting on since 1973. Not surprisingly, Jenkins's exchange with LA Public Access mirrors the experiences of the filmmaker and artist Thomas Allen Harris. His account of anti-Black racism within public television details how token producers of color encountered a "relative lack of power" such that their programming was meant to entertain their white, middle-class audiences and not leave them "annoy[ed]." This reads as: we don't want audiences thinking, just please them—a refrain typical of entertainment. Operating with such an outlook blunts critical thinking in the interest of keeping pleasure front and center. Speaking of his frustration with LA Public Access, Jenkins noted that the "alternative medium [in video] that was to proclaim everyone's freedom of expression meant the freedom to express the status quo's ideal of that 'freedom.'"[26] In short, from Harris to Jenkins, Black practitioners of video art and televisual messaging encountered limitations if their discourse did not conform to the dominant, exclusionary narrative that titillated white middle-class audiences.

All this context above circles back to Jenkins's words in 1972, 1984, and 1990, which repeat different albeit similar exigencies that entertainment places on (Black) cultural production. It is evident that Jenkins's solo angst is a collective one. For the griot, even as a solitary figure, is operating in and out of step with immanence, with history, with words, which, for the historian Djibril Tamsir Niane, have felt "the warmth of . . . [other] human voice[s]."[27] Encountering this reprise in Jenkins's words is a reminder of James A. Snead's treatise on how Black culture embraces the repetitive even as it acknowledges that the return is never "the same thing."[28] Jenkins's grievances are enduring, trenchant—they cut to the core of the image problem even if through roundabout means. For instance, Ferguson is an interlocutor whom Jenkins returns to several times in *Remnants*, a reflexive strategy that imbues their exchanges with a sense of repetition and rehearsal. If Jenkins's Blackness, which is to say his light source, inflects his truth, then *Remnants* illumes the associative thought on the Black political organizing and community activism not directly discussed in the film: the Watts Summer Festival, which was backed by the Los Angeles County Commission on Human Relations, was seen "as a remedy against lingering hostility and pro-riot activism" following the Watts uprisings of August 1965.[29] Taking up this context, Jenkins's editorial cut to the nighttime performance by the funk-rock band War returns us, as griots often do, to the inciting incident on August 11, 1965, when the LAPD assaulted Marquette Frye and his mother, Rena Price.

23   Jenkins, *Doggerel Life*, 60, 113.
24   Fifer, "A Conversation with Ulysses Jenkins."
25   Thomas Allen Harris, "About Face: The Evolution of a Black Producer," in *Black Popular Culture*, ed. Michele Wallace and Gina Dent (Seattle: Bay Press; Dia Art Foundation, 1993), 236–37.
26   Jenkins, *Doggerel Life*, 113.

27   Djibril Tamsir Niane, *Sundiata: An Epic of Old Mali*, trans. G. D. Pickett (Harlow, England: Pearson Longman, 2006), 41.
28   James A. Snead, "On Repetition in Black Culture," *Black American Literature Forum* 15, no. 4 (Winter 1981): 146.
29   Tyler, "Rise and Decline of the Watts Summer Festival," 63.

These are the truths that *Remnants* illuminates if we want to go there with Jenkins's fractured storytelling, which is very much circular in its insistence on creative parity for the video artist. Elsewhere in Snead's essay he contextualizes Jenkins's editorial cuts for us, stating: "Black culture, in the 'cut,' builds 'accidents' into its *coverage*, almost as if to control their unpredictability. Itself a kind of cultural *coverage*, this magic of the 'cut' attempts to confront accident and rupture not by covering them over but by making room for them inside the system itself." [30] I wouldn't call Jenkins's work *magic* per se, but he does revel in the realm of testimonial ritual, which echoes with the playwright Shay Youngblood's claim that "words are impetus for magic, for community." [31] This merging of cuts from Jenkins becomes a type of magical confrontation that opens up and/or ruptures the enclosed circle and, ultimately, the broadcast and television system for a reckoning with what Snead called a "repetition with a difference." Building on this divergent notion of circularity, Jenkins, admittedly, notes that while he works in a "cyclical manner," he's also "interested in the idea of a 'work-in-progress,' where the work never really finishes itself—in other words, it's constantly reevaluating itself and then starting up again." [32] From the lapse evidenced in the making of *Remnants* to Jenkins's critiques of entertainment, it's fair to say both operate as works-in-progress—cultural observances of ritual that testify, and testify again, but from a different angle.

Rather than romanticize myth making, which is the hallmark of entertainment, Jenkins's early brand of television journalism mythologizes by cutting up and poking holes in what Snead calls "the philosophical insight about the shape of time and history." [33] Through *Remnants*, Jenkins evidences how one might trouble the conceit and certainty of the image. Latching on to the echolalic utterance of revolution—from Karenga to Jenkins to Ferguson, and back—reiterates the need for media literacy and a reevaluation of the narratives of progress and content seen in public-affairs television. As Heitner explicates, the rise in Black public programs following the death of Martin Luther King Jr. wasn't to rupture an oppressive system so as to bring about change; rather, these news organizations sought to capitalize on a sociopolitical movement billed as creating "*compelling* tv." [34] The fact that Black suffering provided enough compelling entertainment value for television programming speaks to Jenkins's gripes in 1984. Yet Jenkins was merely rearticulating the pitfalls he had witnessed in the '70s, with public-affairs programs like *Soul!* (1968–73) ending due to funding shortages or *Black Journal* (1968–70, under William Greaves) changing their political approach to shake off the "too radical" tag from PBS executives. [35] Snead would ask whether this choice to pull funding was bound up in "self-aware" progress from white media executives or simply an impulsive "immediacy" (of anxiety and avarice) that initiated these Black television programs in the first place. Well, it was as self-aware as the "closed tautological system" that capital circulates within, where, per Snead, "growth and development" are really just "a decrease in an asset" elsewhere. [36] Funding from the Corporation for Public Broadcasting (CPB) in 1973 was directed toward interracial shows like *Interface*, with the reason being that television programs like

30   Snead, "On Repetition," 150.
31   Shay Youngblood, quoted in Joni L. Jones, "Conjuring as Radical Re/Membering in the Works of Shay Youngblood," in *Black Theatre: Ritual Performance in the African Diaspora*, ed. Paul Carter Harrison, Victor Leo Walker II, and Gus Edwards (Philadelphia: Temple University Press, 2002), 227.

32   Phillips, "Ulysses Jenkins," 113.
33   Snead, "On Repetition," 146.
34   Heitner, *Black Power TV*, 8 (emphasis my own).
35   Heitner, 120.
36   Snead, "On Repetition," 148–49.

Soul! and *Black Journal* were "relic[s] of the segregated past—or at least a past of racial crisis that the nation had worked to surmount—[and that] the CPB could paradoxically position itself as a champion of progress."[37] But if we focus on Jenkins's temporal journey, his inability to finish editing *Remnants* in the '70s highlights that the advances with the passage of civil rights legislation were not far-reaching on a class and even psychosocial level. Moreover, Jenkins still encountered accessibility issues through a racially biased LA Public Access. By repeating his frustrations about entertainment stymieing video art, Jenkins's griot endeavors sought to fracture the false logic of progress by engaging the very closed tautological system—i.e., public television—that he held reservations about.

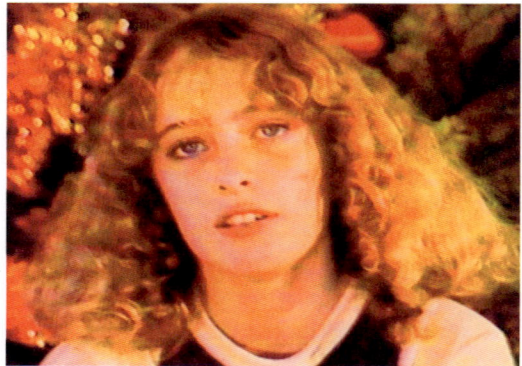

Fig. 5: Ulysses Jenkins, *Holiday Greetings* (video still), 1979–80. Video transferred to DVD, black and white with color, sound, 21:20 min. Courtesy of the artist and Electronic Arts Intermix.

Jenkins serves up a droll critique to the above in *Holiday Greetings* (1979–80), which he produced with a youth video program that aired on public television network Group W Cable (formerly Theta Cable TV). In a video dominated by group exchanges among the youth, Jenkins cuts to a surreal, unexpected close-up of a white young woman with coifed red hair (fig. 5). She delivers a monologue, her eyes innocently fixed right at the viewer, the camera panning out to reveal a Christmas tree behind her. Heed her words:

Whatever happened to our freedom? Where I live, they say we are free. Of course, America is more free than other places of the world. But it's still a one-track world. All you have to do is follow the system, but for some it's not that simple. We have freedom of speeches, religions. Why don't they ever listen to your speeches and religions? Everything takes time, just be patient. The world moves so fast. If you don't go by the system, it could mean you're a failure. It is said never look at the past, always the future. If so, why do they have to look at your past? Of course, you can't change the past. But if you want the future to be different, and you want to be looked up to, you have to go by the system. It's a one-track world. But if there was no system, and this was a free world, there are those who would take advantage. Thank you.

This segment of *Holiday Greetings* reads rather odd since the monologue is astoundingly self-reflexive for a white youth. It's not clear whether she drafted the script, but either way, Jenkins's decision to isolate her lands as a retort against whiteness—or those who take advantage. Moreover, the adolescent implicates herself—or whiteness—and geographically sets apart whom the white media executives prioritize in their television programming. Returning to Snead, this part of *Holiday Greetings* sees Jenkins complicate "the shape of time and history" by revealing that time can be sped up or slowed to a halt depending on whether one abides by the system or disregards it altogether. Jenkins doesn't foretell which one will propel humanity—or

37   Gayle Wald, *It's Been Beautiful: "Soul!" and Black Power Television* (Durham: Duke University Press, 2015), 184.

Black life—forward. But he gives us a clue if we read the monologue prismatically. Jenkins is calling for a splintering of the one-track world, to latch on to the *if* and run with the reality that the system is malleable to the point of nonexistence. Moreover, *if* we regard Theodor Adorno and Max Horkheimer's observation that "respect is vanishing" in the culture industry, then the system Jenkins impugns in *Holiday Greetings* starts appearing increasingly deceptive.[38] And we can extend that to the audience too. Because, drawing from Christine Acham, I think Jenkins, even as he engages the predominantly white middle-class television audience, ultimately wants to shift the question fram-

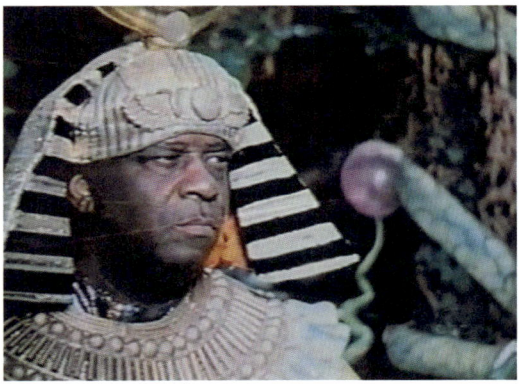

Fig. 6: Ulysses Jenkins, *Planet X* (video still), 2006. Video transferred to DVD, color, sound, 6:19 min. Courtesy of the artist and Electronic Arts Intermix.

ing "the basis of criticism throughout African American television history," which is, "What will white America think?"[39]

I began with an interest in the *how* of Jenkins's practice, which is really an interest in the means for navigating the future. This is top of mind for Jenkins, for his desire to fashion alternate models of Black televisual production and critique separate from entertainment is enduring and there for all to see. Jenkins left us a compass through his video work and performance that isn't rote by any means but prismatic—varied and brilliant in its philosophical positioning of Blackness as a constitutive and destabilizing force for other, unknown, worlds. What this world *is* remains indefinite, which reminds me of Jenkins's paragon, Sun Ra (fig. 6). Similarly moved by griot spirits, Sun Ra maintained that the "net of kindly prisms" guides us away from an "unmeant secret place" that Blackness calls "home." Departing this makeshift home of loopholes and limitations (read: entertainment) for Black image makers demands we attend to the "dark rays of light" that Sun Ra envisioned."[40] Perhaps this Cimmerian luminescence undergirds this new Black universalism from which Jenkins structures multiple outs that allow Blackness to embrace its physics, to find nooks and crannies, such that it can move unhampered, without your interpretation.

38   Theodor W. Adorno and Max Horkheimer, "The Culture Industry: Enlightenment as Mass Deception," in *Dialectic of Enlightenment: Philosophical Fragments*, ed. Gunzelin Schmid Noerr, trans. Edmund Jephcott (Stanford: Stanford University Press, 2002), 130.
39   Christine Acham, *Revolution Televised: Prime Time and the Struggle for Black Power* (Minneapolis: University of Minnesota Press, 2004), 193.
40   Sun Ra, "The Sub-Dwellers" (1972), in *Sun Ra: The Immeasurable Equation; The Collected Poetry and Prose*, ed. James L. Wolf and Hartmut Geerken (Wartaweil, Germany: Waitawhile Books, 2005), 364.

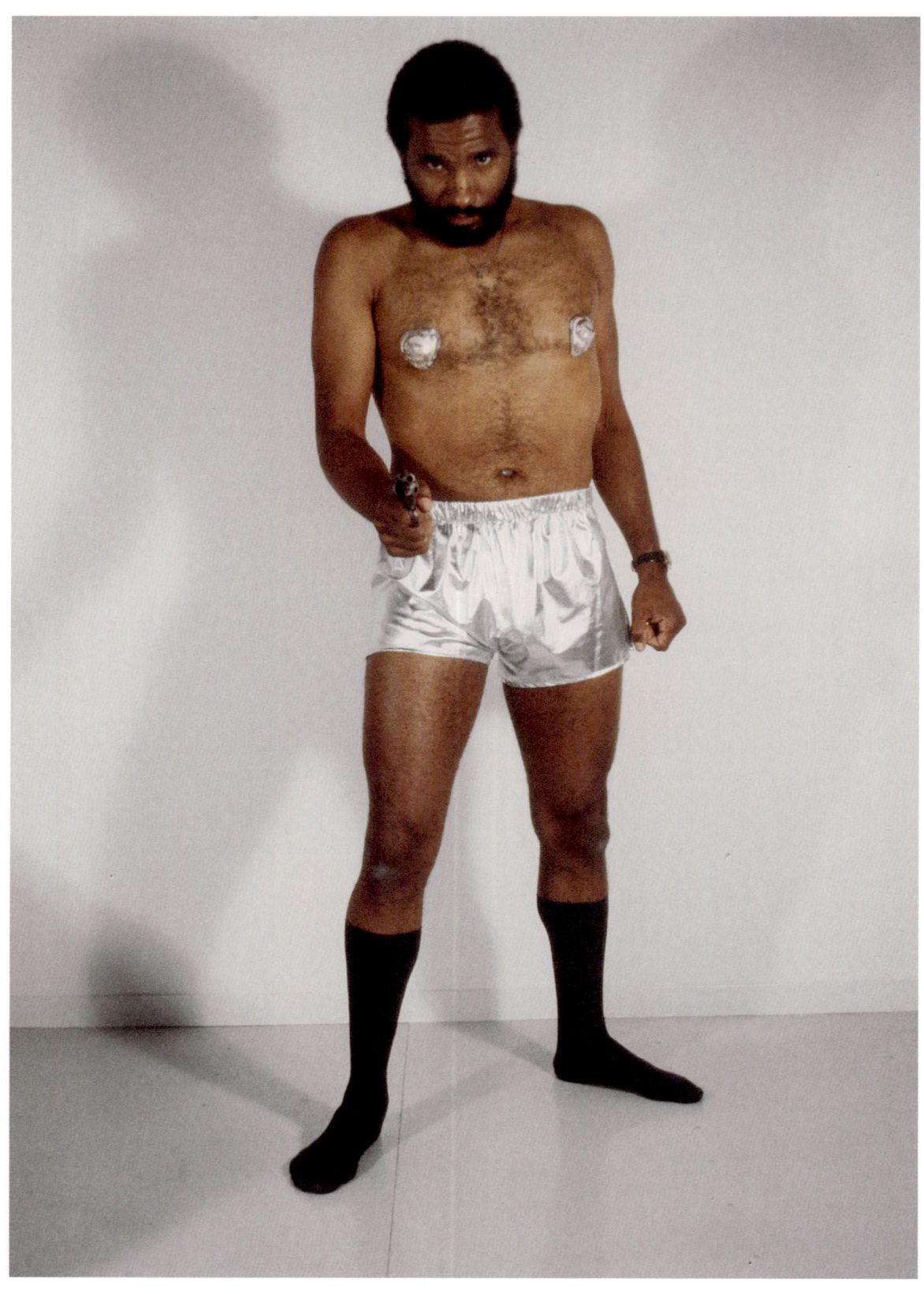

Ulysses Jenkins, *Just Another Rendering of the Same Old Problem*, 1979. Performance. Courtesy of the artist. Photo: Nancy Buchanan.

ARIA DEAN

WRITTEN AND BITTEN

ULYSSES JENKINS AND
THE NON-ONTOLOGY OF BLACKNESS

"Ontology—once it is finally admitted as leaving existence by the wayside—does not permit us to understand the being of the black . . ."
—Frantz Fanon, *The Fact of Blackness*

For all of the vibrancy of the community described by black artists who lived and worked in Los Angeles in the 1970s—including the exhibitions at the Brockman Gallery, gatherings at Studio Z and Othervisions Studio, and collaboration throughout the city—mainstream critical writing's treatment of these artists and the scene that incubated them merely skims the surface. Certainly a number of these artists have, after the fact, gone down in history as important figures. Among them are Senga Nengudi, Barbara McCullough, Fred Eversley, Noah Purifoy, Betye Saar, Charles White, and David Hammons. But many of these artists' careers skew in the direction of being "hometown heroes" in Los Angeles; they are ghettoized to consideration primarily when the art world wants to think local—a consistent trend when it comes to considering art that comes out of Los Angeles—or to think along racial lines.

Video and performance artist Ulysses Jenkins is but one of these under-recognized artists, despite his large and potent body of work and his involvement in collaborations with many artists throughout California through the collective of Othervisions Studio, Electronic Cafe International, and other initiatives. Jenkins, now a professor at the University of California, Irvine, has been included in retrospective exhibitions such as *Now Dig This! Art & Black Los Angeles, 1960–1980* (Hammer Museum) and *Radical Presence: Black Performance in Contemporary Art* (Contemporary Arts Museum Houston). But when his work is discussed, it is almost always in passing—garnering no more than a few paragraphs of interest, the bulk of which considers it a commentary on positive and negative representations and stereotypes of black life[1] — a fate that befalls many a black artist.

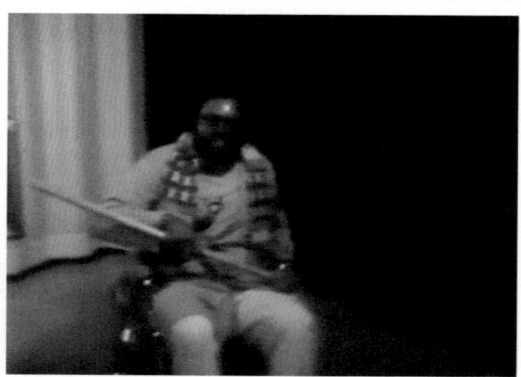

Ulysses Jenkins, *Mass of Images* (video still), 1978. Video transferred to DVD, black and white, sound, 4:16 min. Courtesy of the artist and Electronic Arts Intermix. Photo: Ulysses Jenkins.

These readings of Jenkins's work lean heavily on his 1978 video *Mass of Images*, a recorded performance that does indeed engage black stereotypes perpetuated by the American media. In the work, Jenkins appears on a set accompanied by a stack of televisions, his face obscured by a plastic mask and sunglasses, neck wrapped in American-flag-print scarf, and sporting an Adidas t-shirt underneath a bathrobe, arranged such that only the "ID" of Adidas is visible. The video cuts between this scene and examples of blackface and racist stereotyping from American films and TV. Jenkins repeats a mantra as he settles into a wheelchair and

†   Originally published in *X-Tra* 19, no. 2 (Winter 2017).

1   In the catalog for *Radical Presence: Black Performance in Contemporary Art*, Jenkins's work is described as a "critique [of] the cultural stereotyping of black people in American popular culture." In Roberto Tejada's essay in *Now Dig This!* Jenkins is similarly described as "critiqu[ing] the physical and discursive violence of mainstream representation." See Yona Backer, "Performance Trace: Staged Actions, Live Art, and Performance Made for the Camera," in *Radical Presence: Black Performance in Contemporary Art*, ed. Valerie Cassel Oliver (Houston: Contemporary Arts Museum, 2013), 88; and Roberto Tejada, "Los Angeles Snapshots," in *Now Dig This! Art & Black Los Angeles, 1960–1980*, ed. Kellie Jones (Los Angeles: Hammer Museum, 2011), 20.

wheels himself toward center stage: "You're just a mass of images you've gotten to know / from years and years of TV shows. / The hurting thing; the hidden pain / was written and bitten into your veins / I don't and I won't relate / and I think for some it's too late!"[2]

Continuing the refrain, he gathers his strength and rears to smash the TVs but falters. He gasps and laughs, rather manically, and says, "Oh, I'd love to do this, but they won't let me." He turns toward the camera, repeats the mantra one more time, and then the screen goes dark.

The few published texts on the work that are in circulation—and they are minimal—focus on the inserted panels featuring images of Hattie McDaniel in her all too familiar mammy guise, Bert Williams in blackface, Allen Hoskins playing "Farina" in *The Little Rascals*, and other instances of blackface and racist imagery. The authors argue that Jenkins aims to illustrate the possibility of overcoming the power of these representations. In the catalog for *Now Dig This!*, for example, Roberto Tejada focuses on Jenkins's regaining of his composure following his outburst as signaling the "possibility of . . . self-possession within the mass of images that work to contain black bodies in representation."[3] However, I would argue against Tejada's claim, because this possibility is unrealized in the work. At the video's closing, we leave Jenkins exactly where we found him, repeating the same refrain. Other readings of the video find Jenkins generally critiquing cultural stereotypes, again performing the work that has come to be expected of the black artist of his time.[4]

Across all readings of *Mass of Images*, the lack of interest in Jenkins's failure to destroy the television sets is surprising. If the conceptual thrust of the work is meant to be the black-artist-as-subject's triumph over his flattened, essentialized, racist image—as readings so far have claimed it to be—then we must ask the question: Why doesn't Jenkins smash them? He tells us why. It is because "they won't let" him. The line "they won't let me" betrays a wholehearted desire to commit the act. Jenkins wants to smash the televisions but someone is stopping him. This moment, this break in the otherwise meditative pacing and relative calm of the video, becomes a focal point and

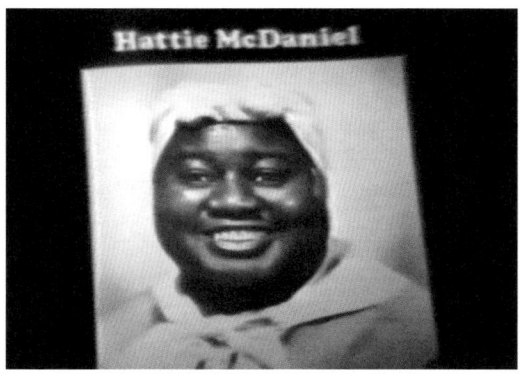

Ulysses Jenkins, *Mass of Images* (video still), 1978. Video transferred to DVD, black and white, sound, 4:16 min. Courtesy of the artist and Electronic Arts Intermix. Photo: Ulysses Jenkins.

in turn positions desire as the unseen force propelling the work. Jenkins noted, in a 2008 interview, that he very carefully positioned the bathrobe over his Adidas t-shirt such that only the "ID" is visible to the viewer as a sly nod to Freud, signaling that he is concerned primarily with the libidinal economy of the work.[5] Here, we are not

2   It should be noted that the video's audio is transcribed sometimes as "written and bitten into your veins" and at other times as "written and bitten into your brains." "Veins" appears more often, so I've used it here. Ulysses Jenkins, *Mass of Images*, video, 1978.

3   Tejada, "Los Angeles Snapshots," 69–89.

4   For example, see Backer, "Performance Trace," 20.

5   "Modern Art in Los Angeles: African American Avant-Gardes, 1965–1990," panel discussion with Ulysses Jenkins, Maren Hassinger, Barbara McCullough, and Senga Nengudi, moderated by Kellie Jones and Judith Wilson, Getty Research Institute, January 16, 2008. For more information, see http://www.getty.edu/visit/events/avantgardes.html.

quite within the domain of ethics or politics—the domains that the Black National-ist agenda and Jenkins's Black Arts Movement contemporaries would have had him occupy. The only politics here is a desire to be himself.[6]

Focusing on this break and viewing *Mass of Images* as an exercise in failure, rather than a victory over representation, we follow Jenkins into a rather unusual realm of inquiry, one that makes sense to have downplayed when it comes to his-toricizing black art of the period. Jenkins and his Los Angeles contemporaries, such as Senga Nengudi, Maren Hassinger, Barbara McCullough, and (for a brief period) David Hammons, were often accused of making art that was not political enough or "black enough" due to their interest in new media and abstraction and their willing-ness to draw on sources from outside of the black tradition.[7] Following Jenkins down this rabbit hole unravels much of the twentieth century's work toward a black politic of representation and provides a counter-argument against attempts by Black Arts Movement leaders, such as Larry Neal and Ron Karenga, toward a black aesthetic and a black art that articulates a self-determined blackness through images that "speak to and inspire black people."[8] Jenkins departs from this concern over what Frank Wilderson III calls the "hegemonic value" and pedagogical power of visual represen-tations of blackness and black people, which ruled black art criticism and black cine-matic theory of the time. Instead, Jenkins is interested in questioning the very nature of blackness itself.

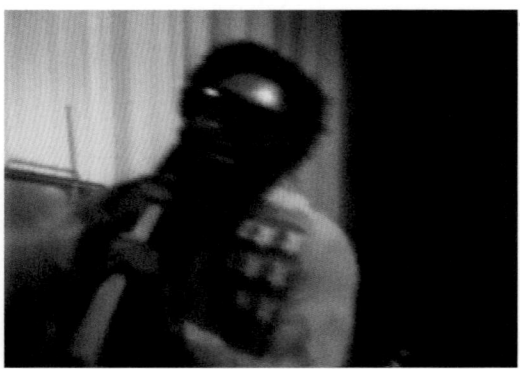

Ulysses Jenkins, *Mass of Images* (video still), 1978. Video trans-ferred to DVD, black and white, sound, 4:16 min. Courtesy of the artist and Electronic Arts Intermix. Photo: Ulysses Jenkins.

During the period from the creation of *Mass of Images* through the performance *Adams Be Doggereal* (1981), one finds Jen-kins asking a specific set of questions. These works should be viewed as a marked period in Jenkins's oeuvre, one that goes beyond "cultural critique," reaching into a zone of inquiry less acceptable to the mainstream. During this period, which includes the video/performance *Two-Zone Transfer* as well as the performance *Just Another Rendering of the Same Old Problem* (both 1979), we witness a narrative unfolding, one that originates in Jenkins's massive failure to assert a legible ontology of himself as a black subject capable of wreaking havoc over the images imposed on him and ends with an abandonment of this pursuit. By the end of this period, Jenkins—in a semi-linear progression—has moved away from grappling with the slippage between the black subject and its rep-resentation and toward a non-ontological blackness, or what he deems a new black universalism.

6   Rebecca Peabody, "African American Avant-Gardes, 1965–1990," *Getty Research Journal*, no. 1 The University of Chicago Press on behalf of The J. Paul Getty Trust, 2009), 214.
7   Their work was in apparent opposition to the criteria of black art set out by Maulana Ron Karenga and others. In "Black Cultural Nationalism": "black art must be functional, that is 'useful' ... Black art must expose the enemy, praise the

people and support the revolution." Valerie Cassel Oliver, "Through the Conceptual Lens: The Rise, Fall, and Resurrec-tion of Blackness," in *Double Consciousness: Black Concep-tual Art Since 1970*, ed. Terry Adkins, Valerie Cassel Oliver, and Franklin Sirmans (Houston: Contemporary Arts Museum, 2005), 19.
8   Maulana Ron Karenga, "On Black Art," *Black Theater* 3 (1969): 9–10.

Let us begin again, from here. Jenkins started where many young black artists find themselves. Studying at Santa Monica College (SMC) and later at Otis College of Art and Design, "in the shadow of Hollywood,"[9] Jenkins was aware of the conflicting interests of the entertainment industry and the African-American community. The works he developed following shortly after his enrollment at SMC take to task the media's role in perpetuating these stereotypes, exploring the resultant exacerbation of a black "double-consciousness," to borrow W. E. B. Du Bois's terminology.[10] *Mass of Images* is chronologically the first of these critiques, followed by

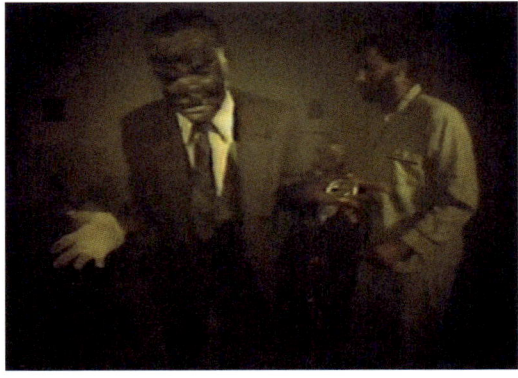

Ulysses Jenkins, *Two-Zone Transfer* (video still), 1979. Video transferred to DVD, color, sound, 23:52 min. Courtesy of the artist and Electronic Arts Intermix. Photo: Ilene Segalove.

Two-Zone Transfer and *Just Another Rendering of the Same Old Problem* (1979). *Two-Zone Transfer* follows closely in the footsteps of *Mass of Images*, with Jenkins zeroing in on blackface and minstrelsy's effects on black Americans. The video, also staged as a performance at Otis College, opens with Jenkins boarding a city bus, where we witness white riders' suspicion of him as a black man. Jenkins drifts off to sleep, and a figure in a dream says, "You know why you can't sleep; it's the same old problem that every black person in this country has had." Jenkins replies: "You mean the misunderstandings I encounter, or the same old, basic image problem?"[11] The "image problem" spoken of is the career-defining conundrum of black representation.

However, *Two-Zone Transfer* marks a shift in Jenkins's approach to the image problem, away from the traditional inquiries of first-wave black filmmaking and film theory—described by Frank Wilderson as an intense preoccupation with "identifying and critiquing the recurrence of stereotyped representation in Hollywood films,"[12] and exemplified in the writings of such critics as Don Bogle, Thomas Cripps, and Gladstone L. Yearwood. Instead, Jenkins looks to the source of the problem, interrogating the history of early twentieth-century vaudeville. On-screen, Jenkins is joined by three actors—Kerry James Marshall, Greg Pitts, and Ronnie Nichols—who wear masks in the likeness of presidents Nixon and Ford. In a strange layering of whiteface and blackface, the masks are smeared unevenly with black paint. The men brag about the history of minstrelsy in the United States and how they have, for years, manipulated and misused African-Americans' images and culture in order to distort society's understanding of black life.

Here, Jenkins recognizes blackness itself as an image rather than focusing on its inaccuracy when contrasted with what might be posed as an authentic black life, once again departing from the efforts of black art and cinematic theory of the time. "The image problem" is not that the image fails to correspond to reality, but that the image has partly crafted reality, inextricably linking Jenkins's own experience—as

9   Tejada, "Los Angeles Snapshots," 79.
10   "Double Consciousness" is explained by Du Bois as "a peculiar sensation ... this sense of always looking at one's self through the eyes of others." W. E. B. Du Bois, *The Souls of Black Folk*, introduction by David Levering Lewis (1903; New York: Modern Library Edition/Random House, 2003), 5.

Quoted in Cassel Oliver, "Through the Conceptual Lens," 17.
11   Ulysses Jenkins, *Two-Zone Transfer*, video, 1979.
12   Frank Wilderson III, *Red, White, & Black: Cinema and the Structure of U.S. Antagonisms* (Durham, NC: Duke University Press, 2010), 7.

exemplified by his earlier interaction on the bus—to popular images of blackness and black people. The developing line of thought here resonates with Frantz Fanon's realization of blackness as some "impure product."[13] As Fred Moten reads Fanon's "The Fact of Blackness" (in *Black Skin, White Masks*), blackness has always been and always will be "a function of a making that is not its own, an intentionality that could never have been its own."[14]

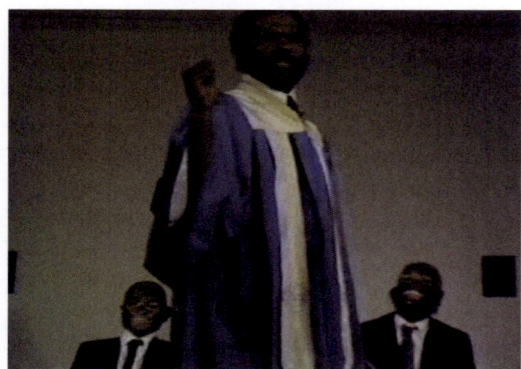

Ulysses Jenkins, *Two-Zone Transfer* (video still), 1979. Video transferred to DVD, color, sound, 23:52 min. Courtesy of the rtist and Electronic Arts Intermix. Photo: Ilene Segalove.

Traces of this position are also visible in the earlier *Mass of Images*. In Jenkins's refrain, he repeats: "The hurting thing / the hidden pain was written and bitten into your veins." If we take "the hurting thing / the hidden pain" as a reference to suffering as a constitutive element of black lived experience, then *Mass of Images* shares *Two-Zone Transfer*'s emphasis on the origin of blackness as external to itself. Here, his use of "written" could be read as a gesture toward a biologically determined blackness, perhaps a tongue-in-cheek shout out to out-of-fashion scientific racism. Jenkins is a black person, an individual of African descent. Blackness is "written" into his DNA. In contrast, "bitten into your veins" points to blackness as a virus or contagion—a theme that we find throughout rhetoric around blackness and black cultural production, from racist associations between blackness and actual disease to the tendency to laud black music as "contagious" and black joy as "infectious." Whether "written" or "bitten," blackness appears caught in an apparent contradiction. Jenkins, in effect, admits the seemingly paradoxical distinction between written black and bitten blackness. Jenkins himself is black in all his appearances and in his biographical experience, but his blackness is, again, an "impure product." It is an external contagion, circulating independent of Jenkins's own embodiment, "bitten into his veins" by mass media, engineered by white America long before his birth.

Two-Zone Transfer has, in essence, a dramatic "to be continued" ending. After the history lesson in *Two-Zone Transfer*, the video cuts to Jenkins, dressed as a preacher, delivering a sermon about the biblical figure Noah; in the following scene, he performs a rendition of a James Brown song with the actors, now unmasked, singing back-up. The video ends with Jenkins waking up from the dream and saying, invigorated, "After a dream like that, I know I've got direction. I know what I'm up against."[15]

Imagine a commercial break, and the next episode begins.

13   Fred Moten, "The Case of Blackness," *Criticism* 50,   14   Moten, "The Case of Blackness," 185.
no. 2 (Spring 2008): 185.   15   Jenkins, *Two-Zone Transfer*.

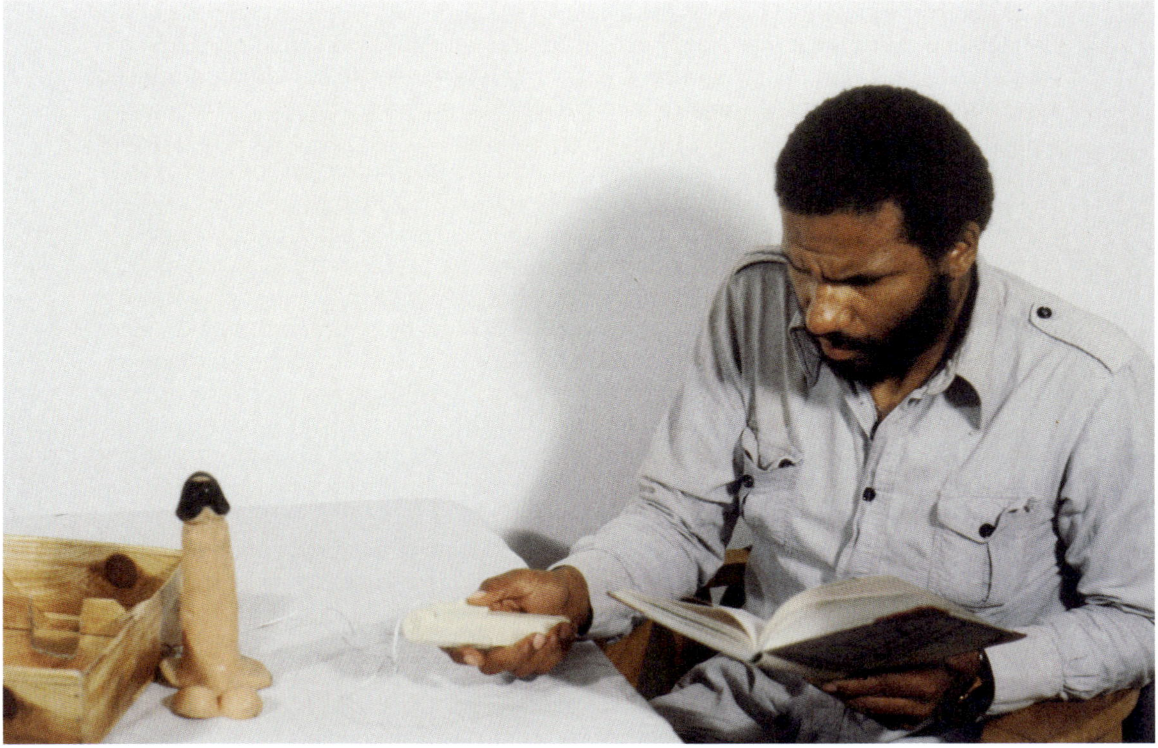

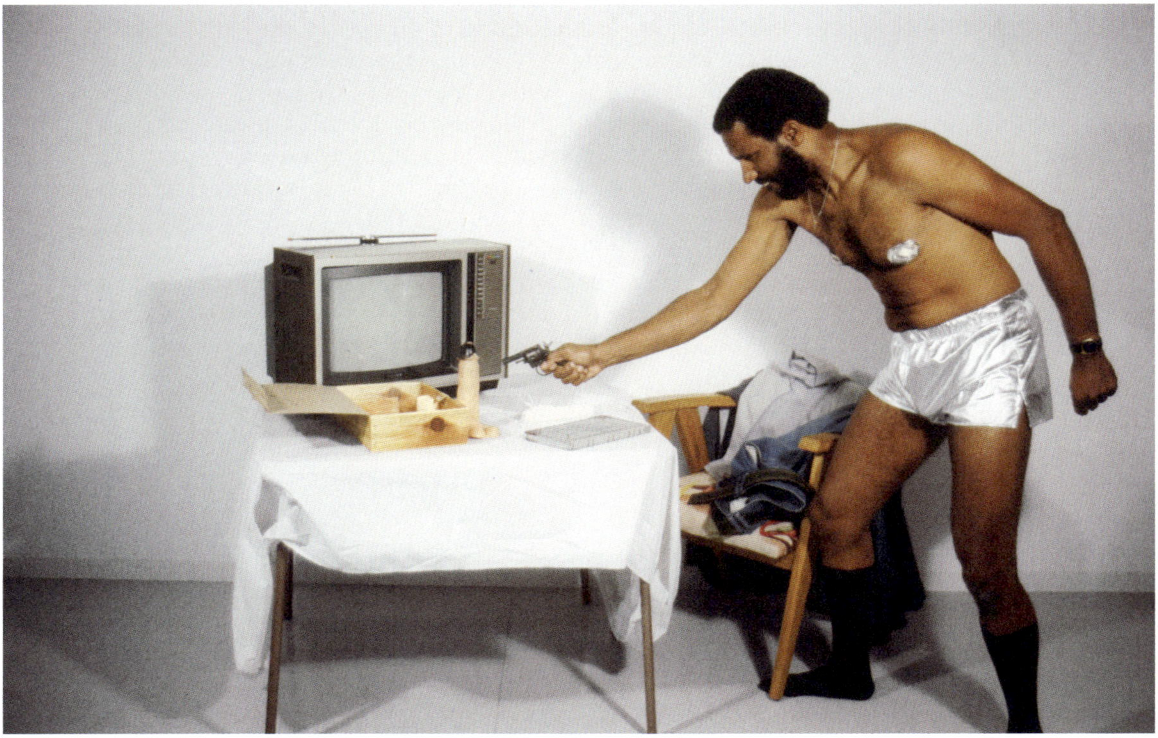

Ulysses Jenkins, *Just Another Rendering of the Same Old Problem*, 1979. Performance. Courtesy of the artist. Photo: Nancy Buchanan.

Later in 1979, *Just Another Rendering of the Same Old Problem* opened at Otis College in a gallery that was empty except for a small table upon which sits a television set. Ulysses Jenkins, dressed as a janitor, tidies the small set while a confused audience waits for his performance to begin. Jenkins surprises them by sitting down at the table and opening a book; through his reading he discovers that "the African-American male is perceived as a sex object in the Blacksploitation [era] of the 1970s."[16]

Jenkins pulls a cigar box from under the table, from which he procures a vibrating dildo. Importantly, it is a "white" dildo, with the glans, or head, painted black—a form of "blackface." Jenkins then disrobes, "revealing pasties with Superman's 'S,' a rhinestone in his bellybutton, and silver boxer shorts,"[17] suddenly embodying the sexualized black male that he's read about. Jenkins reacts by pulling out a fake pistol and shooting the dildo. The dildo falls into the view of a closed-circuit video camera, which in turn magnifies it on the monitor's screen. It visibly gyrates from the impact of the shots. As recounted on Jenkins's website, "the artist realizes [that this is] the perception he confronts in contemporary society and continues [to] shoot the dildo. This stereotype won't die ... so he realize[s] he has to manually turn off [the television] and walk away."[18]

The entire scene echoes "The Fact of Blackness," in which Fanon writes: "I came into the world imbued with the will to find meaning in things, my spirit filled with the desire to attain to the source of the world, and then I found that I was an object in the midst of other objects."[19]

In "The Case of Blackness," Moten argues that "The Fact of Blackness" is a mistranslation; it should read: "The Lived-Experience of the Black," which would more openly signal Fanon's phenomenological interests. Moten narrates Fanon's realization of the ontological impossibility of a black subjectivity within civil society.[20] Fanon argues, "The black man has no ontological resistance in the eyes of the white man."[21] Ontology—by way of Hegel—is attainable only when a consciousness confronts an "equally independent and self-contained" other. "Moreover, this other must have 'nothing in it which is not itself the origin.'"[22] For the black (non)subject, this is an impossibility from the outset, as blackness itself is a condition whose very existence is contingent upon and derived from whiteness, making "the black" an always already impure other. In *Just Another Rendering of the Same Old Problem*, Jenkins thus parallels Fanon; the artist realizes that he himself exists at the limit—and beyond the limit—of ontology, unable to overtake his own representation, in this instance, as a sexual object. Caught in a literal closed circuit of representation between the dildo, its image, his own body, and the text that describes the processes acting upon him, he is left with no ability to contest his own objectification. Exhausted by his ongoing battle with the black image—which is exemplified in this work and others, as well as in his day-to-day life—Jenkins withdraws fully.

16   Othervisions Studio, "Just Another Rendering of the Same Old Problem," http://www.ulyssesjenkins.com/justanother.html.

17   Paul Von Blum, "Ulysses Jenkins: A Griot for an Electronic Age," *Journal of Pan African Studies* 3, no. 2 (2009): 135.

18   Othervisions Studio, "Just Another Rendering of the Same Old Problem."

19   Frantz Fanon, "The Fact of Blackness," in *Black Skin, White Masks*, trans. Charles Lam Markmann (London: Picador, 1970), 82.

20   Moten, "The Case of Blackness," 179.

21   Fanon, "The Fact of Blackness," 83.

22   Kara Keeling, "In the Interval: Frantz Fanon and the 'Problems' of Visual Representation," *Qui Parle* 13, no. 2 (Spring/Summer 2003): 91–117.

Jenkins moves on to a much larger question, an inquiry that entirely exceeds cultural critique. Now freed from the stalemate between black life and the white gaze through his own withdrawal, he asks: If blackness cannot *be* in the eyes of civil—white—society, if black people cannot articulate themselves as black *individuals*, untethered to blackness, then what is it, in fact, to be black? What is the character of blackness?

As Jenkins approaches *Adams Be Doggereal* in 1981, he has already parsed out the difference between blackness and the black individual, and understands the onto-logical impossibility of the latter. He has renounced his desire to just be himself, understanding now that he, as a black man, is always already "All Blacks," as Fanon would say. Or, as Cedric Robinson wrote, Jenkins has renounced actual being for an acceptance of the historical being, the "ontological totality."[23] He has always already "consent[ed] not to be a single being."[24] As Kara Keeling writes, "The Black therefore exists as a collective subject whose governing fiction is not personal but social."[25]

With this distinction in mind, it is difficult to find the exact language to speak of where Jenkins finds himself at this juncture, for his concern appears at once as *neither* for "the Black" *nor* for blackness, as well as for *both* the black *and* for blackness. This is to say, Jenkins is thinking *the gap* between the two, or as Fred Moten so eloquently phrased it in "The Case of Blackness": "[T]he wary mood or fugitive case that ensues between the fact of blackness and the lived experience of the black and as a slippage enacted by the meaning—or, perhaps too 'trans-literally,' the (plain[-sung]) sense—of things when subjects are engaged in the representation of objects."[26]

Moten, too, lingers in the gap, in the mistranslation of Fanon's "lived-experi-ence" as "fact," of the phenomenologically black and the ontologically voided black-ness. Thinking this gap, Jenkins builds upon Fanon and anticipates Moten's similar negotiations, resonances that situate him within some sort of Afro-pessimist/Black Optimist tradition[27] (if we can even claim there is such a tradition). In this continuum, Afro-pessimism is something like a "[theory] of black positionality" that spreads out-ward from Fanon's (non)ontology rather than a school of thought.[28] Moten writes that one of the great beauties of Afro-pessimist thought is that it "allows and compels one to move past that contradictory impulse to affirm the interest of negation and to begin to consider *what nothing is*."[29] This is where we find Jenkins in *Adams Be Doggereal*.

In the performance, Jenkins's nothing, his approximated black nothingness, takes the form of the glass prism, collectively discovered by the artist and his col-laborators in a pile of dirt in his studio. Jenkins recalls the object as symbolizing a "new self."[30] The prism is materially present yet curiously empty, its primary function being to act as a filter for light. A prism can be used, as Sir Isaac Newton discovered long ago, to reflect and refract light—that is, to disperse white light into beams of different colors. Prior to Newton, it was believed that white light was colorless; his

23   Cedric Robinson, *Black Marxism: The Making of the Black Radical Tradition* (Chapel Hill: University of North Carolina Press, 2000), 171.
24   Moten often references this phrase of Édouard Glissant. See "One World in Relation: Édouard Glissant in Conversation with Manthia Diawara," *Nka: Journal of Contemporary African Art*, no. 28 (2011): 4–19, doi:101.215 /10757163-1266639.
25   Keeling, "In the Interval," 100.
26   Moten, "The Case of Blackness," 179.
27   While often in dialogue and agreement with those considered Afro-pessimists, Moten prefers to label his work as "black optimism." However, he notes that Afro-pessimism and black optimism "are not but nothing other than one another." Fred Moten, "Blackness and Nothingness (Mysti-cism in the Flesh)," *The South Atlantic Quarterly* 112, no. 4 (Fall 2013): 742.
28   Wilderson III, *Red, White, & Black: Cinema and the Structure of U.S. Antagonism*, 6.
29   Moten, "Blackness and Nothingness (Mysticism in the Flesh)," 741. Italics in the original.
30   "Modern Art in Los Angeles: African American Avant-Gardes, 1965–1990," panel discussion.

experimentation with prisms proved that it was quite opposite, that it is comprised of all of the colors of the rainbow.

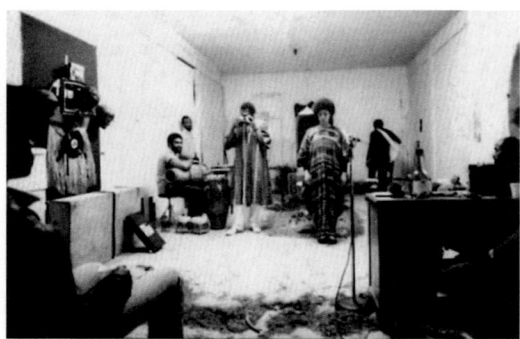

Ulysses Jenkins, *Adams Be Doggereal*, 1981. Performance. Courtesy of the artist. Photo: Bruce W. Talamon.

Jenkins's use of the prism can be theorized in a number of ways, all of which might be said to negotiate the simultaneous plentitude and void that blackness presents. First, we might read the prism as a filter of sorts, where blackness might be a lens through which to view the world. We see a similar position in William Pope.L's *Black Factory*. On the occasion of that work's first instantiation, Pope.L declared that "blackness is a lever to talk about otherness, . . . just a funnel."[31] A prism is a starting point from which to think a multitude of positions—a rather humanist, multiculturalist conclusion.

Second, Jenkins might be proposing a radicalized departure from Pope.L's stance, one where the prism—considering its role in proving that white light is not colorless—might speak to the notion that all other positions have been and must be articulated through and against "the Black." This, again, follows in the Afro-pessimist line of thinking, where blackness is the non-communicable body against which white civil society constitutes itself. Third, the prism rests between emptiness and fullness. It is, as noted above, at once materially present and transparent; it also contains the potential for the apparent emptiness of white light and fullness of the rainbow. In this case, it embodies the paradoxical emptiness and fullness, plenitude and nothingness of a black (non)ontology.

Looking back upon his own work from this period, Jenkins says that his goal was always to illustrate the possibility of a new black universalism.[32] It is impossible to say whether this was fully realized—or what that would even look like in practice. However, we can say that, in *Adams Be Doggereal*, Jenkins does realize some sort of expansion of blackness that begins to repair or move beyond its originary ontological failure. The prism effectively positions blackness as a stance from which all else must be thought, much like François Laruelle's *uchromia*, wherein we might "think from the point of view of Black as what determines color in the last instance rather than what limits it."[33] From here, blackness, in all of its para-ontological glory, destabilizes not only its own existence but also all other racial ontologies that it exists to constitute. And from here, thinking "blackness as what determines color," blackness as the starting point and not the limit, we might throw into question other artistic and philosophical interests in the color itself—and therefore reassess the position of all those whom it marks as well. Thinking of blackness, "the Black," in this way activates its darkness and allows a consideration of its depth, its ability to reflect and absorb. As Laruelle writes, "a phenomenal blackness entirely fills the essence of man."[34]

31   Joshua Feist, "William Pope.L Interview Excerpt," posted March 15, 2010, https://www.youtube.com /watch?v=e-7KNINpA6w.
32   "Modern Art in Los Angeles: African American Avant-Gardes, 1965–1990," panel discussion.
33   François Laruelle, "On the Black Universe: In the Human Foundations of Color," trans. Miguel Abreu, in *Hyun Soo Choi: Seven Large-Scale Paintings* (New York: Thread Waxing Space, 1991), 2–4, http://www.recessart.org /wp-content/uploads/Laruelle-Black-Universe1.pdf, accessed 6/4/2016.
34   Laruelle, "On the Black Universe."

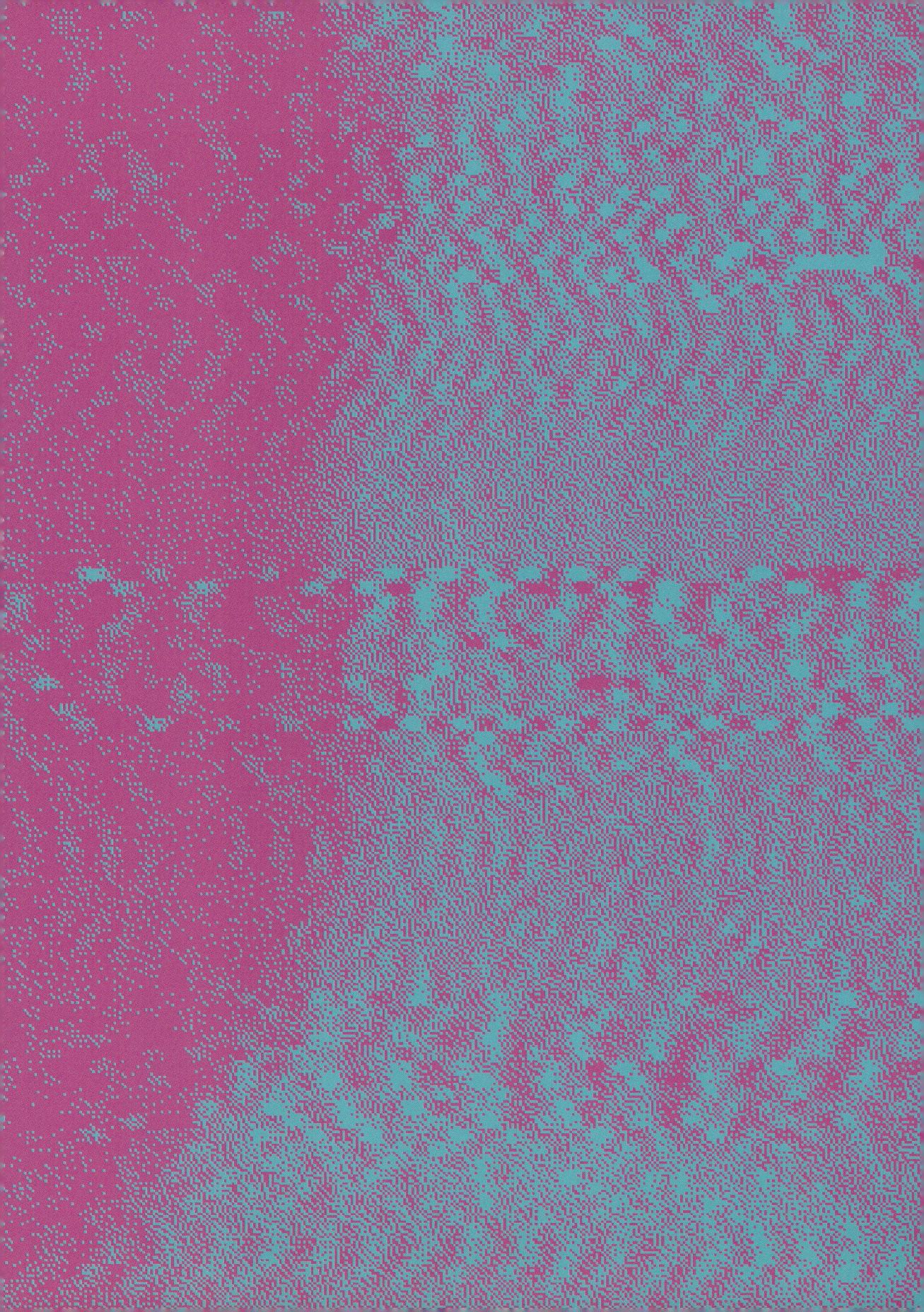

REMNANTS OF THE

WATTS FESTIVAL

1972–73, compiled 1980, 55:44 min.

This videotape presents an overview of what was a
historical event in the Black and Brown community of the
Southeast Central area of Los Angeles. —UJ

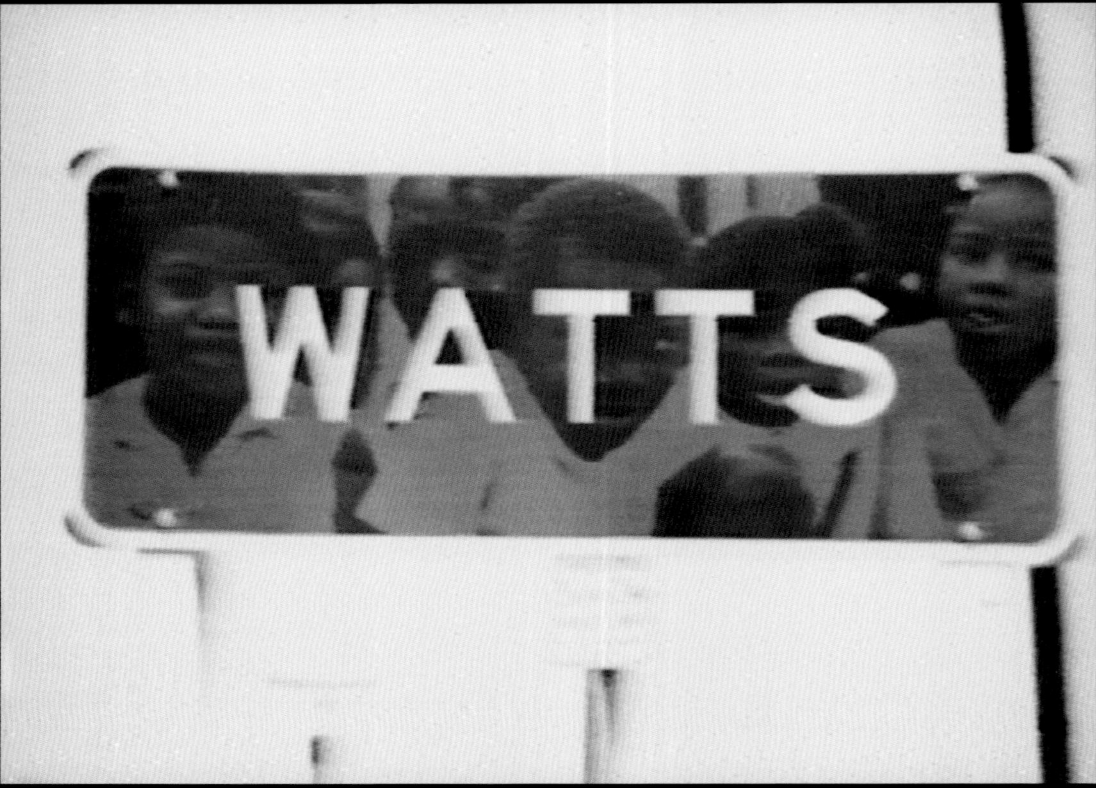
WATTS

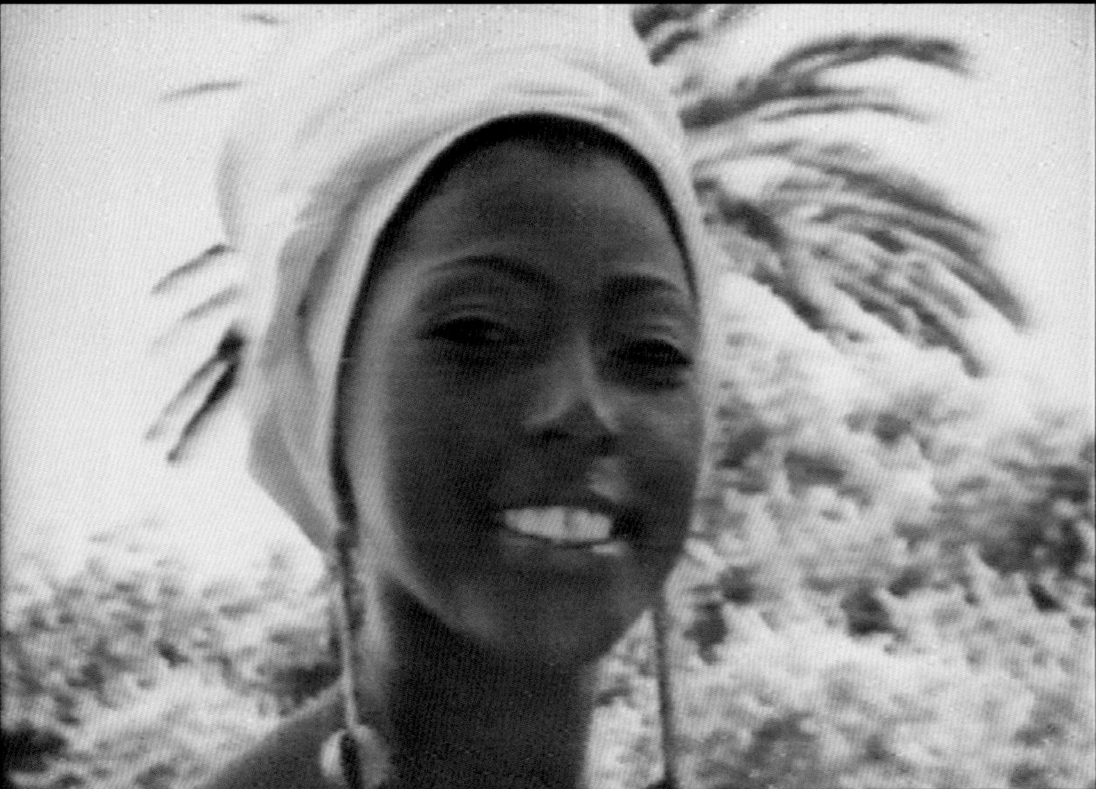

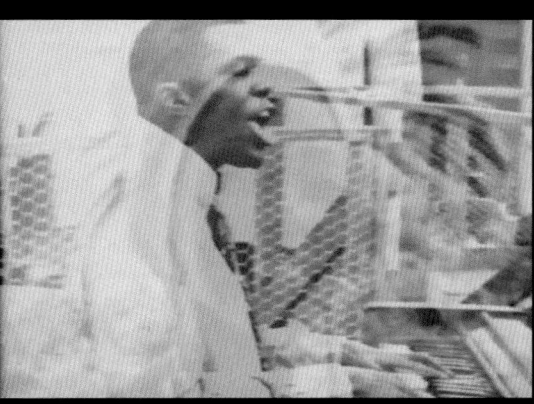

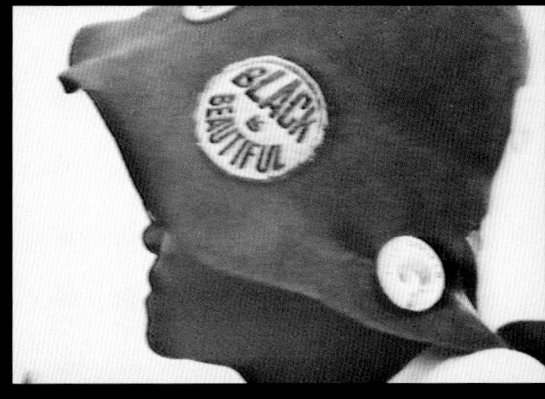

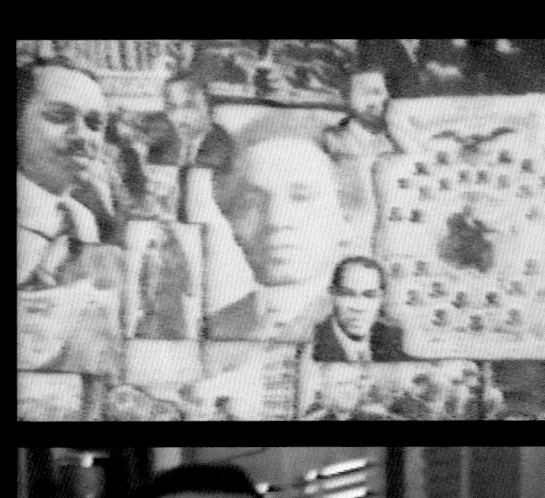

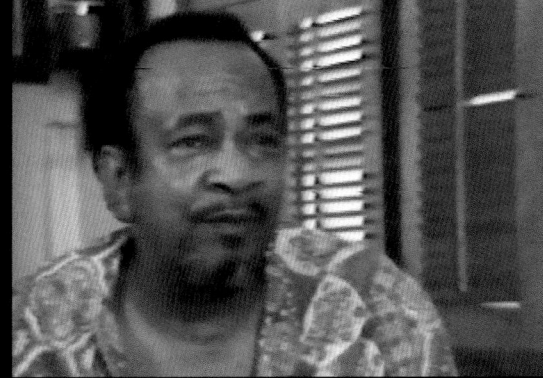

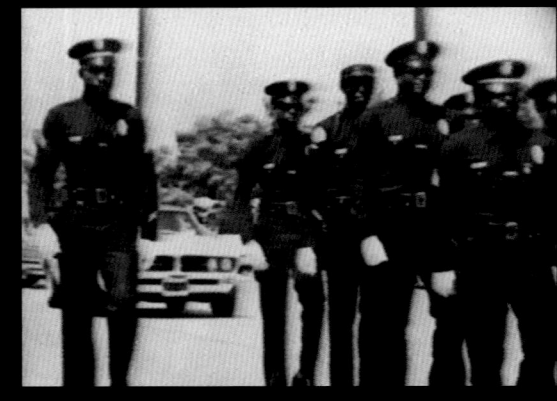

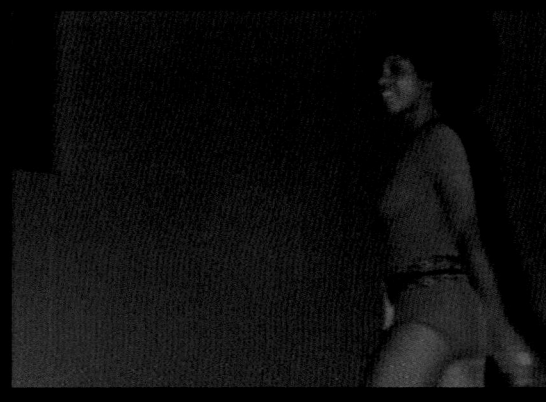

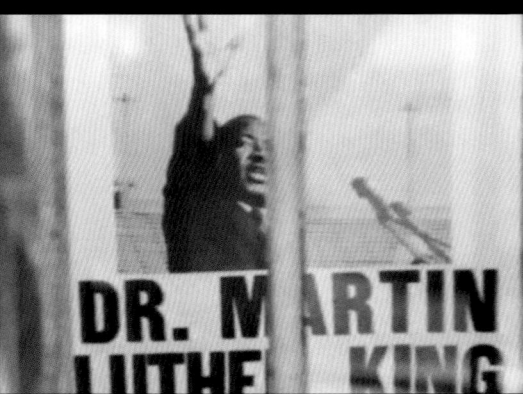

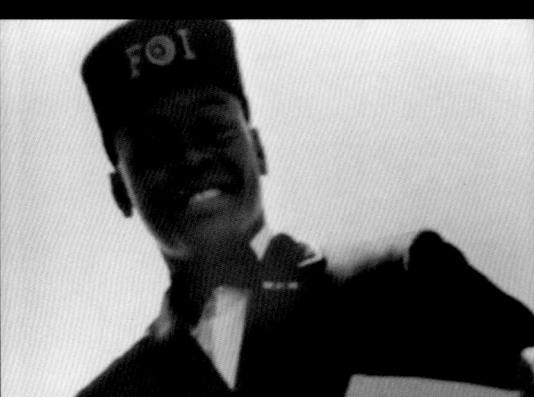

DISTRICT F

1977, 62 min.

The purpose of this tape was to create a sociological
overview for the administration and faculty of Santa
Monica College in conjunction with the Equal Opportunity
Program. The title comes from the geographical area
designated by the Los Angeles Unified School District,
known as "District F," which incorporated the incoming
minority population east of La Cienega Blvd. —UJ

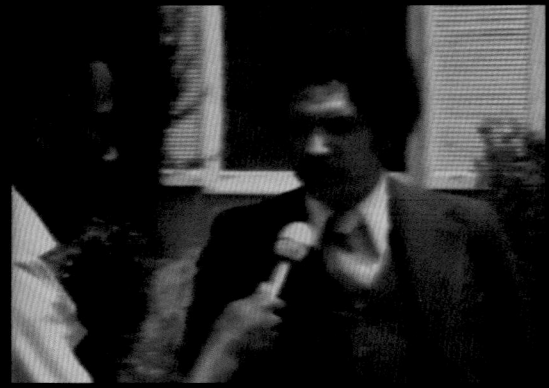
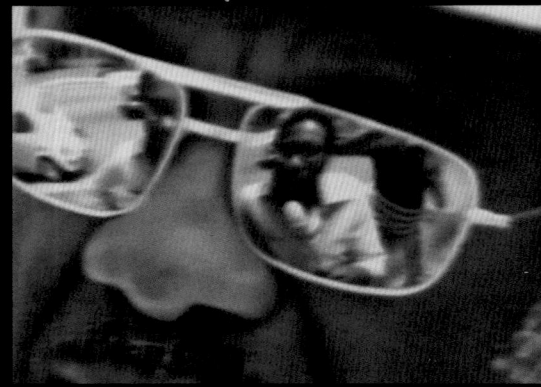
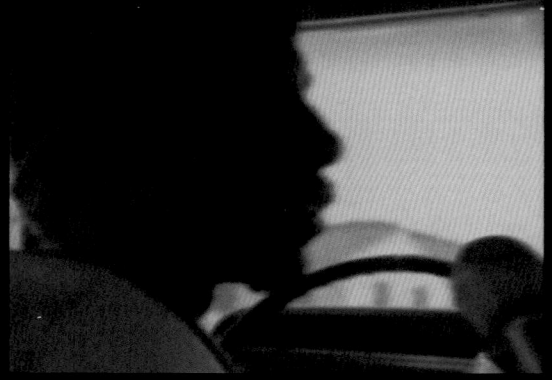
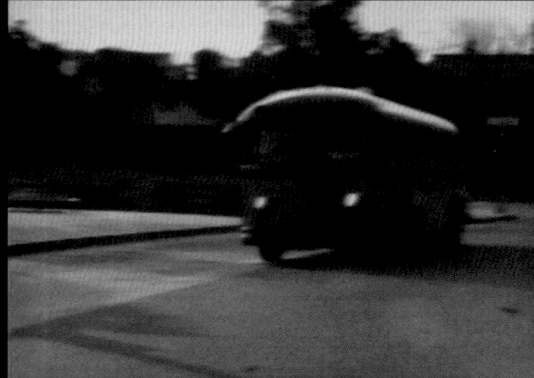

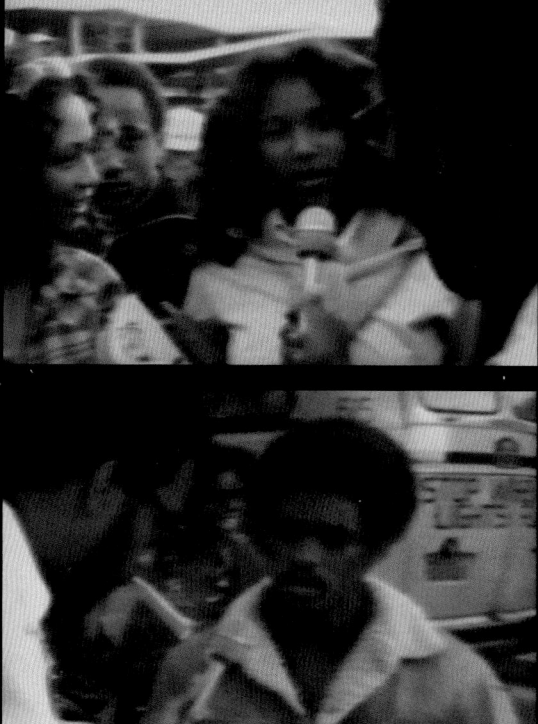

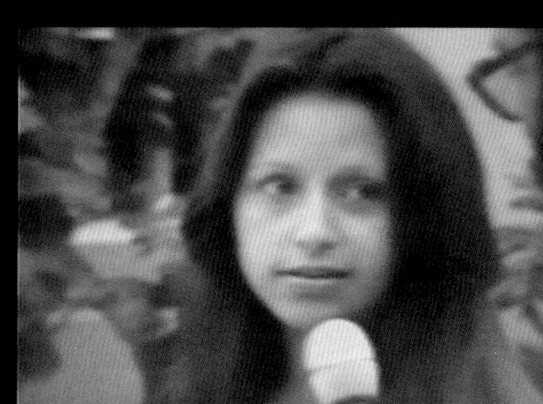

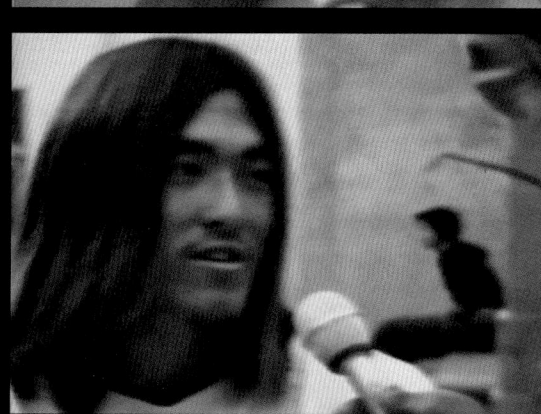

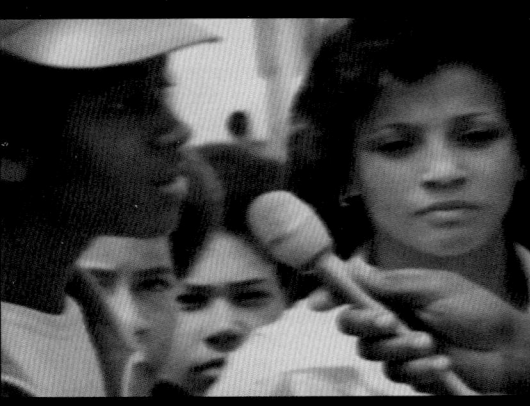
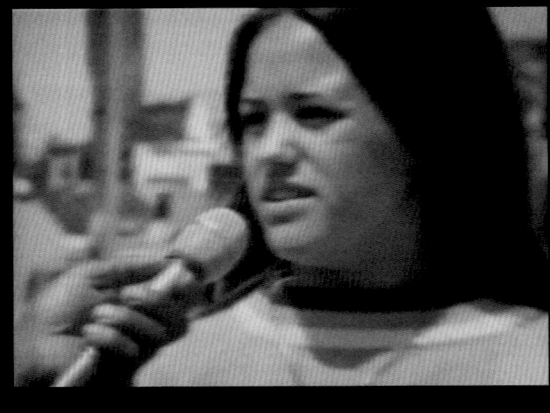
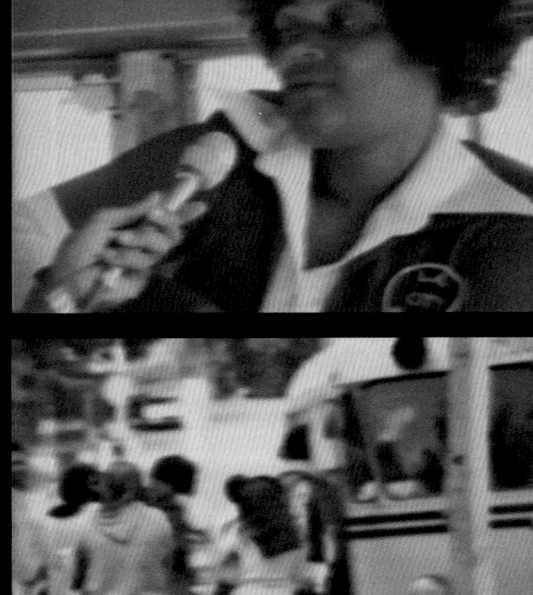

KING DAVID

1978, 17:30 min.

A collaborative portrait of David Hammons with LaMonte
Westmoreland as commentator. A visit with the artist
at his summer studio where he discusses his philosophies
and his work. —UJ

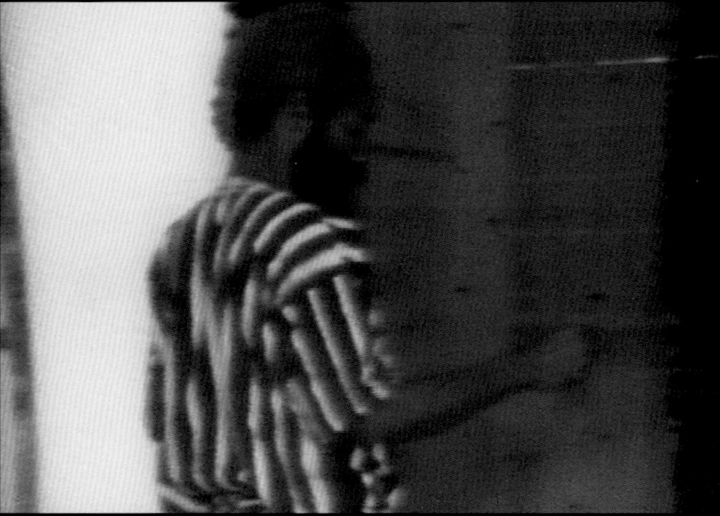

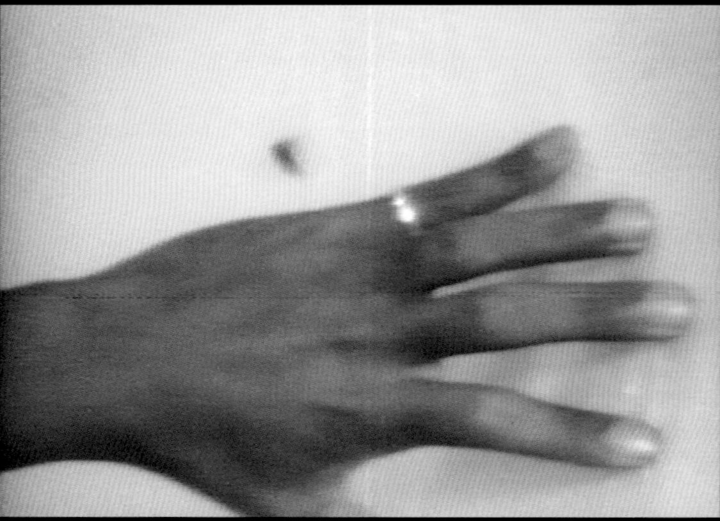

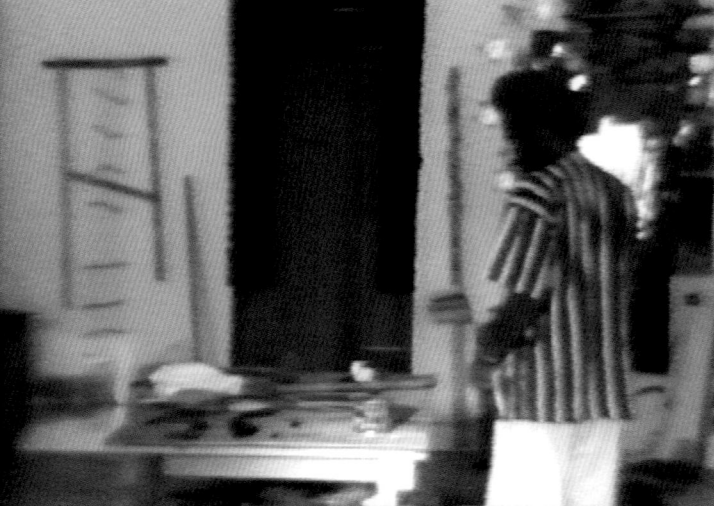

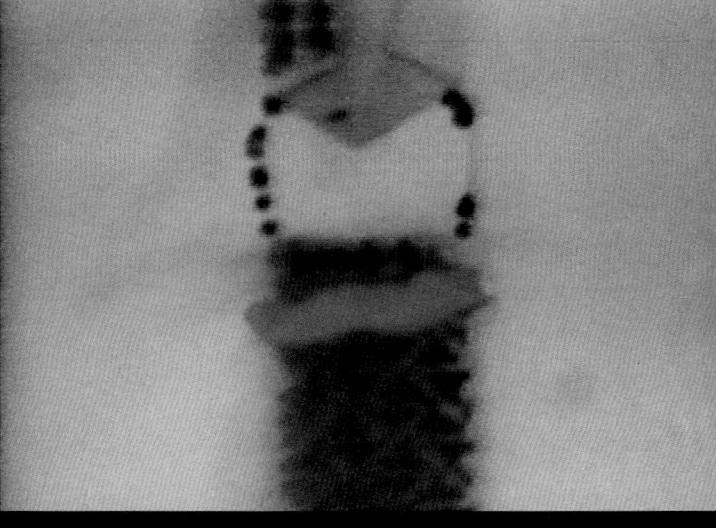

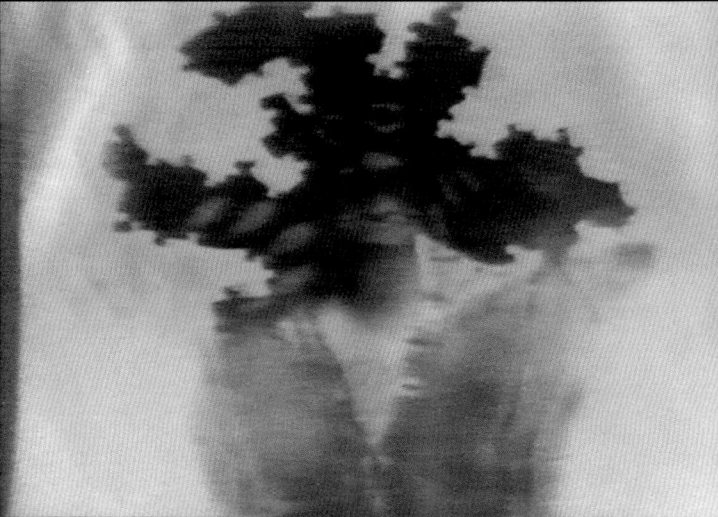

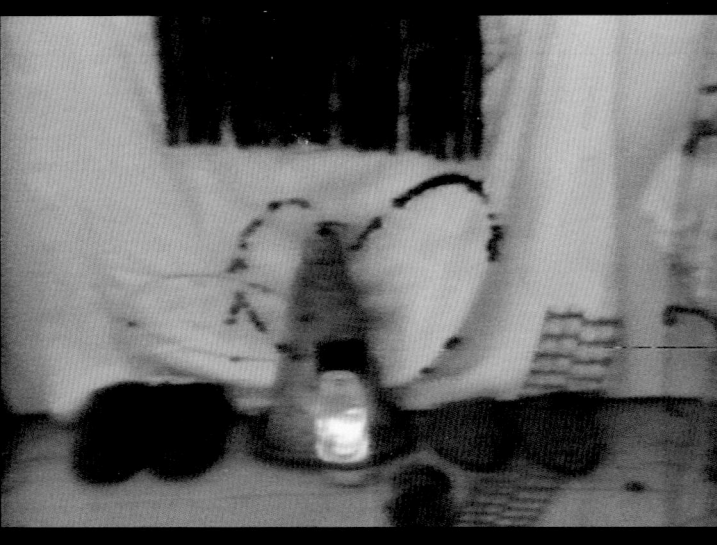

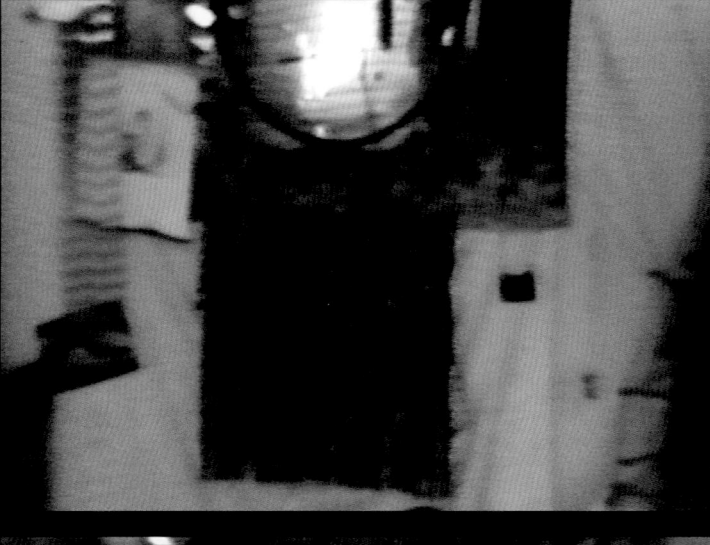

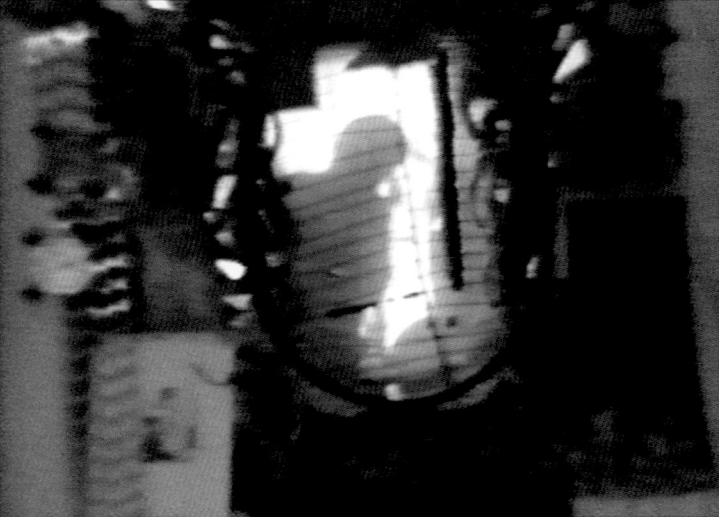

MASS of IMAGES

1978, 4:16 min.

This is my first video performance, a visual collage that takes a critical view of African American stereotypes in American media. —UJ

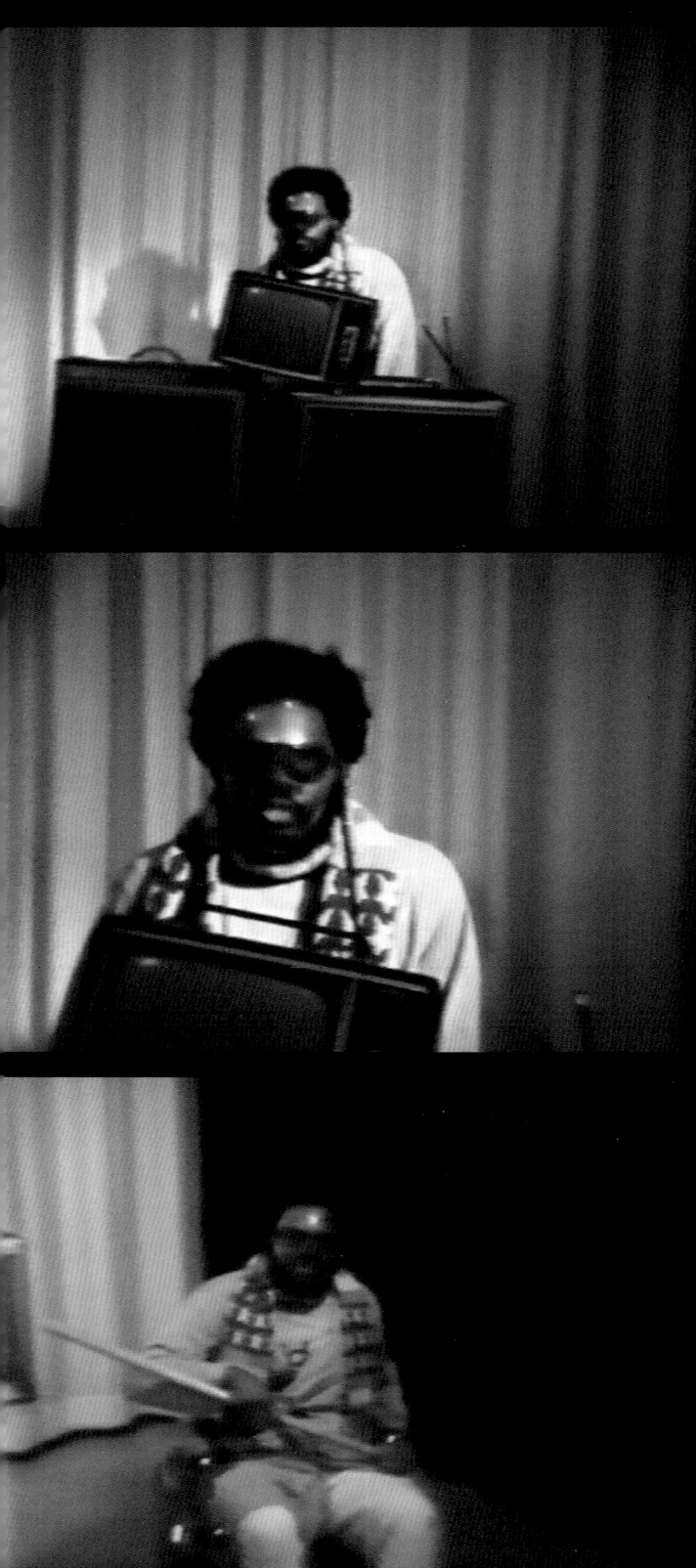

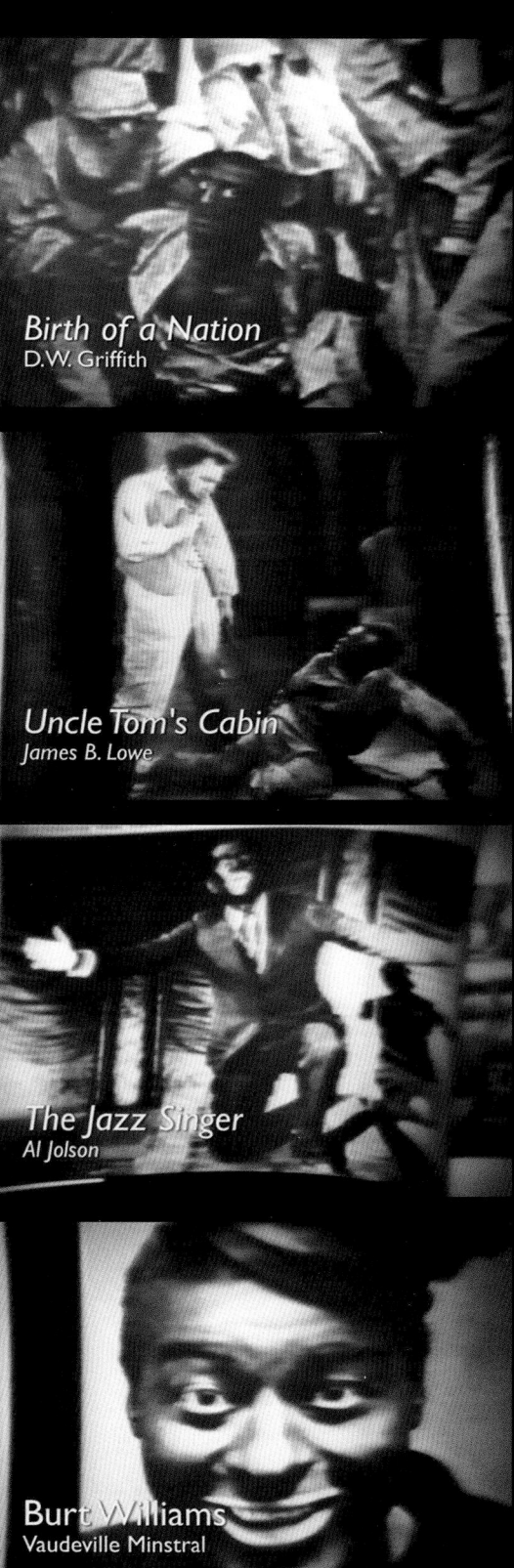

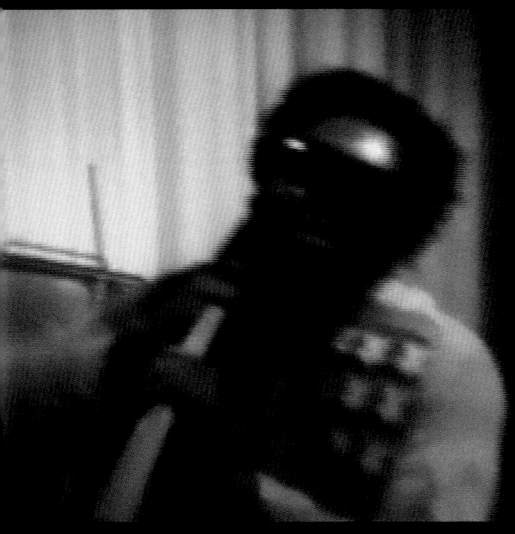

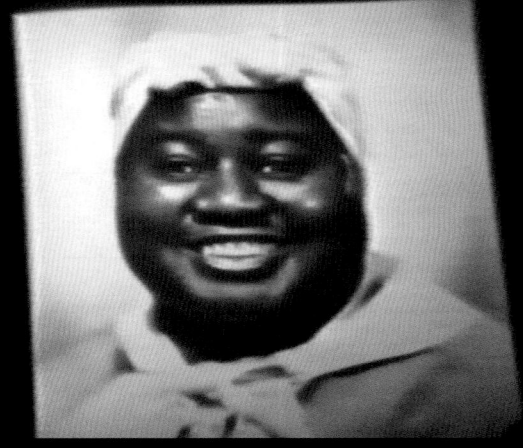

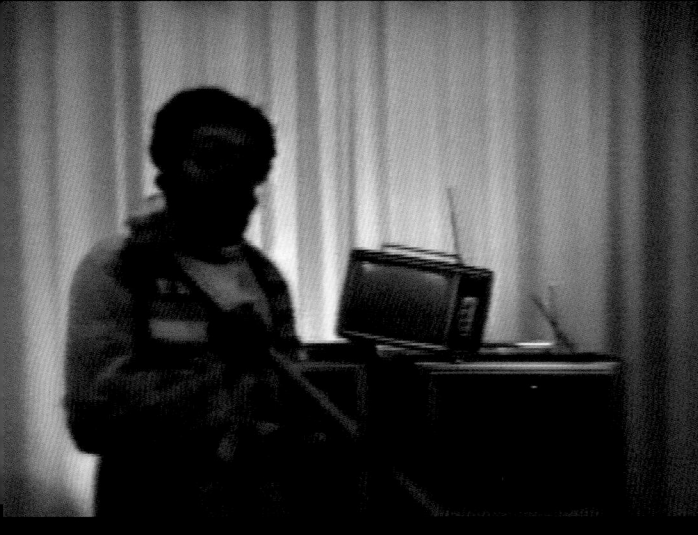

TWO - ZONE TRANSFER

1979, 23:52 min.
Performed on November 21, 1978, at Otis Art Institute,
Los Angeles

A narrative fiction look at the source of Afro-American
stereotypes. The main character, having a restless
night, has a dream that leads his subconscious into
the history of the minstrel: an American entertainment
institution from which the stereotypical image of
Black people derived. —UJ

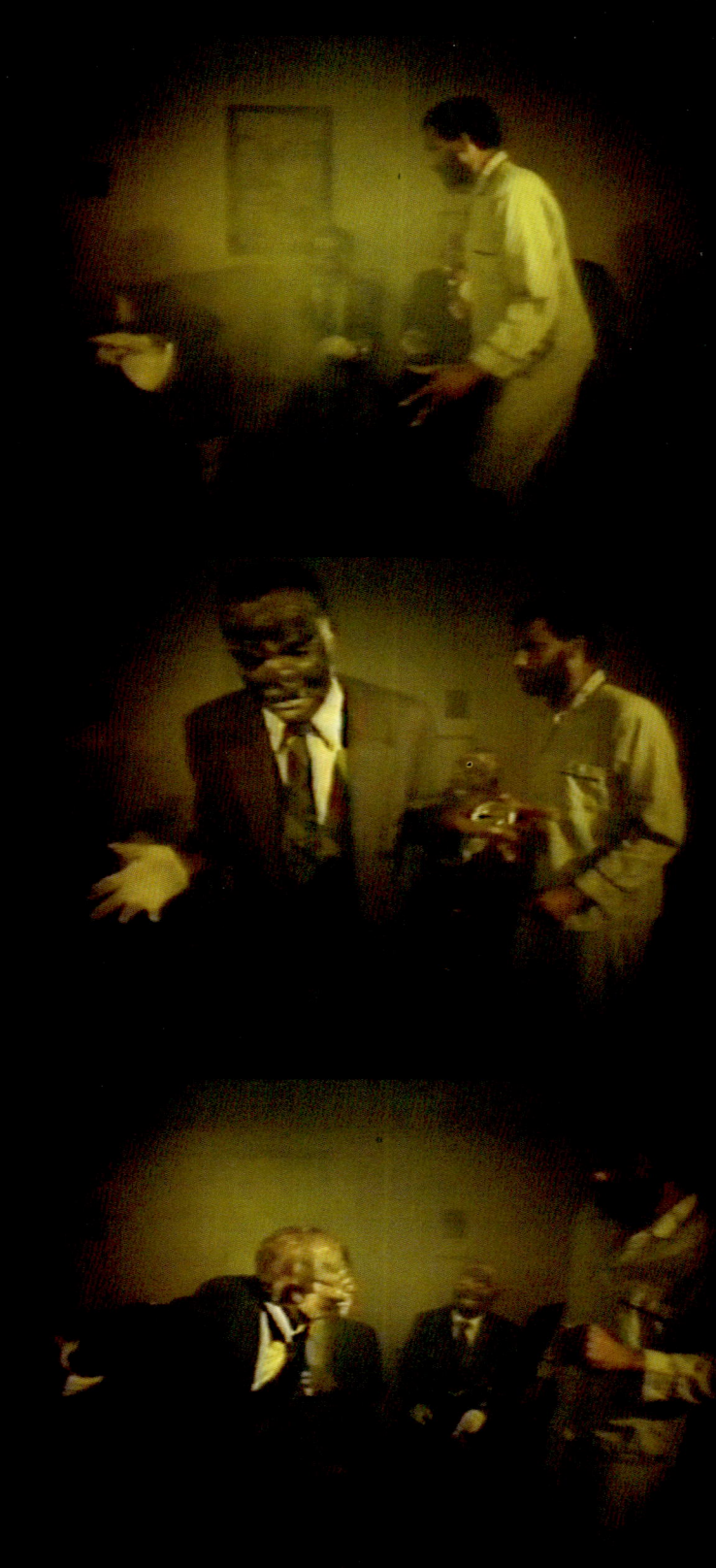

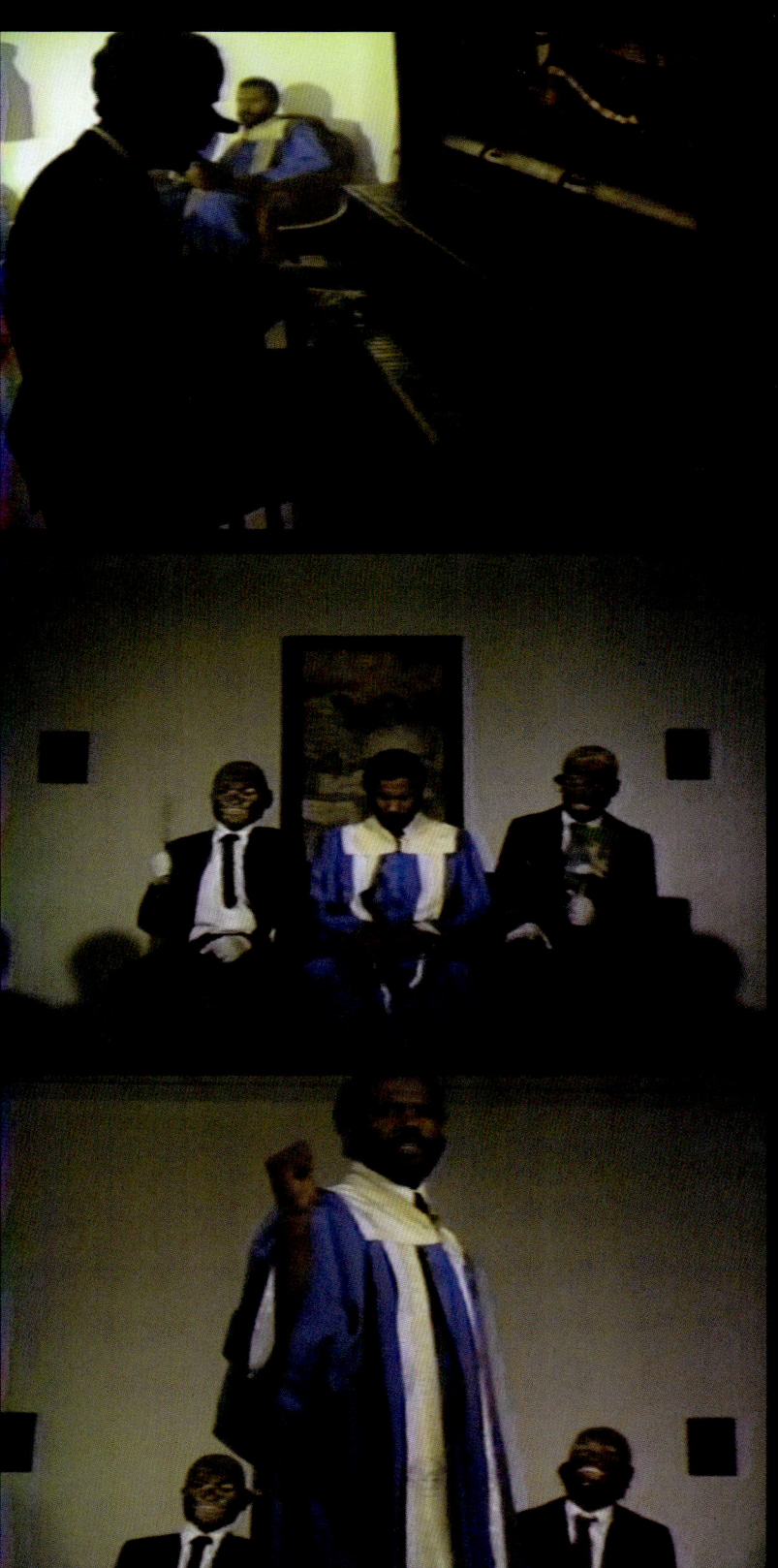

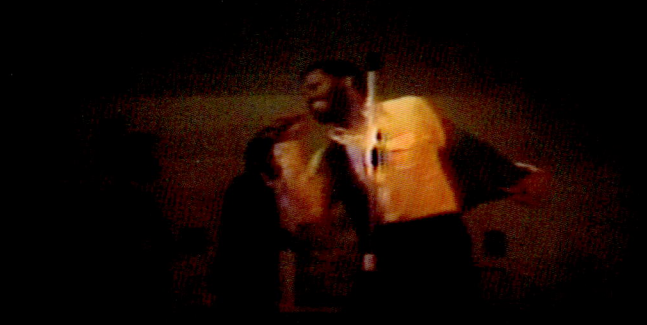

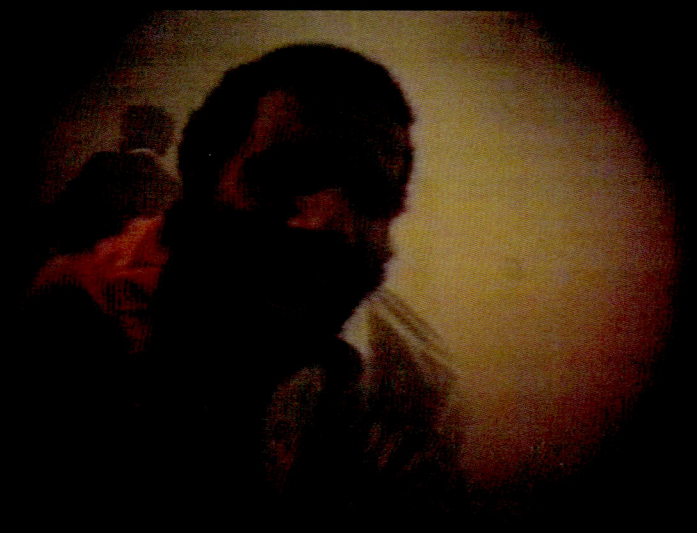

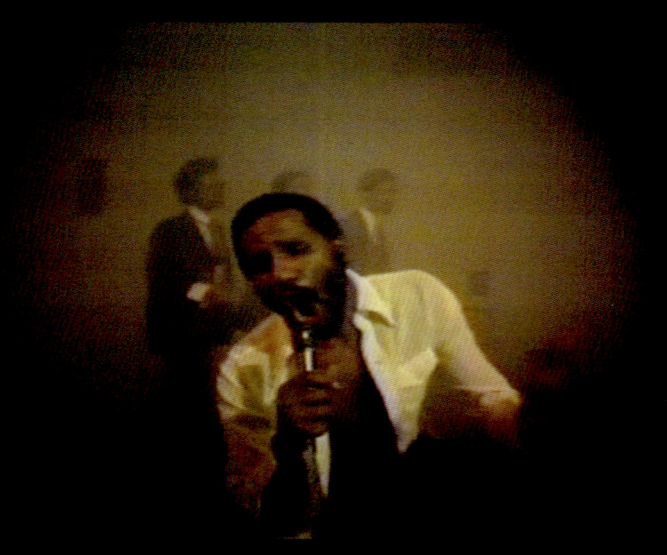

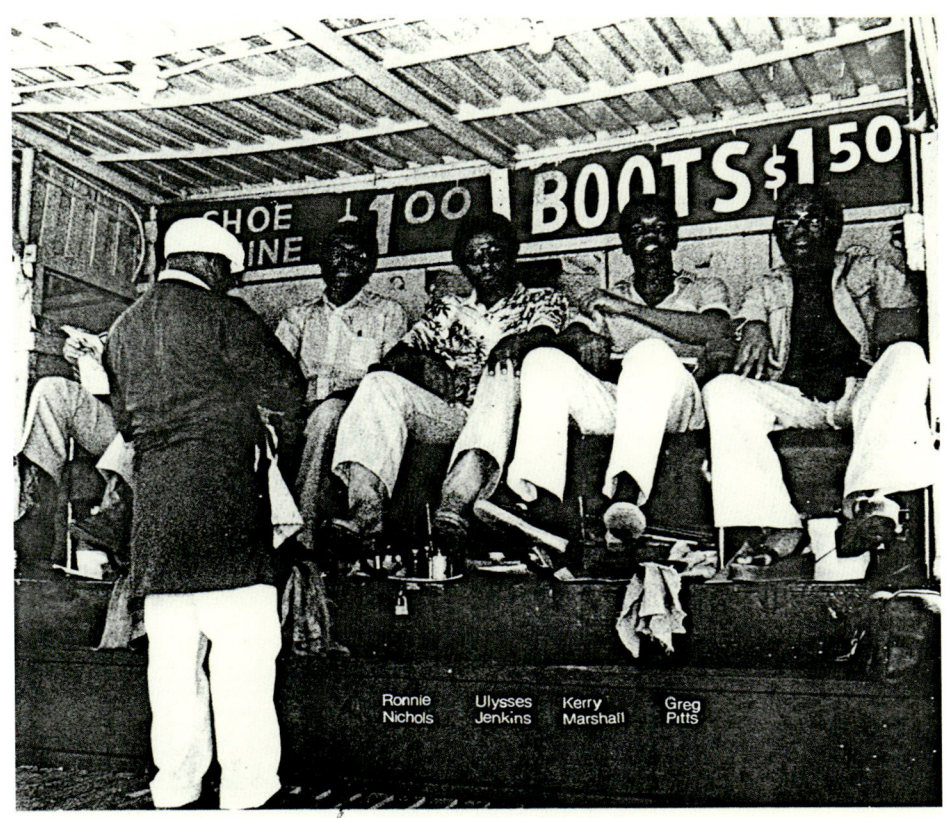

TWO·ZONE TRANSFER

NOVEMBER 21 -DECEMBER 1

RECEPTION 7 p.m.   PERFORMANCE 8 p.m.
TUESDAY · NOVEMBER 21

Otis Art Institute   2401 Wilshire Blvd   L. A., California
North Gallery   Tues.-Sat. 10·3 p.m.

Poster for *Two-Zone Transfer* performance, 1978, designed by Kerry James Marshall. Courtesy of the Collection of Kerry James Marshall.

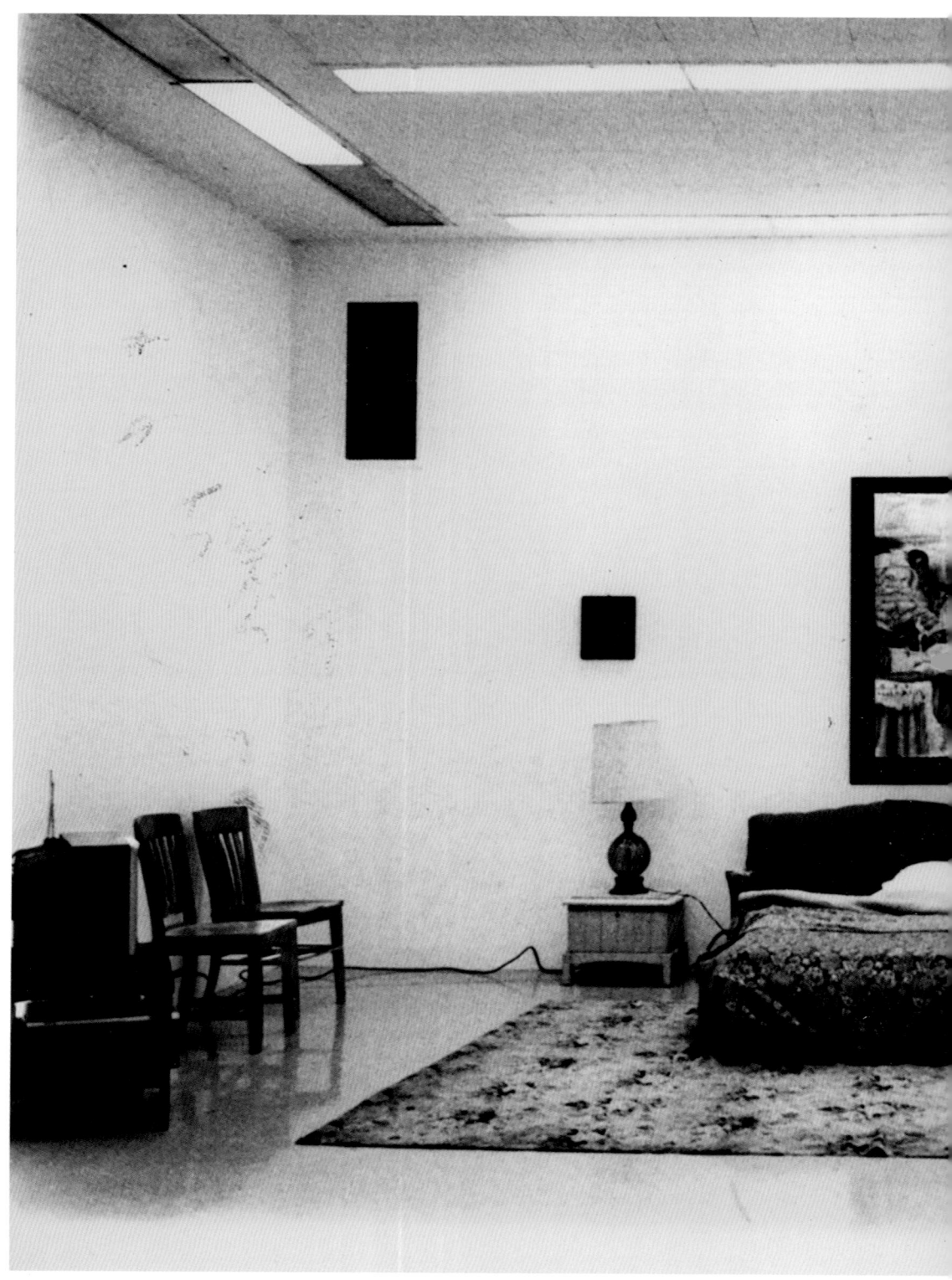

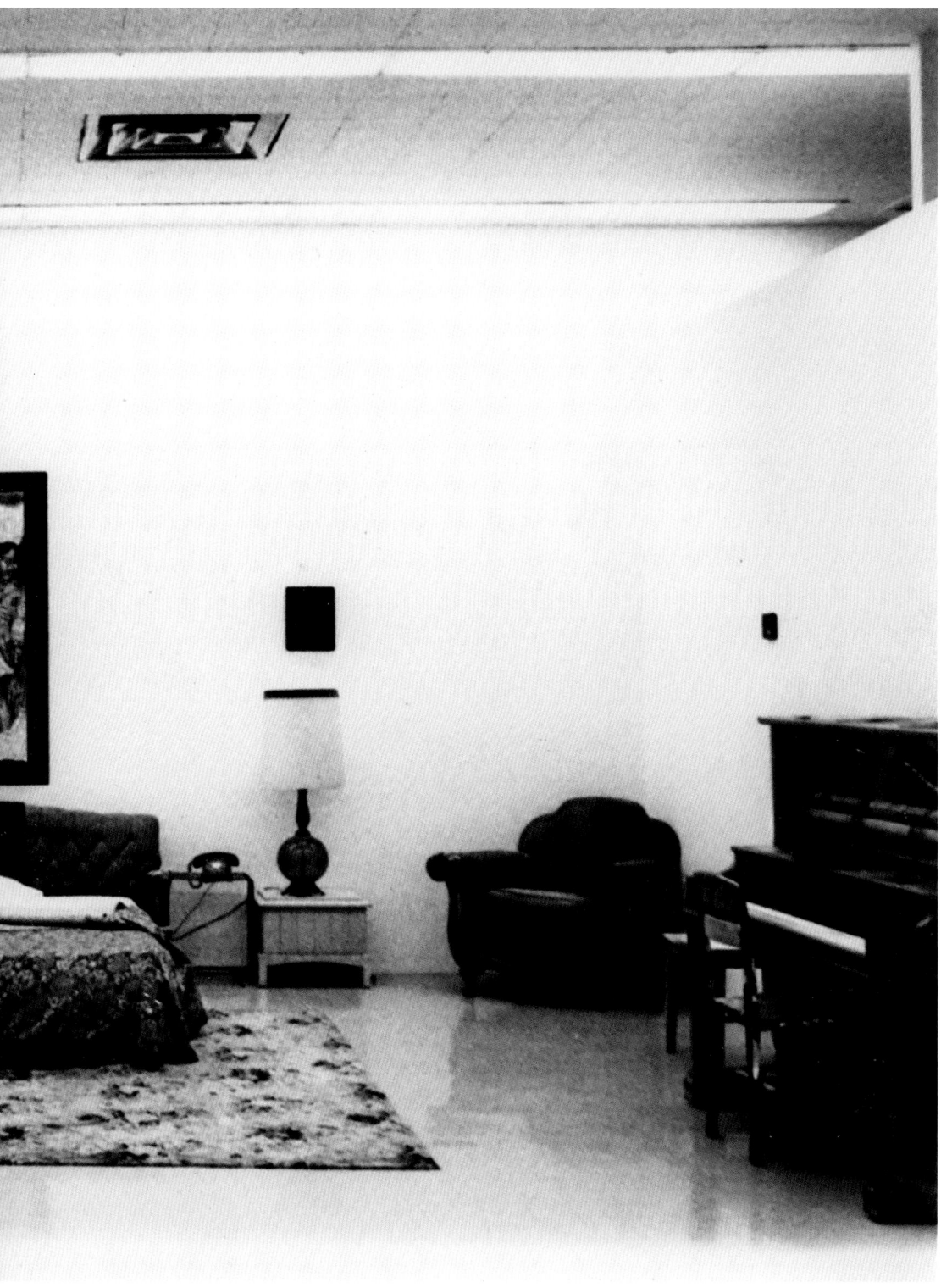

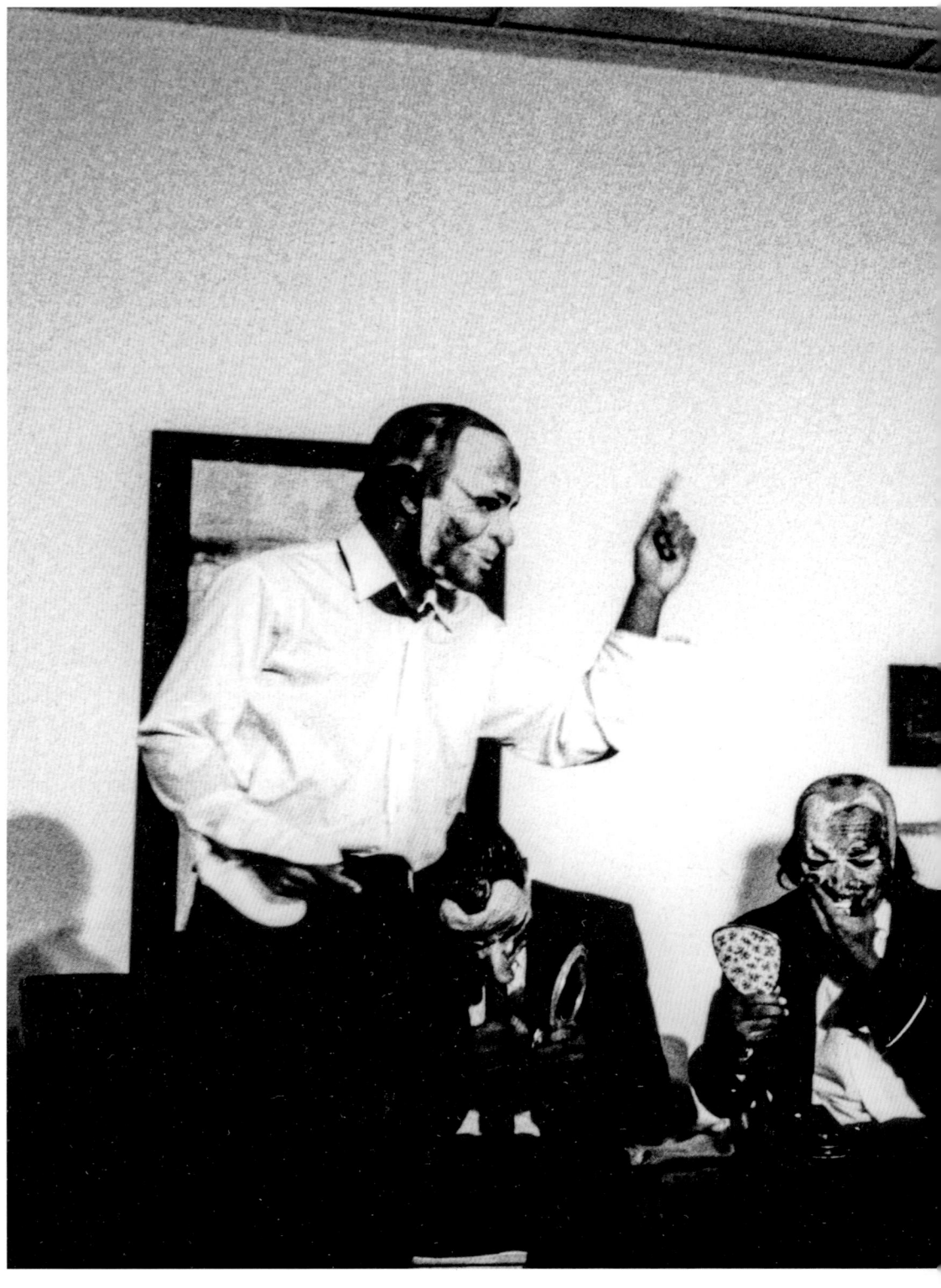

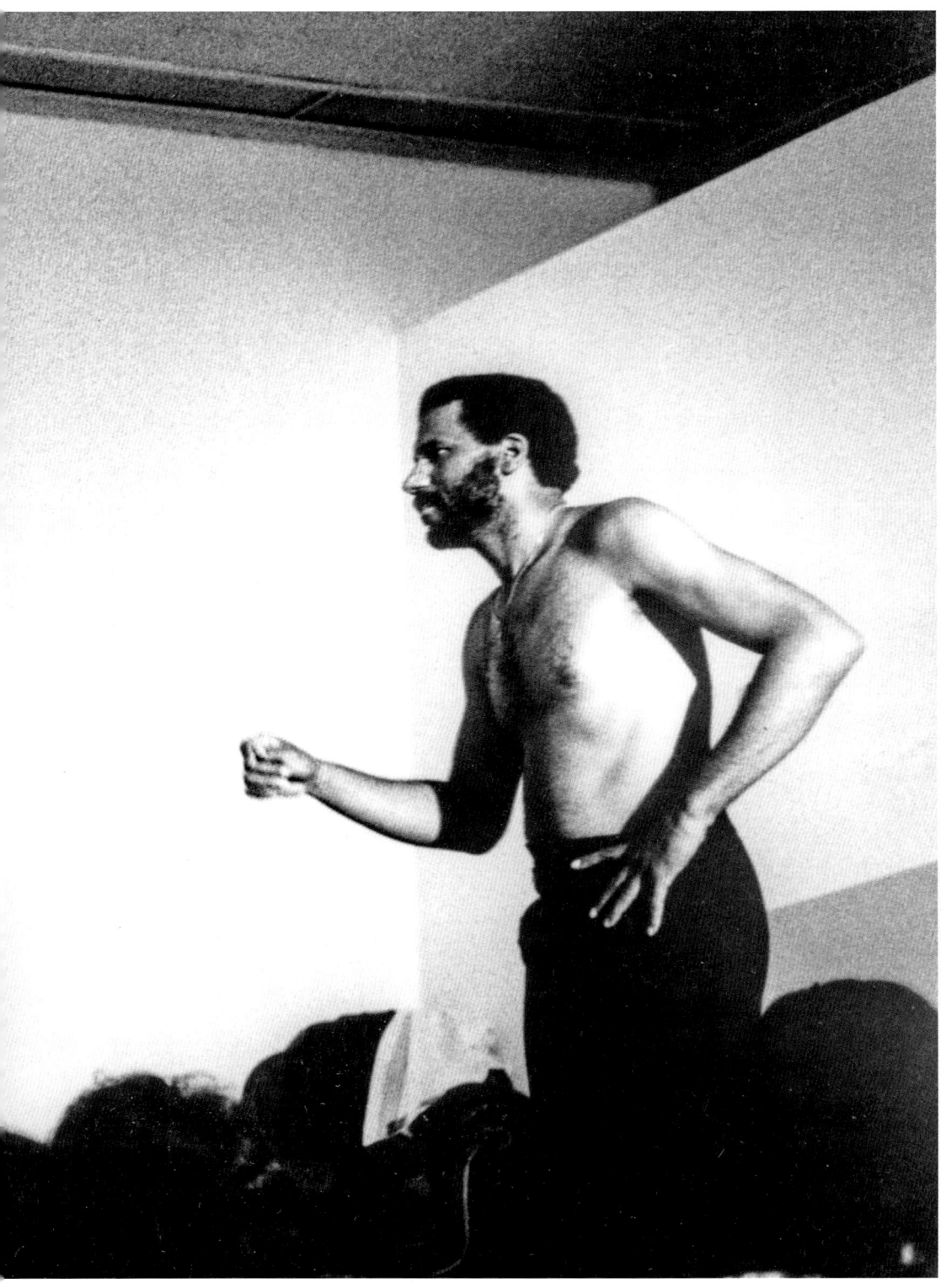

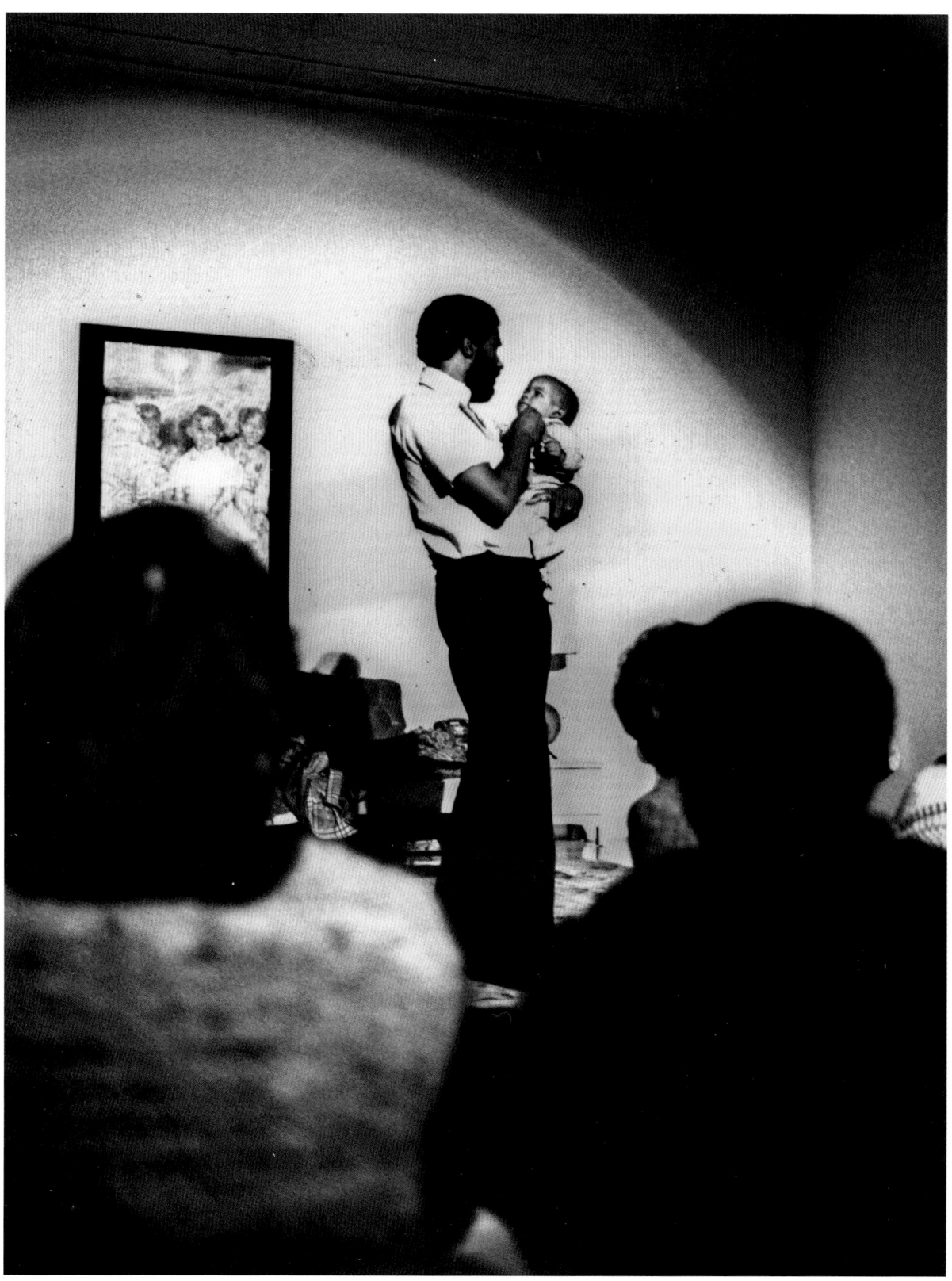

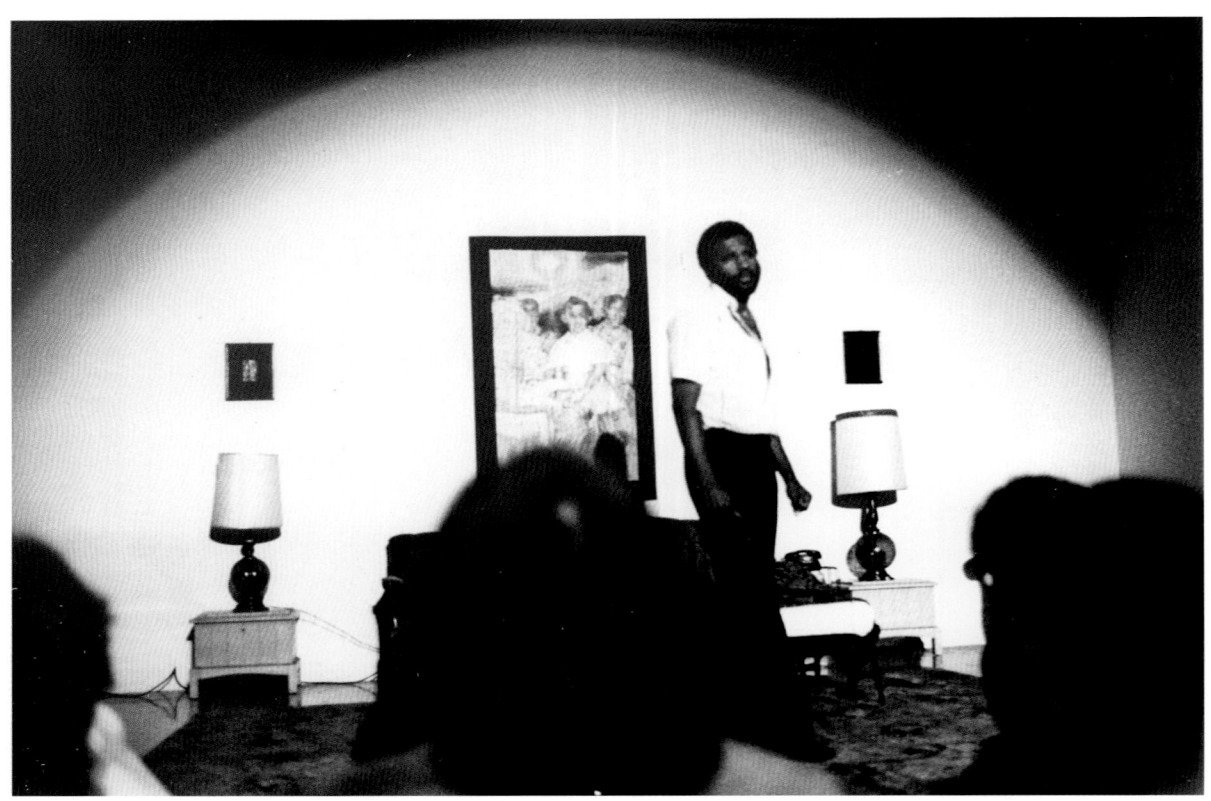

Two-Zone Transfer performance, 1978. Courtesy of the artist. Photo: Ilene Segalove.

JUST ANOTHER
RENDERING OF THE SAME
OLD PROBLEM

1979
Performed on May 8, 1979, at Otis Art Institute,
Los Angeles.

The birth of such consciousness / has always read /
phallic and grotesque / let go let go. —UJ

Opposite: Contact sheet with photographs of Ulysses Jenkins, *Just Another Rendering of the Same Old Problem*, performance, 1979. Photographer unknown.

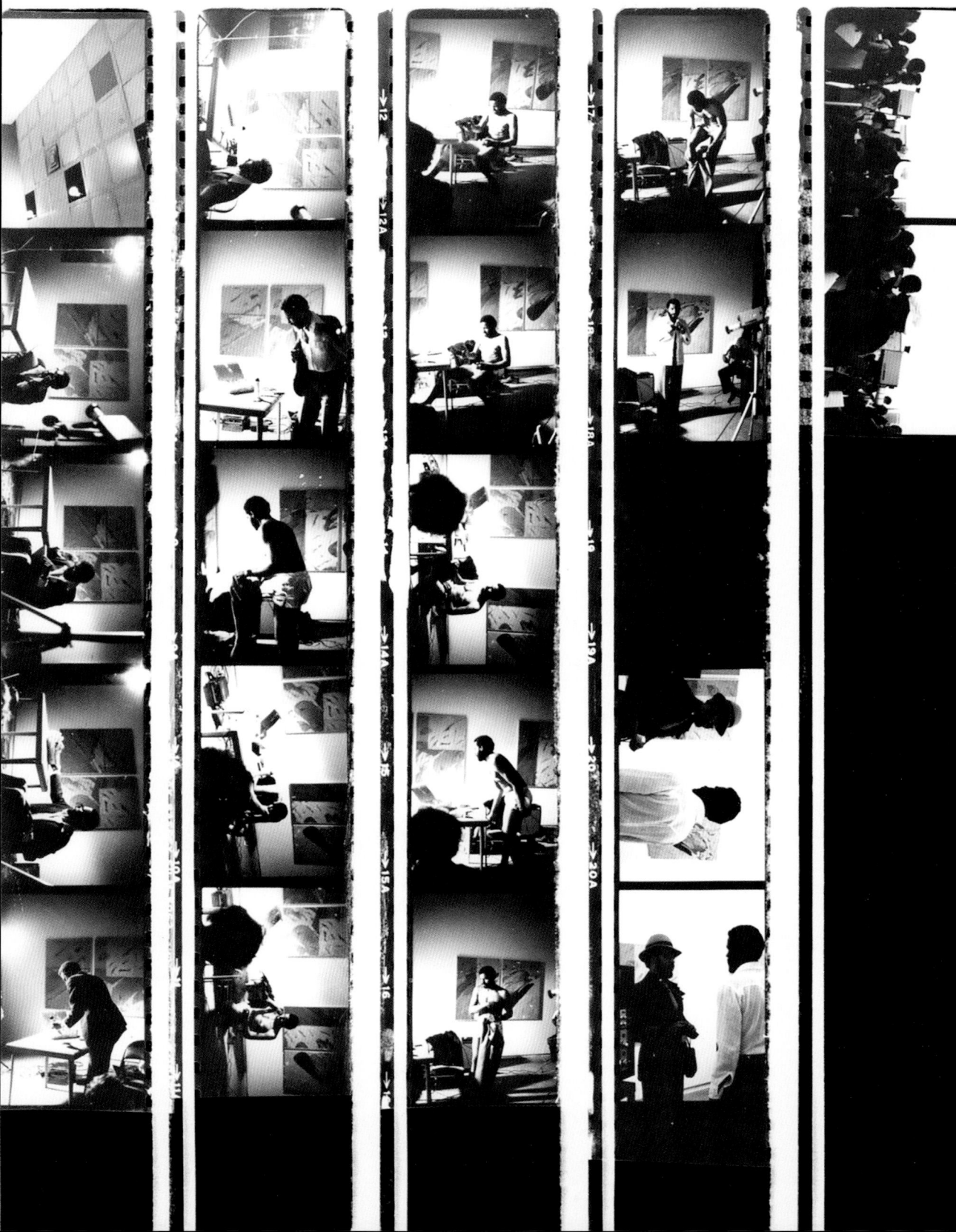

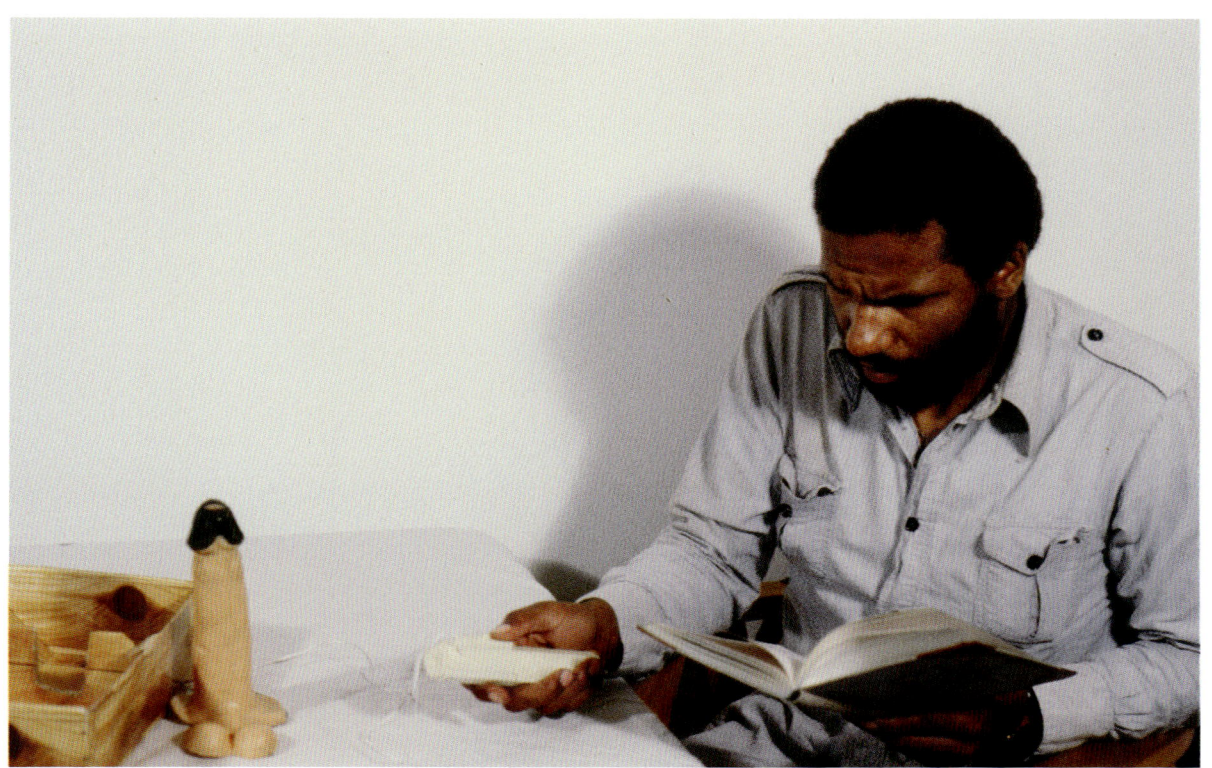

Ulysses Jenkins, *Just Another Rendering of the Same Old Problem*, 1979. Performance. Courtesy of the artist.
Photo: Nancy Buchanan.

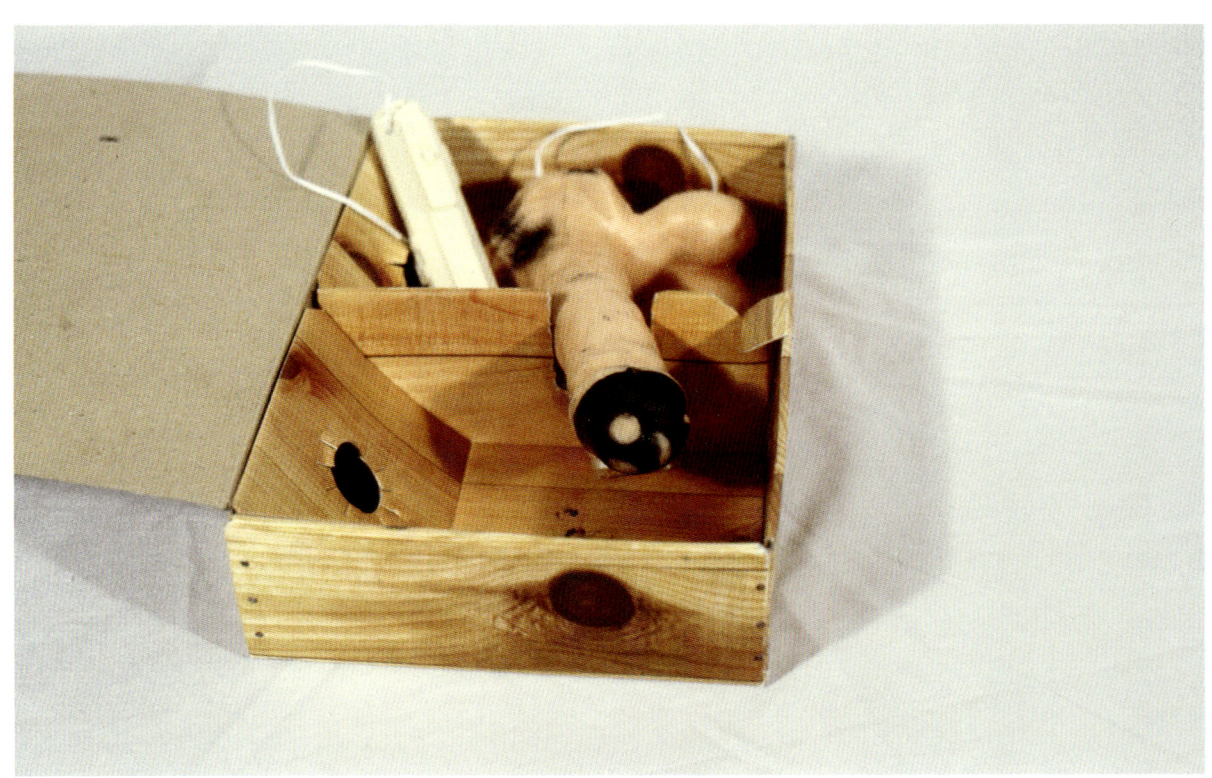

Ulysses Jenkins, *Just Another Rendering of the Same Old Problem*, 1979. Performance. Courtesy of the artist.
Photo: Nancy Buchanan.

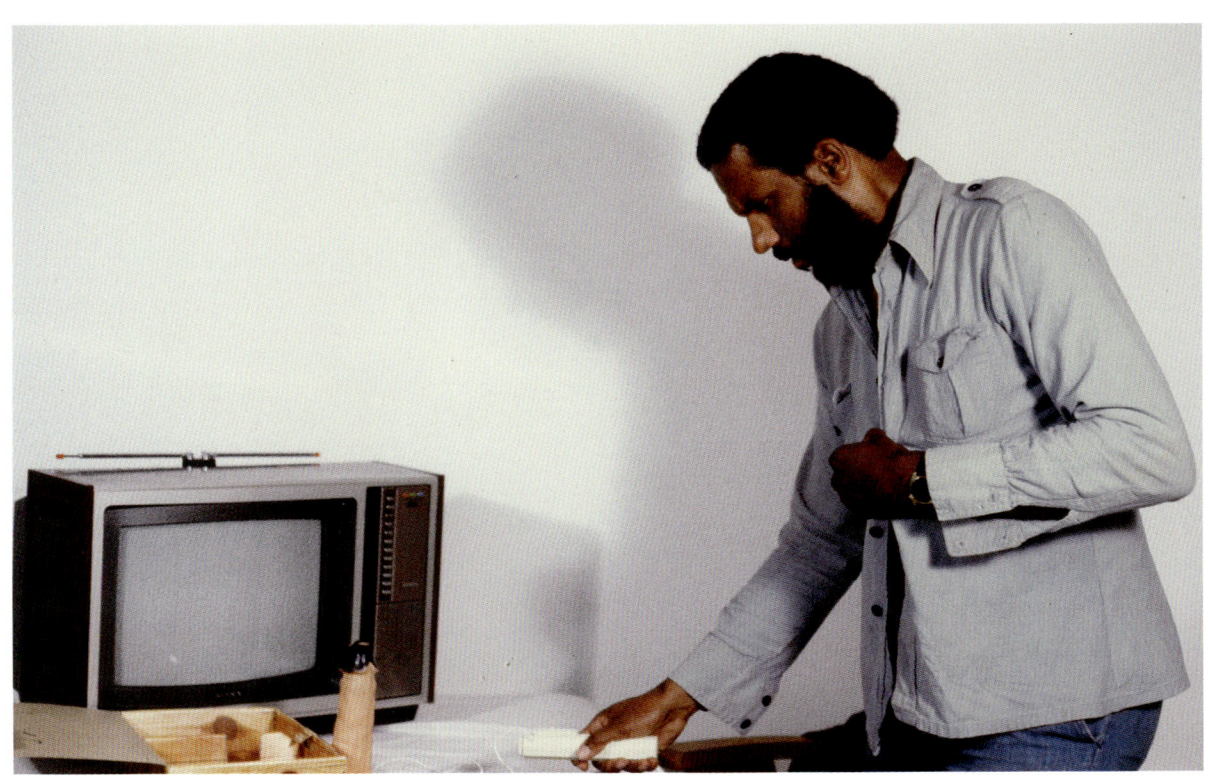

Ulysses Jenkins, *Just Another Rendering of the Same Old Problem*, 1979. Performance. Courtesy of the artist.
Photo: Nancy Buchanan.

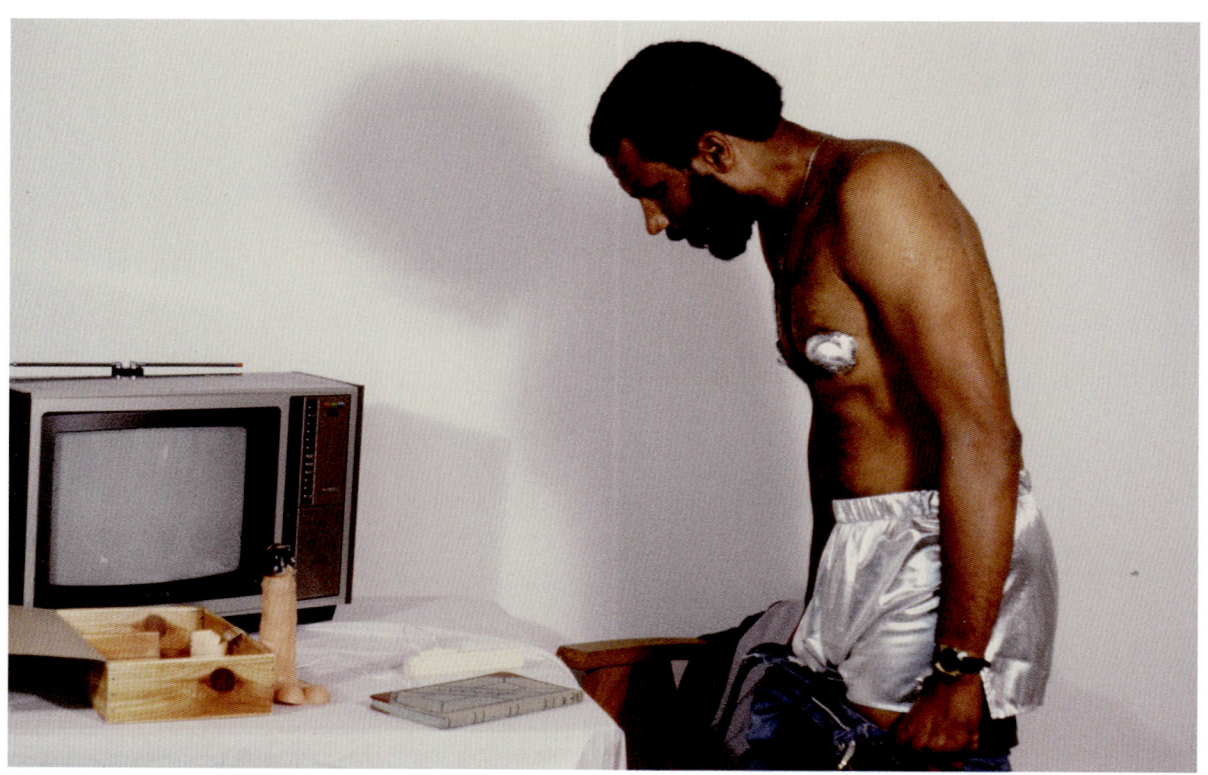

Ulysses Jenkins, *Just Another Rendering of the Same Old Problem*, 1979. Performance. Courtesy of the artist.
Photo: Nancy Buchanan.

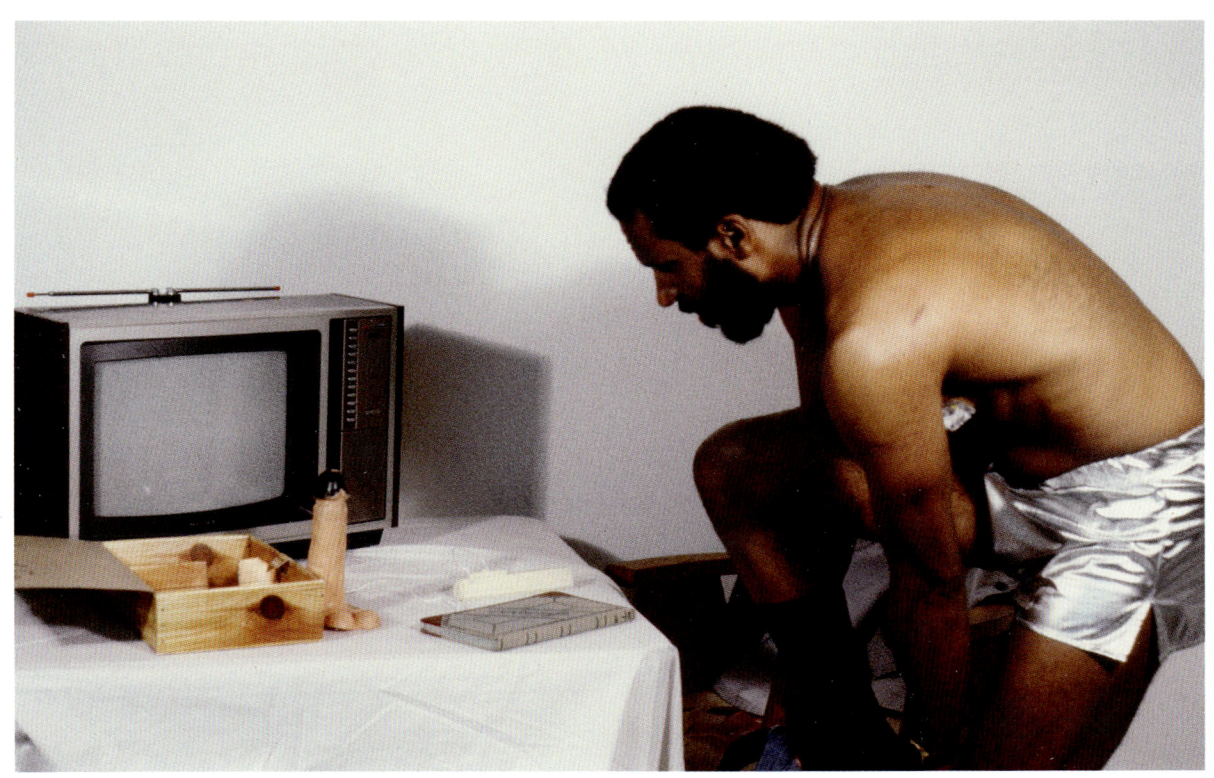

Ulysses Jenkins, *Just Another Rendering of the Same Old Problem*, 1979. Performance. Courtesy of the artist.
Photo: Nancy Buchanan.

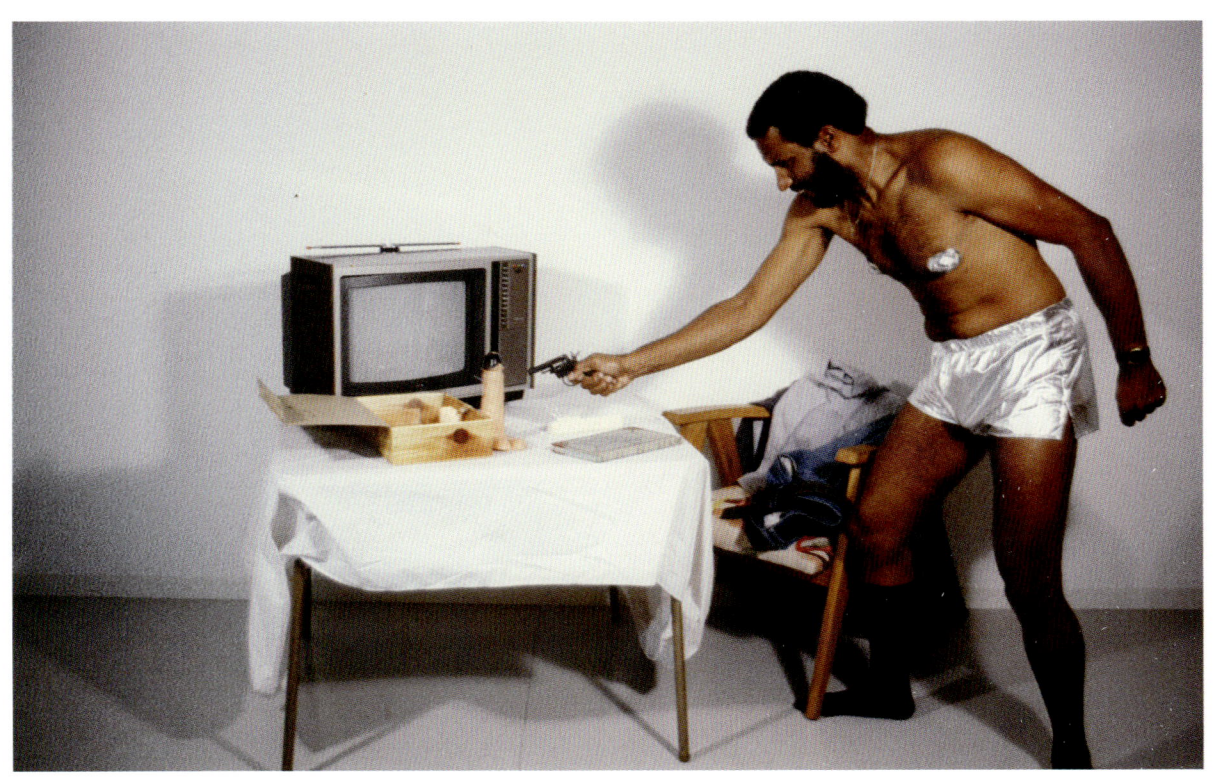

Ulysses Jenkins, *Just Another Rendering of the Same Old Problem*, 1979. Performance. Courtesy of the artist.
Photo: Nancy Buchanan.

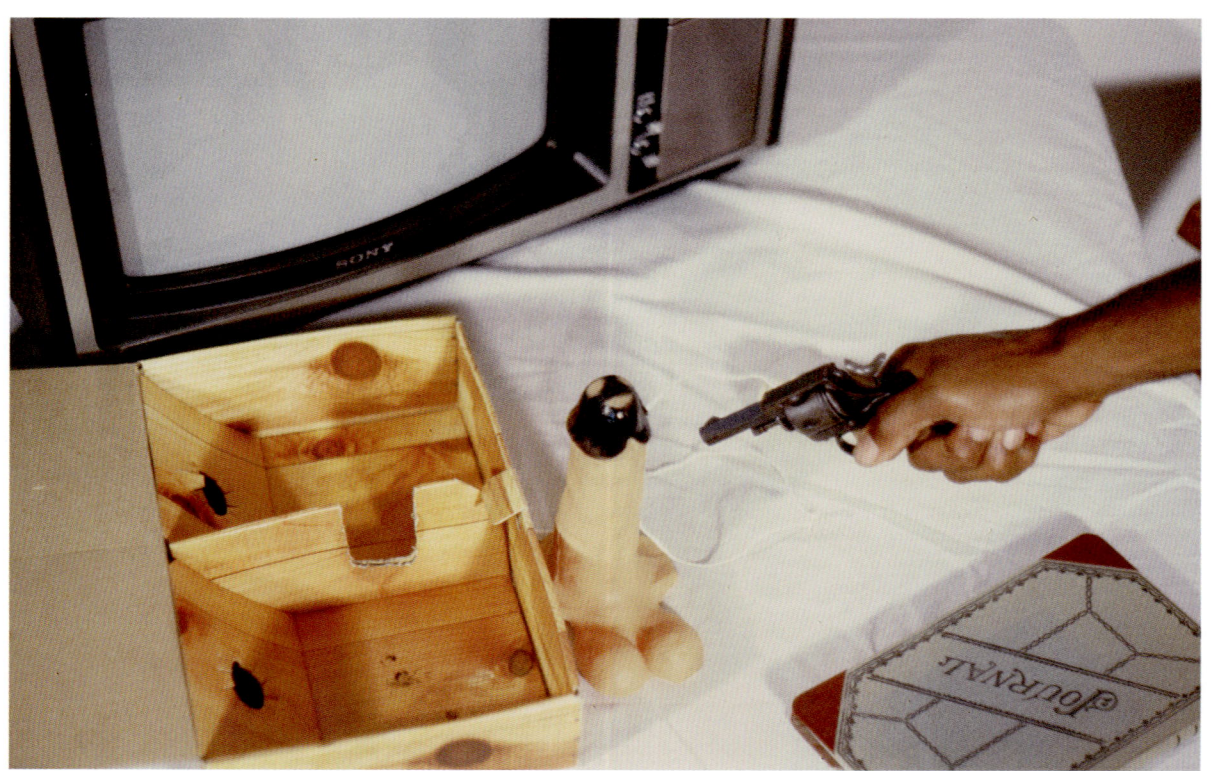

Ulysses Jenkins, *Just Another Rendering of the Same Old Problem*, 1979. Performance. Courtesy of the artist. Photo: Nancy Buchanan.

HOLIDAY GREETINGS

1979–80, 21:20 min.

I conceived of and created the Alternative Media Program
in Mar Vista, California, to provide use of videotape
as an art form for young people. *Happy Holidays* was the
second video in a series of three. The concept involved
the commercialization of Christmas, sex and violence, and
the hostage crisis in Iran. —UJ

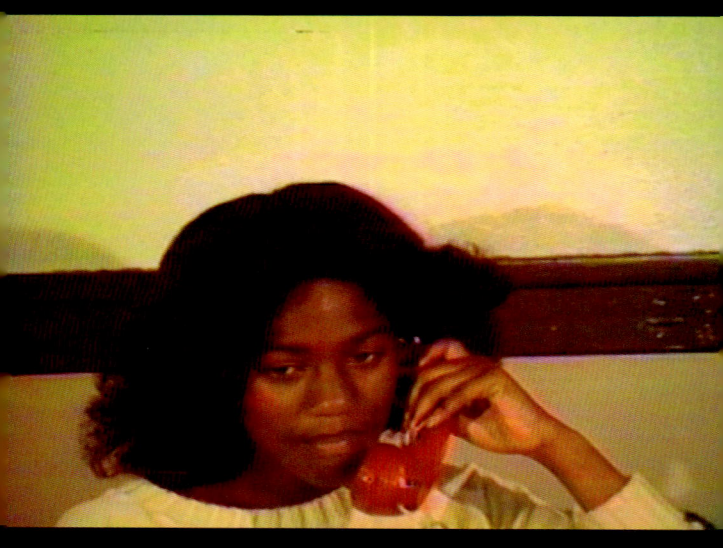

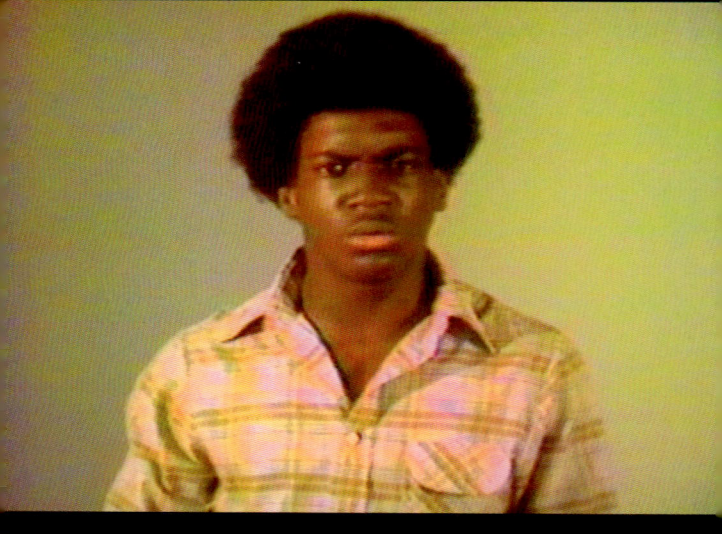

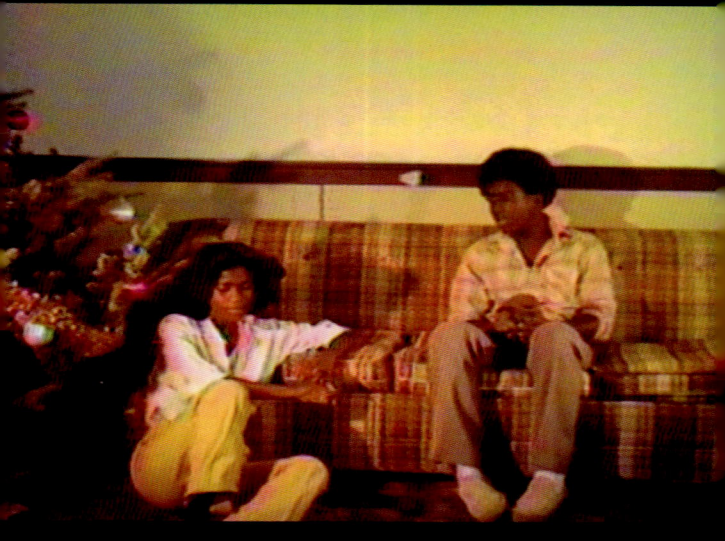

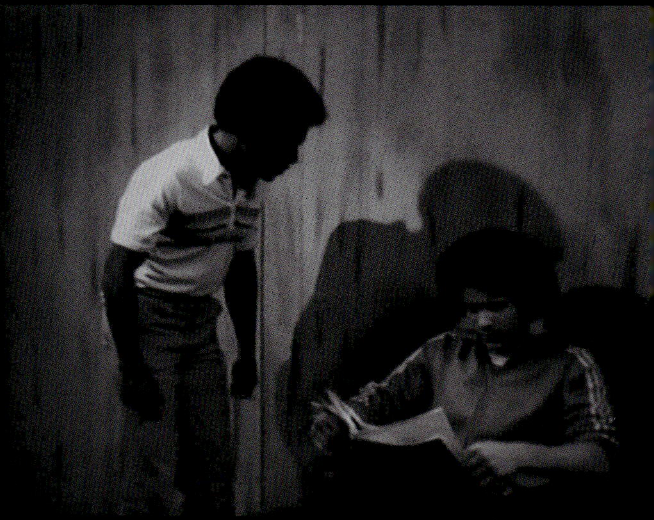

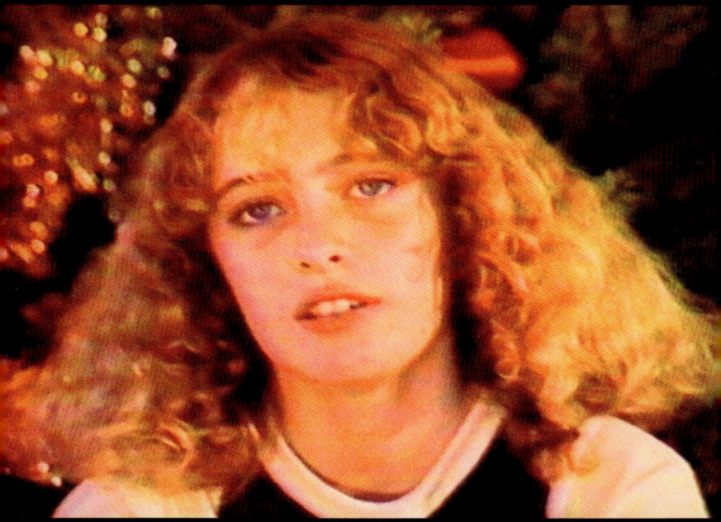

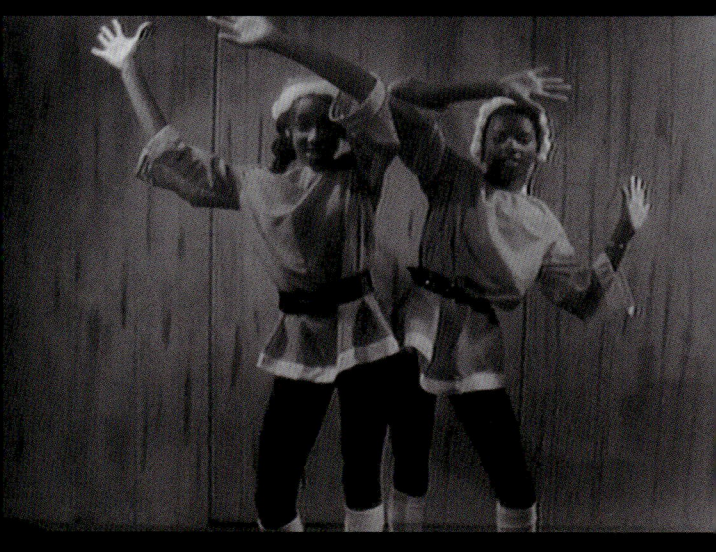

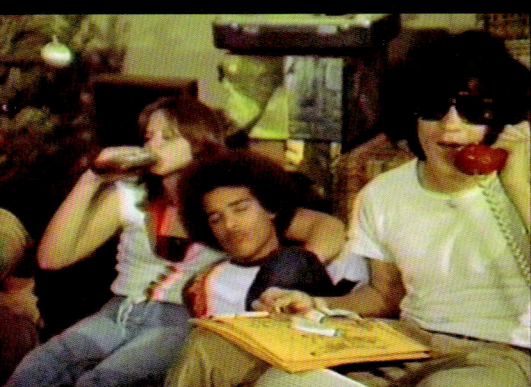

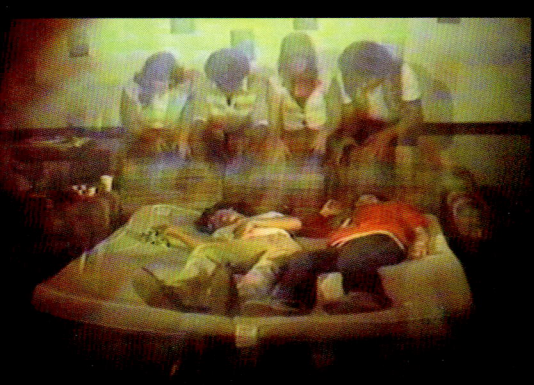

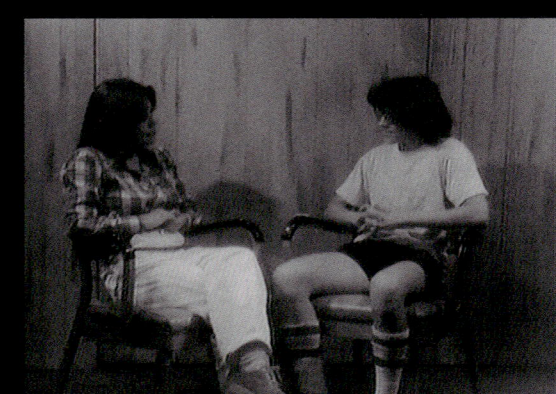

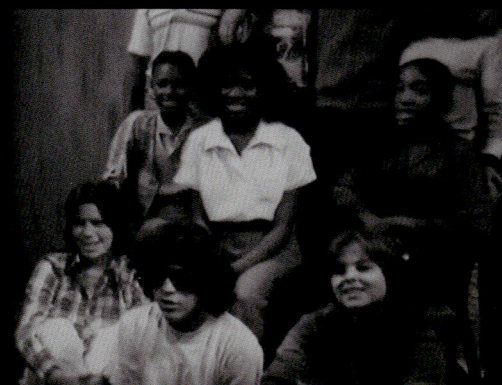

INCONSEQUENTIAL

DOGGEREAL

1981, 15:19 min.

The vertigo within this videotape presents contradictions
that question issues surrounding compatibility,
poetic lyricism, and traditional intonations associated
with normal television consumption. —UJ

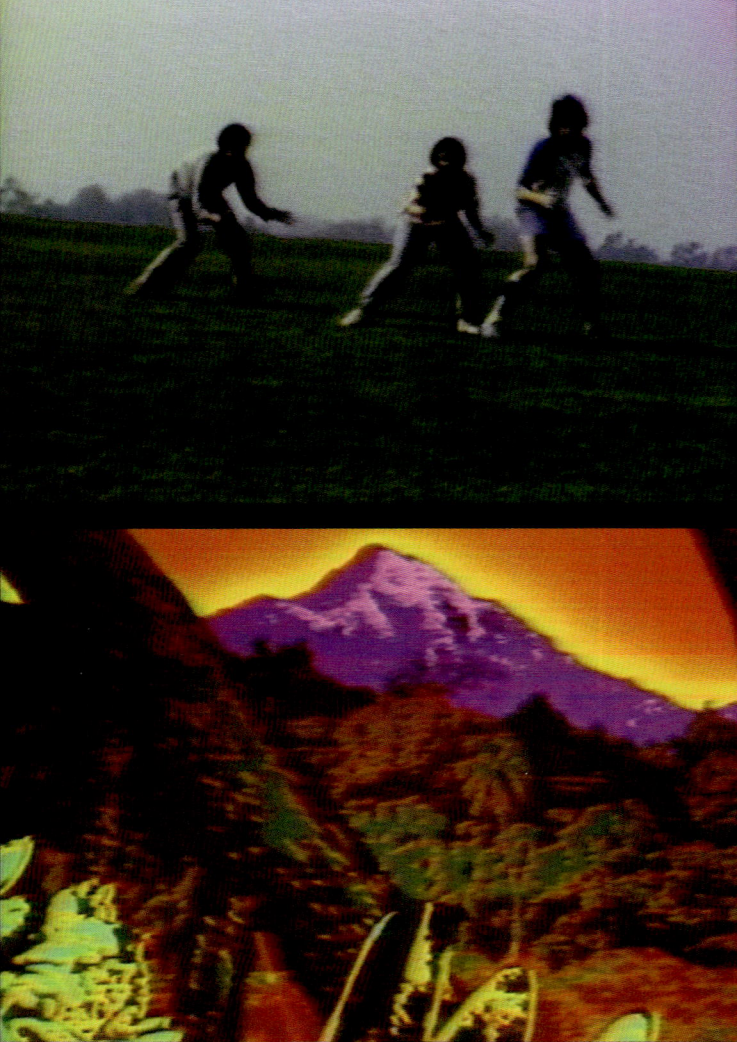

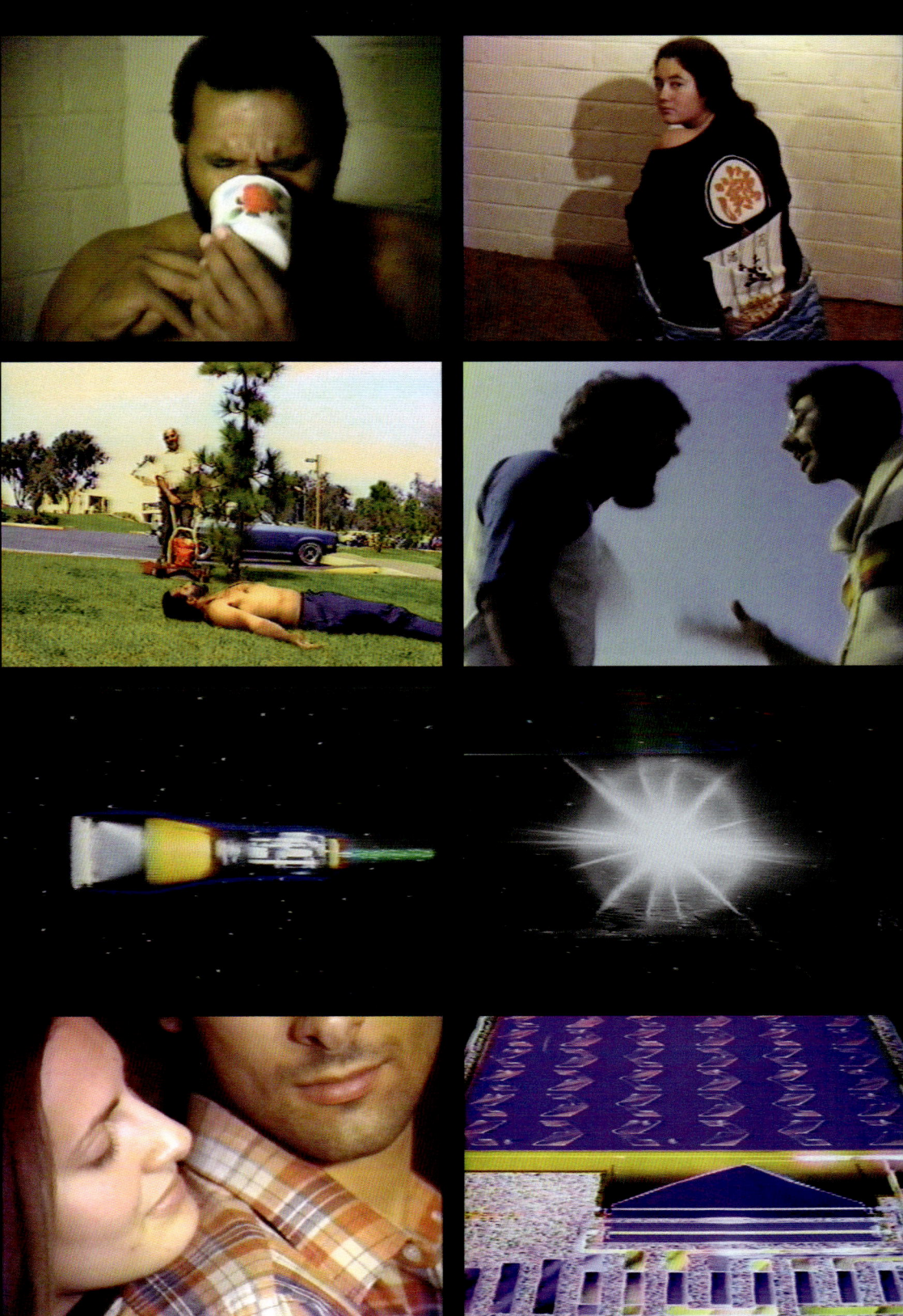

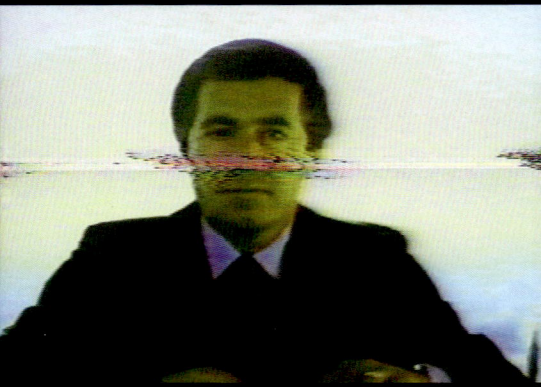
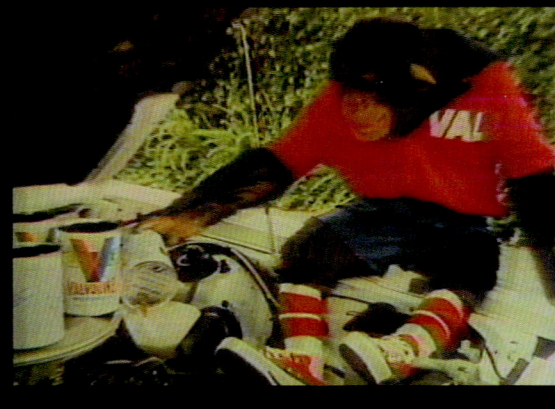
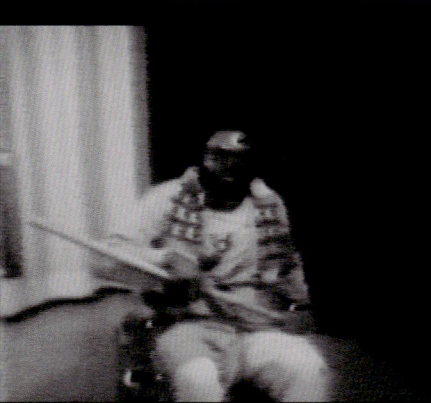
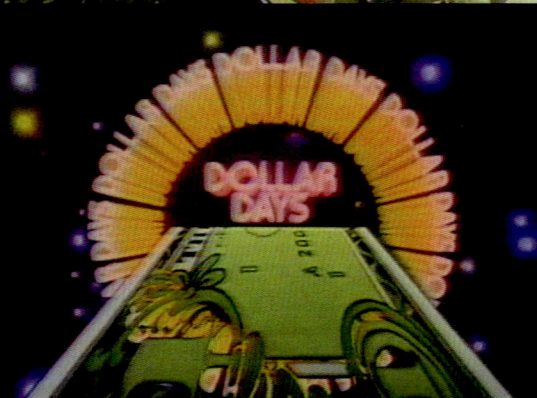
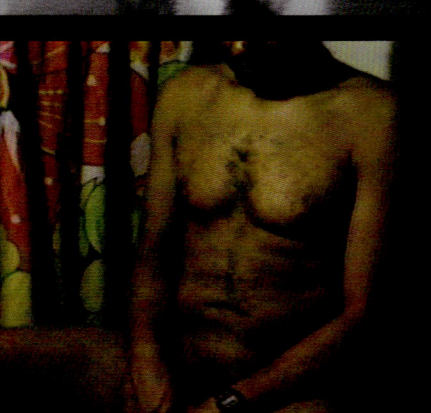
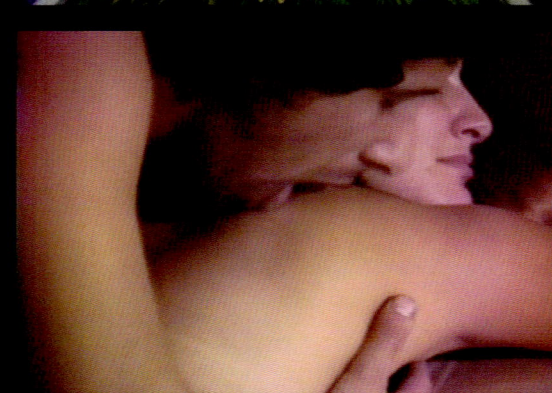
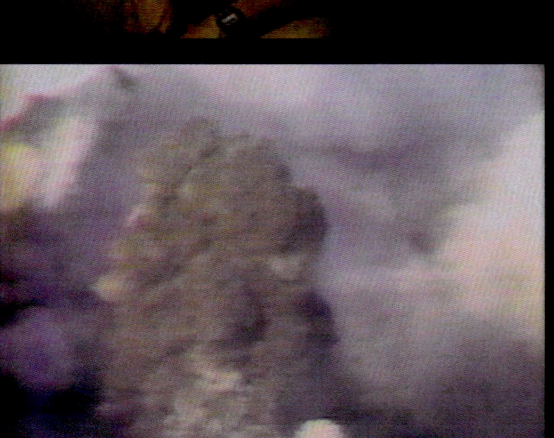
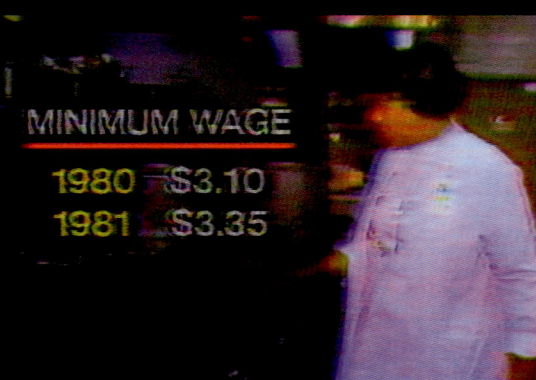

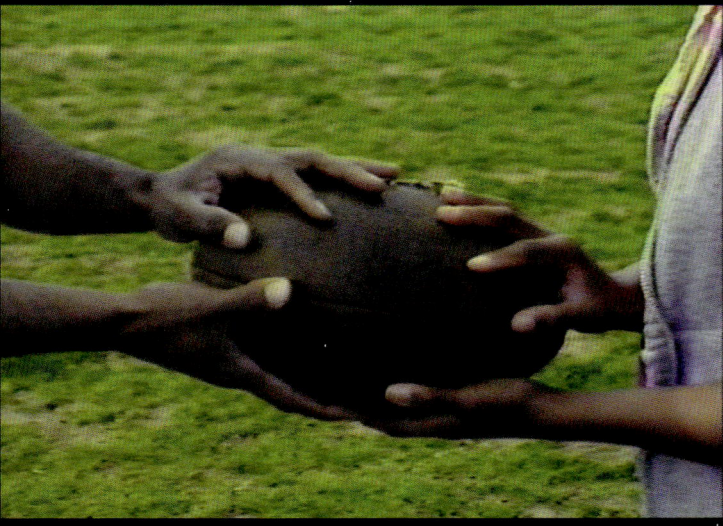

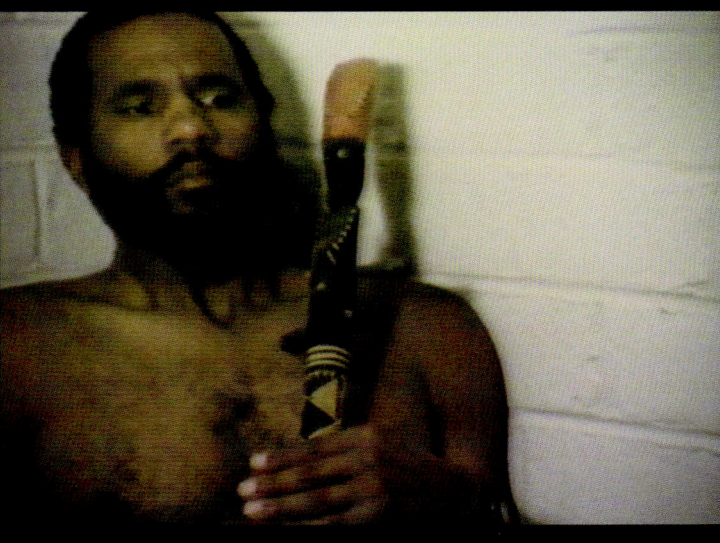

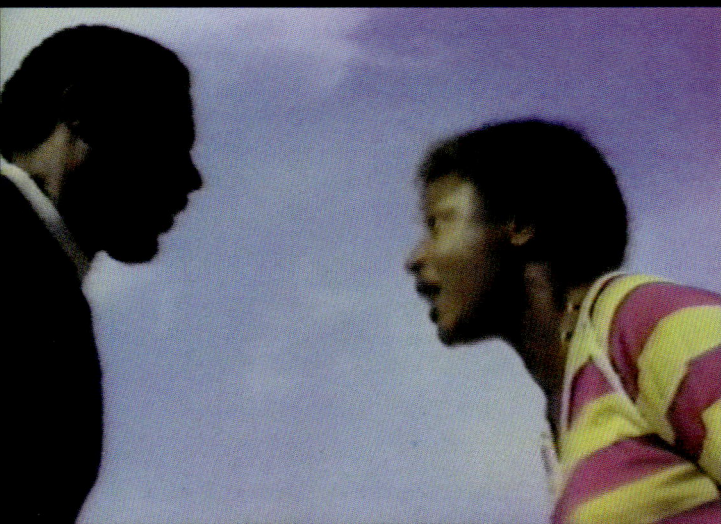

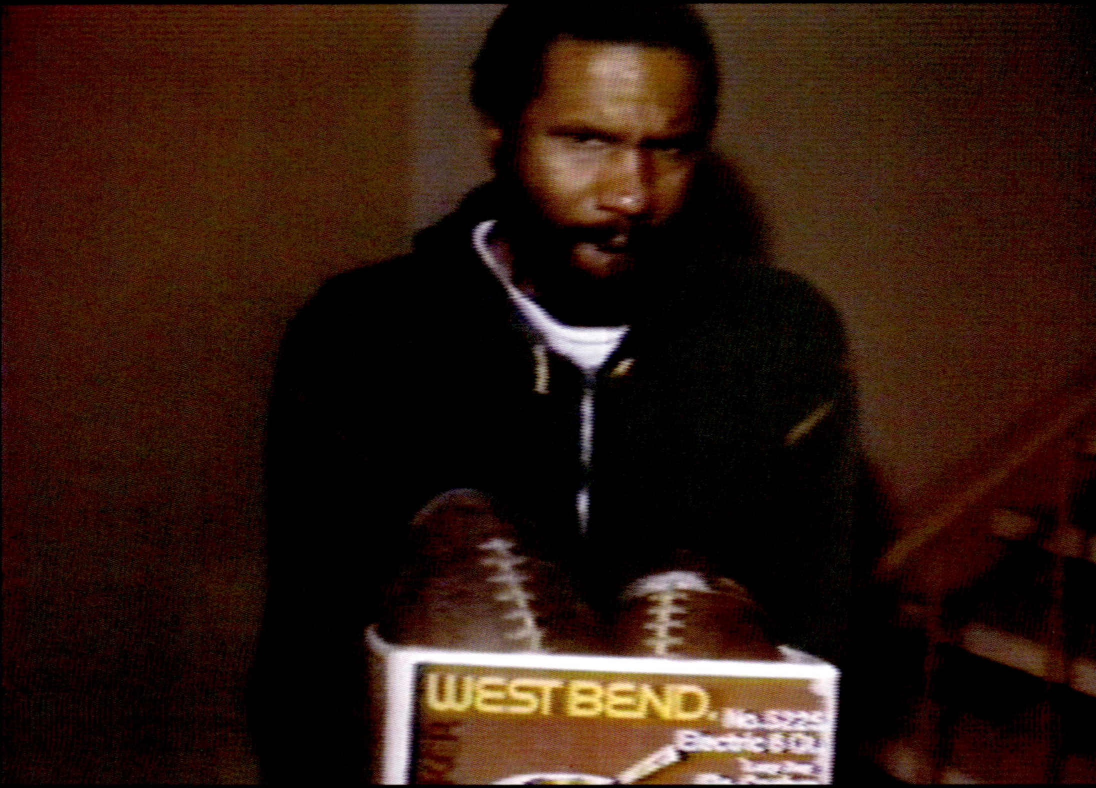

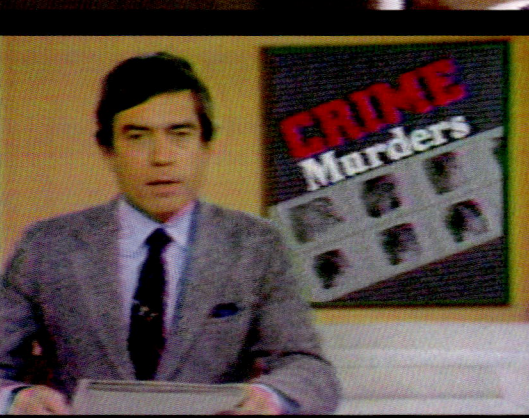

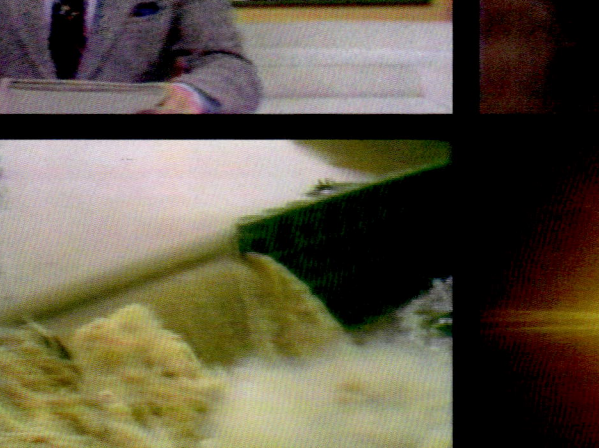

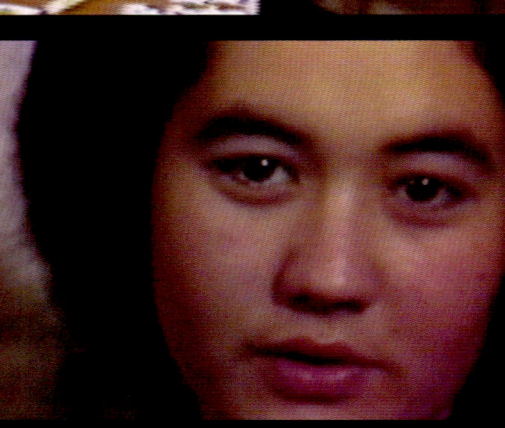

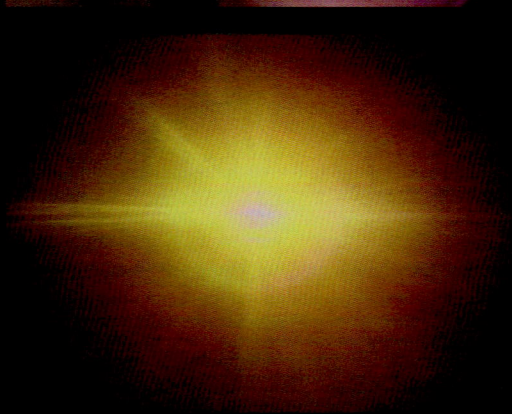

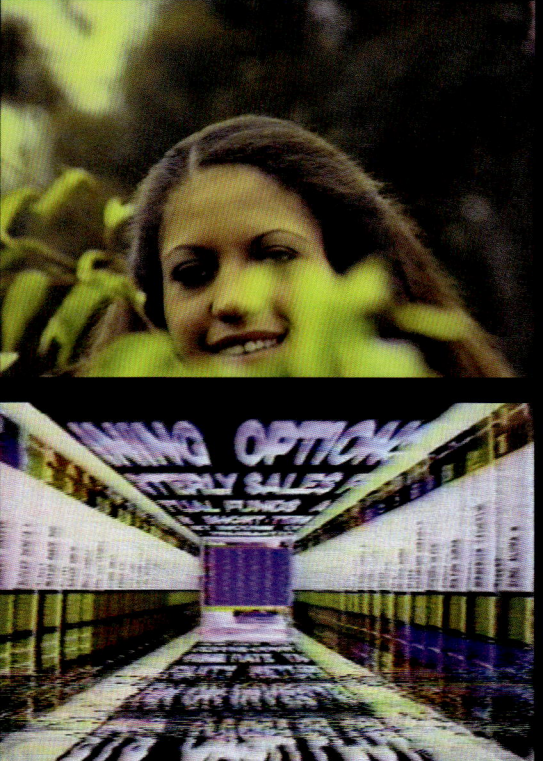
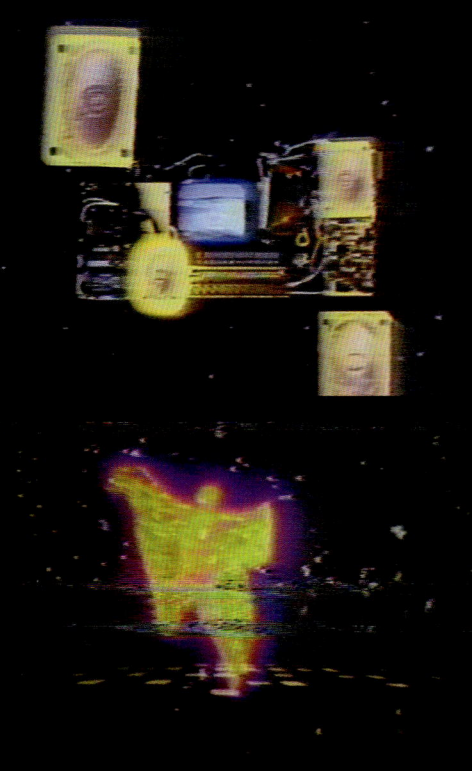

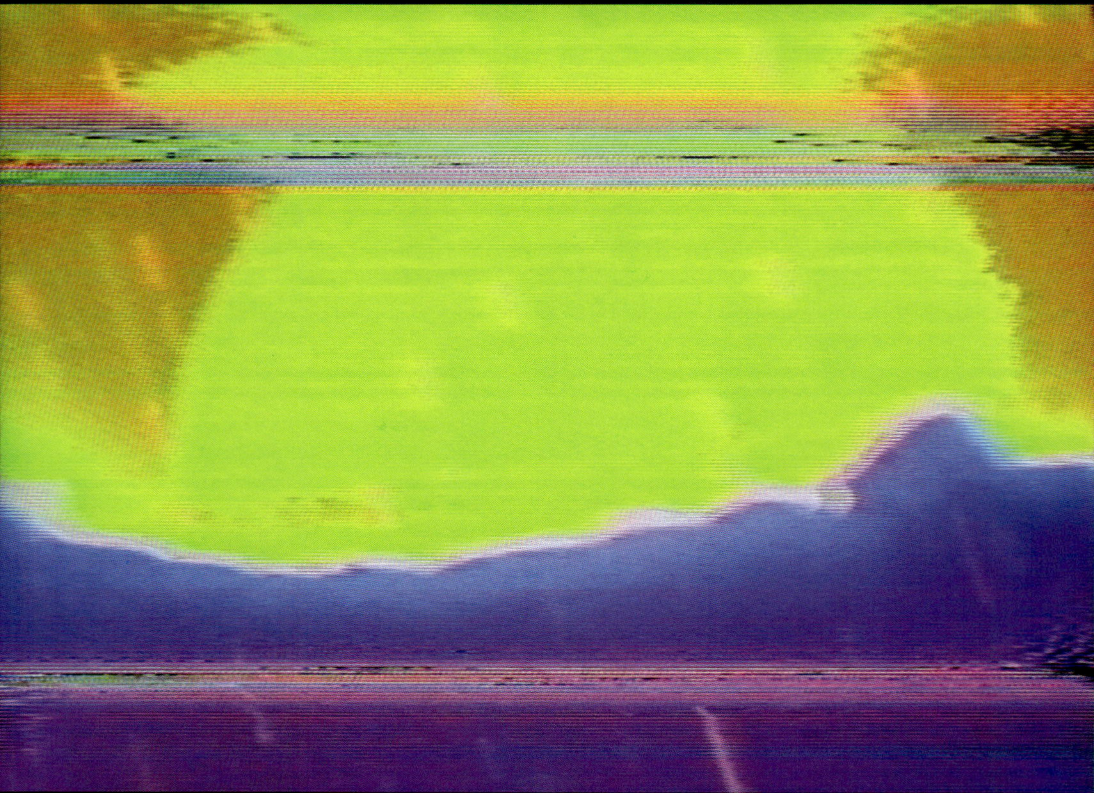

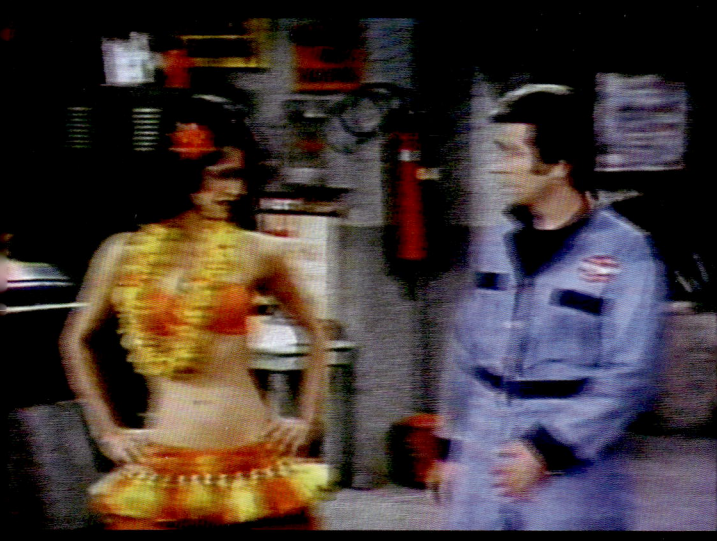

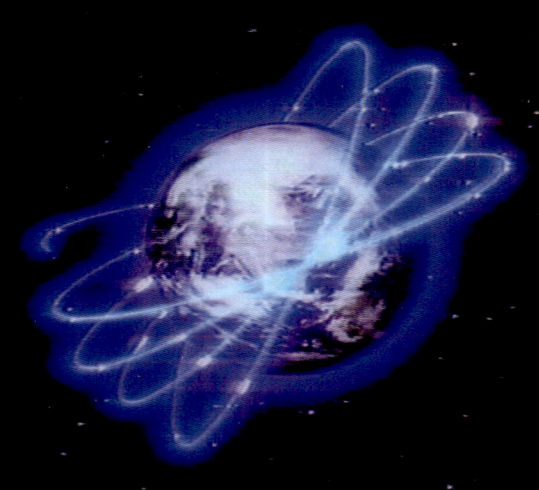

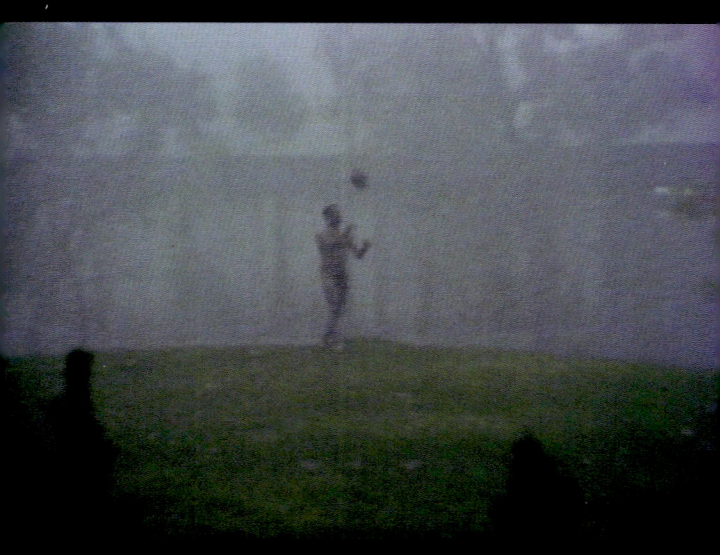

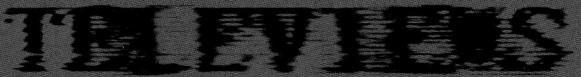

TELEVIEWS

&

CABLE RADIO

1981, 11:18 min.

Video documentary that explores the alternative modes
of expression via future contemporary electronic media.
Two locations within the University of California,
San Diego, campus (Walk's Pub and the Media Center and
Communications complex) were interconnected by video
via microwave link, enabling simultaneous interaction
between both locations. —UJ

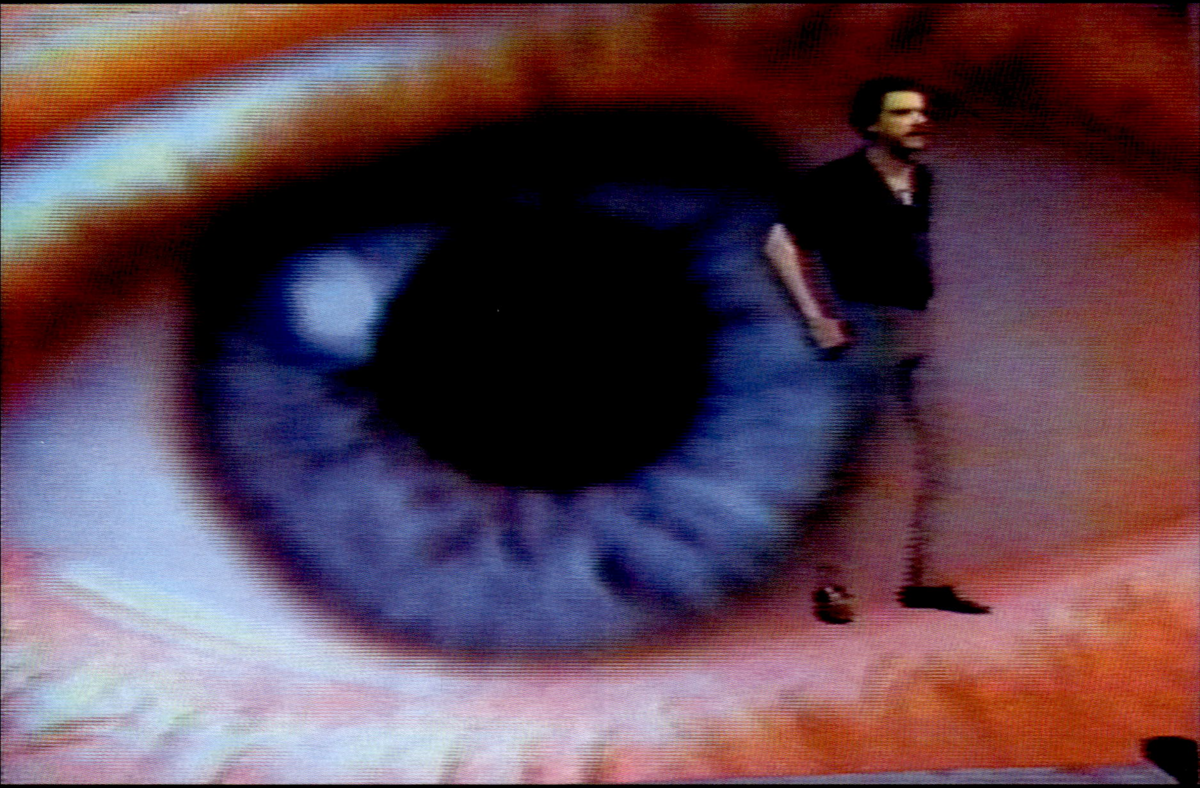

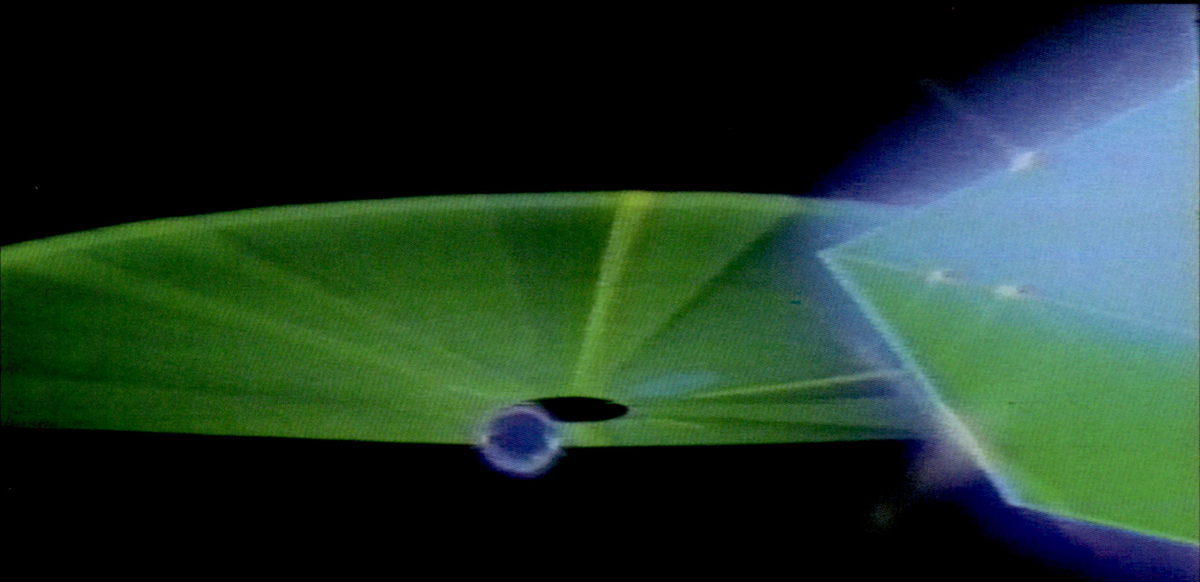

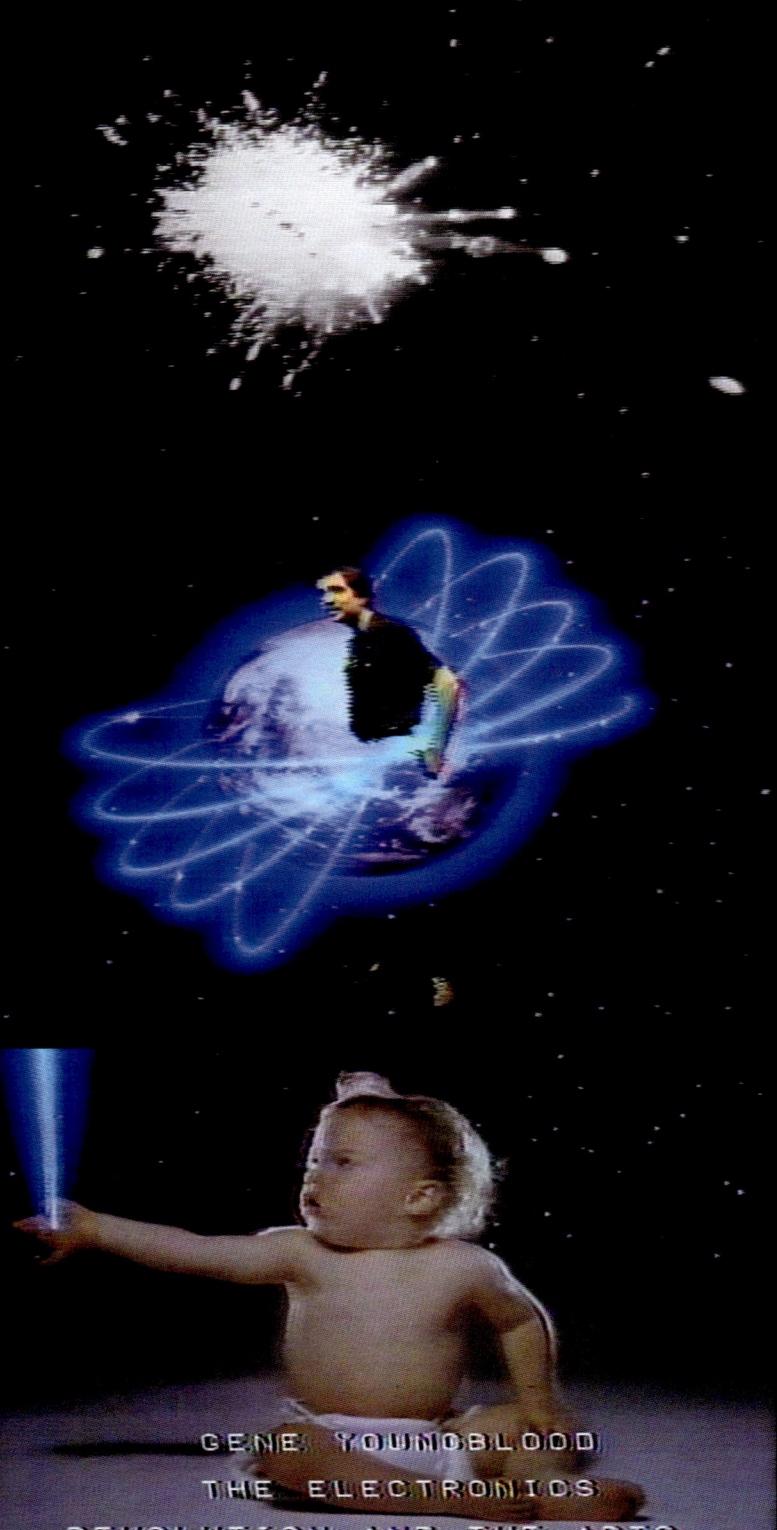

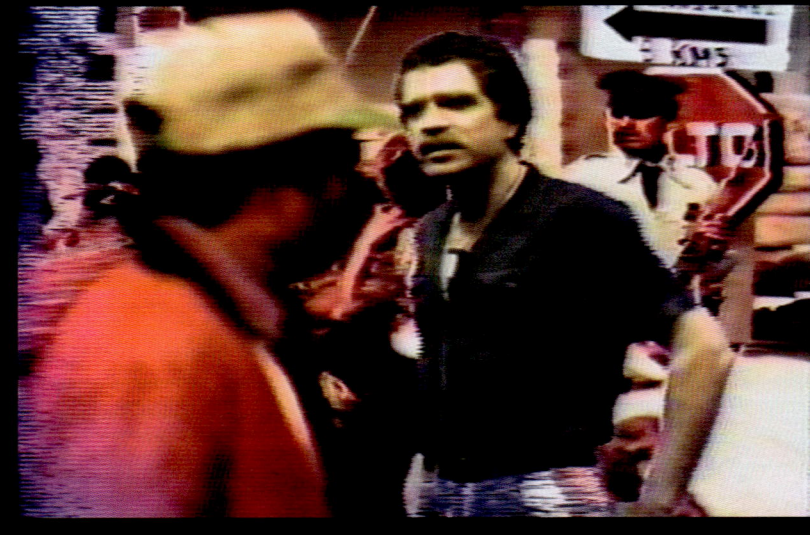

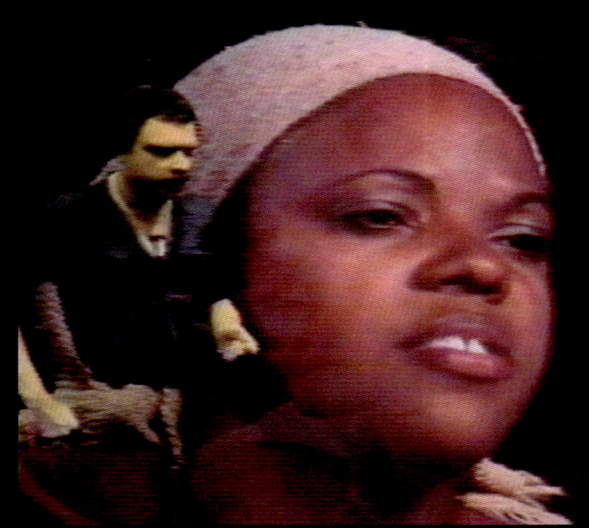

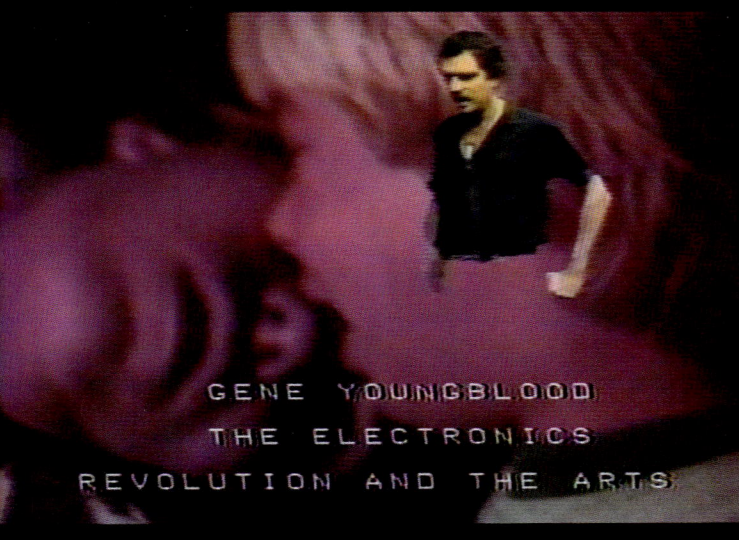

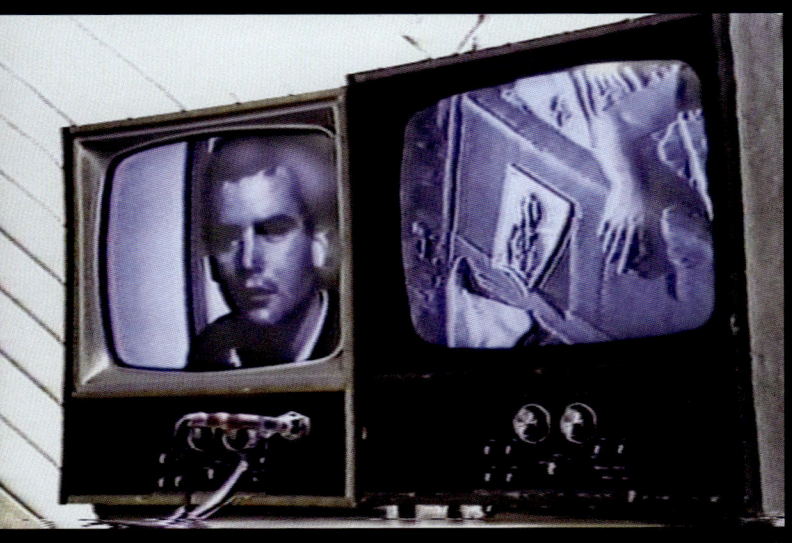

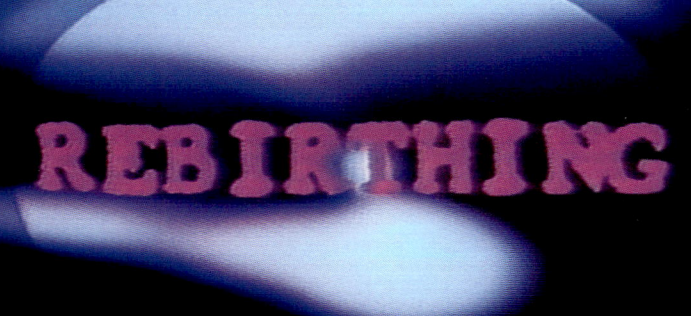

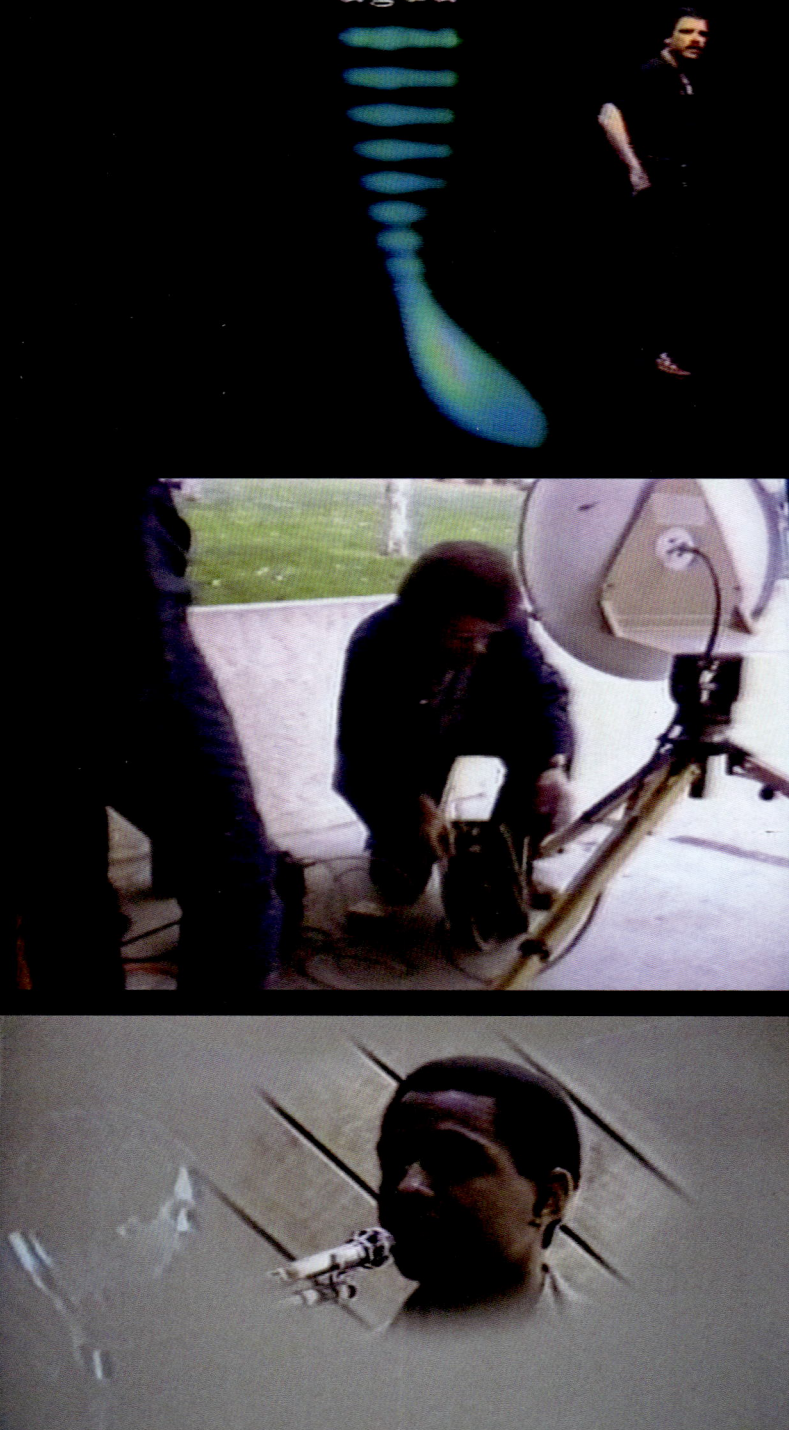

MOMENTOUS OCCASIONS:
The Spirit of *CHARLES WHITE*

1977/1982, 19:41 min.

Video documentary that covers Charles White's
retrospective exhibition at the Los Angeles Art Gallery
and his activities as professor of art at Otis Art
Institute in the fall of 1977. —UJ

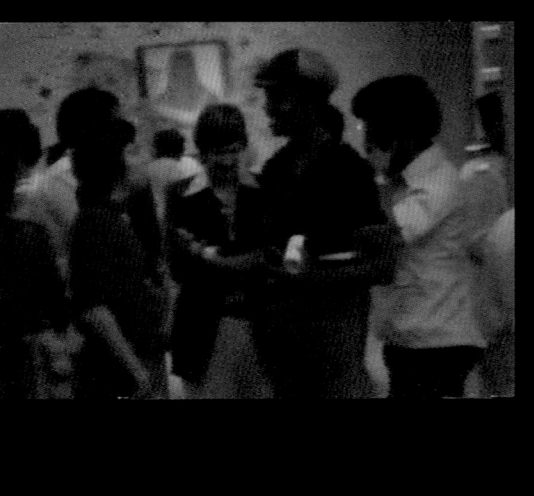

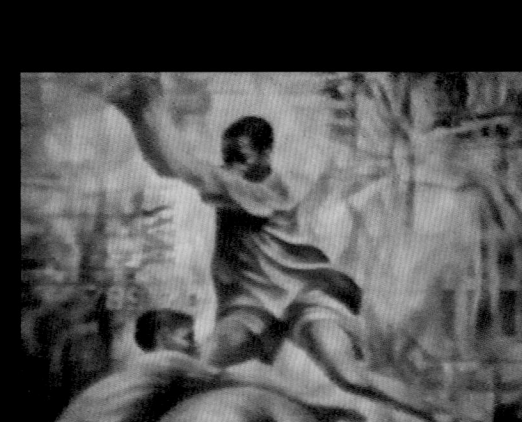

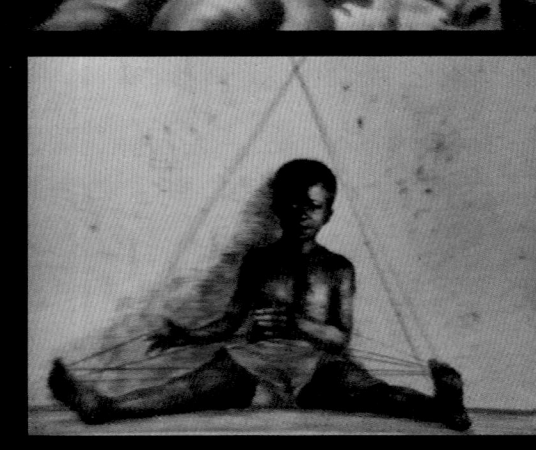

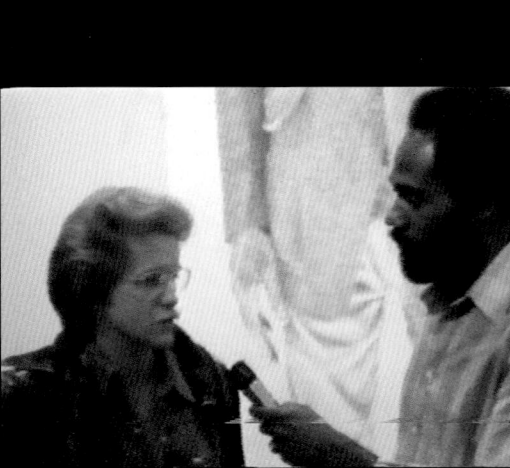

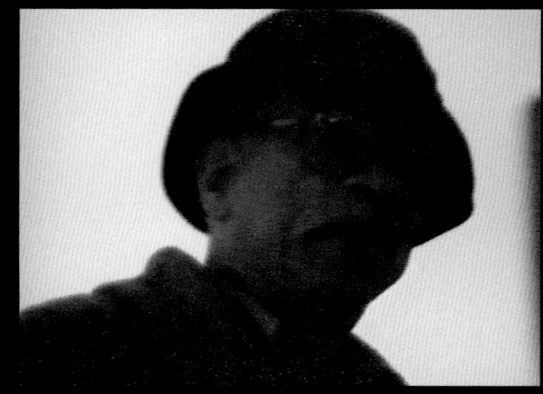

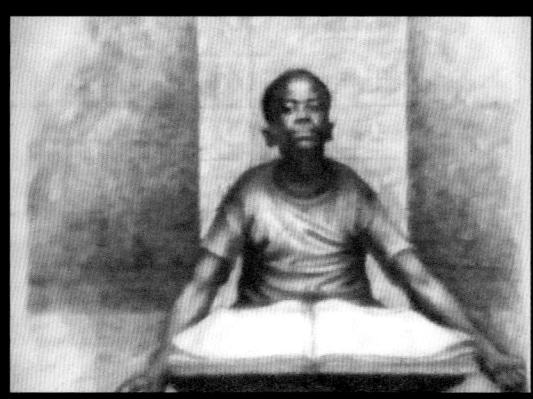

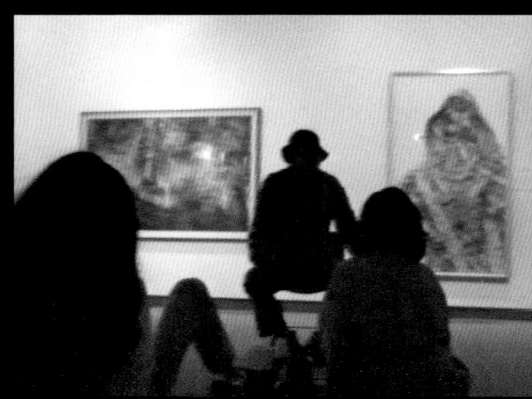

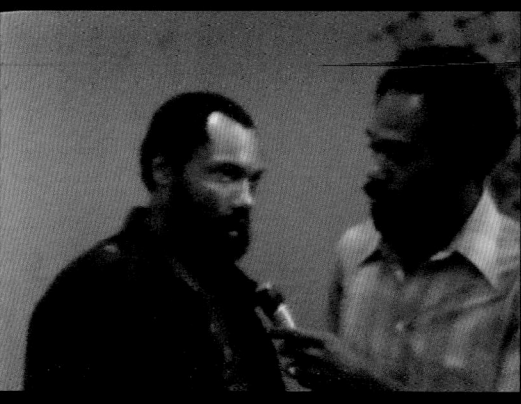

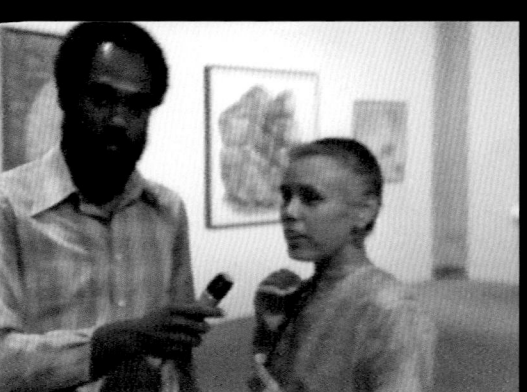

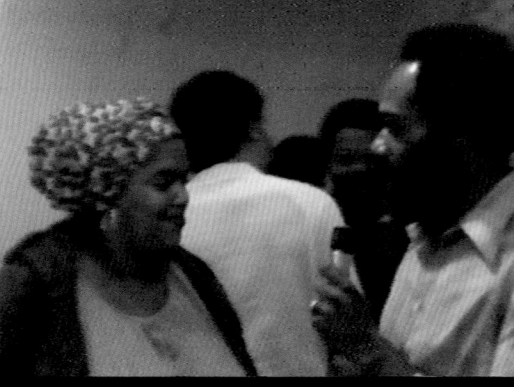

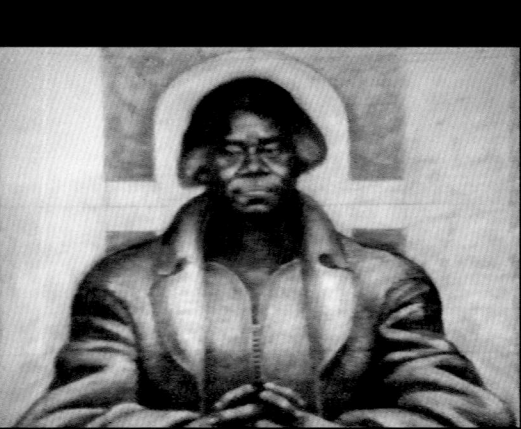

DREAM CITY

1983, 5:19 min.

Originally recorded and performed on September 18, 1981,
at Rachel Rosenthal's Espace DbD, this video reinterprets
a metaphoric ritual in time. —UJ

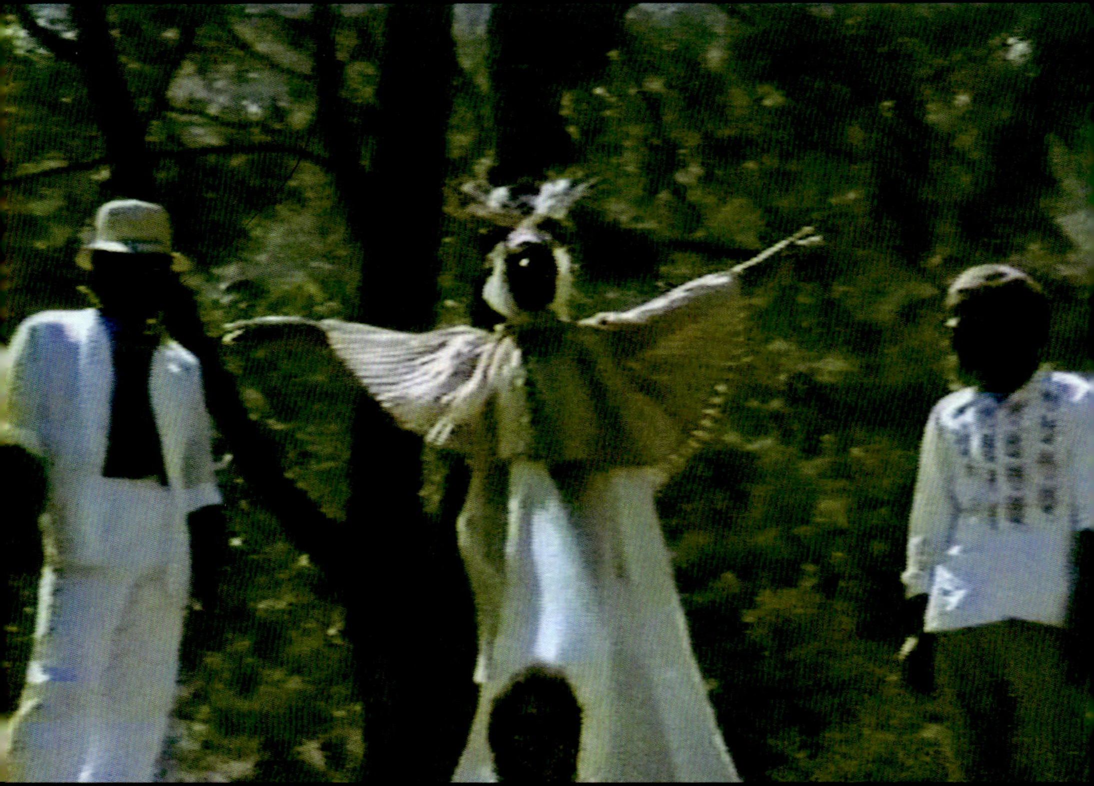

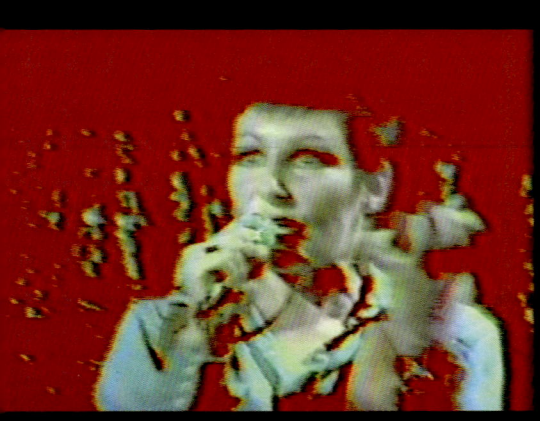
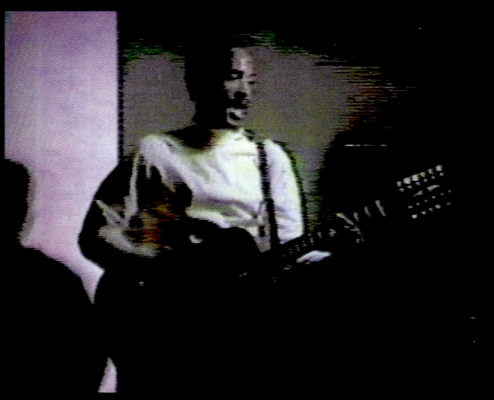

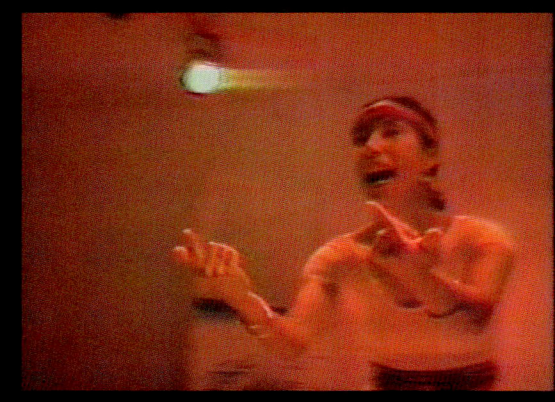

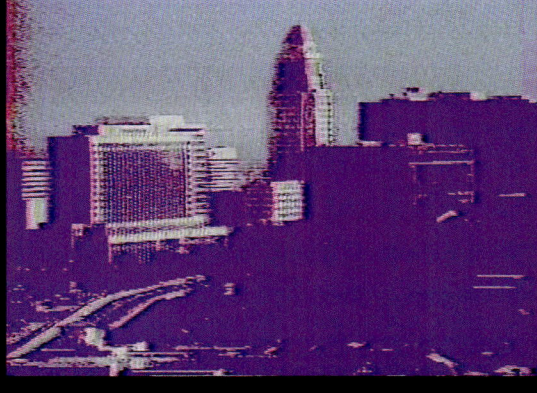

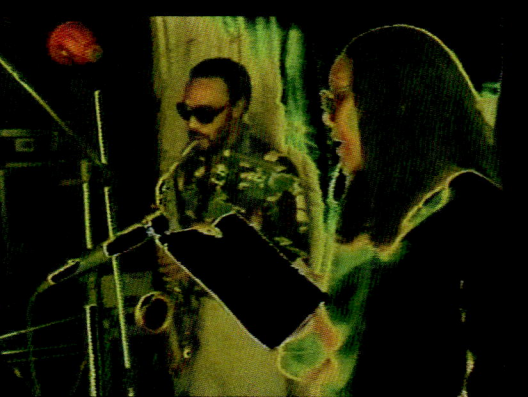

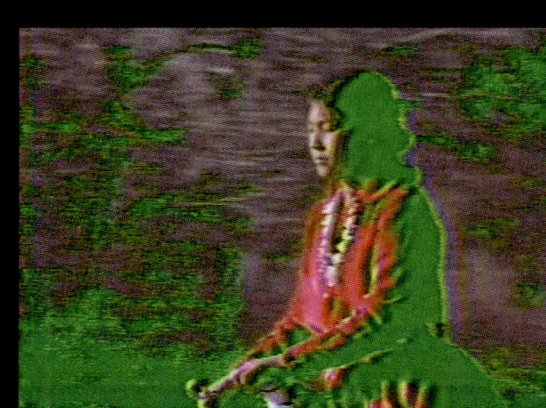

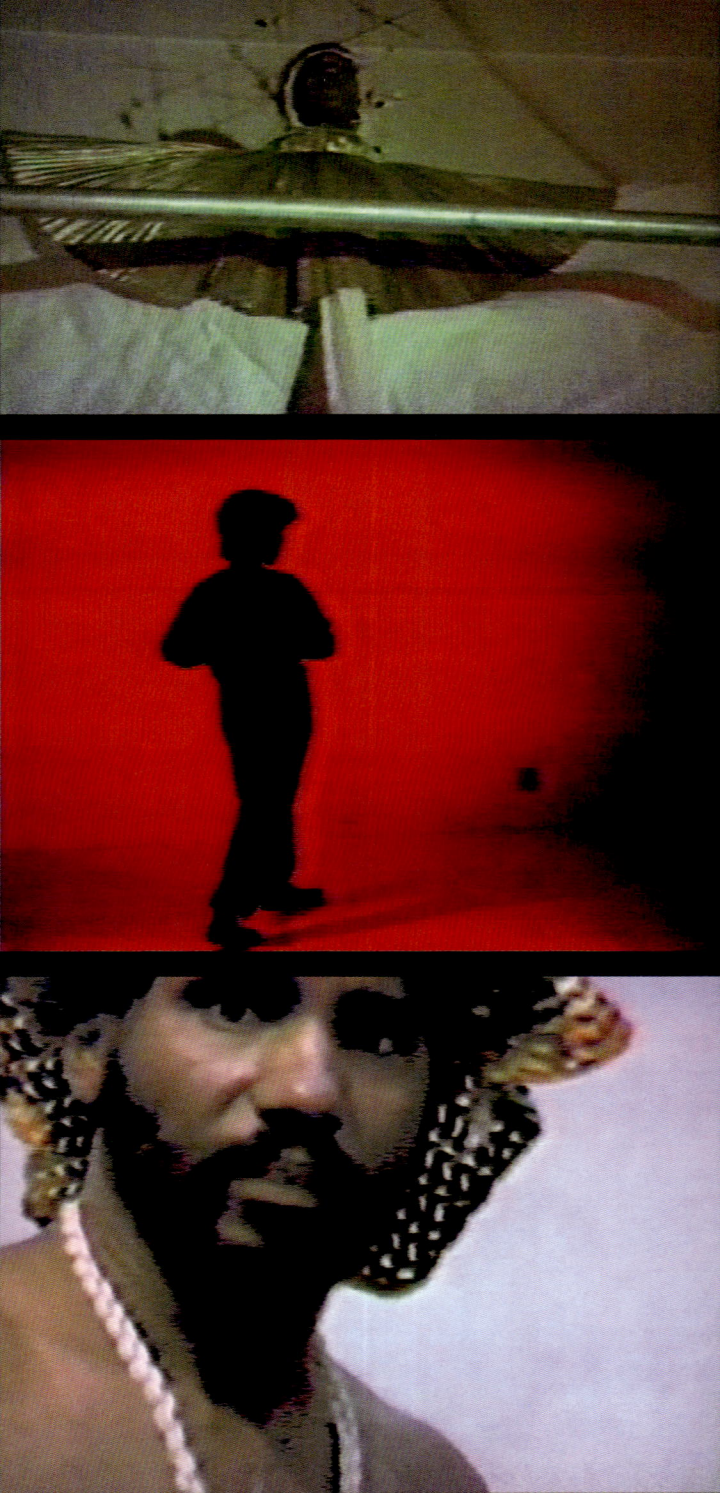

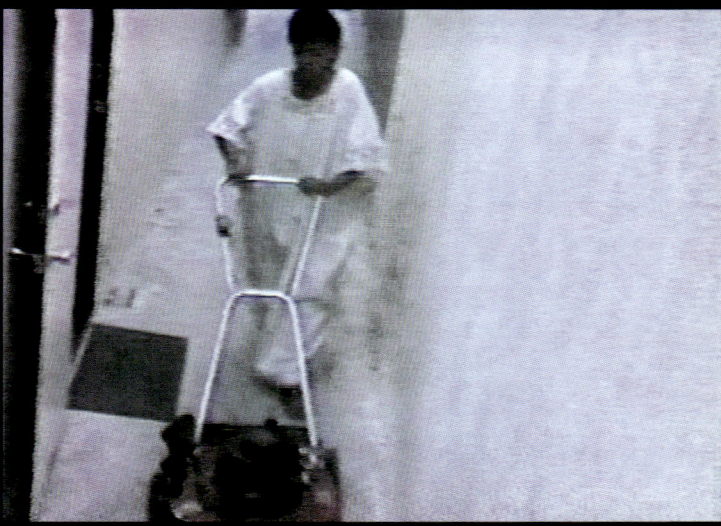

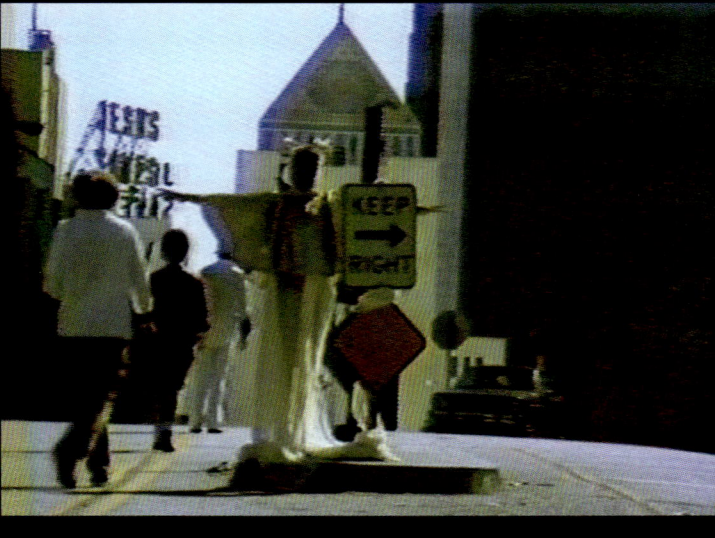

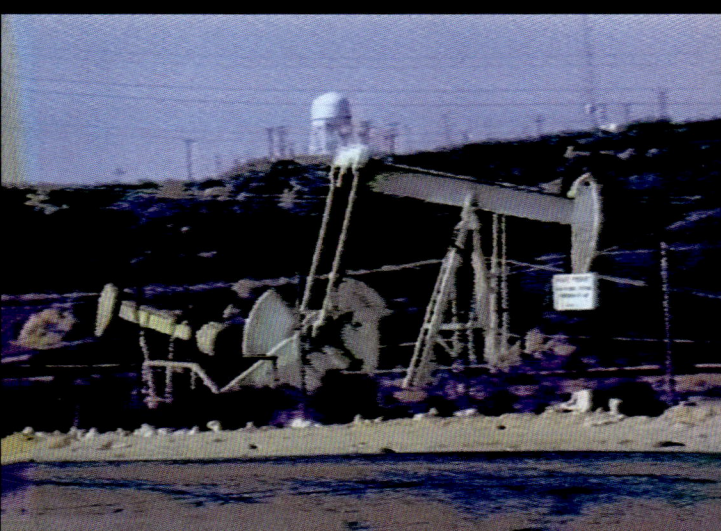

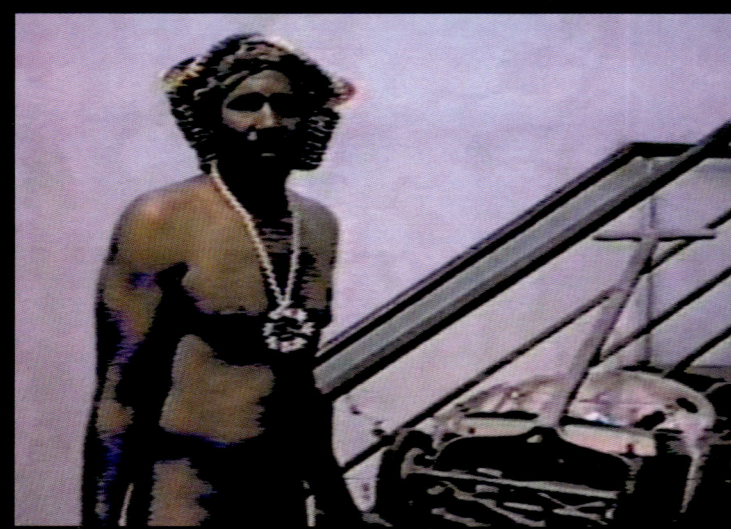

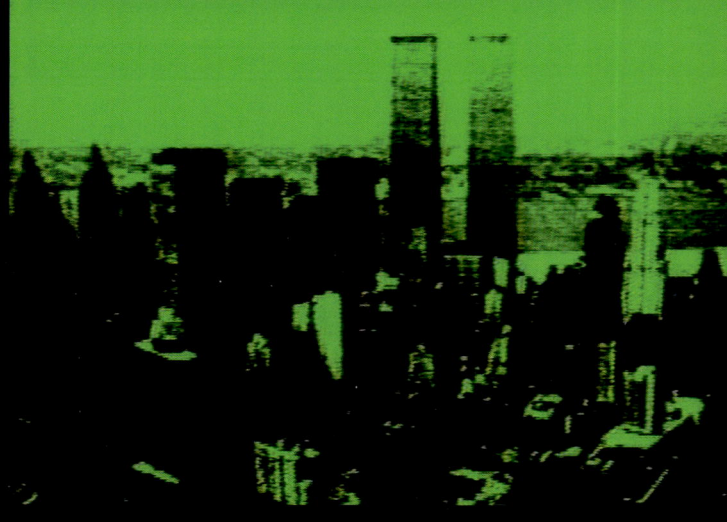

''LASISI''

1983, 12:50 min.

This videotape is a video-documentary of original
indigenous African fusion music by musician Lasisi filmed
at the ComeBack Inn in Venice, California. —UJ

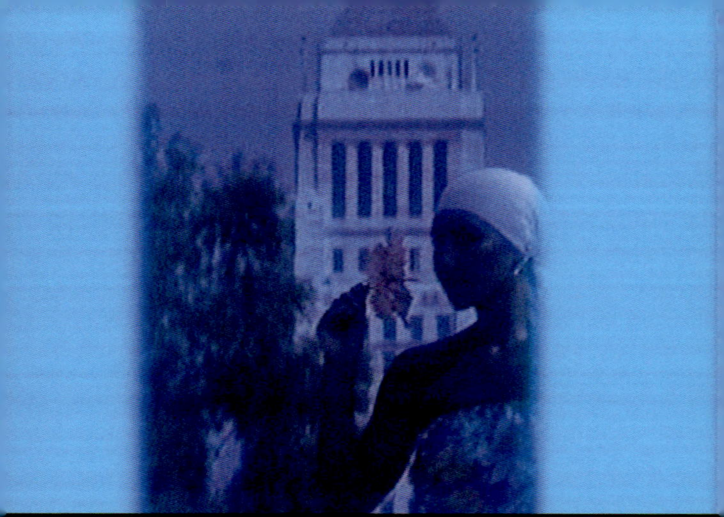

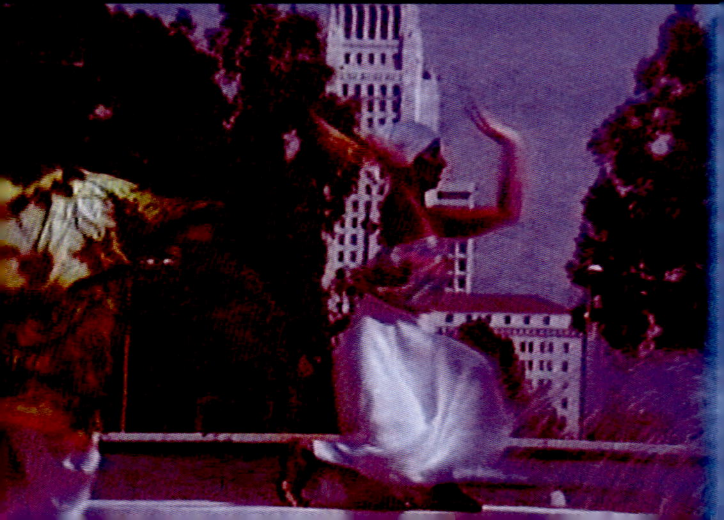

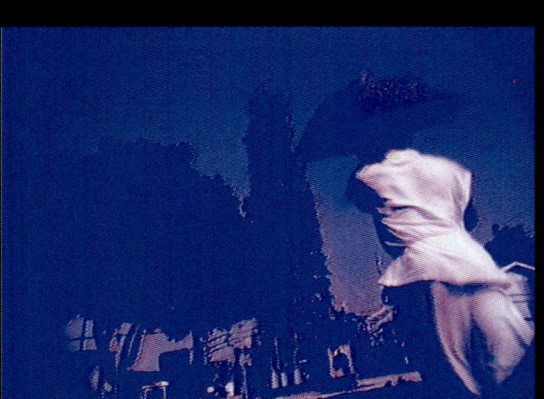

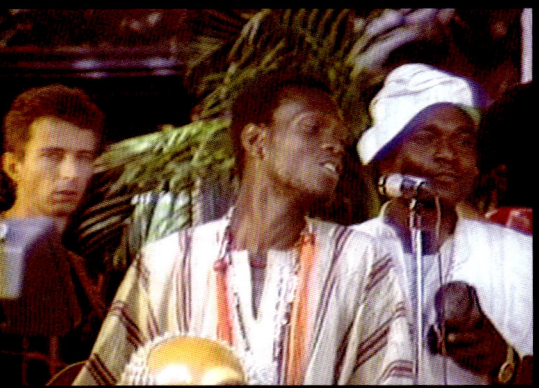

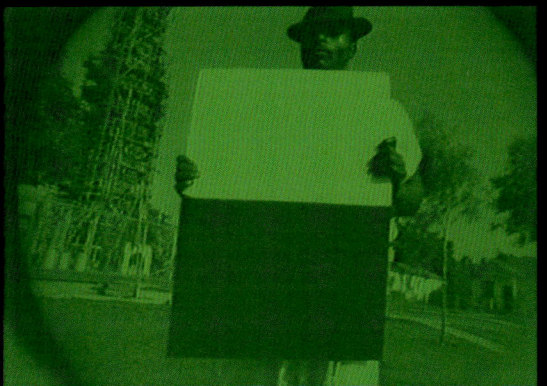

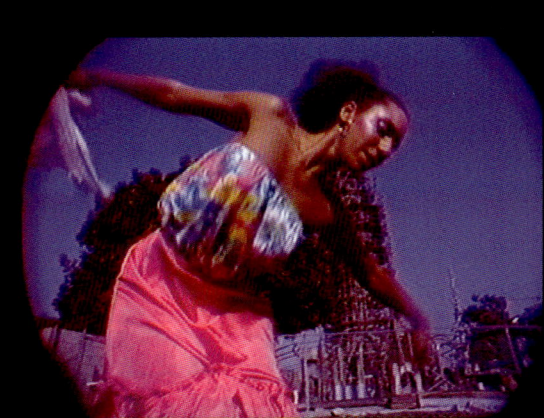

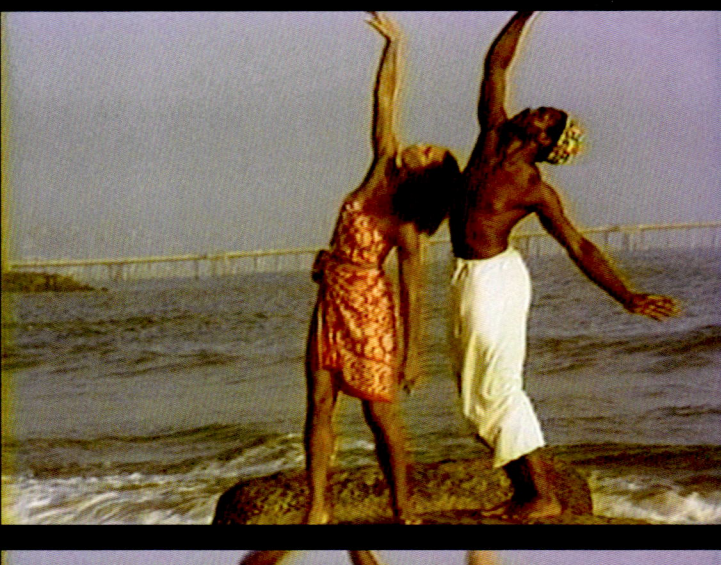
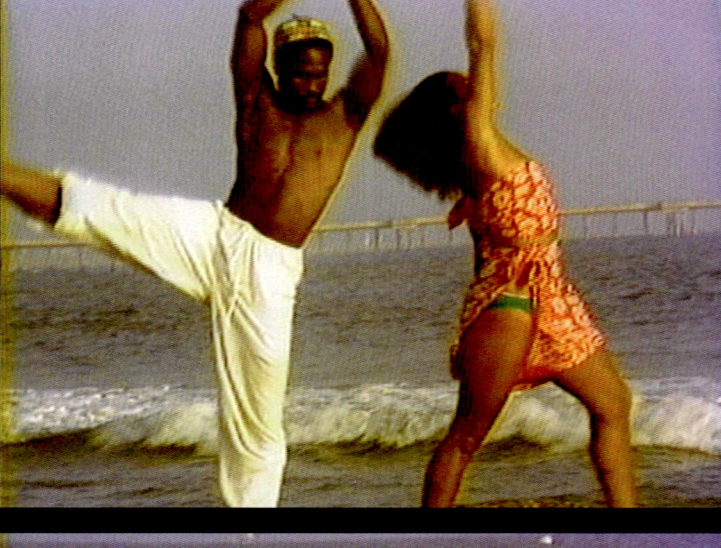
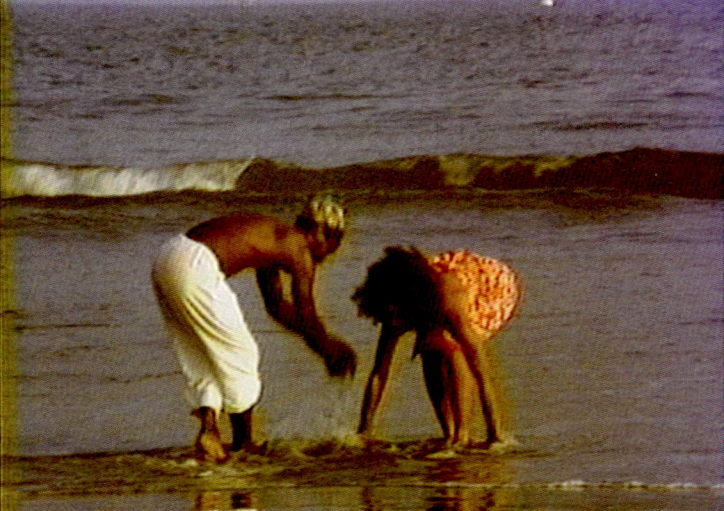

Z-GRASS

VIDEOTAPE
BY
ULYSSES JENKINS

C.1983

1983, 3:03 min.

Computer-generated images designed with an electronic
paint program entitled ZGrass. This composition is
based on the function inherent to the ZGrass command
vocabulary. —UJ

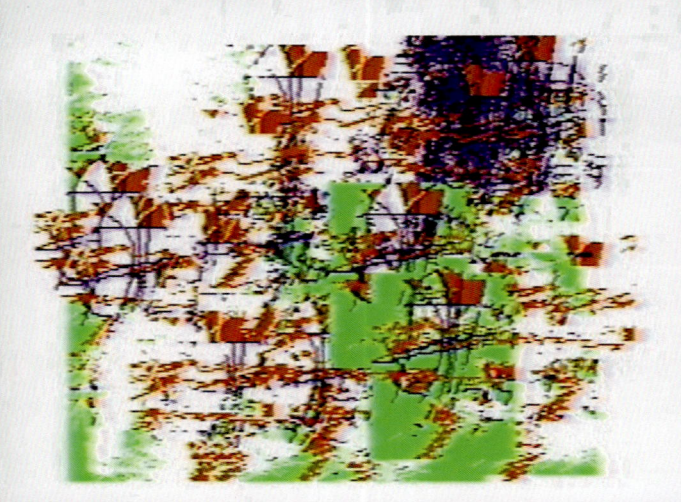

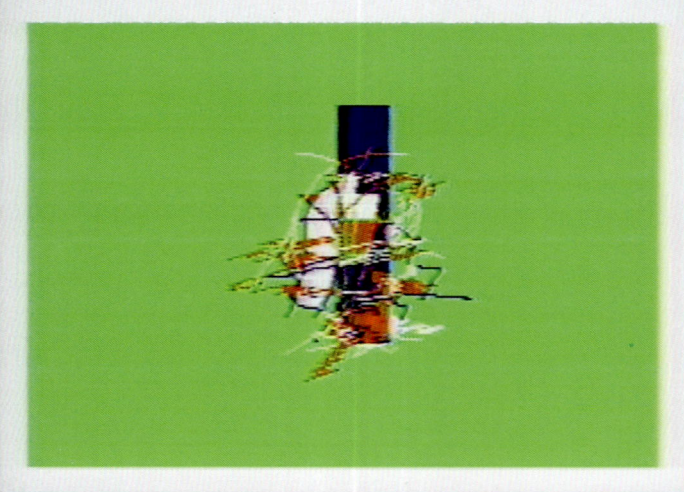

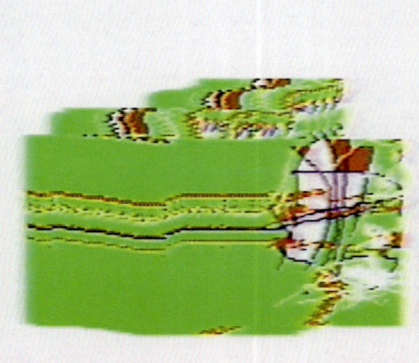

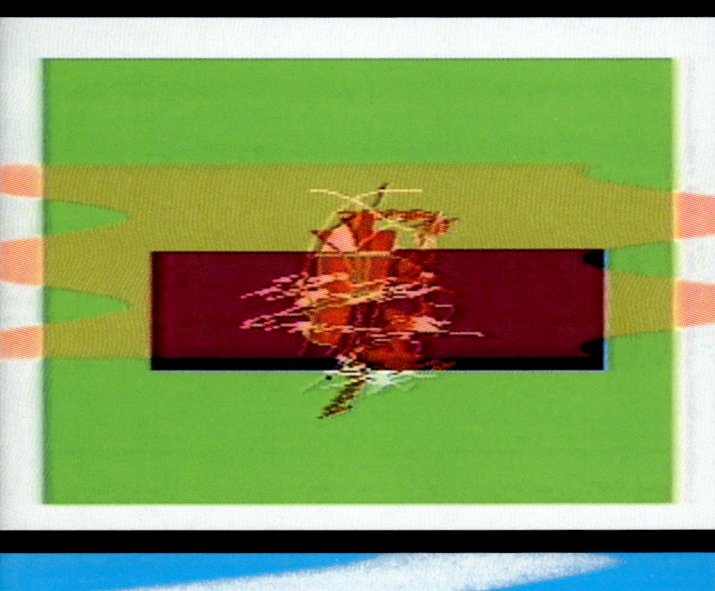

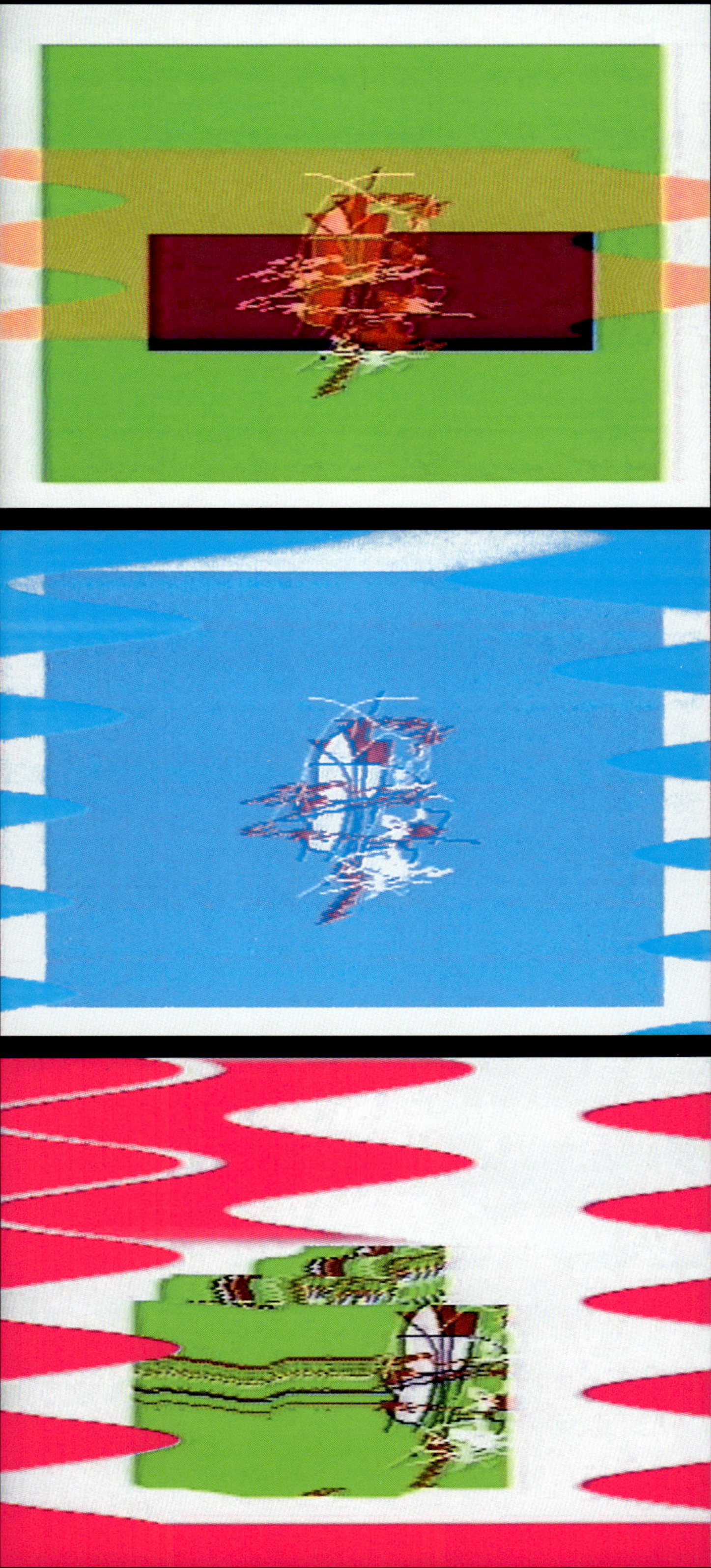

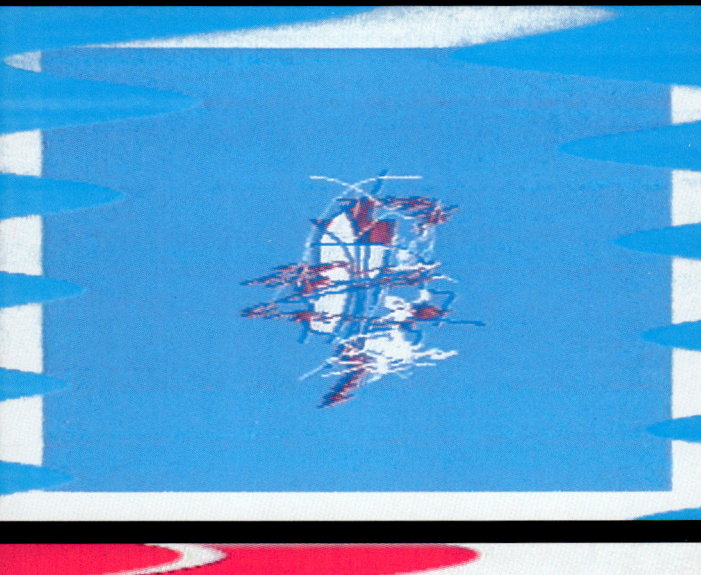

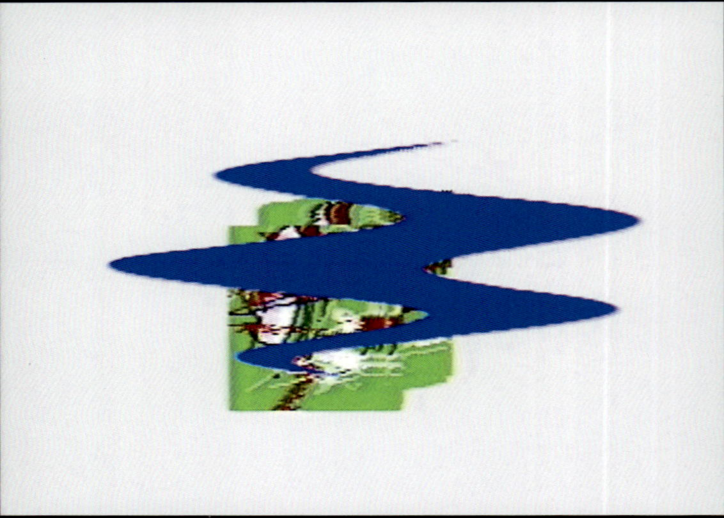

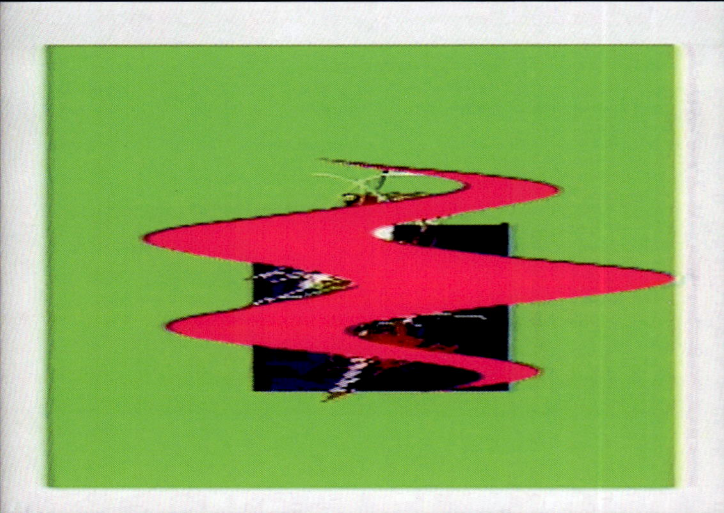

WITHOUT
YOUR
INTERPRETATION

1984, 13:53 min.

This videotape is a video-performance from a live performance near the Los Angeles River at the Art Dock. The performance continues the artist's premise of "Doggereal." This ritual of social crisis and survival represents a collaborative effort of third-world sensibilities in various disciplines by these artists. —UJ

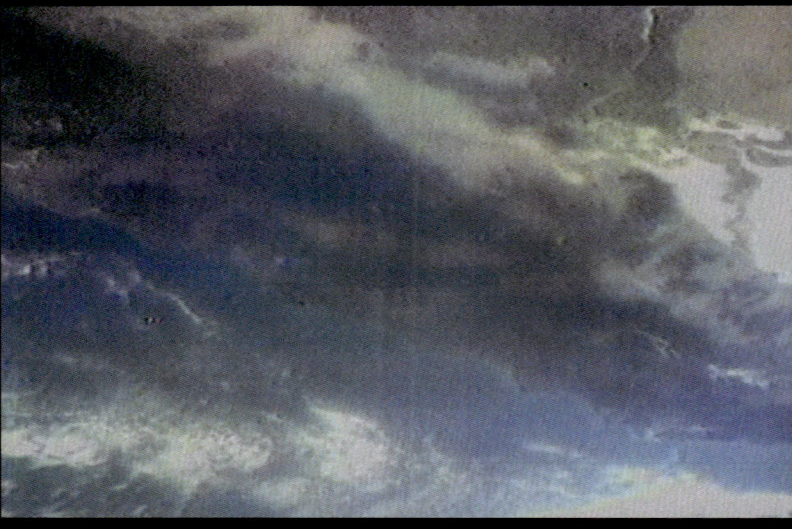

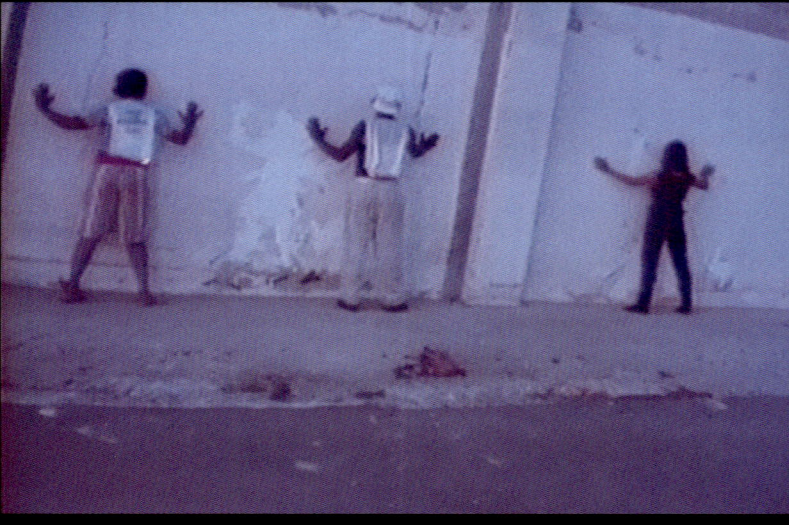

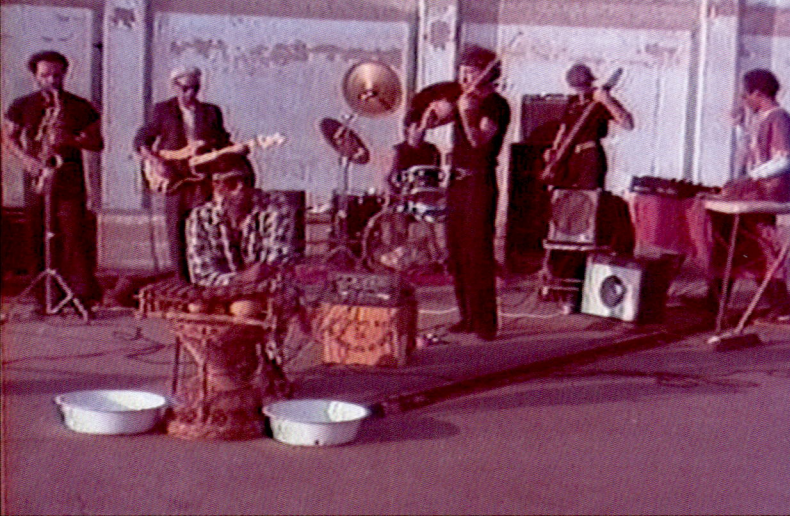

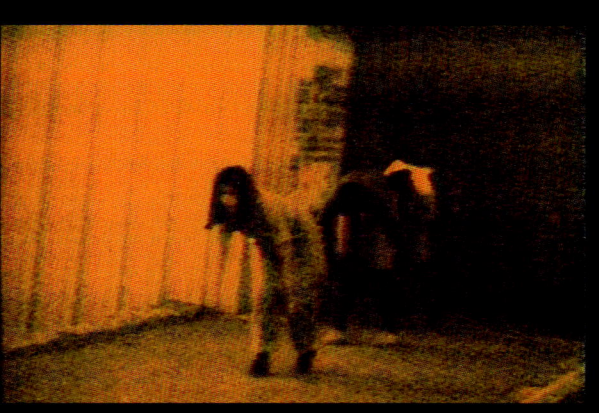
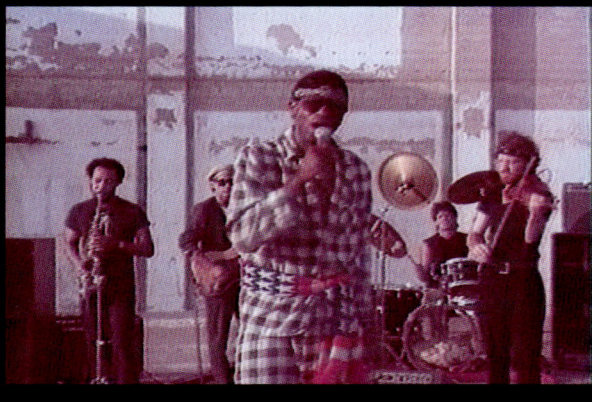

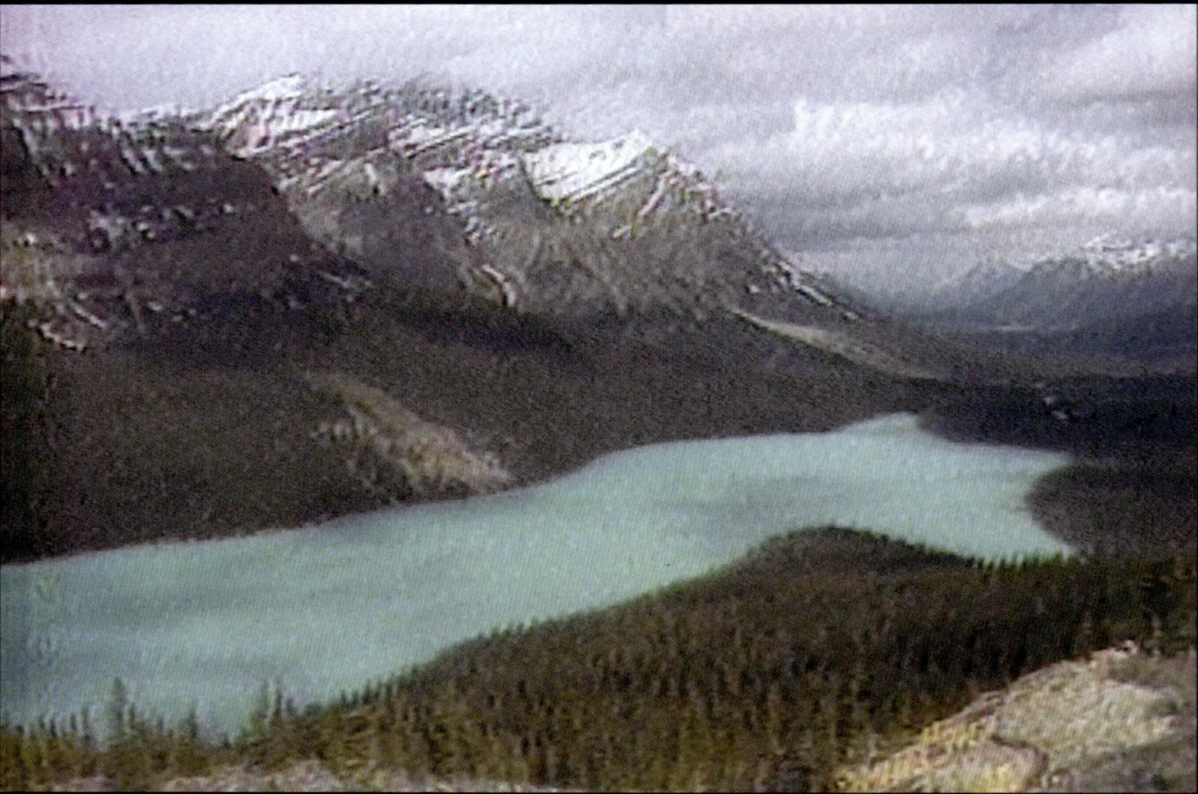

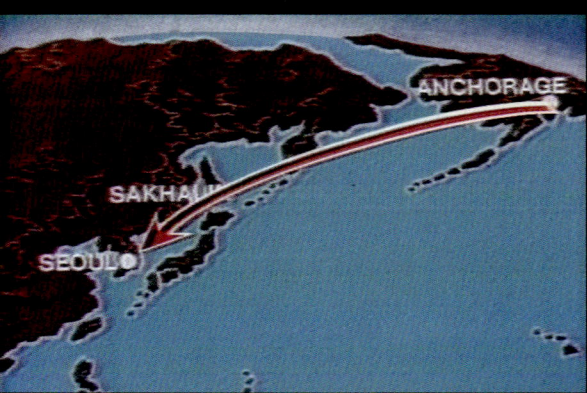
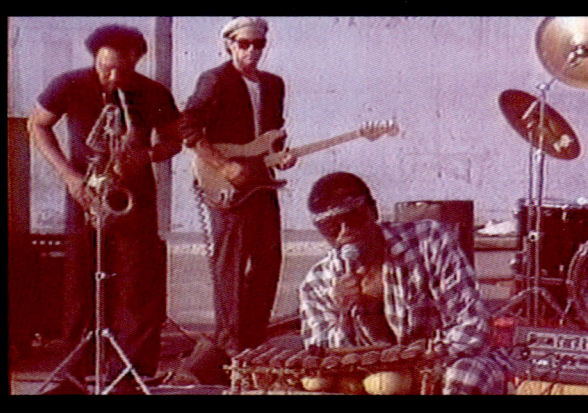

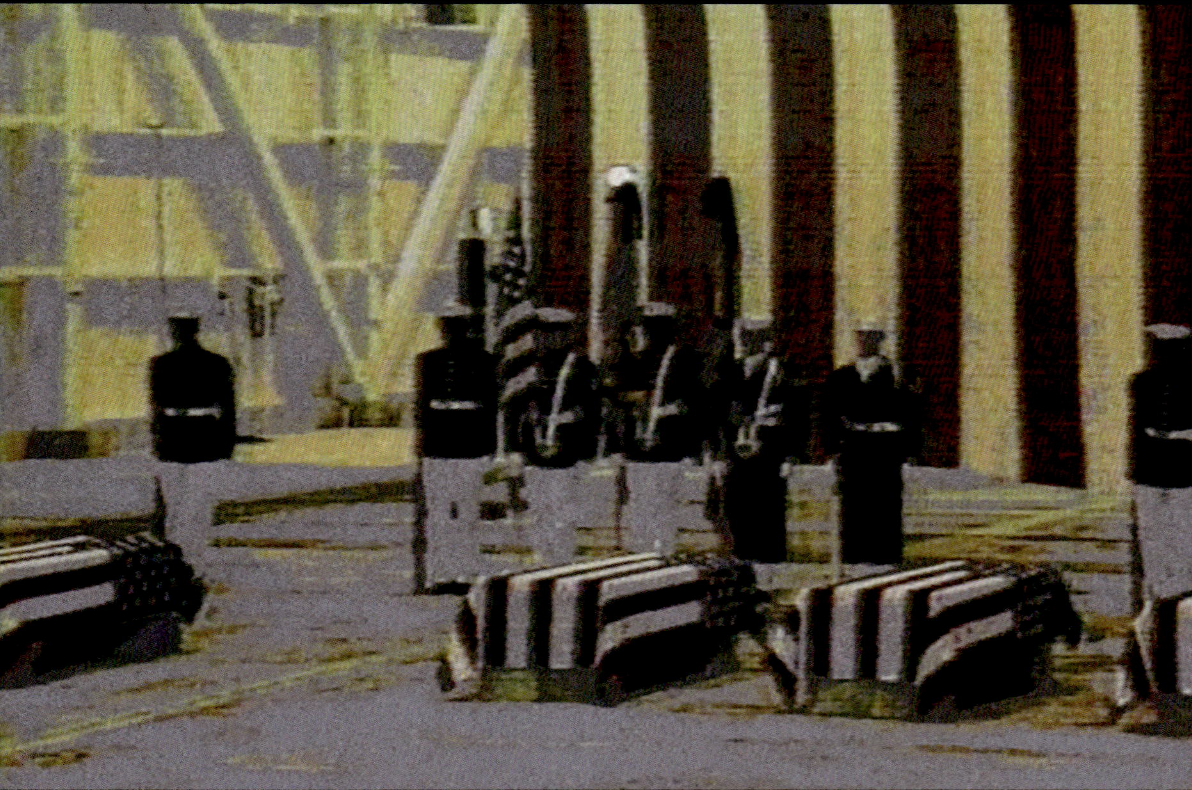

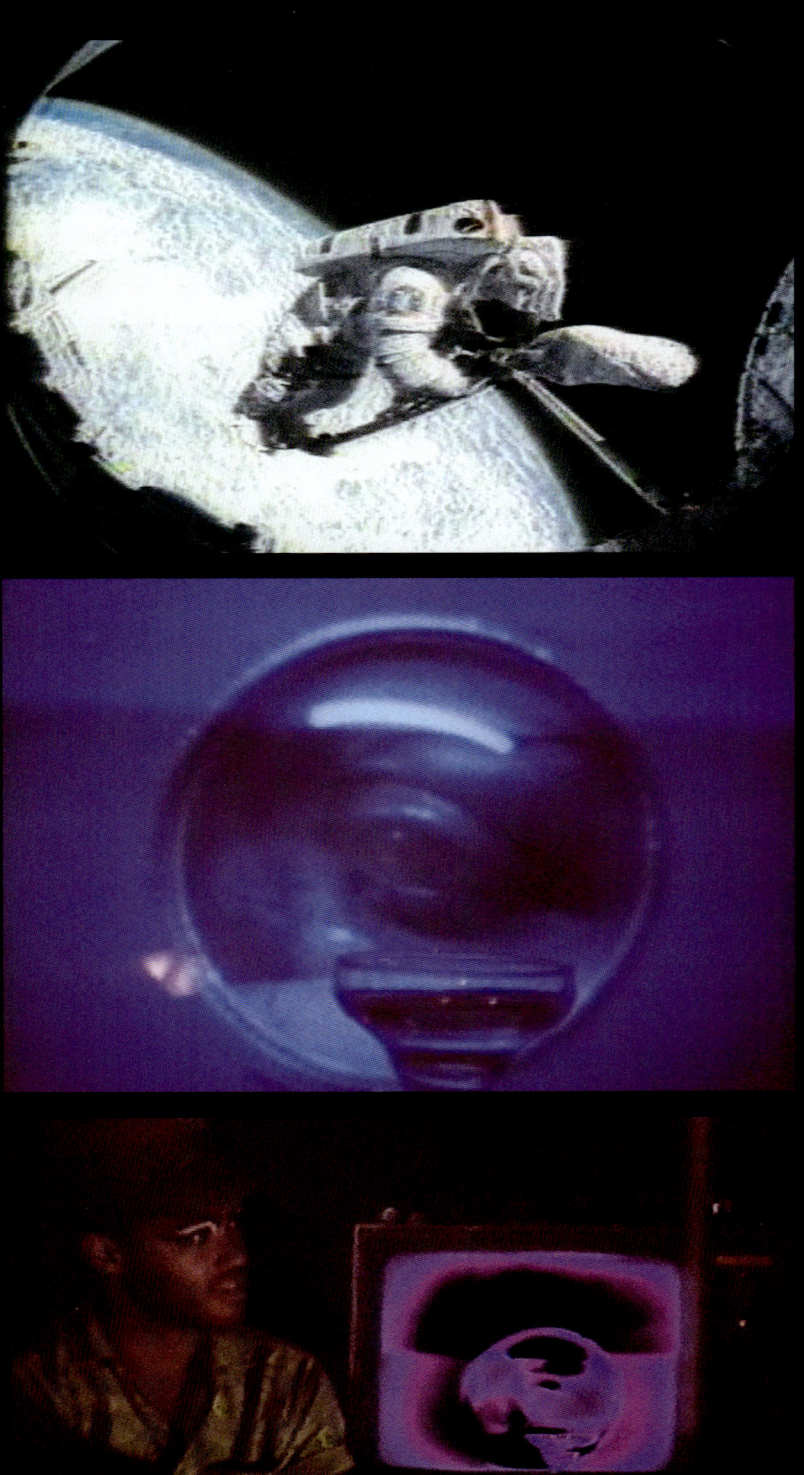

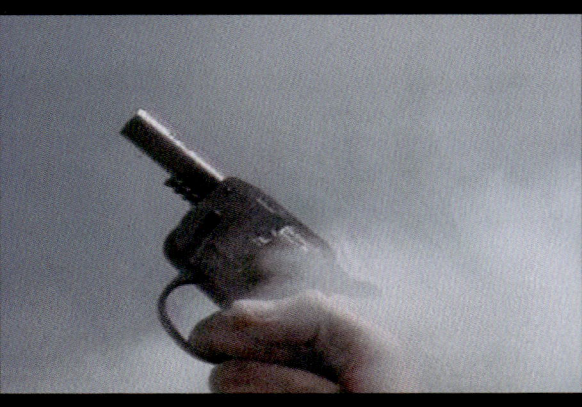
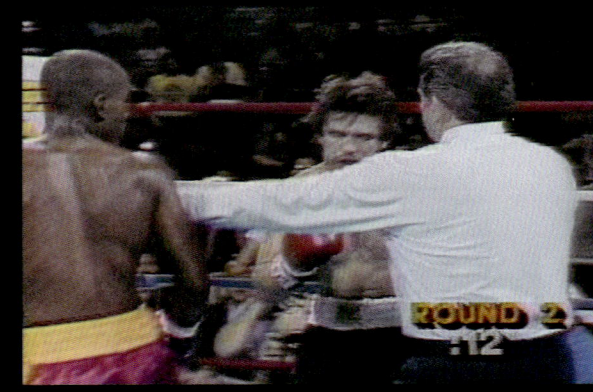
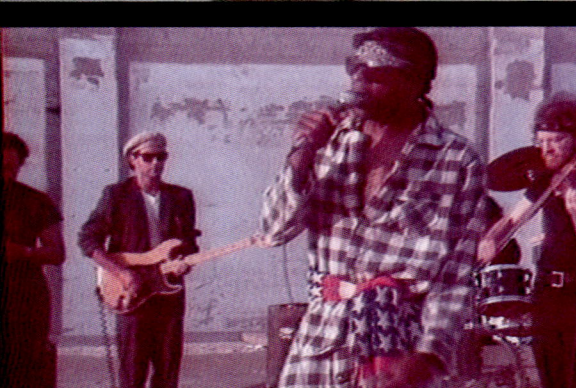
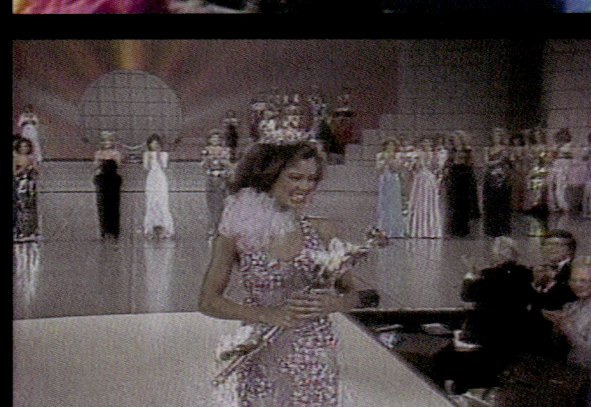
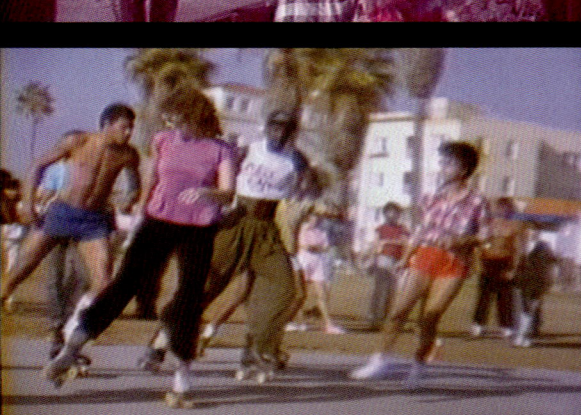
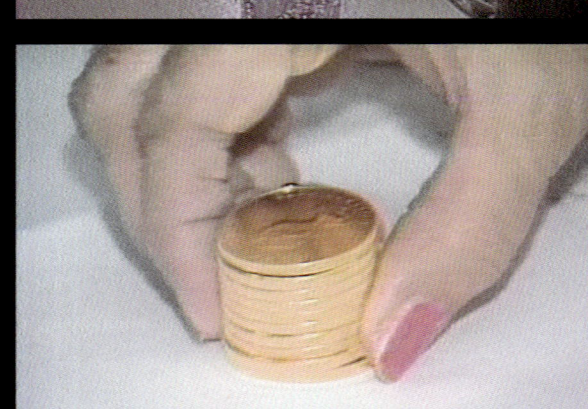
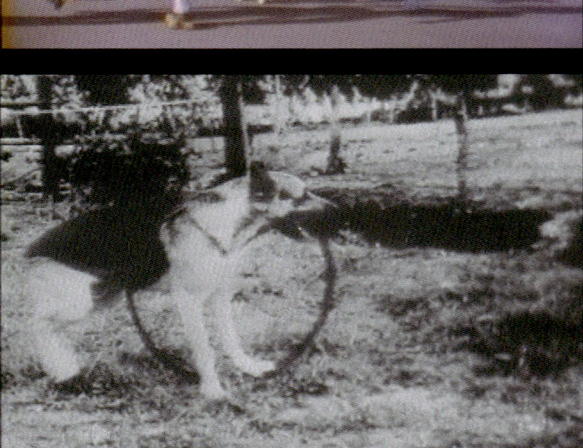
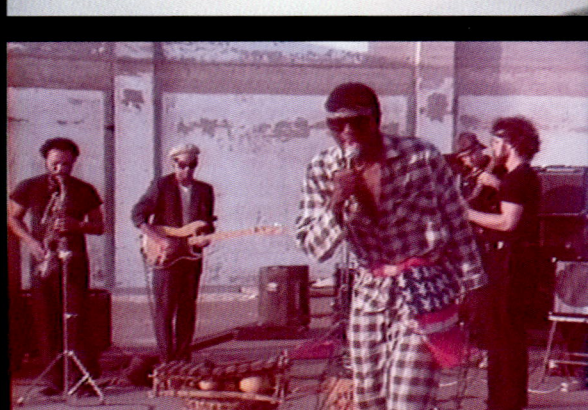

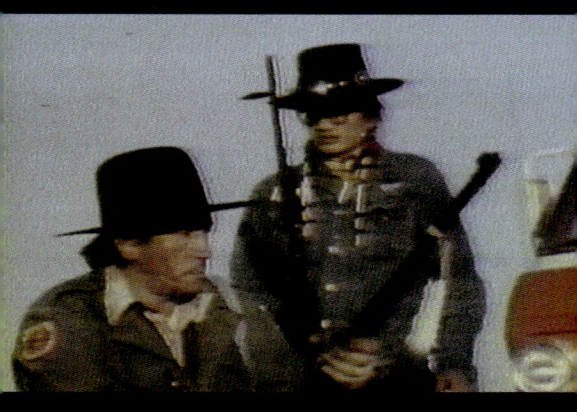

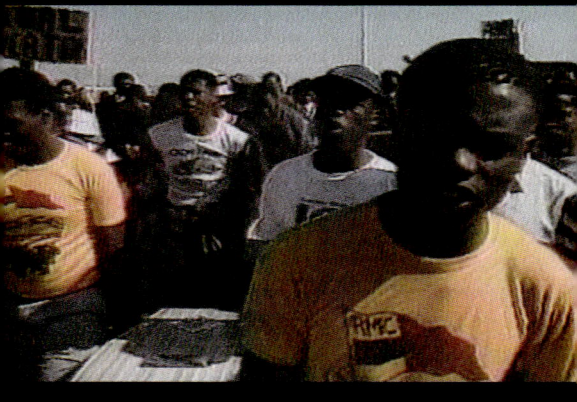

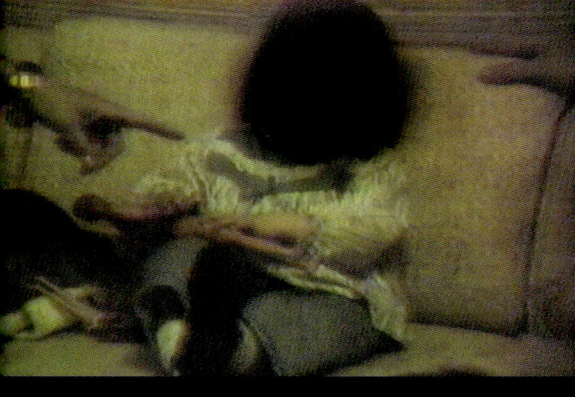

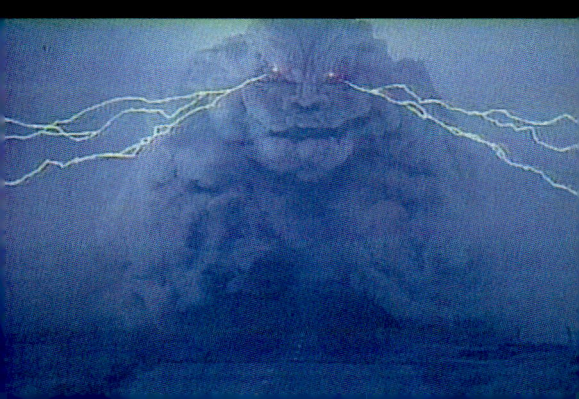

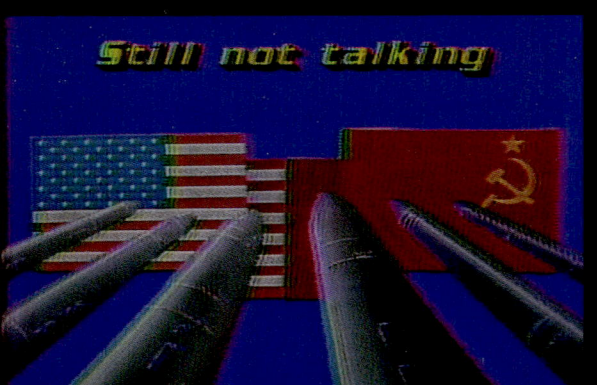
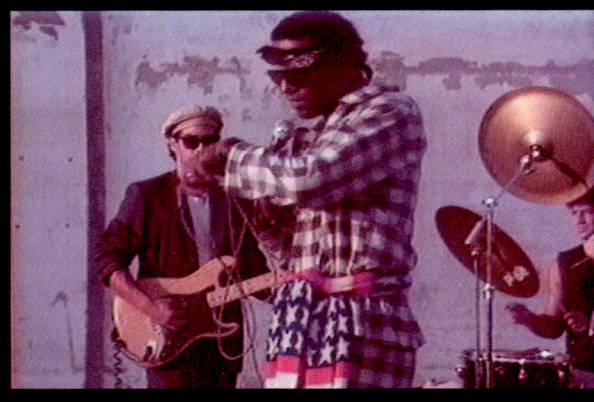
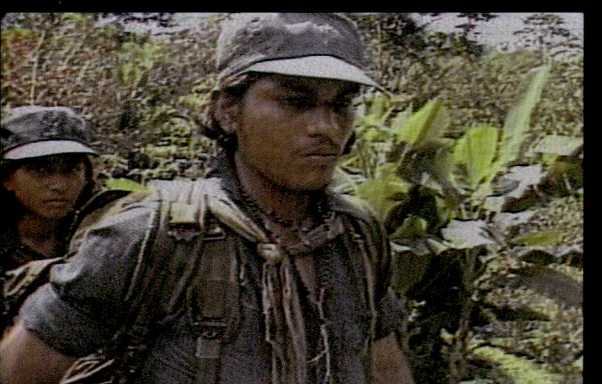
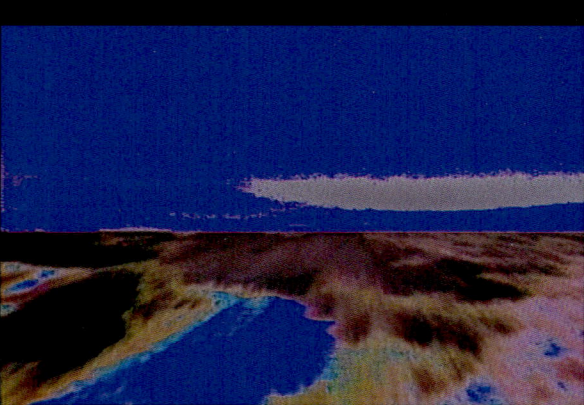

PEACE and ANWAR SADAT

1985, 21:32 min.

This composition provides a tribute to the world's most
formidable peace activist, Anwar Sadat. The video
paints visions of issues concerning Earth's flirtation
with the apocalypse. —UJ

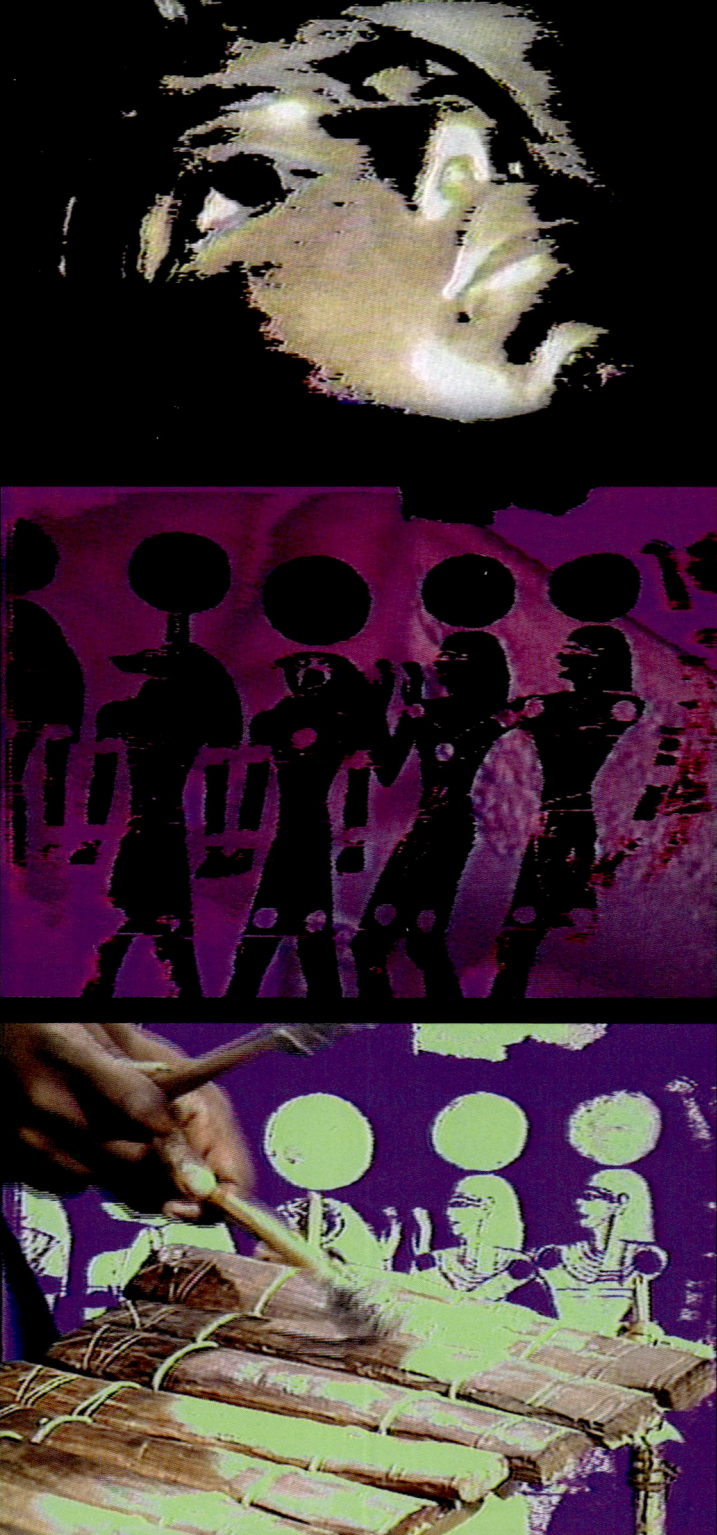

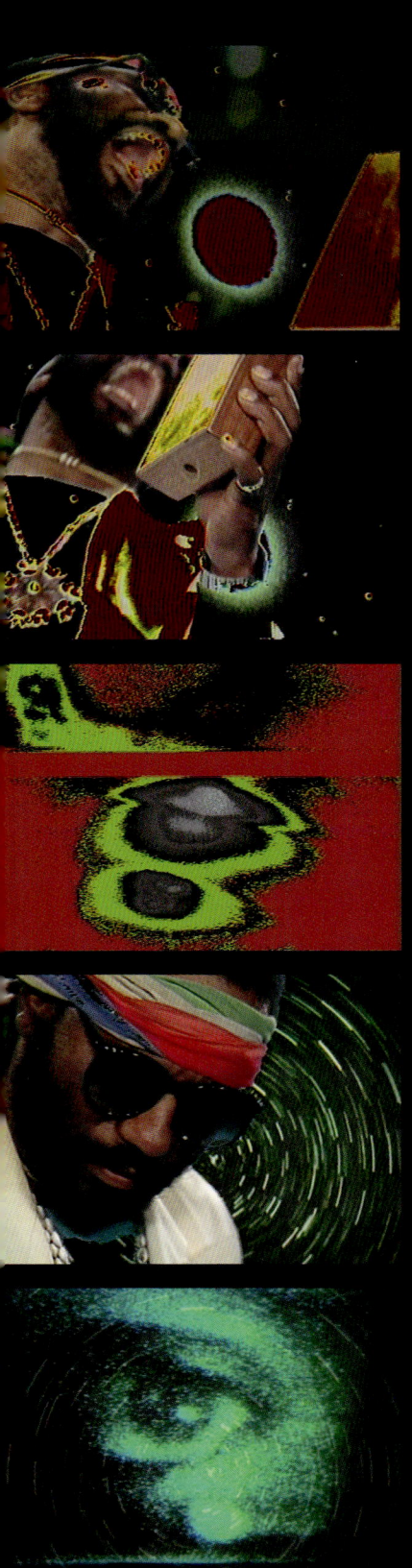
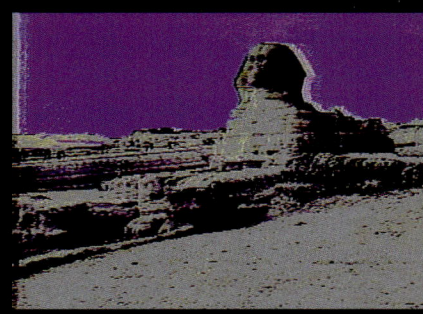
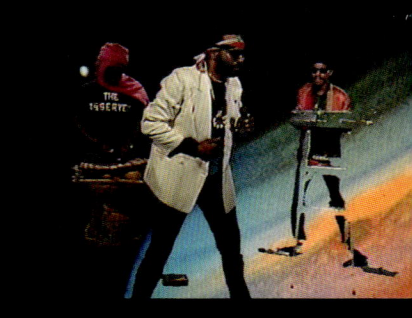
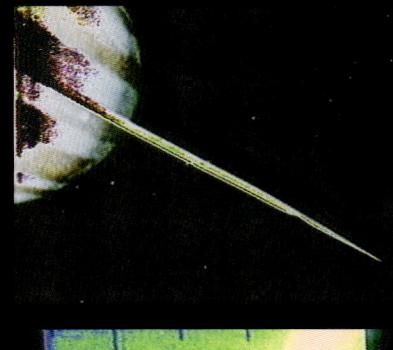
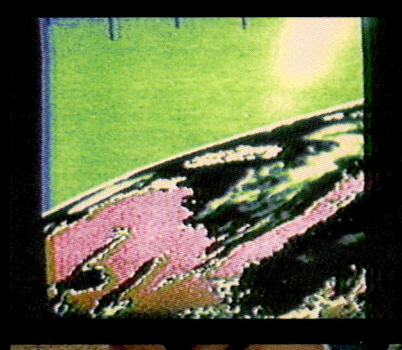
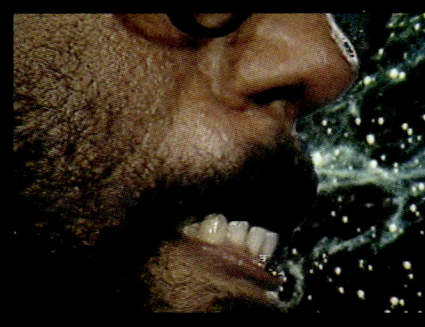

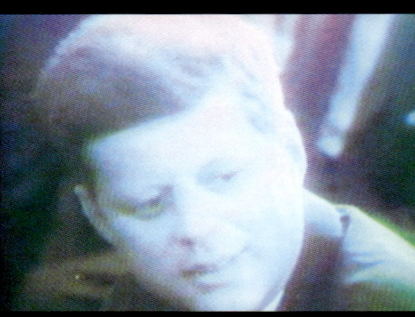
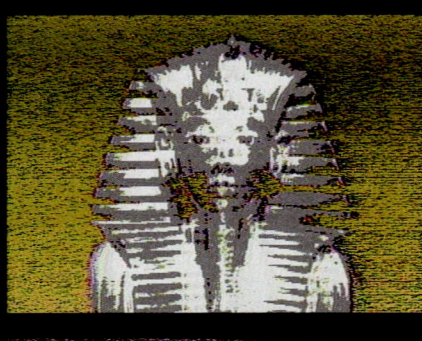
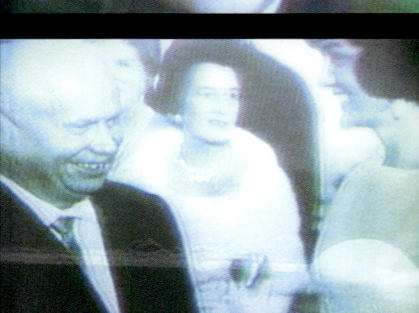
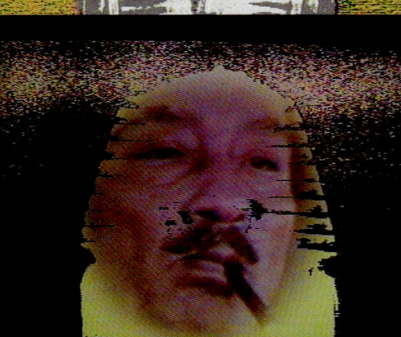
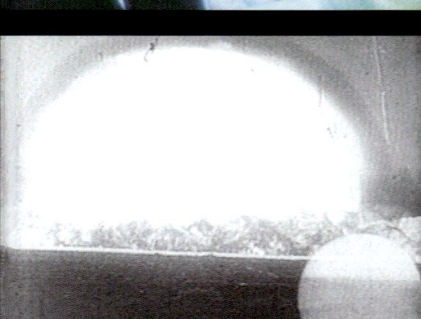
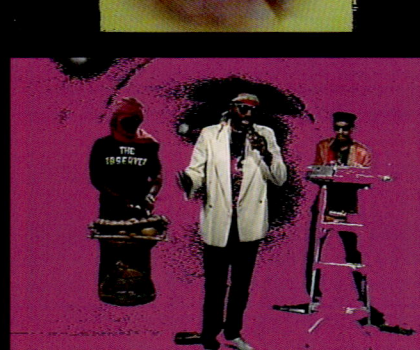
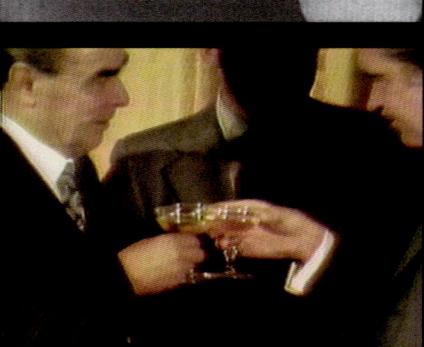
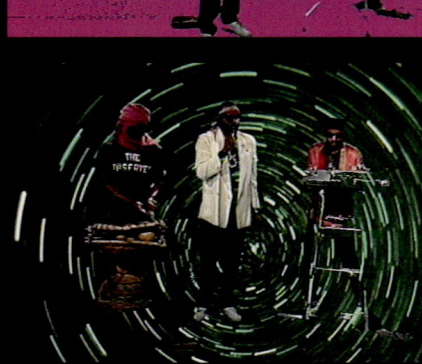
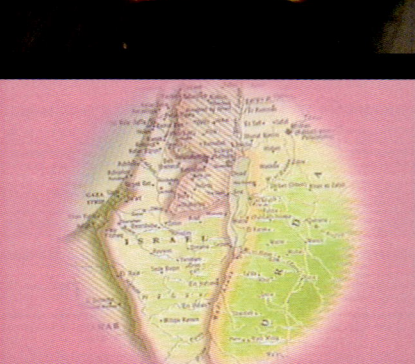
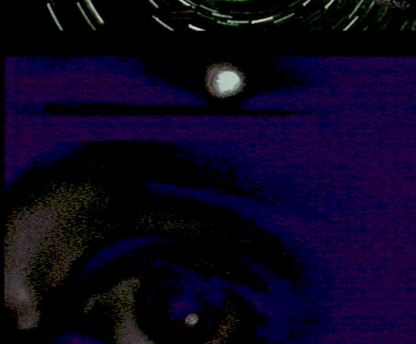

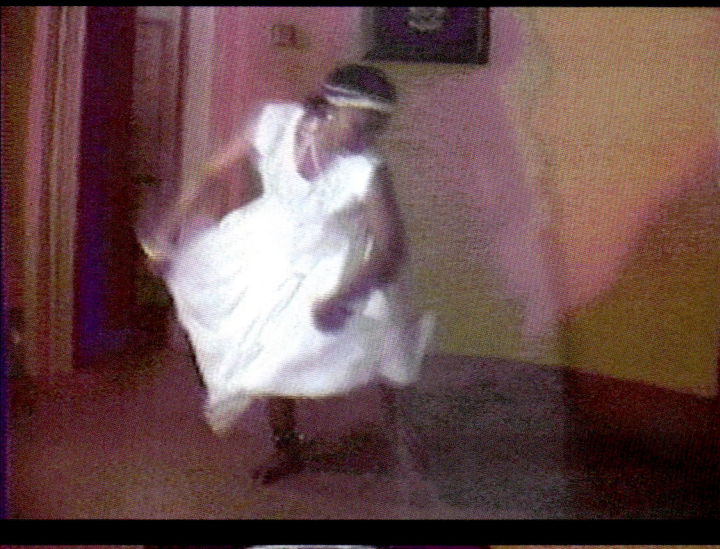

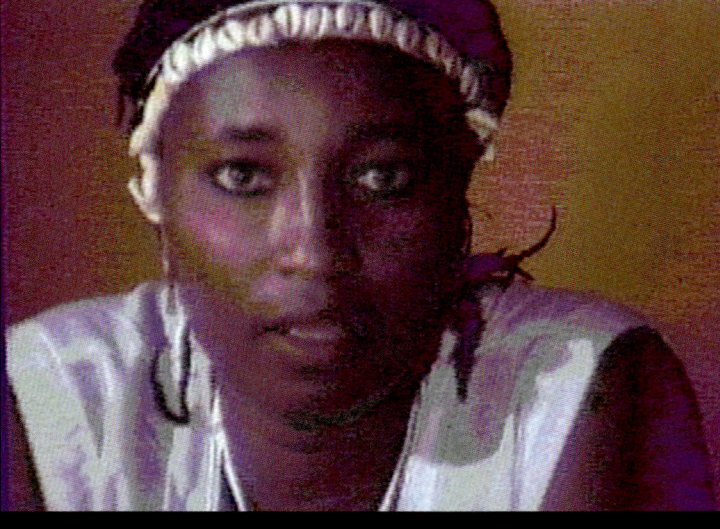

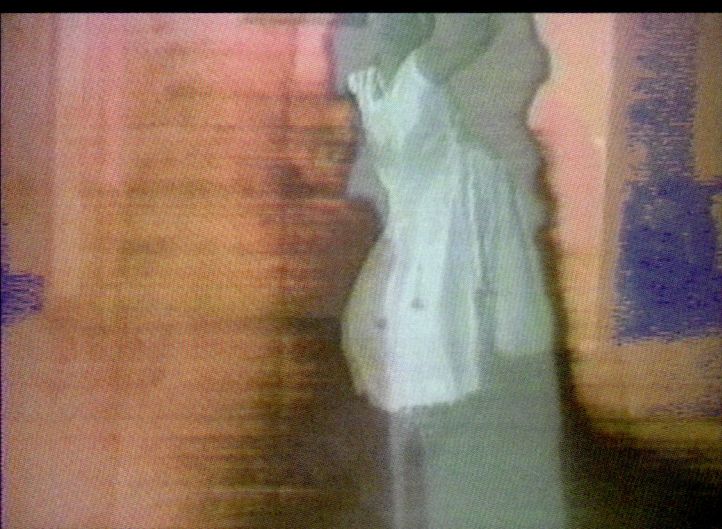

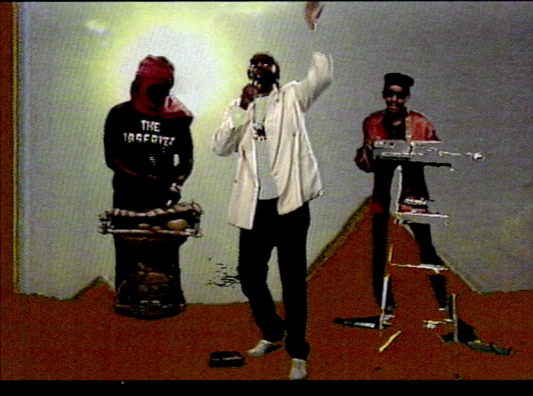

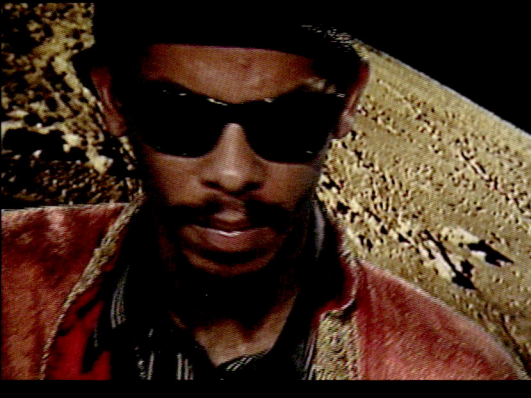

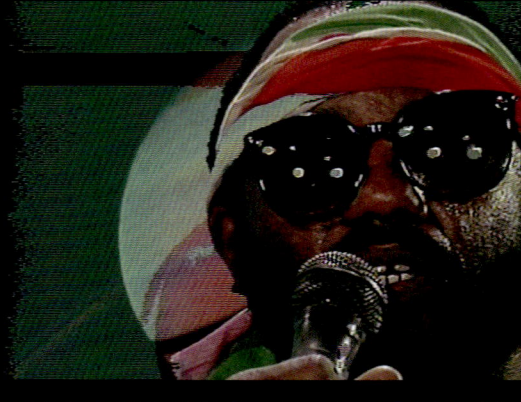

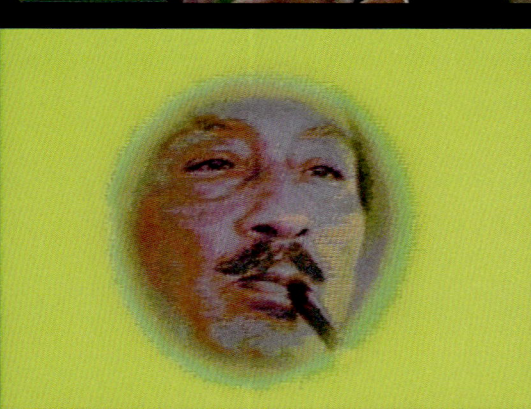

CINCO DE MAYO

1986
GARDENA.CA.

1986, 10:58 min.

Highlights from the first Cinco de Mayo parade from the
City of Gardena. Recorded on Saturday, May 3, 1986,
for Group W Cable.

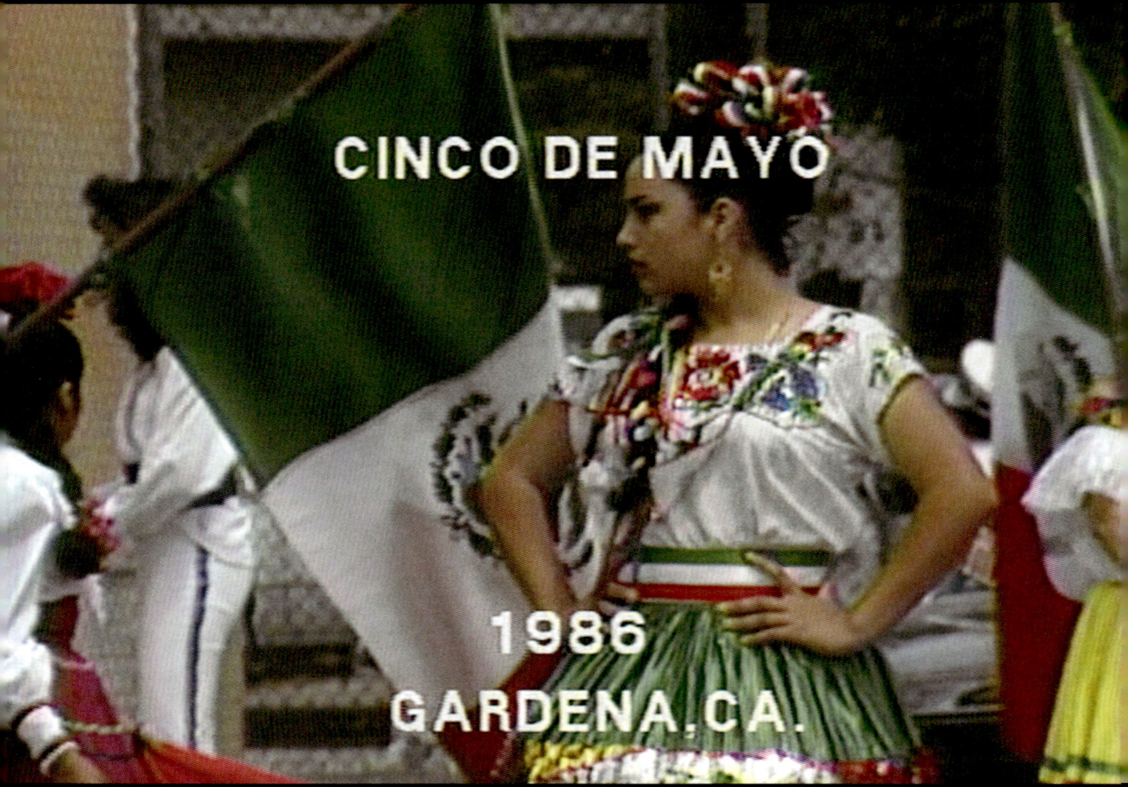
CINCO DE MAYO
1986
GARDENA.CA.

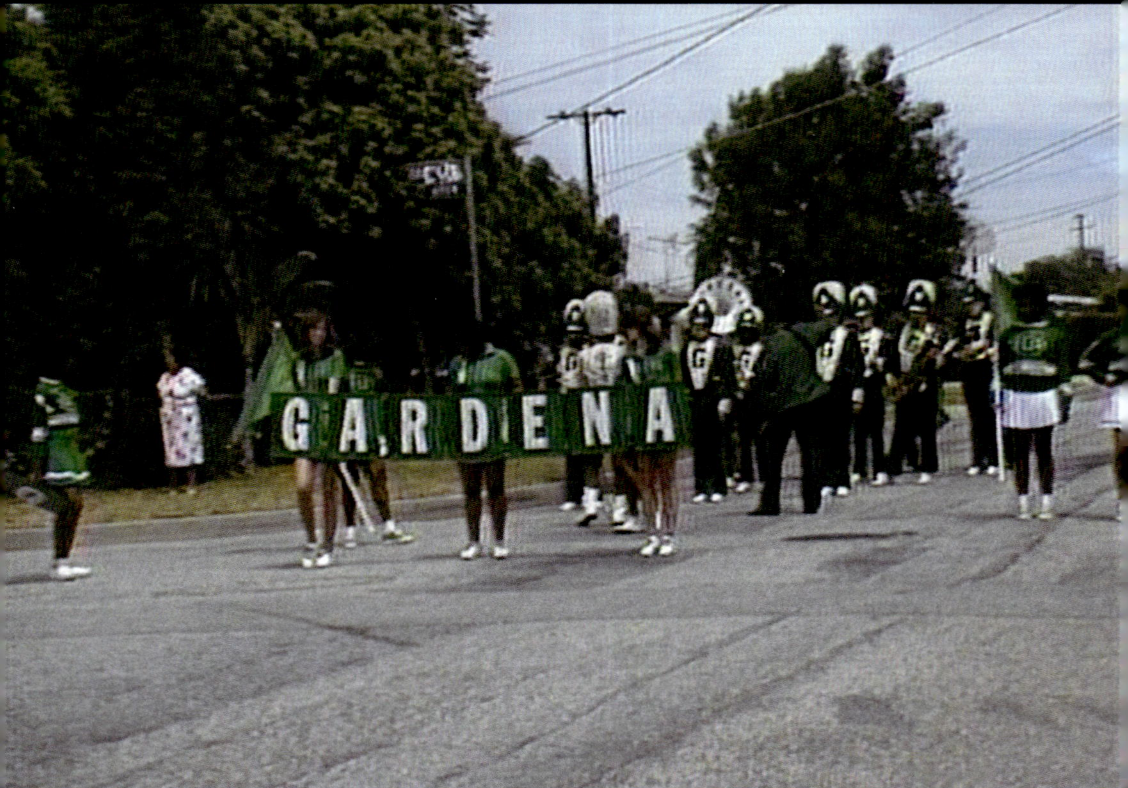
GARDENA

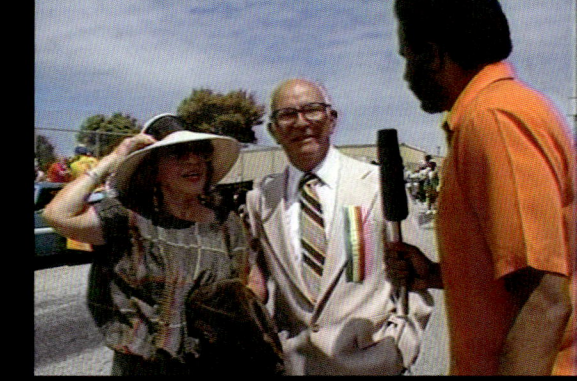

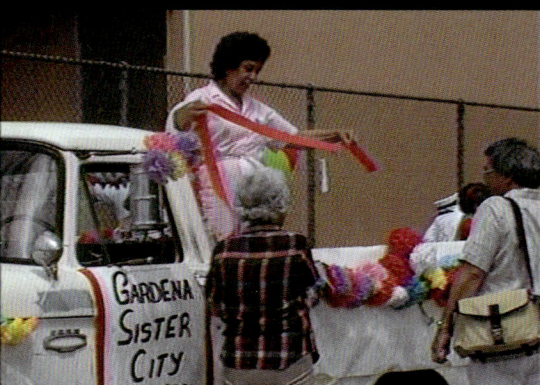

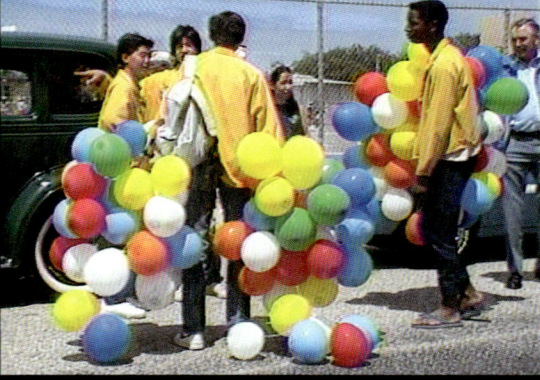

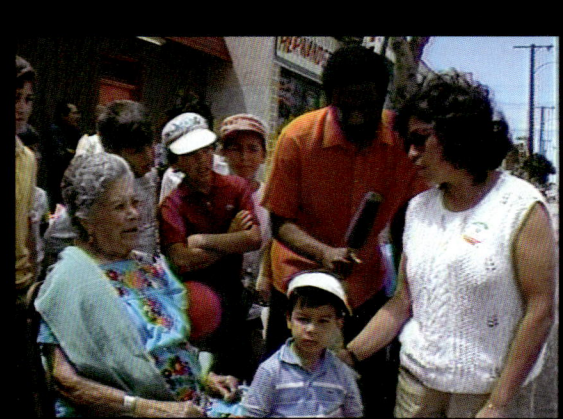

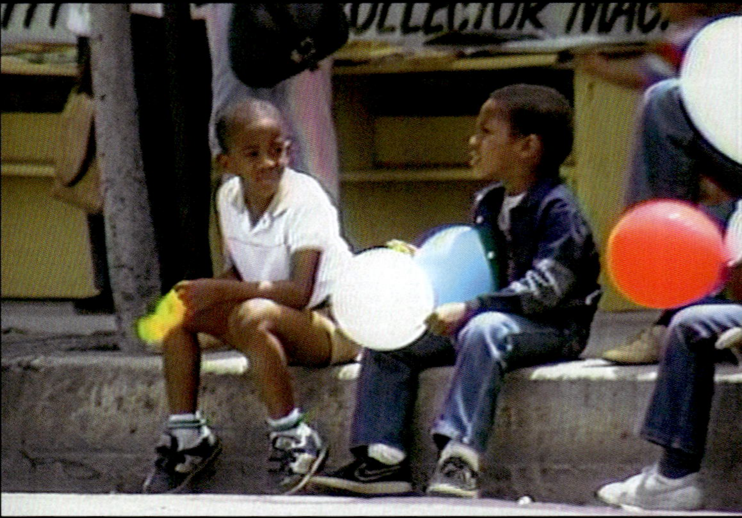

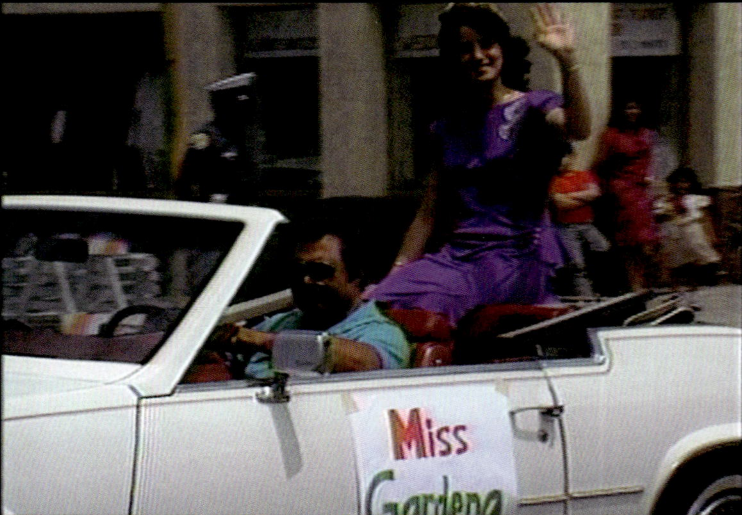
Miss

 #9

Fat and Fucked Up, 1987, 27:39 min.
The Last Minstrel Show from Below the Underground,
1987, 29:31 min.
Primal Synthesis, 1987, 31:26 min.

Episodes from Othervision's cable TV program #9.

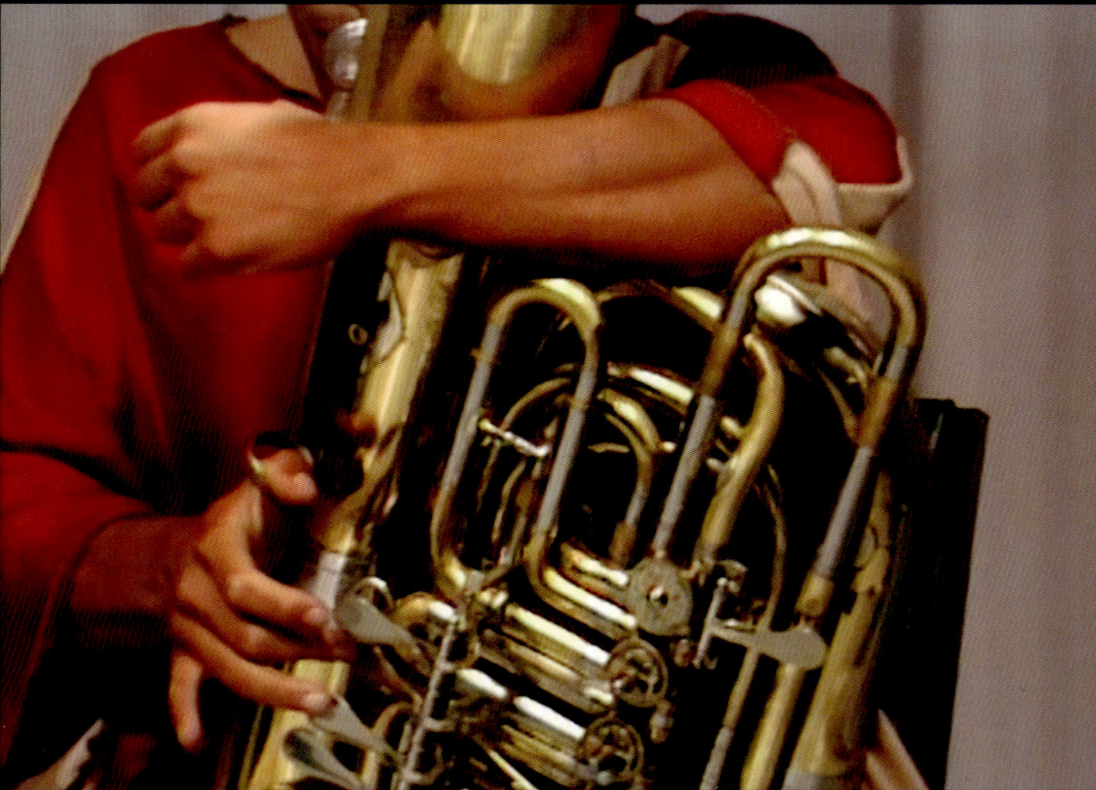

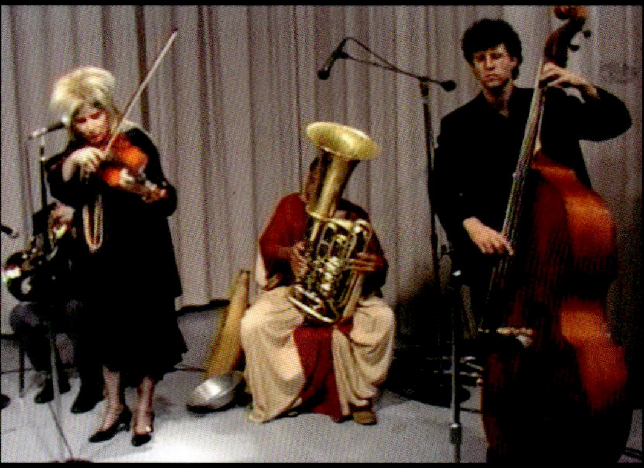

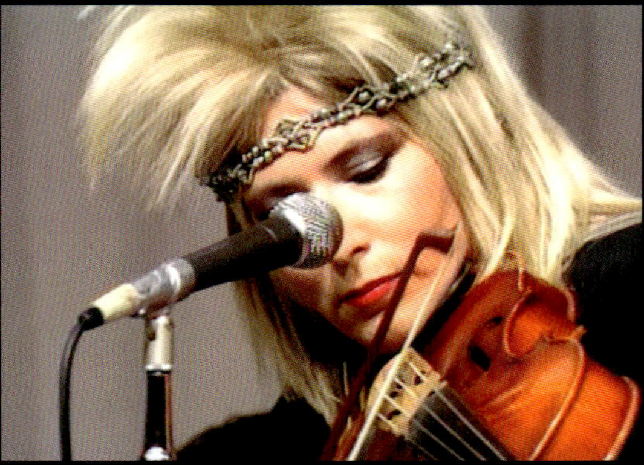

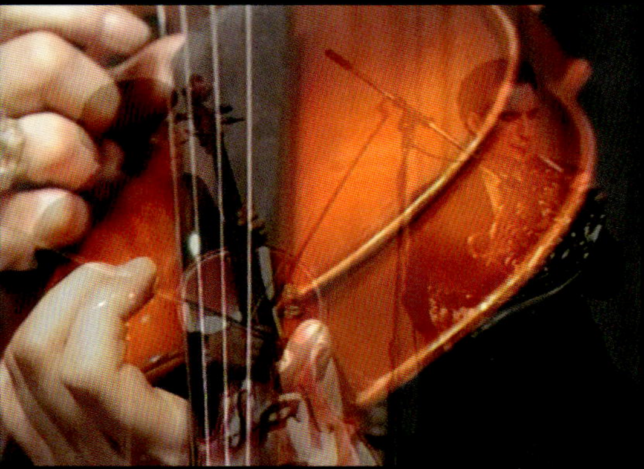

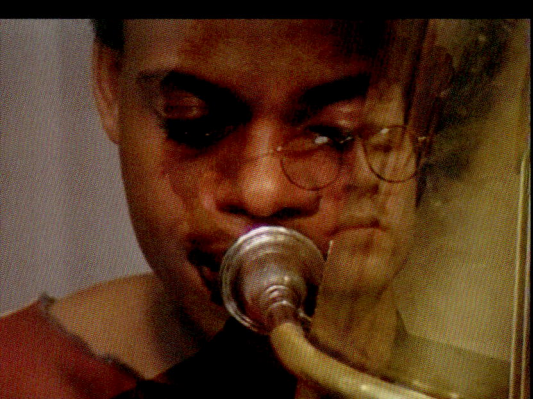

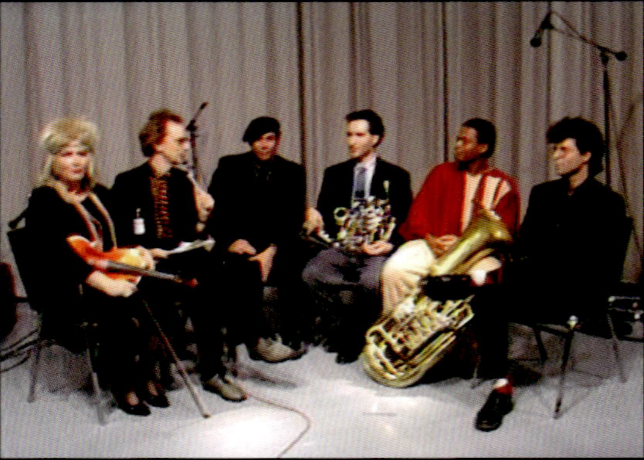

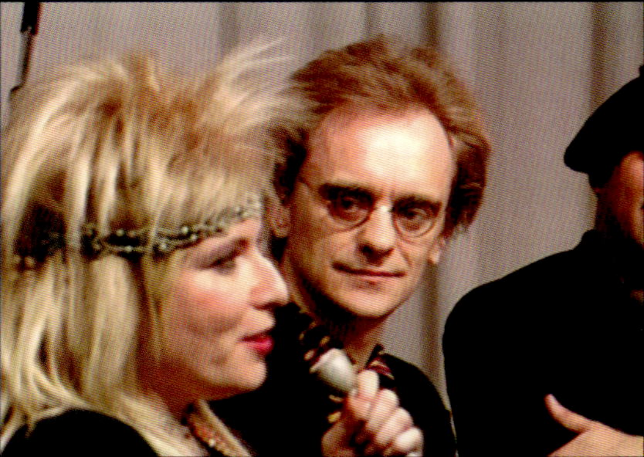

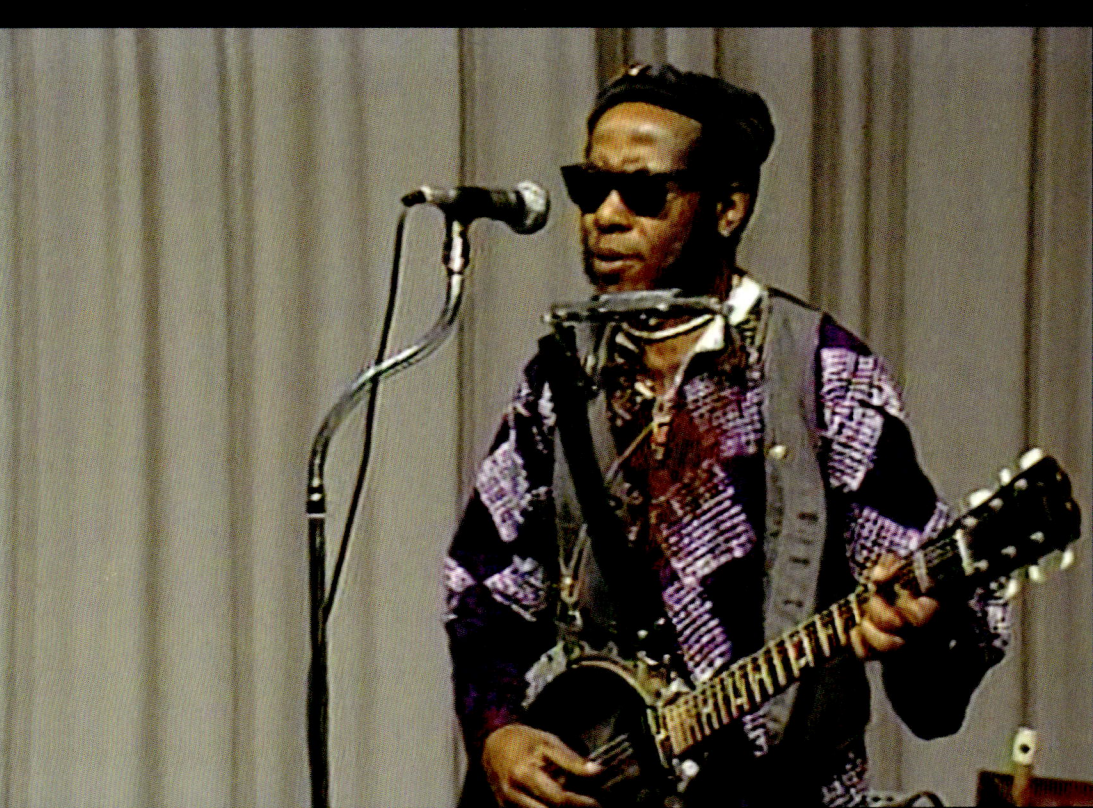

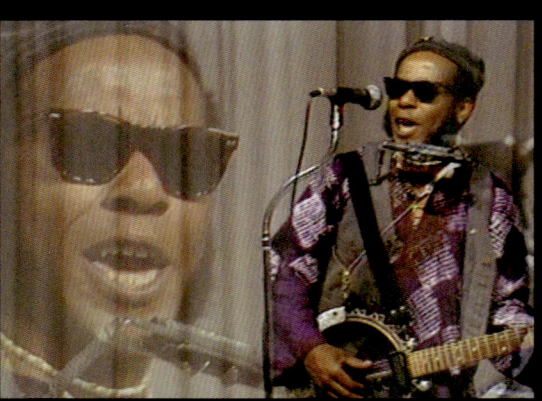

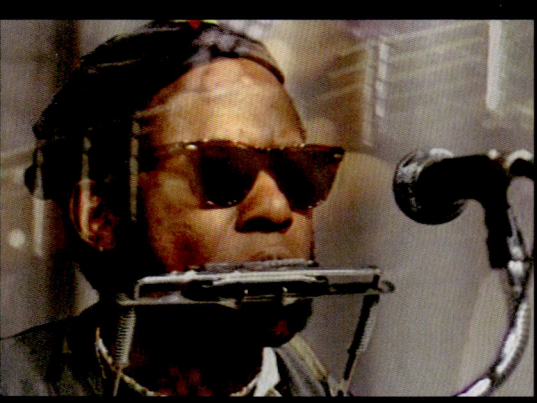

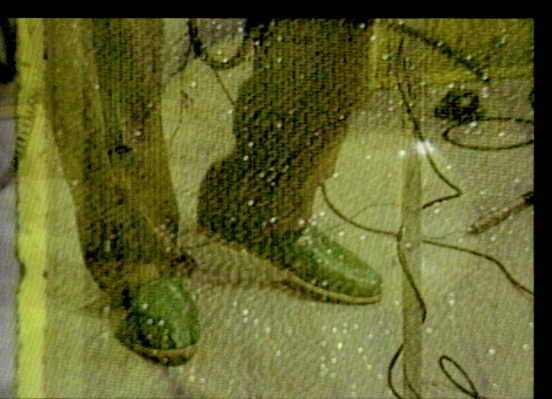
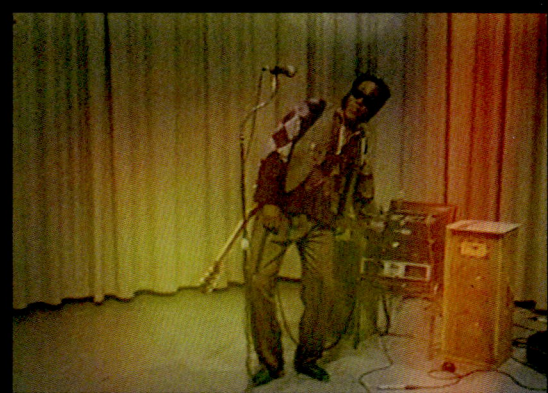

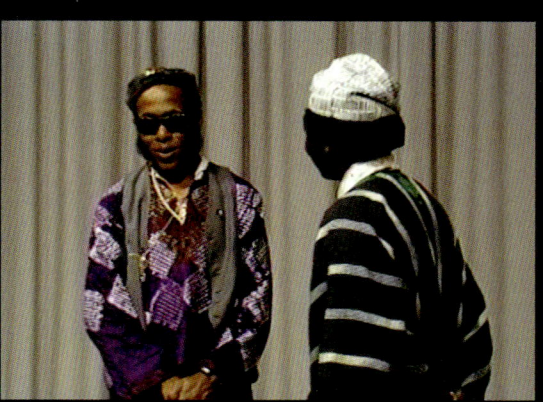

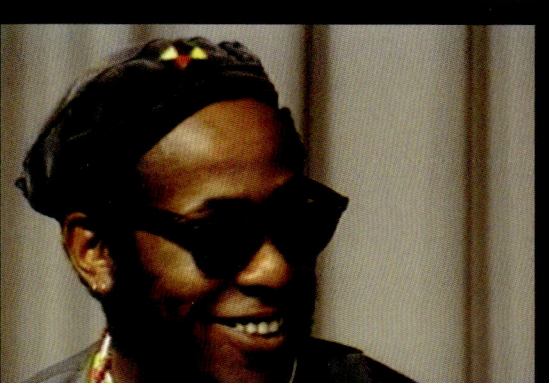

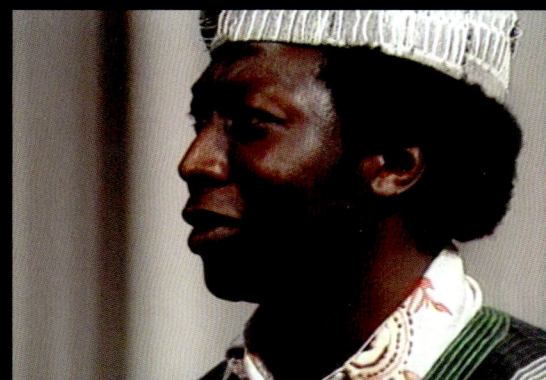

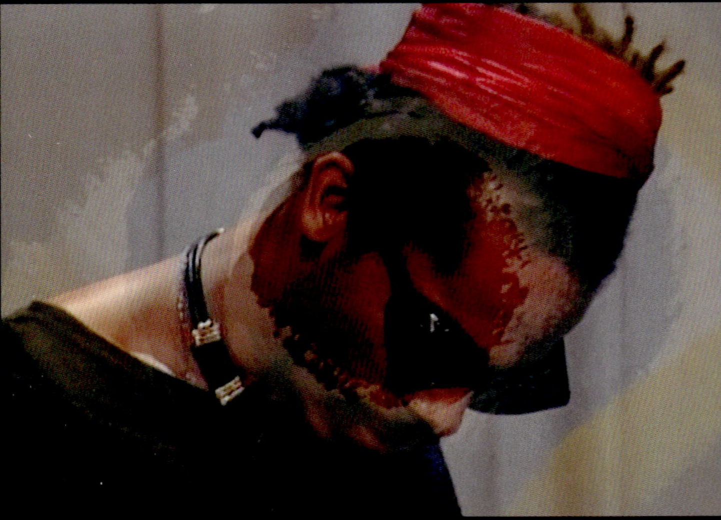

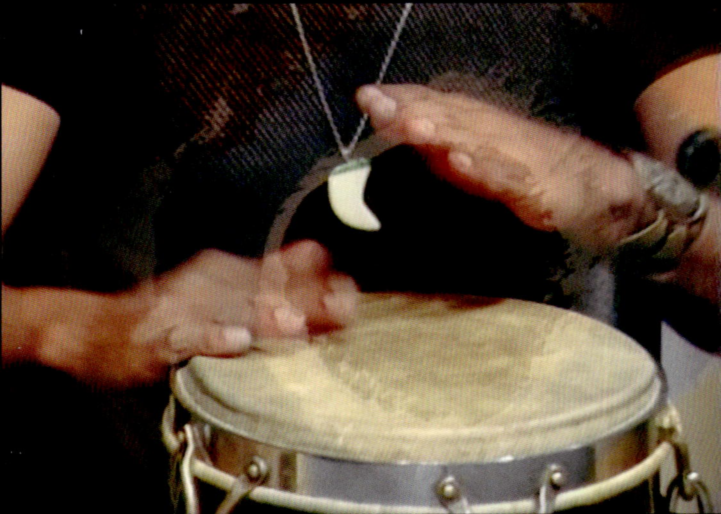

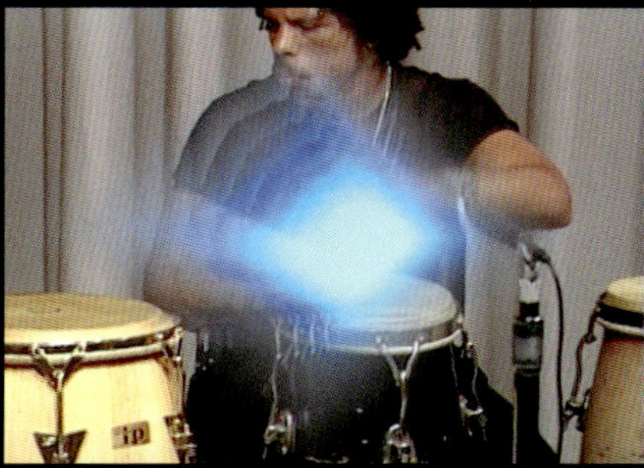

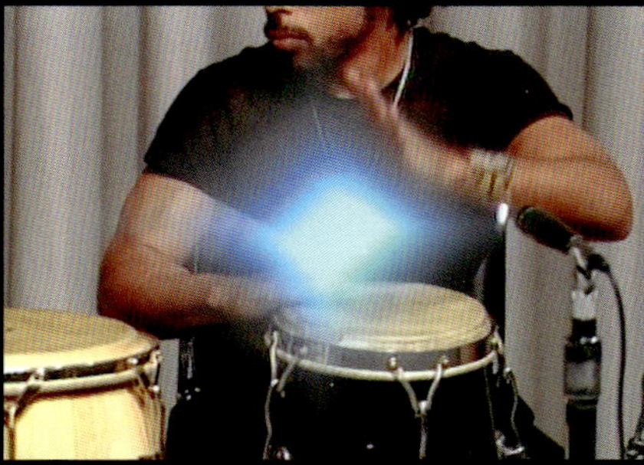

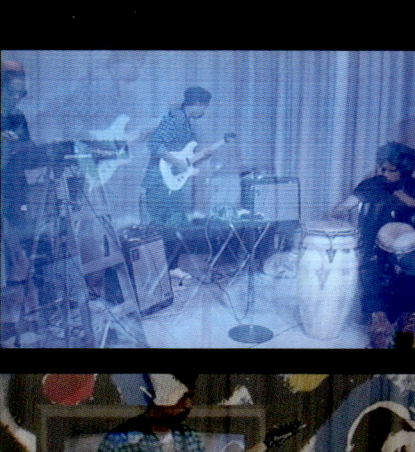
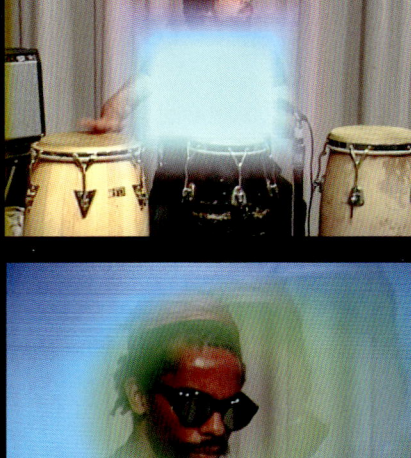
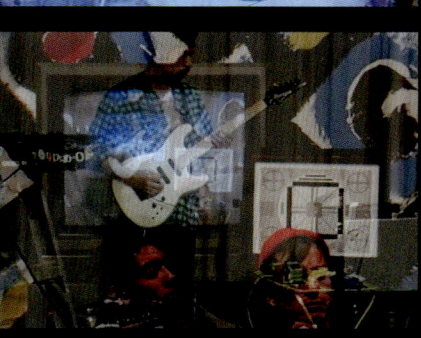
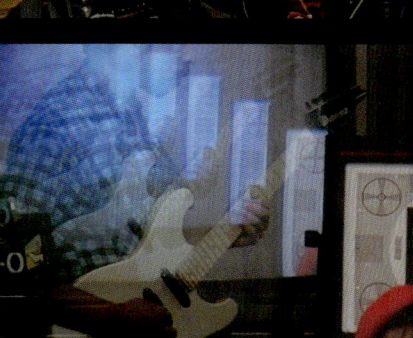
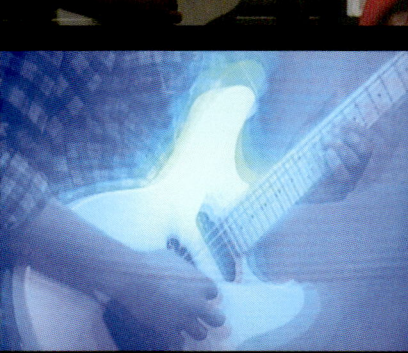
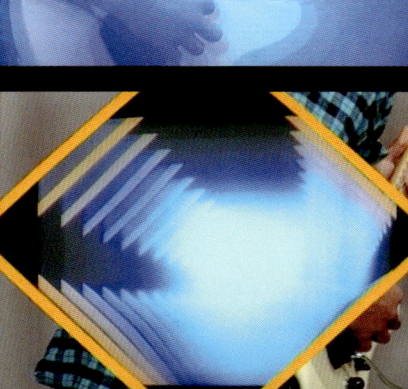
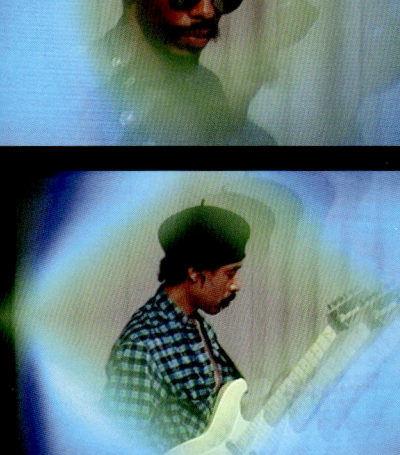

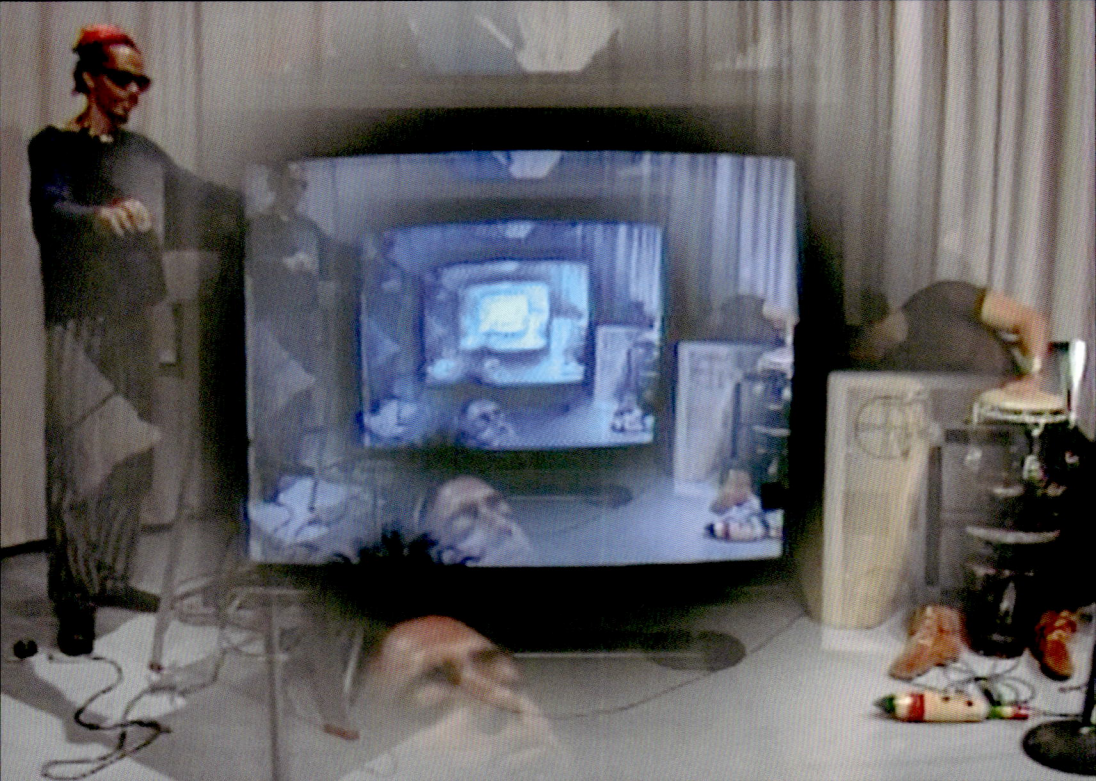

NO SUPPER

© 1987
HARRY GAMBOA JR.

1987, 25:35 min.

Debut of Harry Gamboa's play *No Supper*. Produced by
Ulysses Jenkins and South Bay Cablevision for the TV
program *Theatré Twenty Two*.

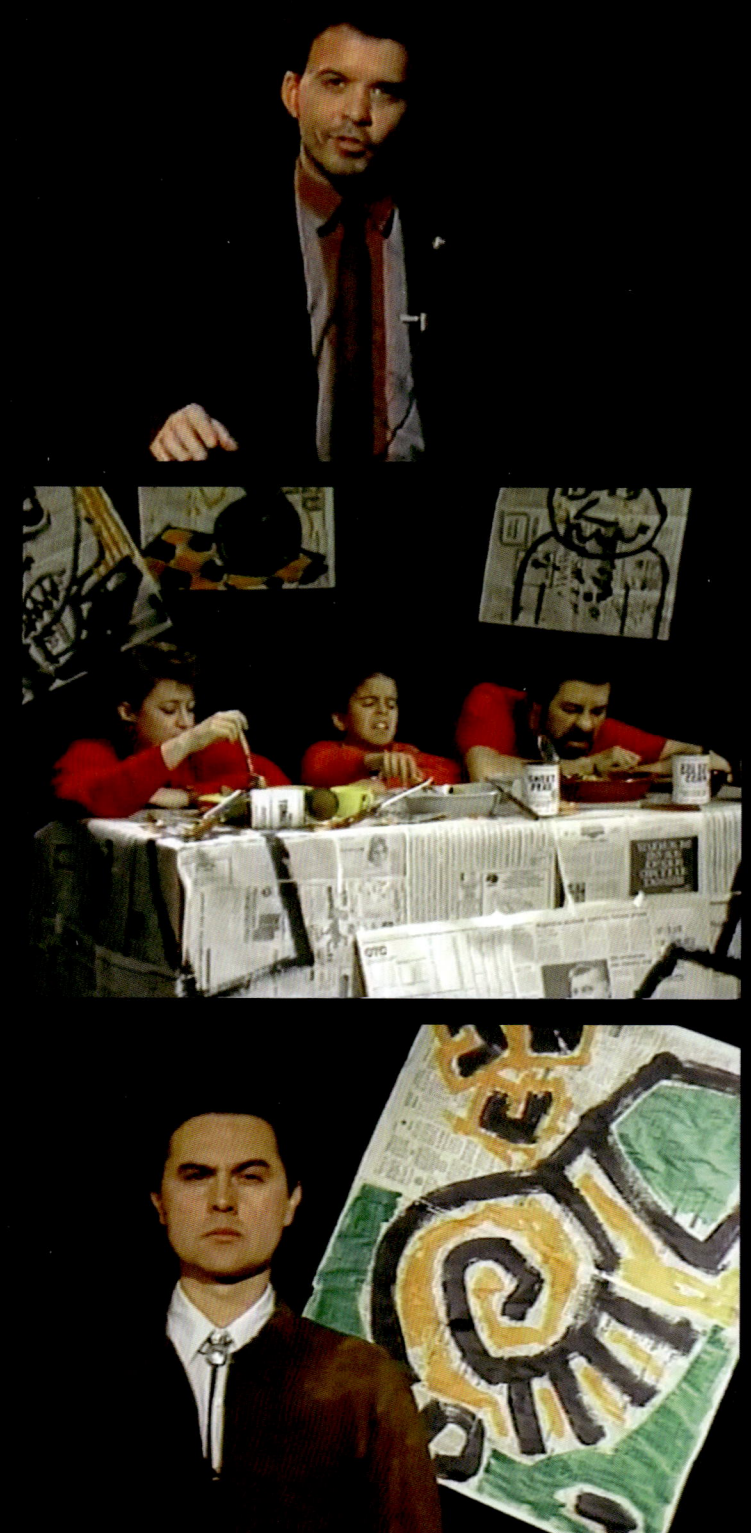

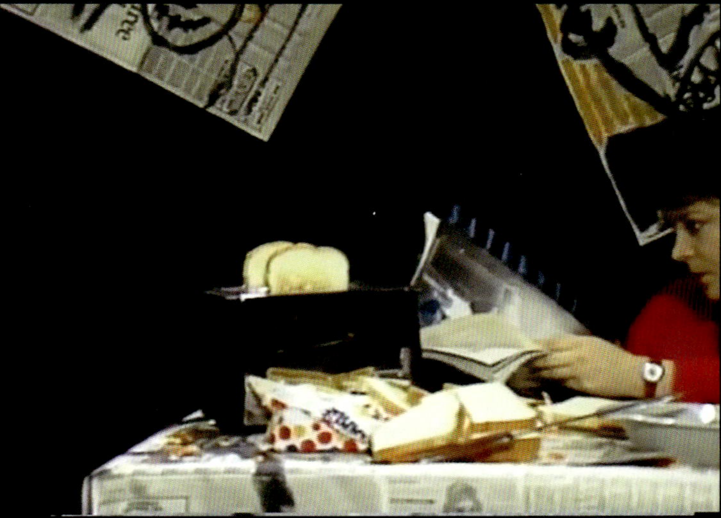

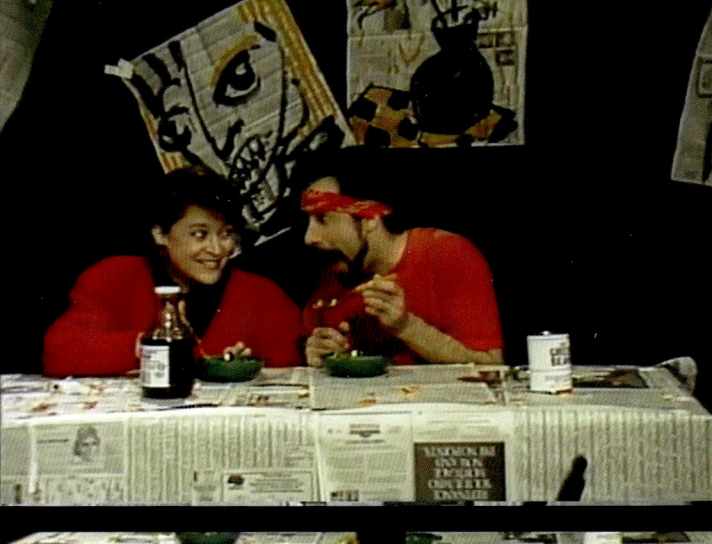

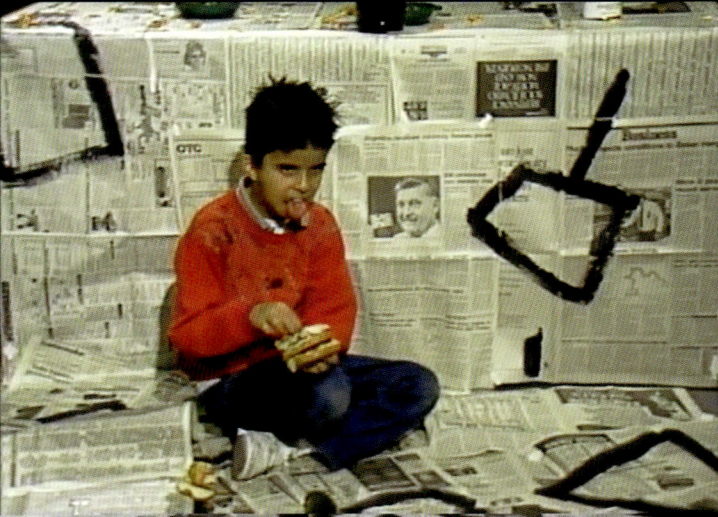

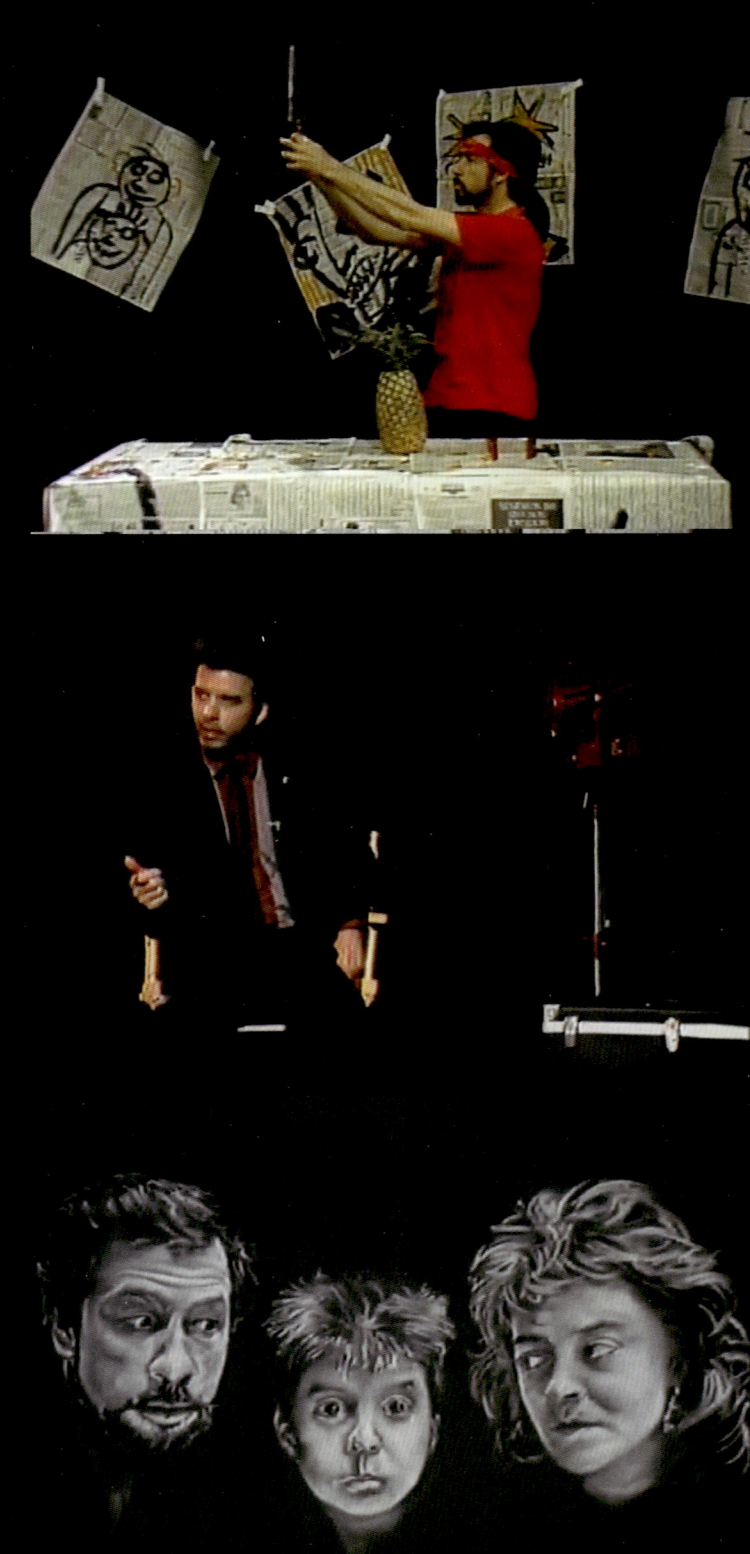

stinji

1988, 31:03 min.

A composition that is a fictional narrative and
satirical metaphor. The story portrays the day in the
life of a Los Angeles performance artist. —UJ

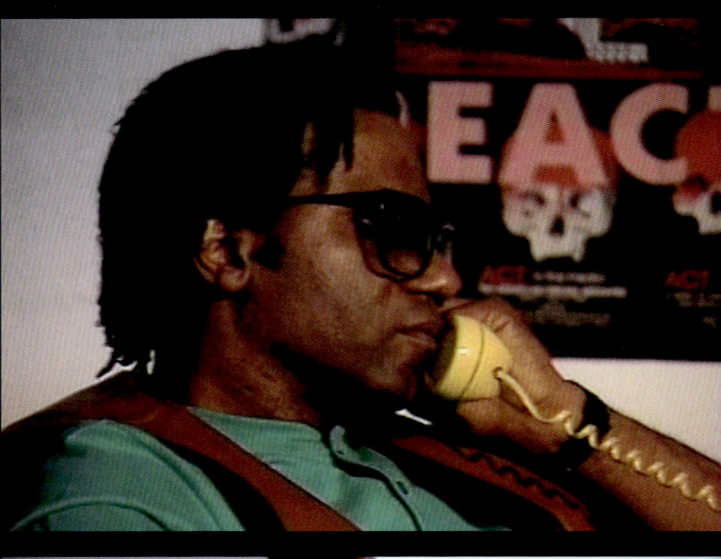

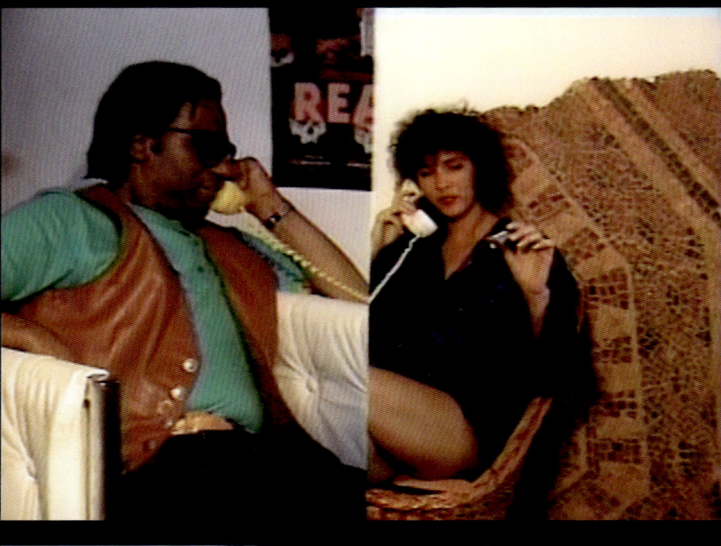

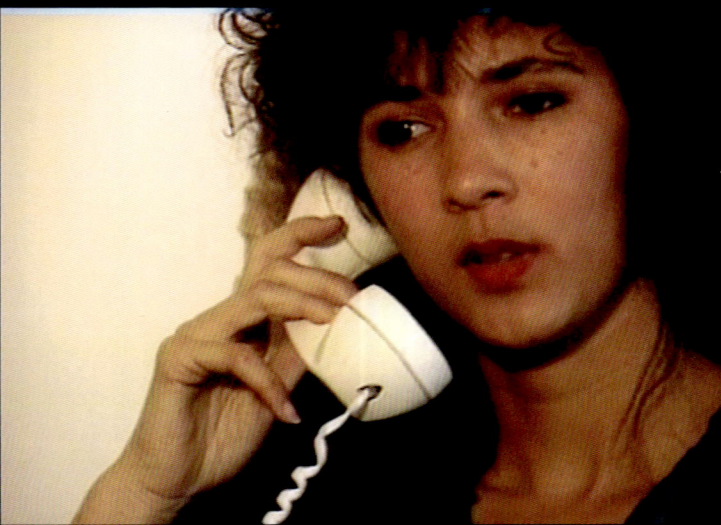

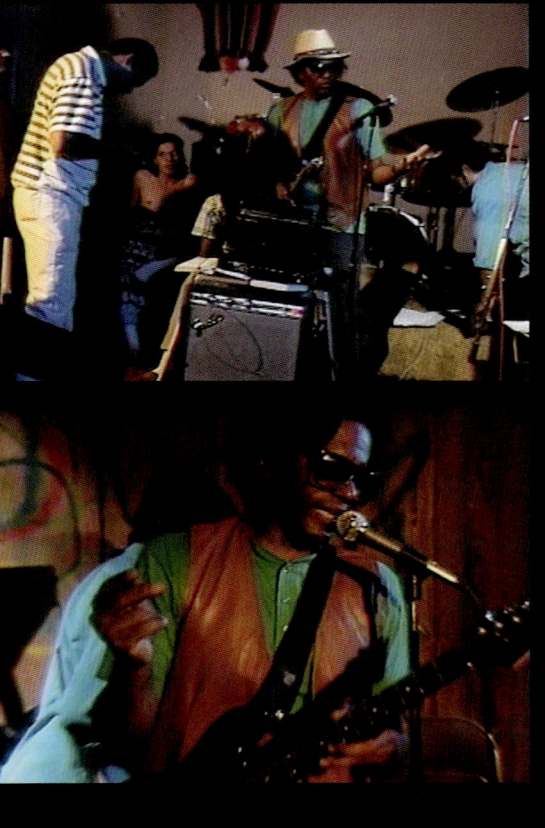

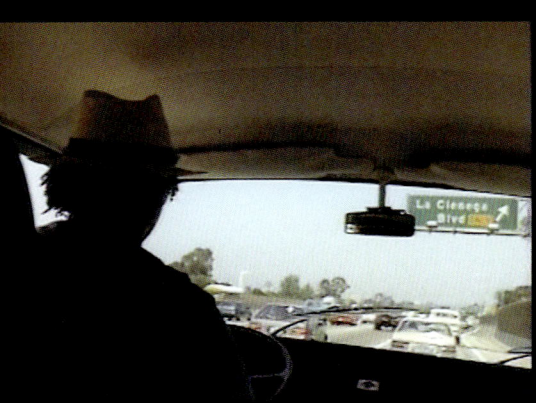

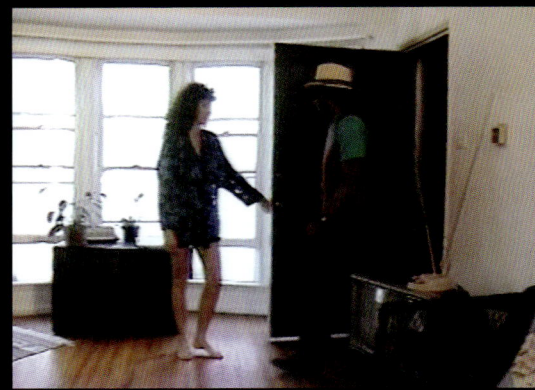

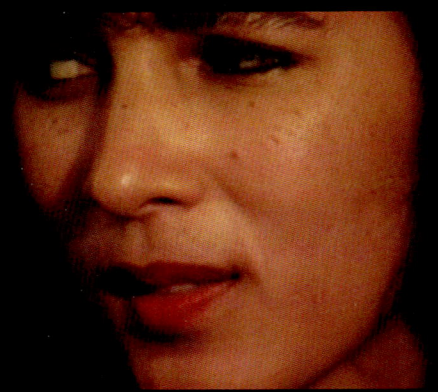
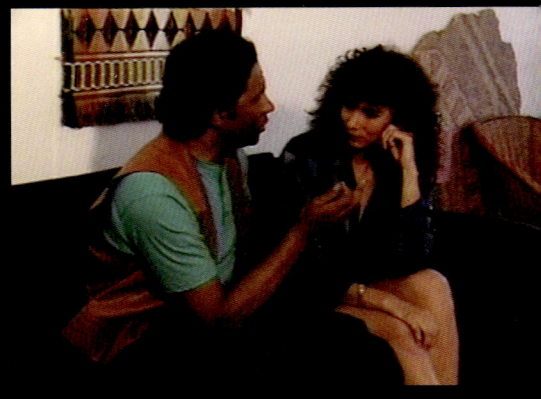
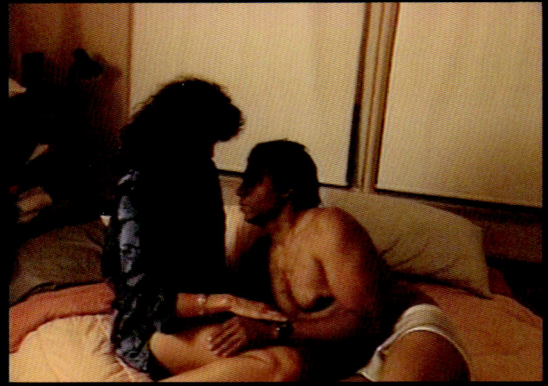
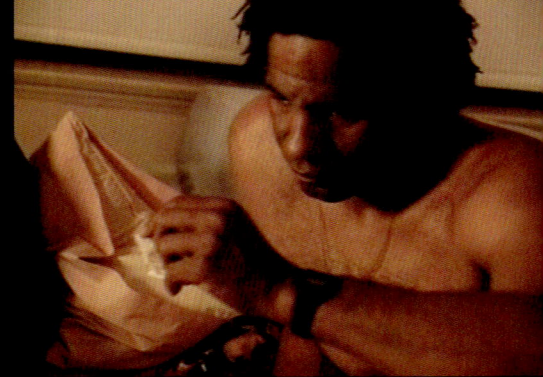

CAKE WALK

A Performance by
HOUSTON CONWILL

1983/1989, 26:26 min.

A video documenting Houston Conwill's performance *Cake Walk* at Just Above Midtown gallery in New York.

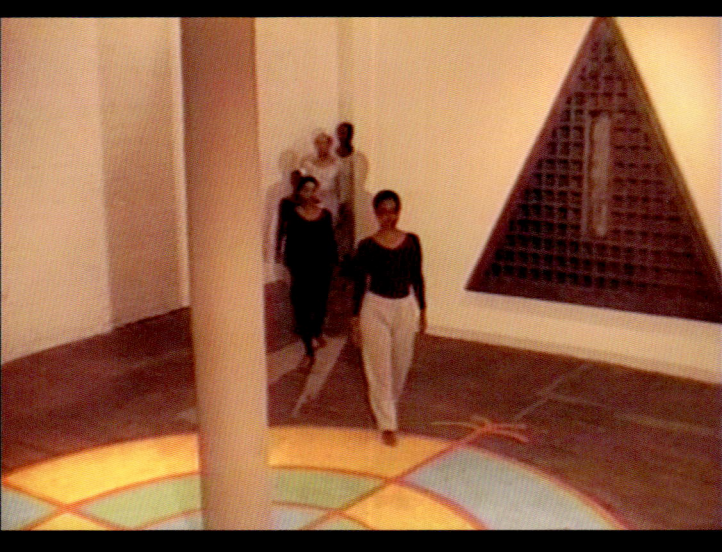

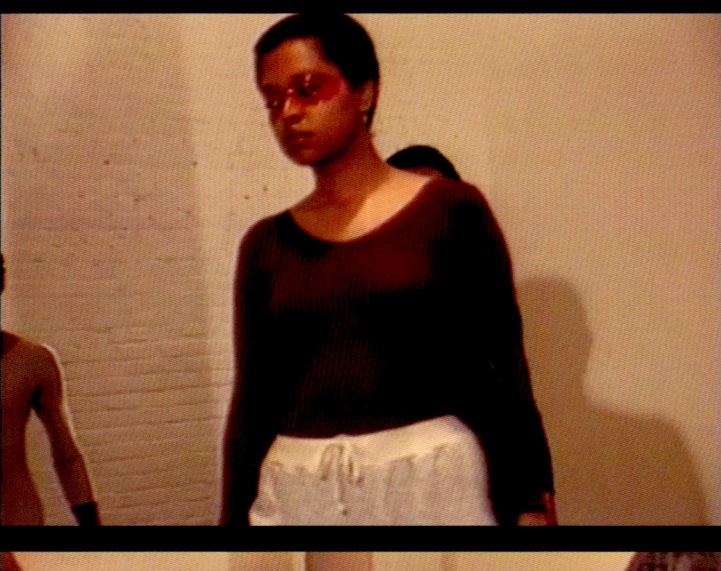

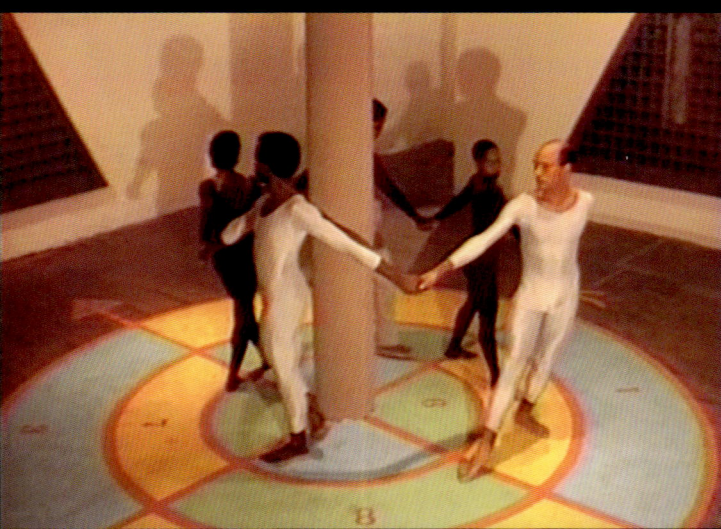

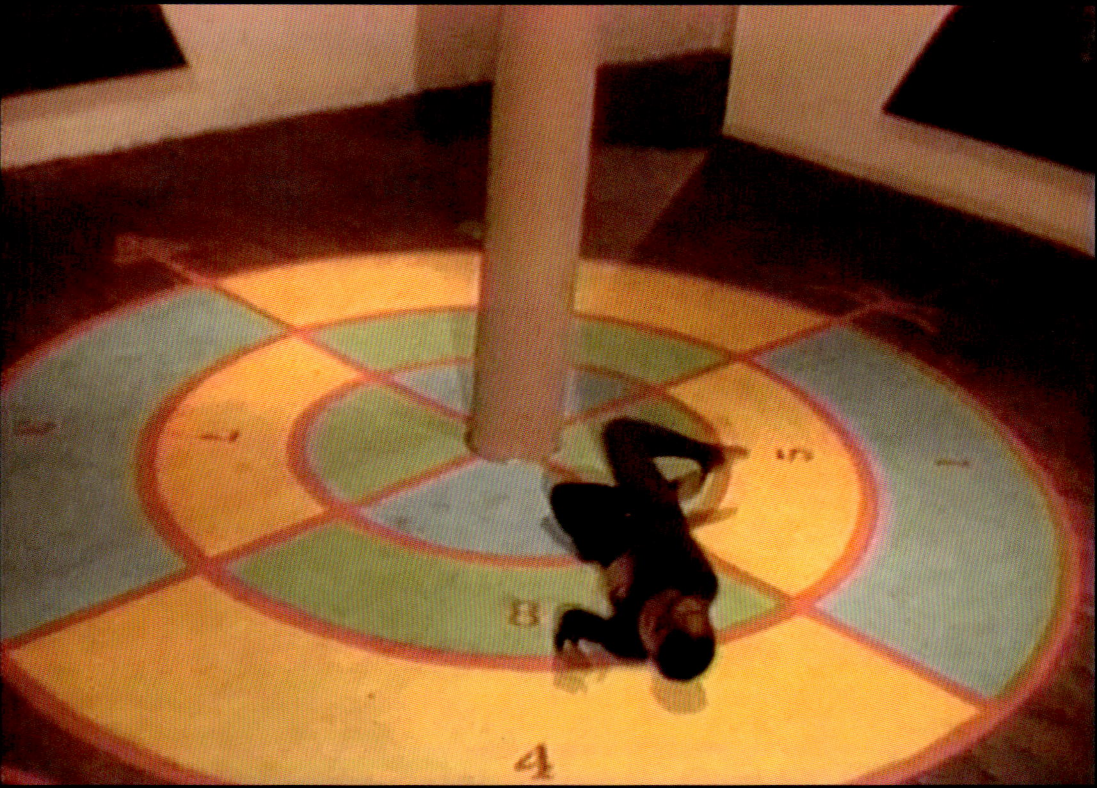
5
8
4

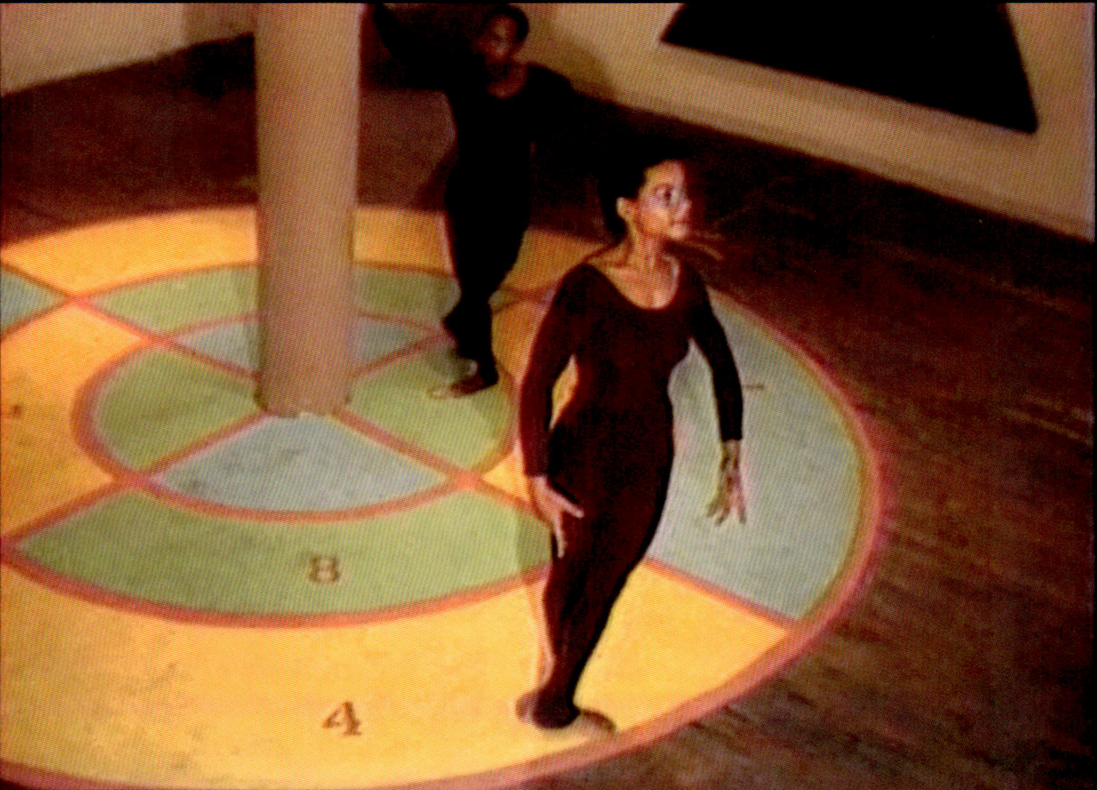
8
4

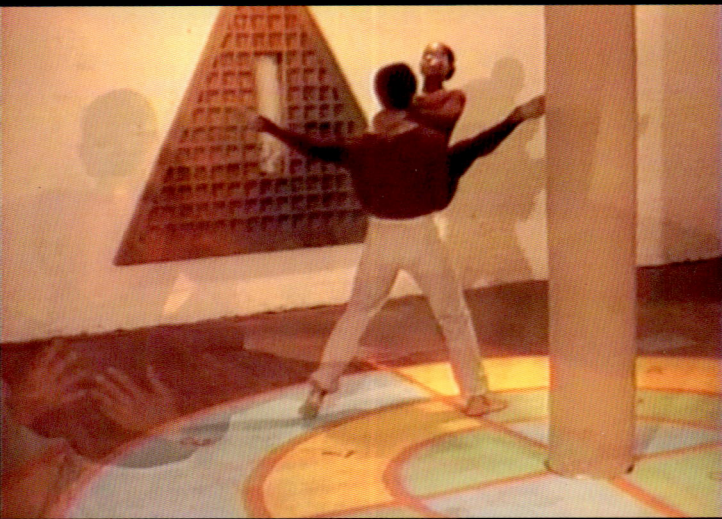

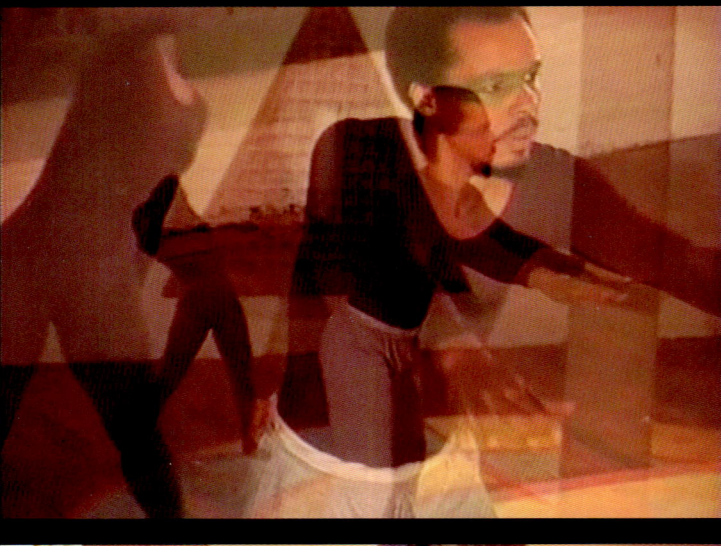

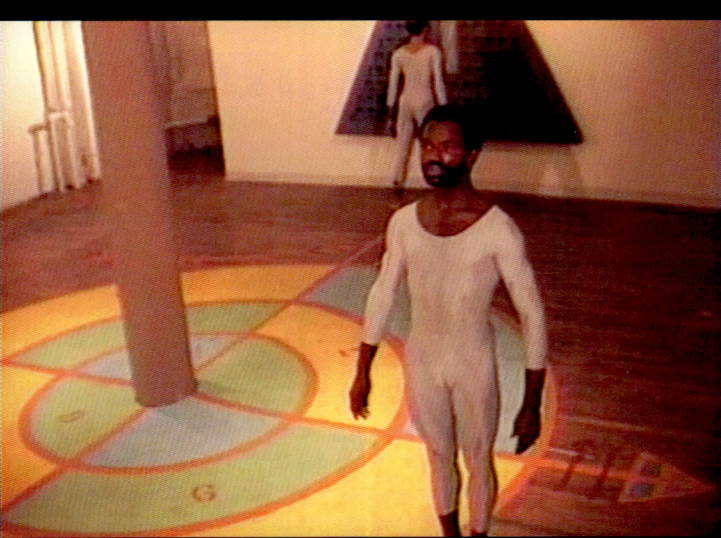

SELF DIVINATION

1989 (Part I of *The Video Griots Trilogy*)
11:56 min.

An insightful myth concerning the contemplation of an
African American male's journey through his intuition,
which provides the sojourner to reflect, respect,
and realize that his life as metaphor can lead unto
enlightenment. —UJ

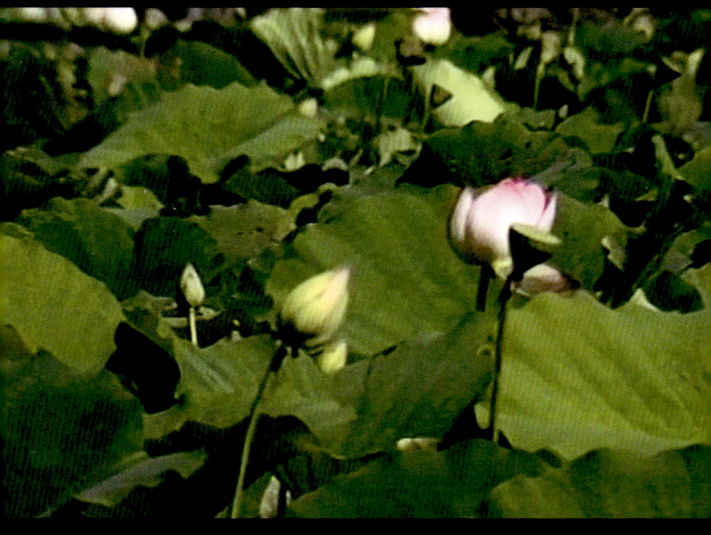

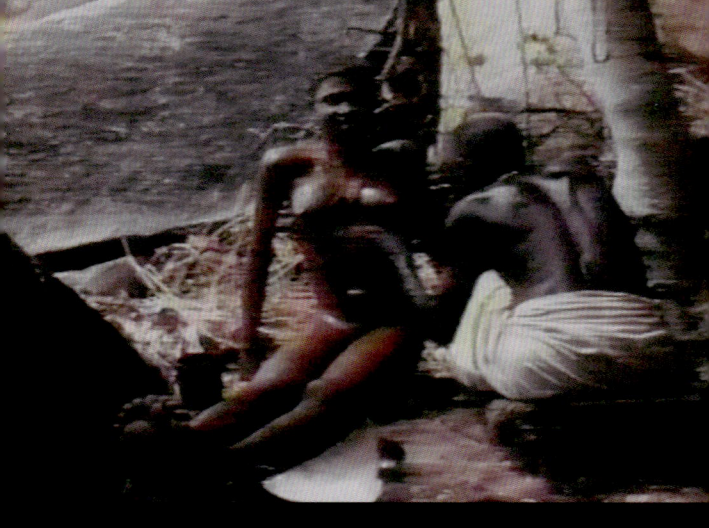

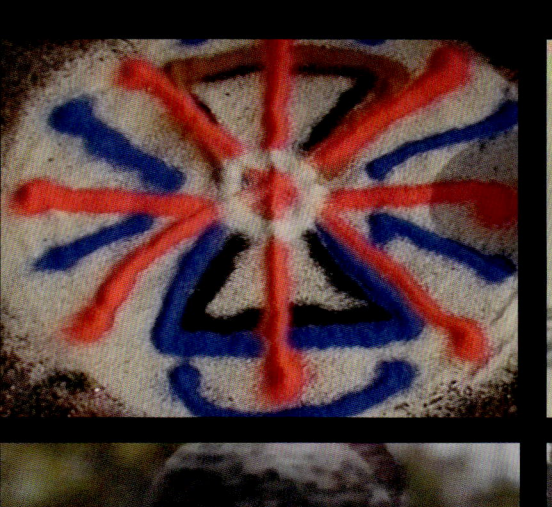
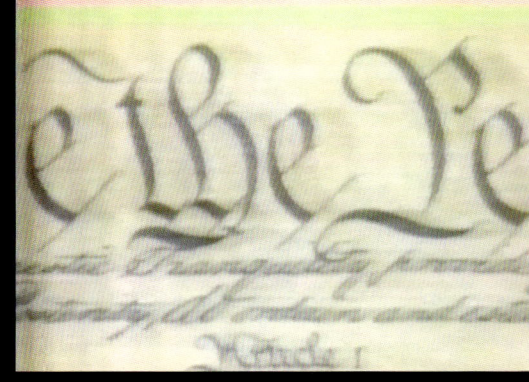
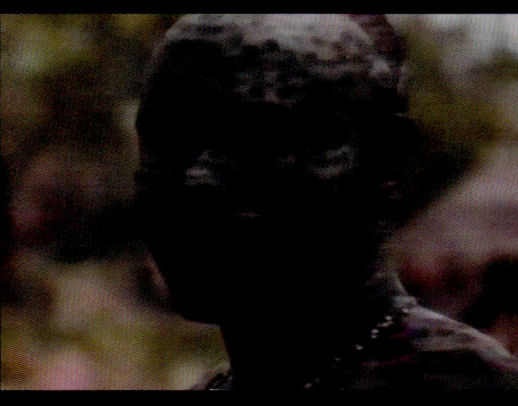
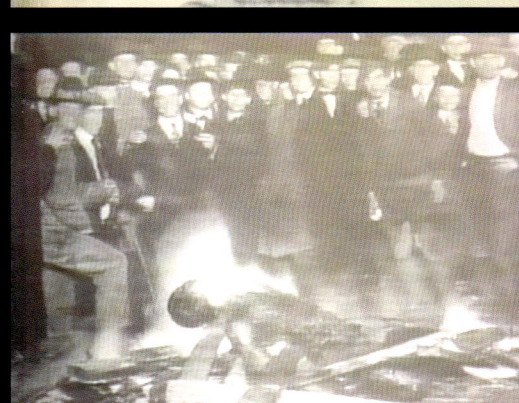
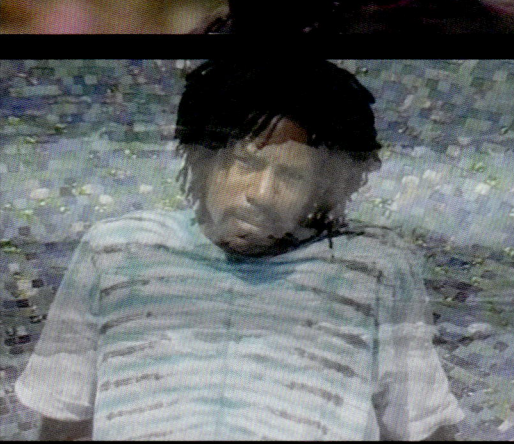
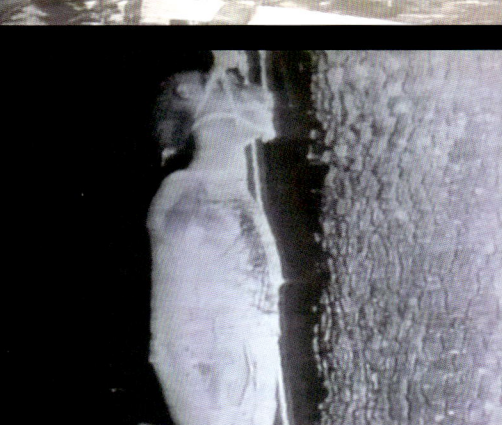
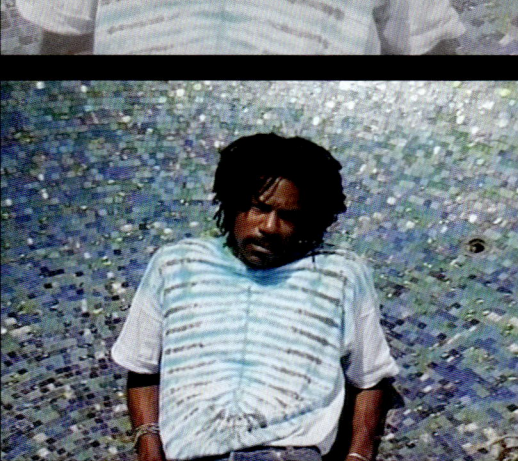
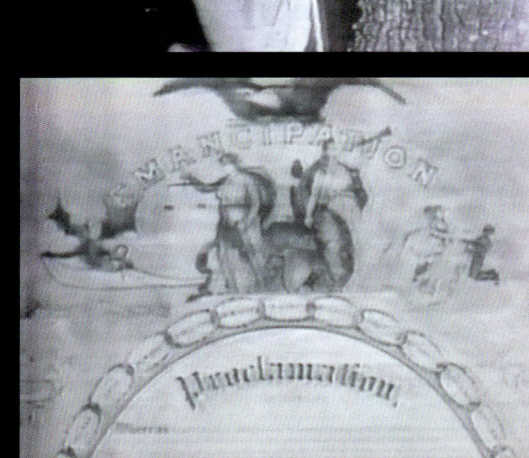

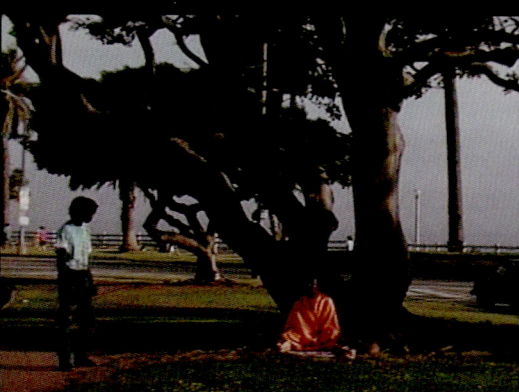

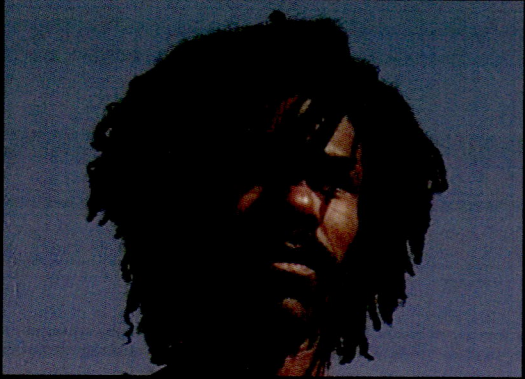

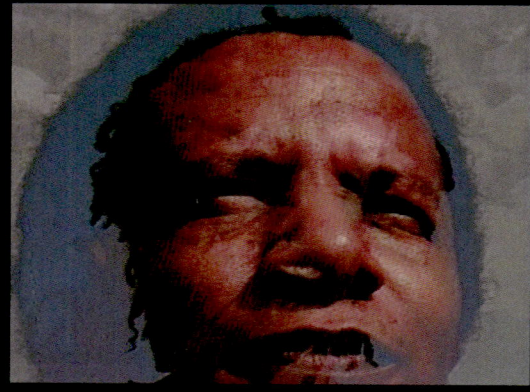

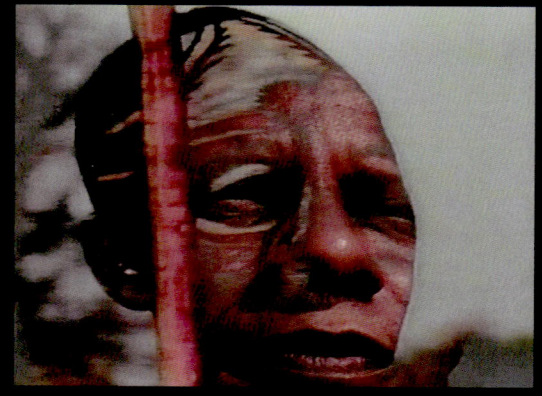

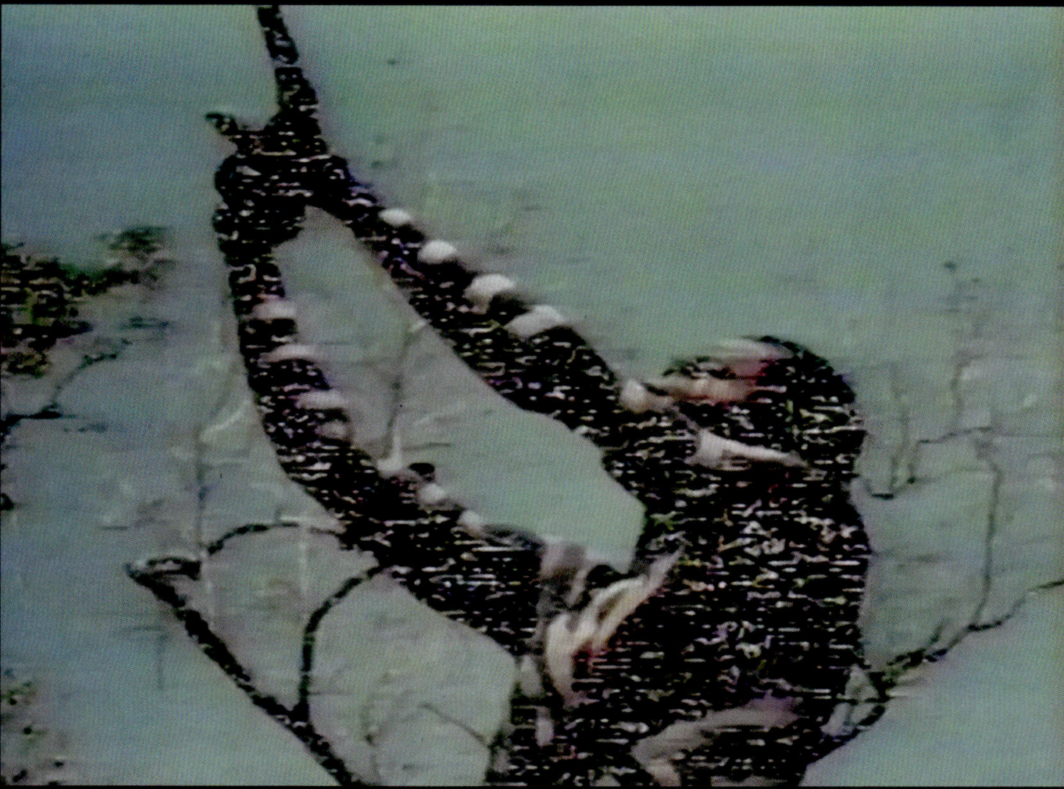

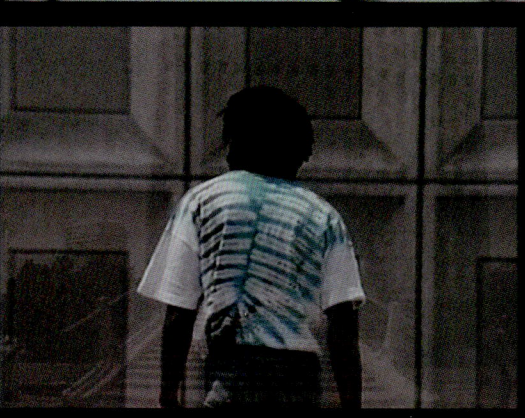

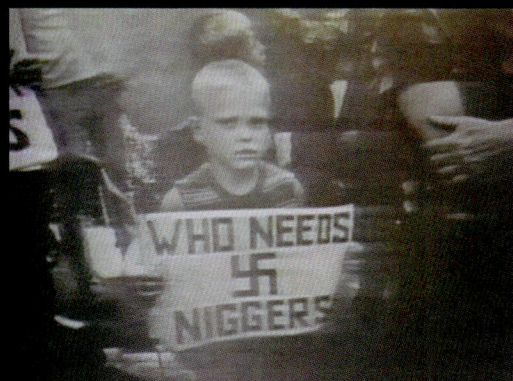

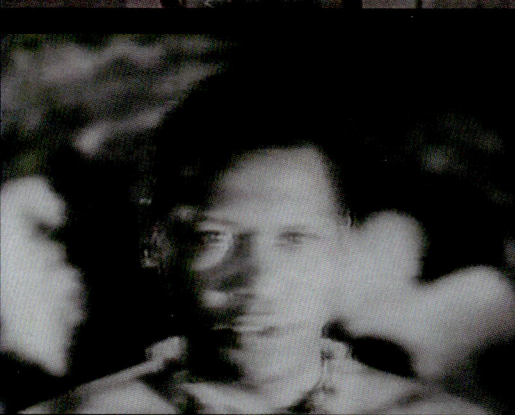

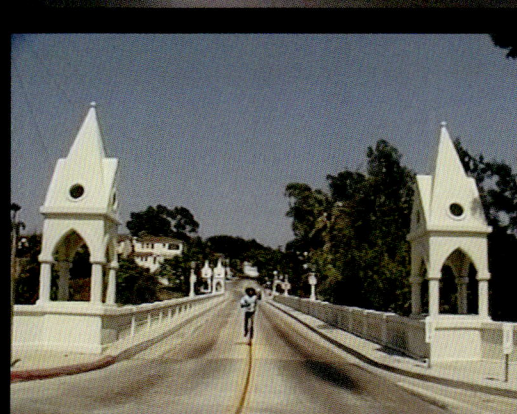

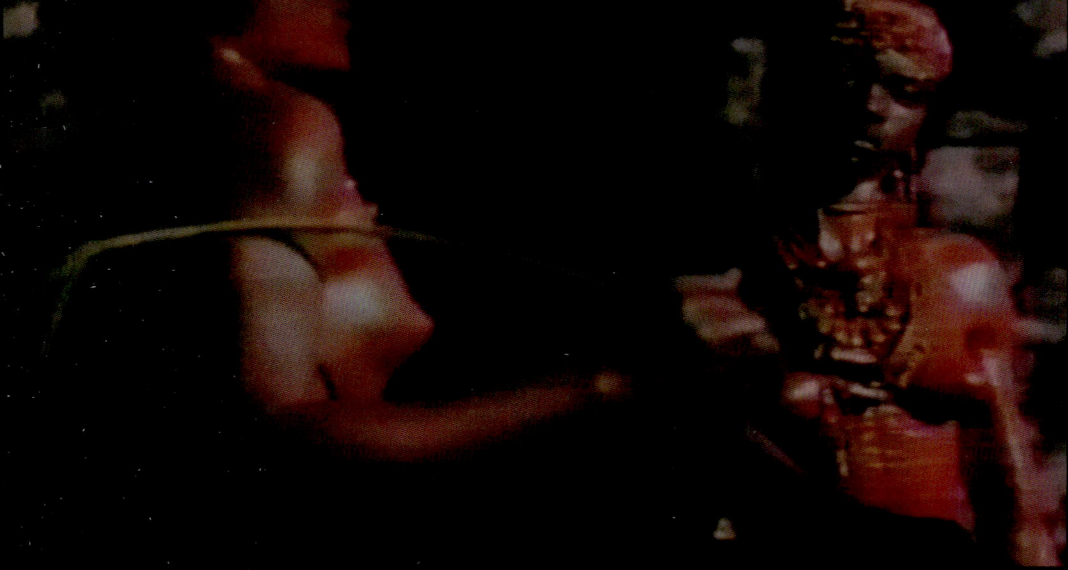

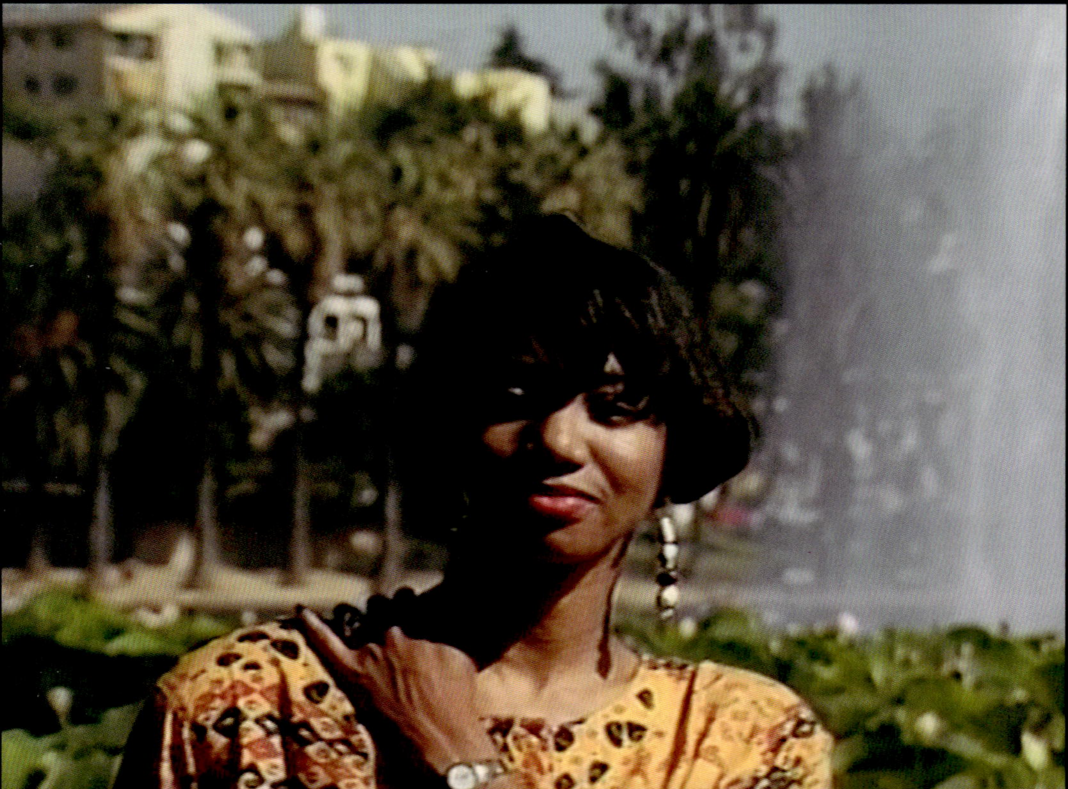

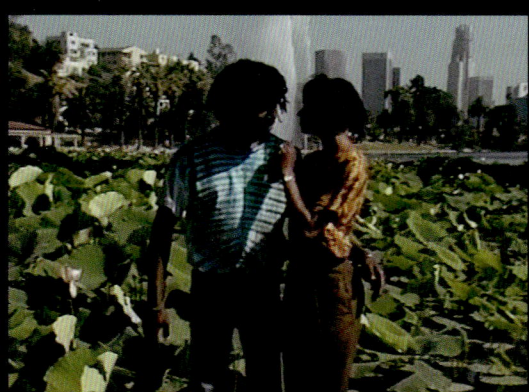

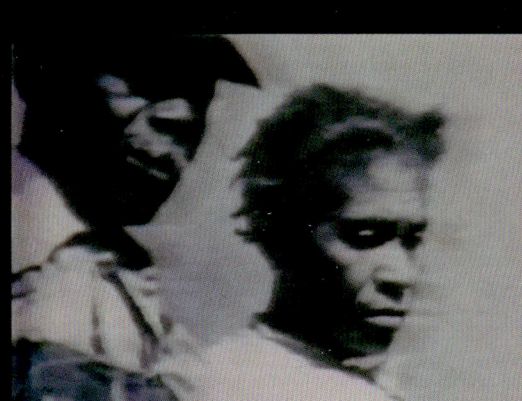

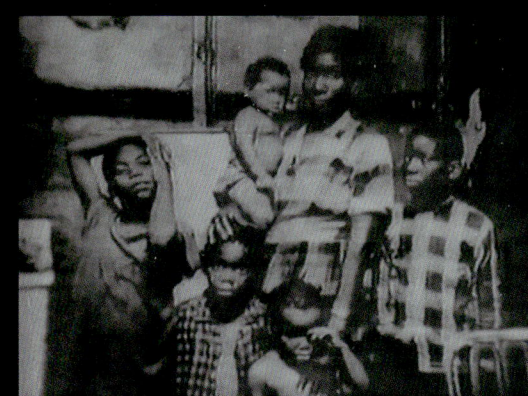

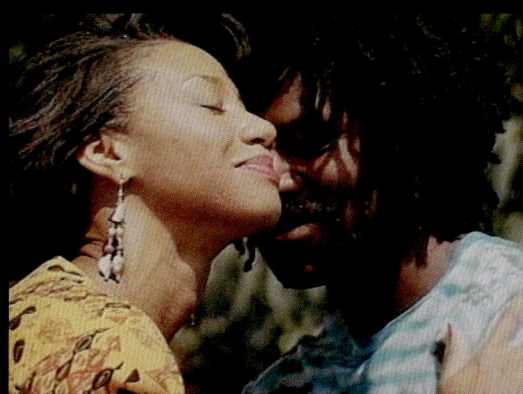

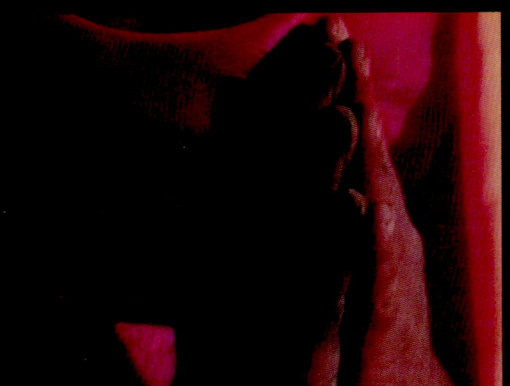

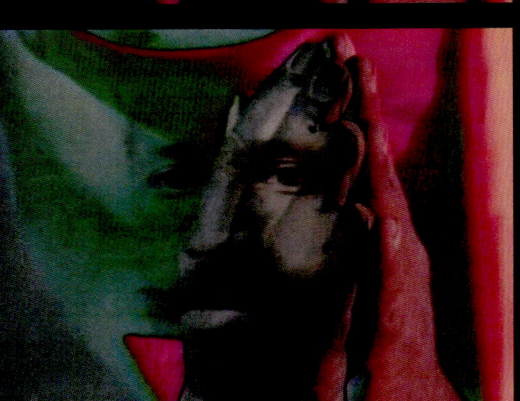

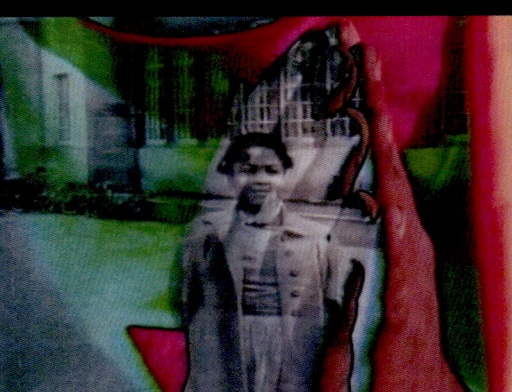

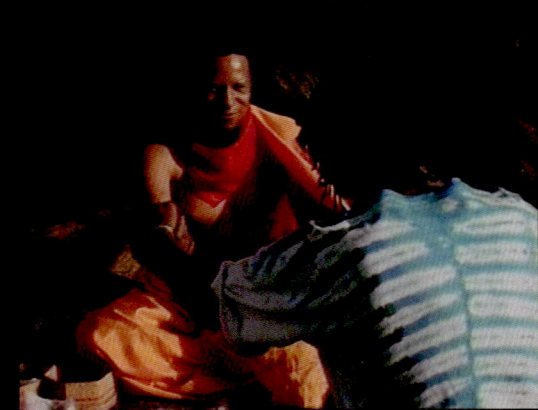

Mutual Native Duplex

1990 (Part II of *The Video Griots Trilogy*)
11:53 min.

A symbolic myth exploring the relative positions of
African Americans and Native Americans. —UJ

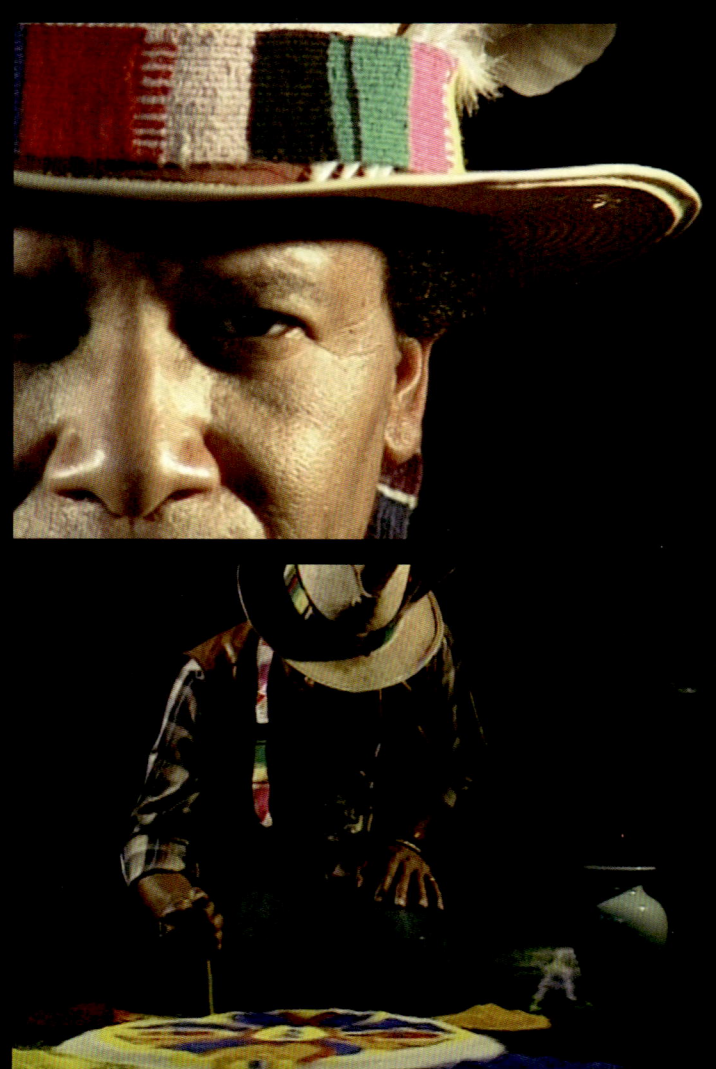

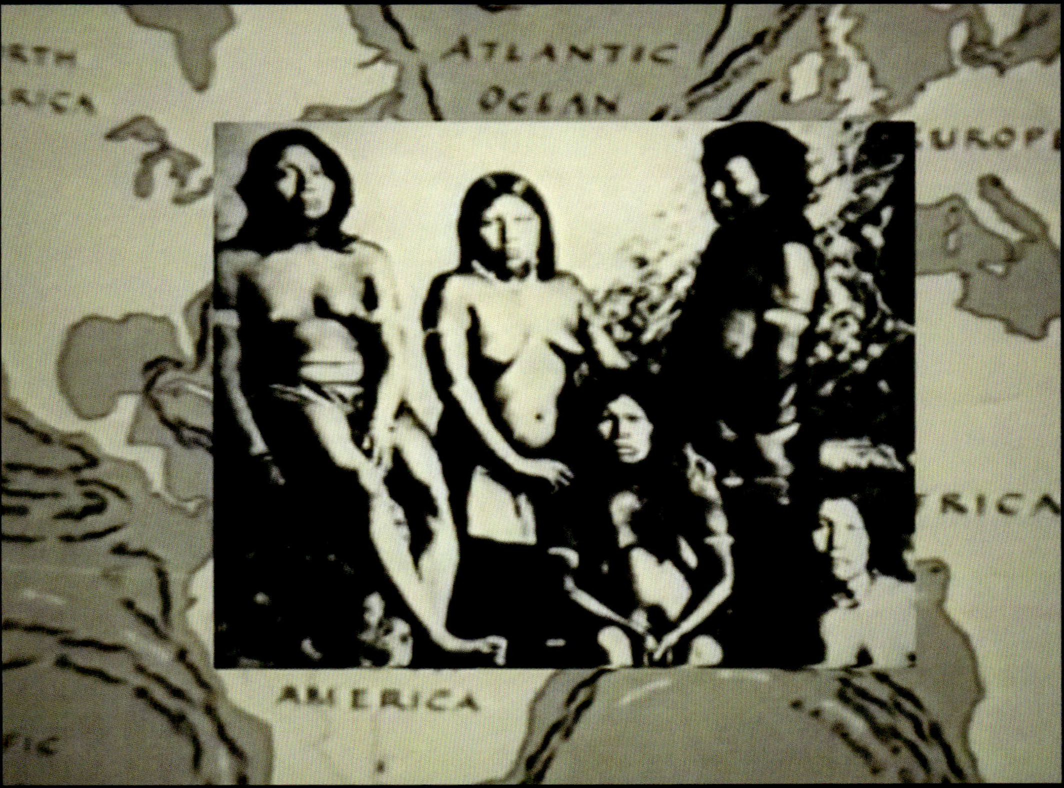

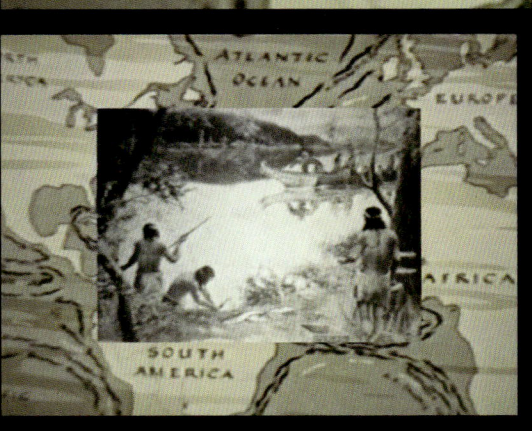

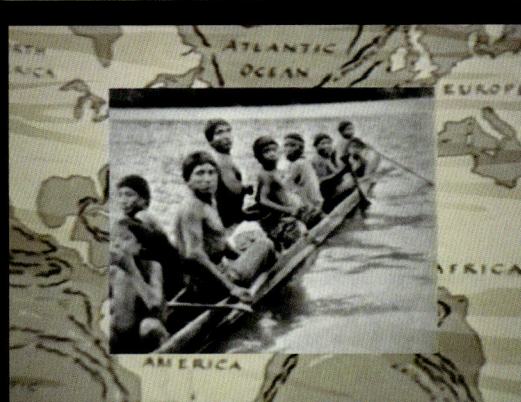

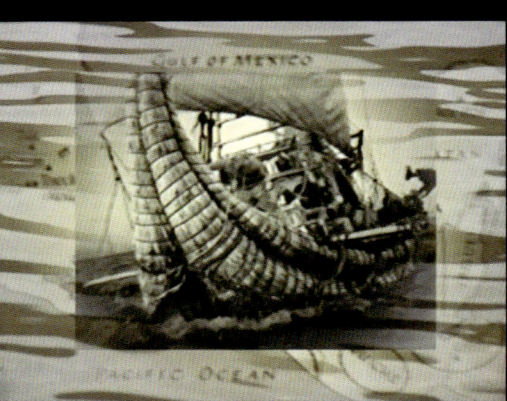

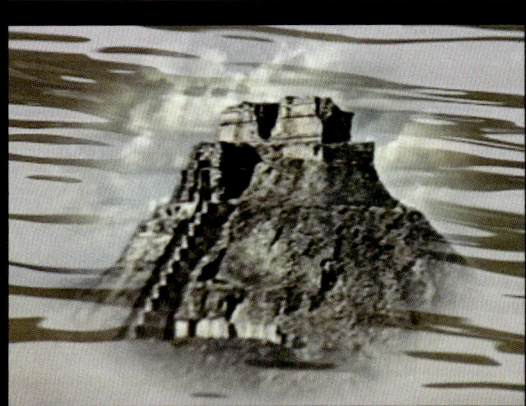

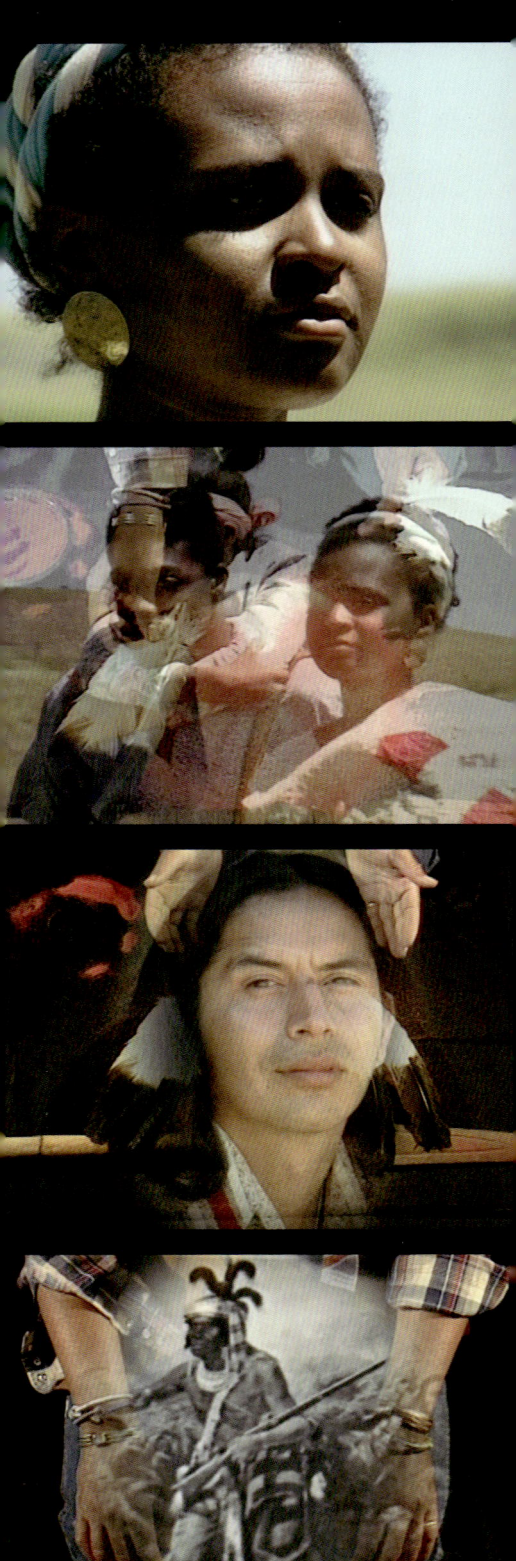

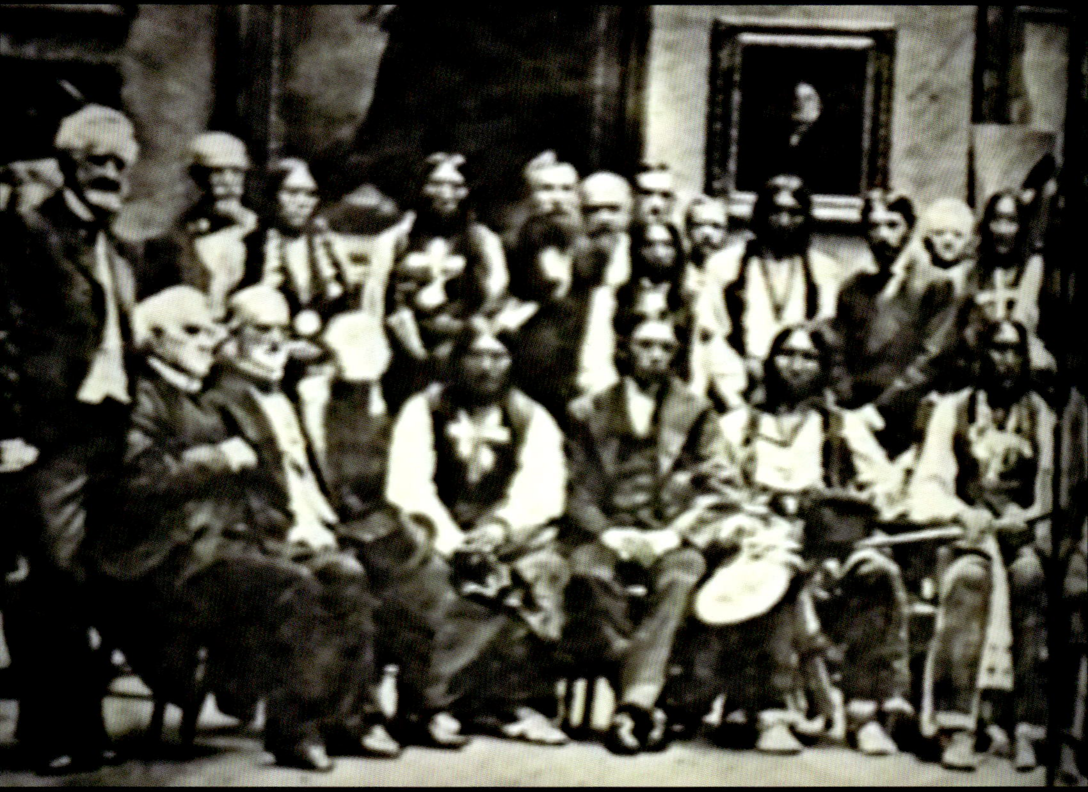

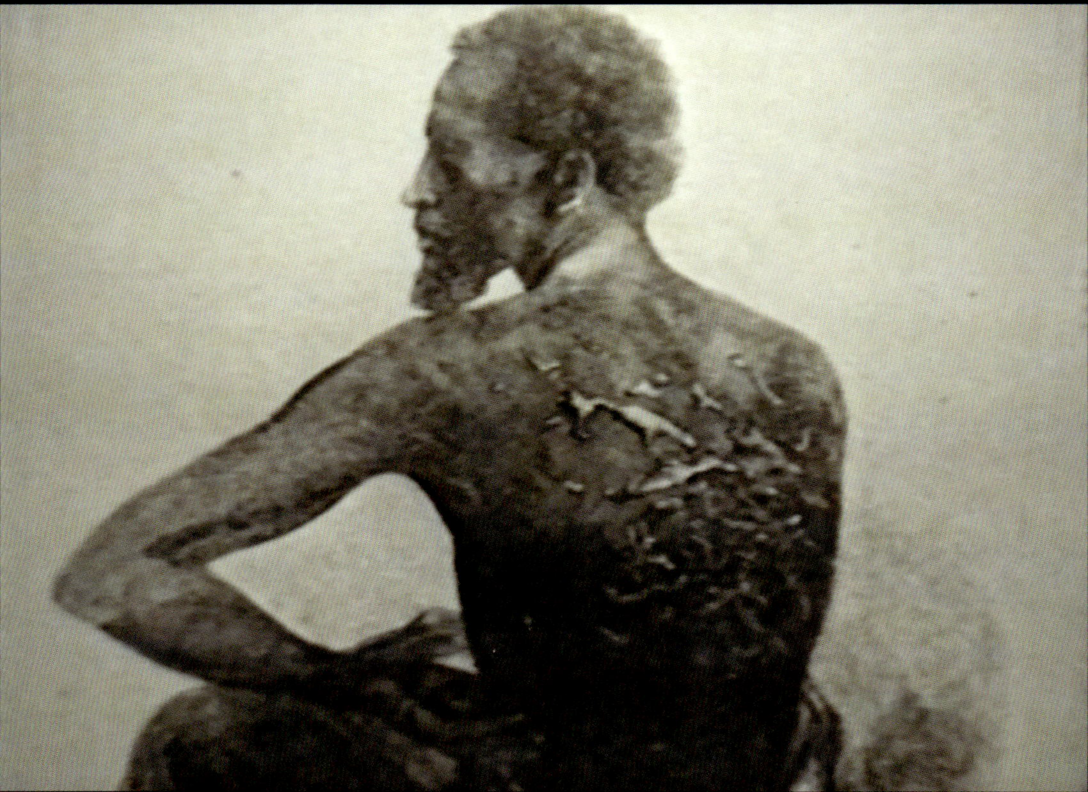

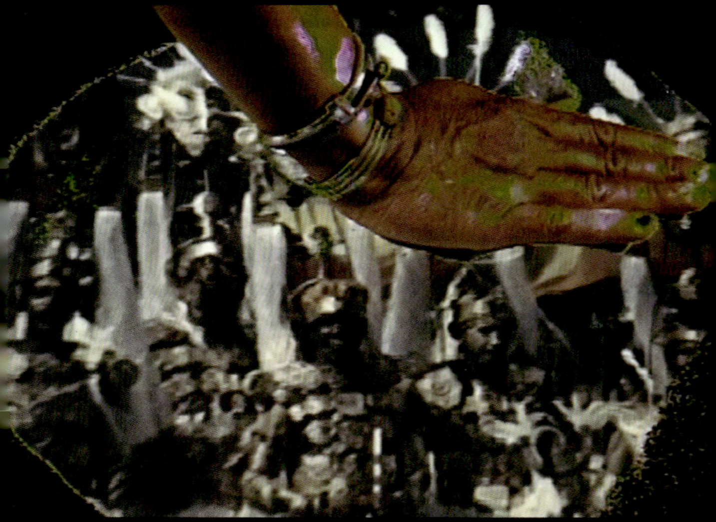

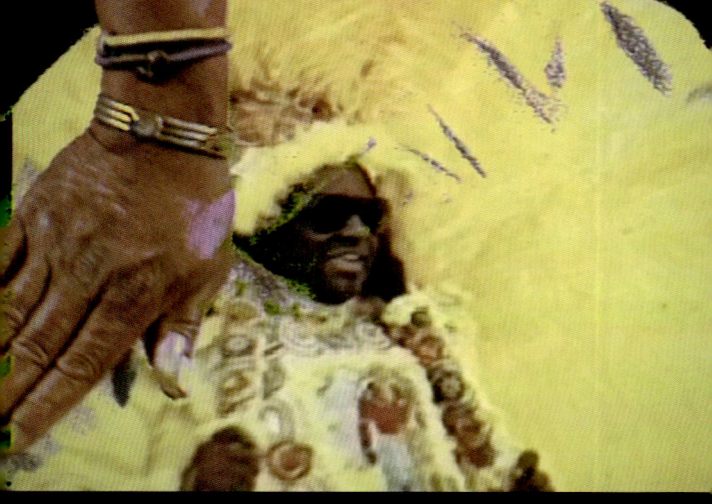

"BAY WINDOW"
a videophone
ritual
performance

1991, 84 min.

This is the video documentation of a videophone
performance art event that could be considered as an
early version of Al Gore's film *An Inconvenient
Truth* via videophones. —UJ

THE COOKIE JAR
IS EMPTY
INTERNATIONAL
protest

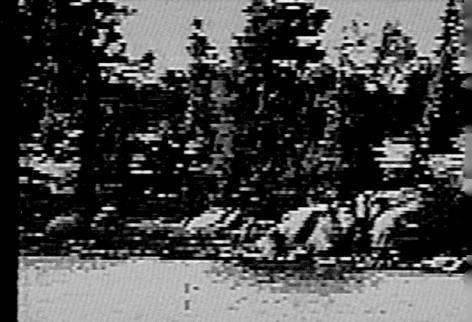

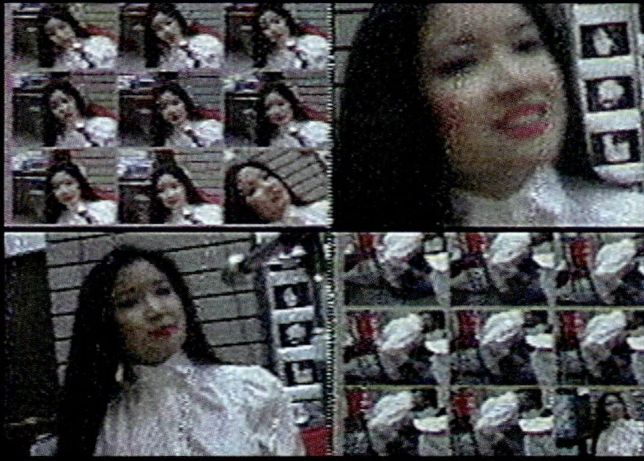

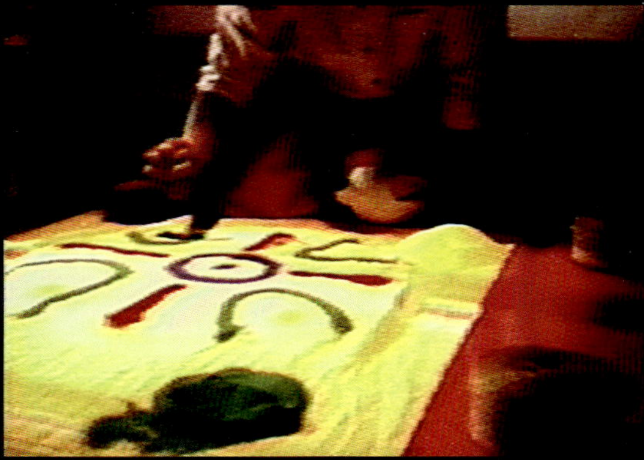

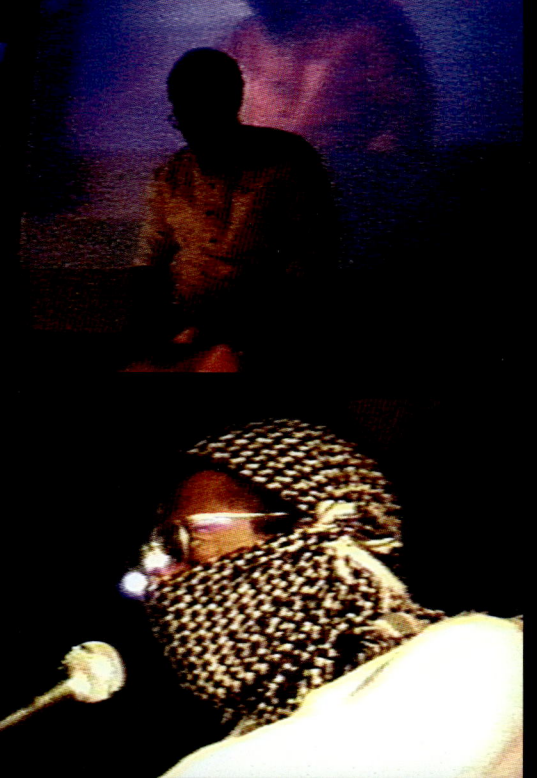

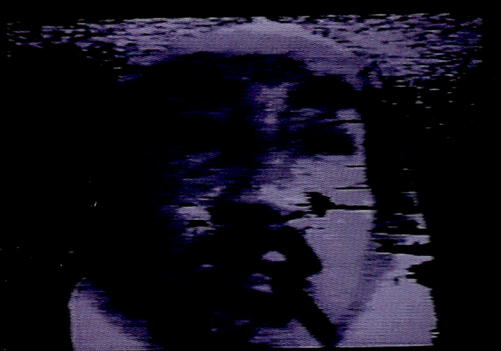

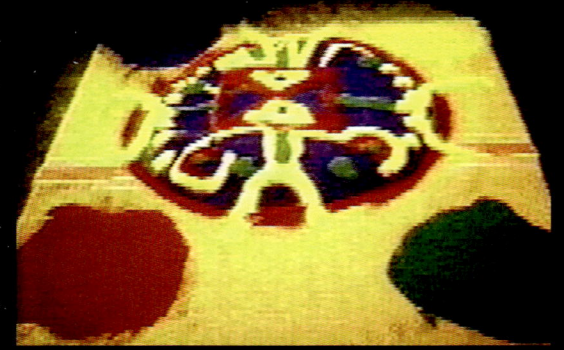

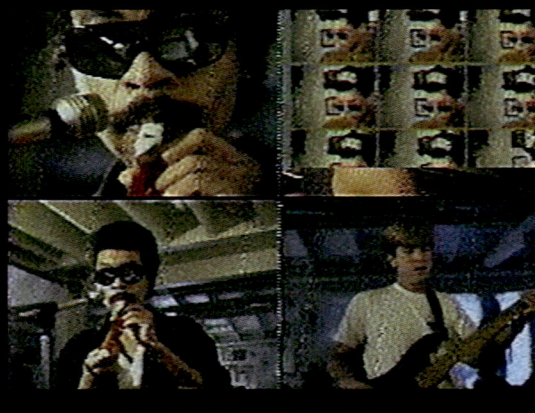

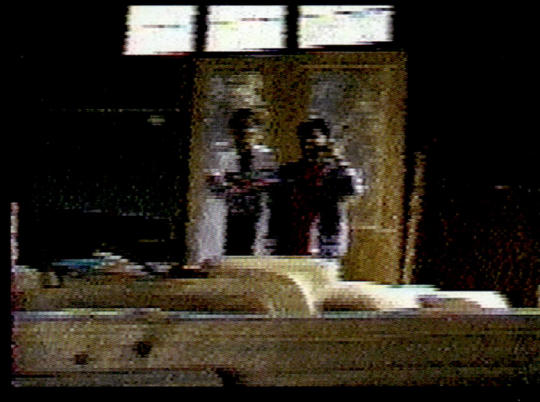

The Nomadics

1991 (Part III of *The Video Griots Trilogy*)
12:36 min.

A video composition that traces the sojourner of the
East African people's movements and cultural influences
as cultivators of early human civilizations. —UJ

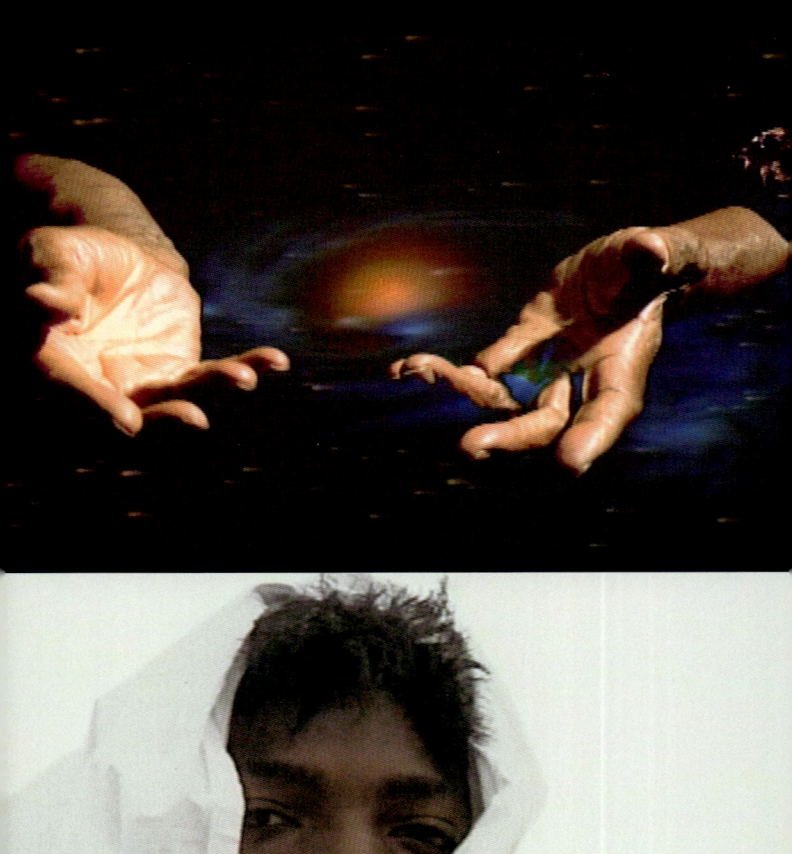

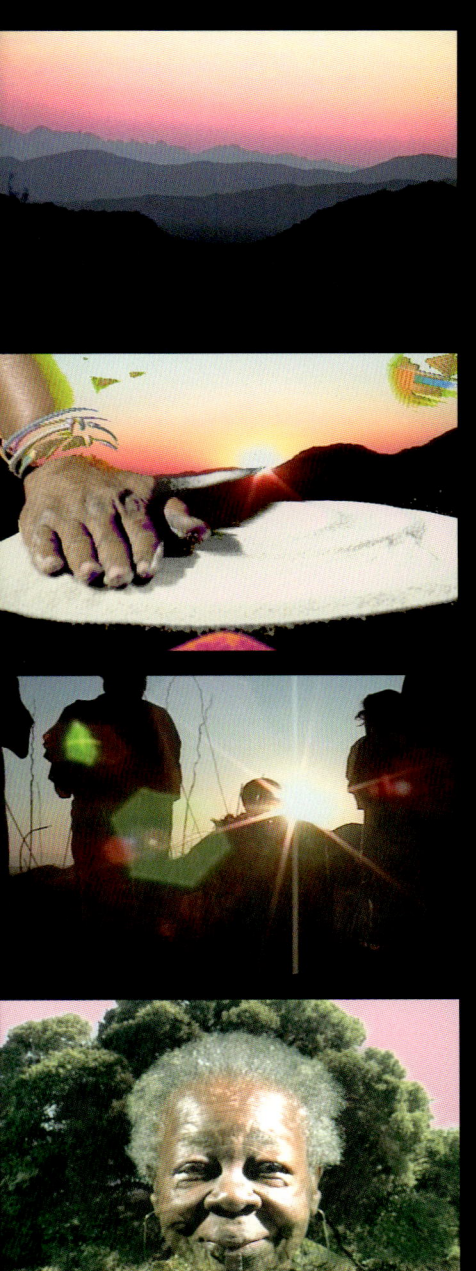

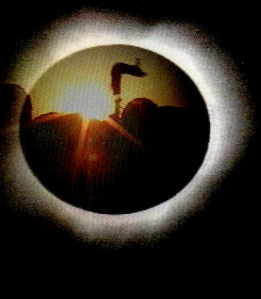

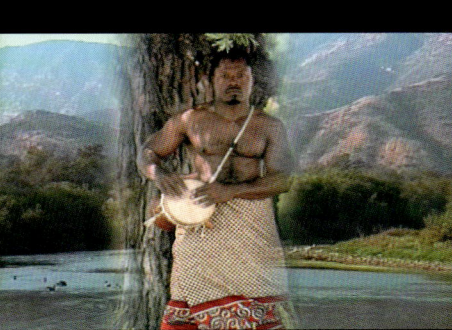

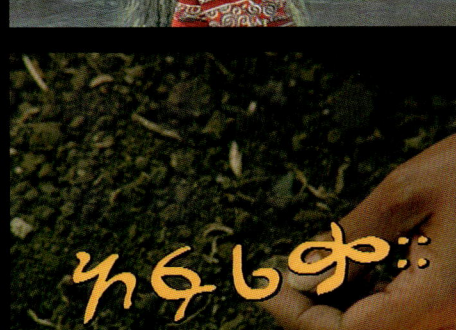

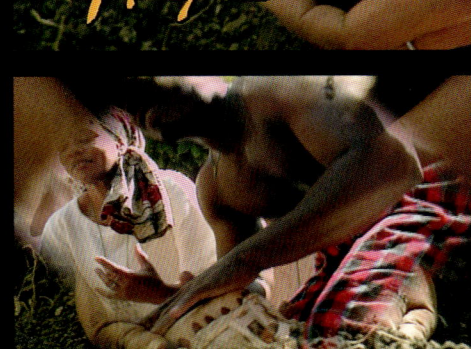

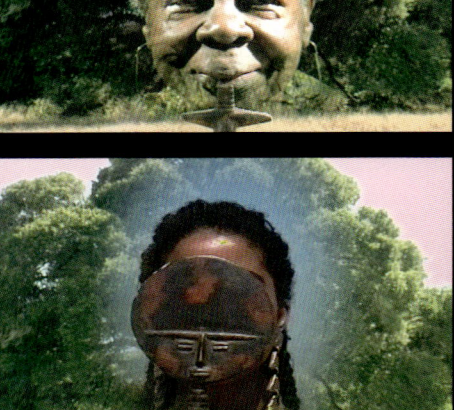

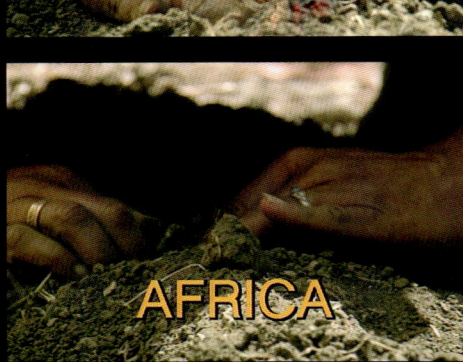

AFRICA

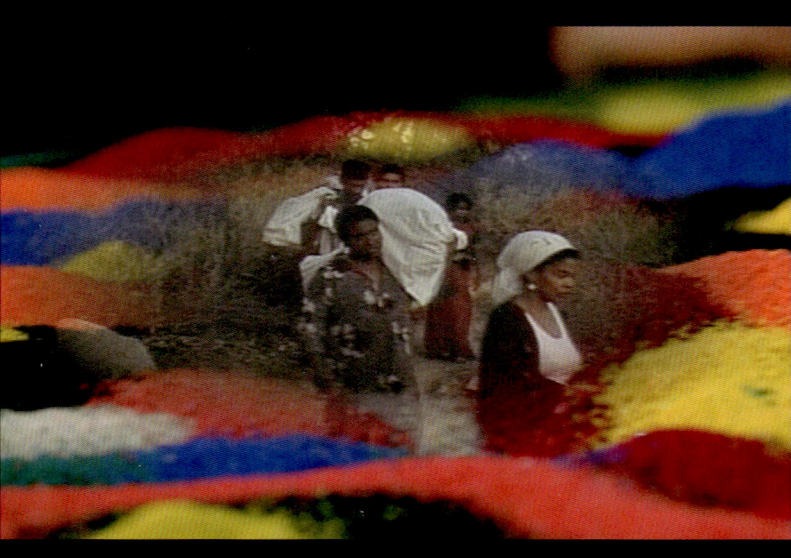

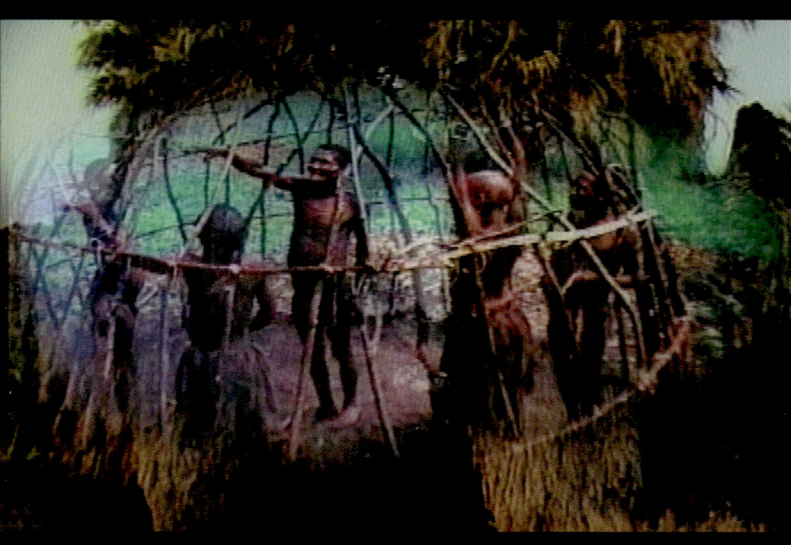

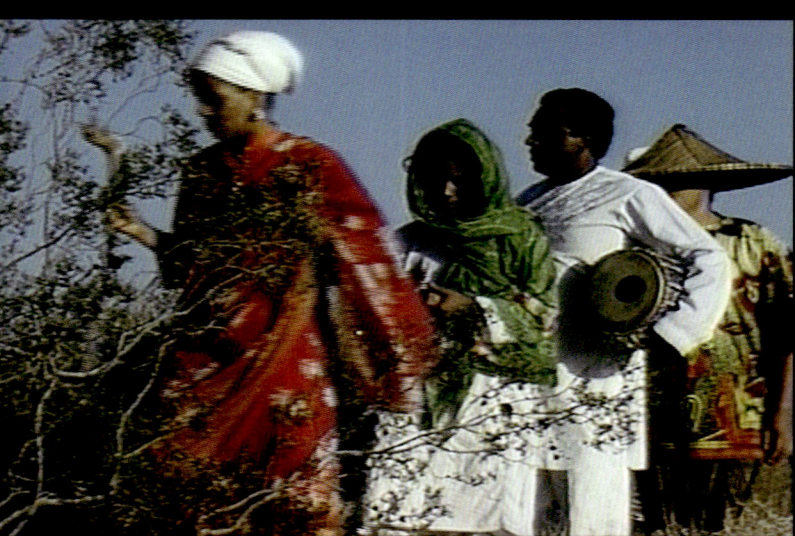

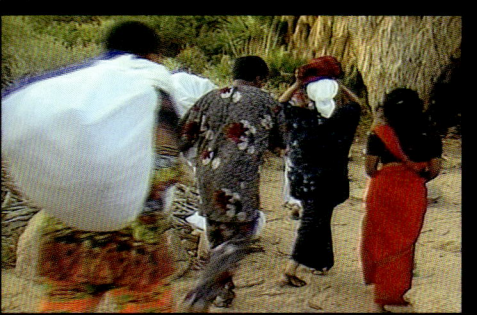

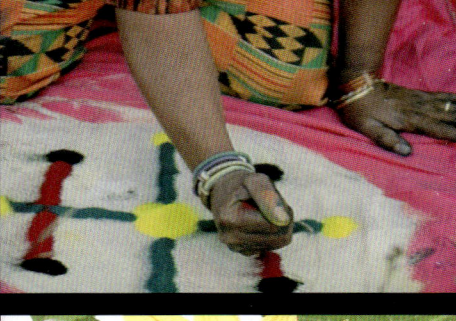

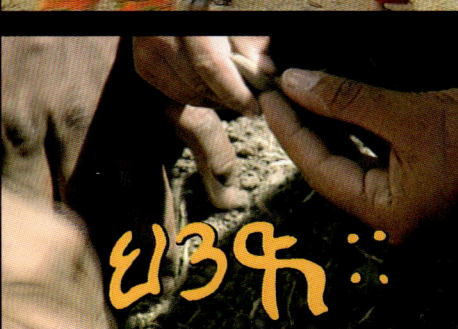

ይንዱ።

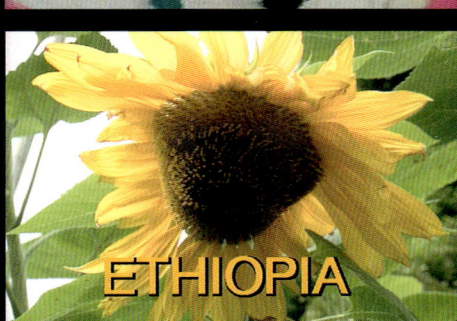

ETHIOPIA

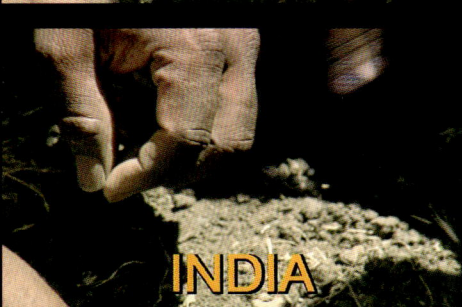

INDIA

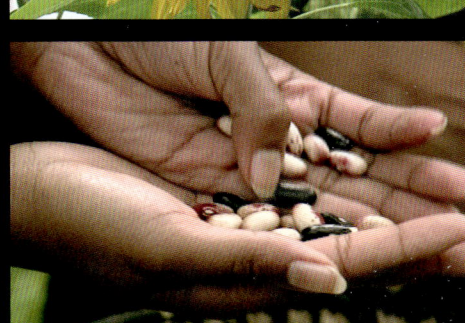

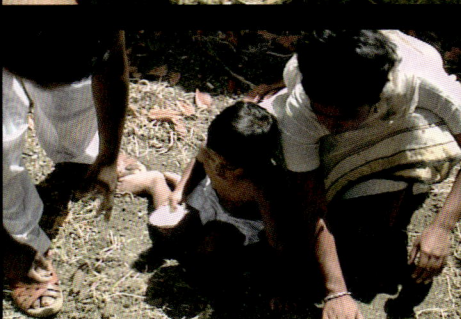

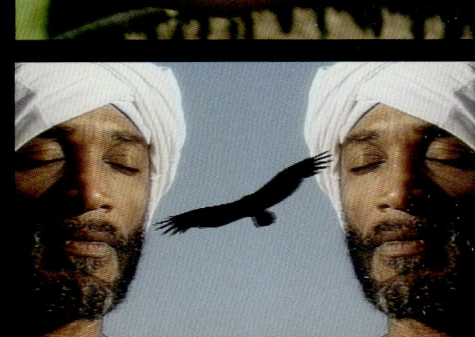

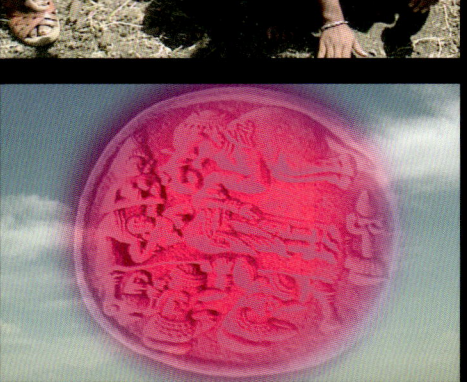

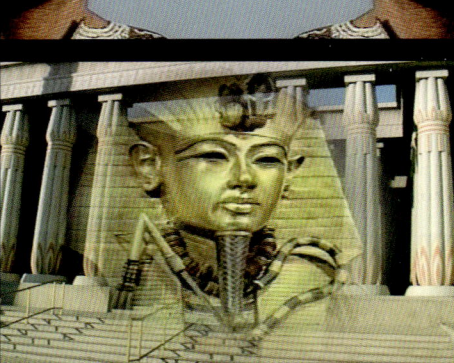

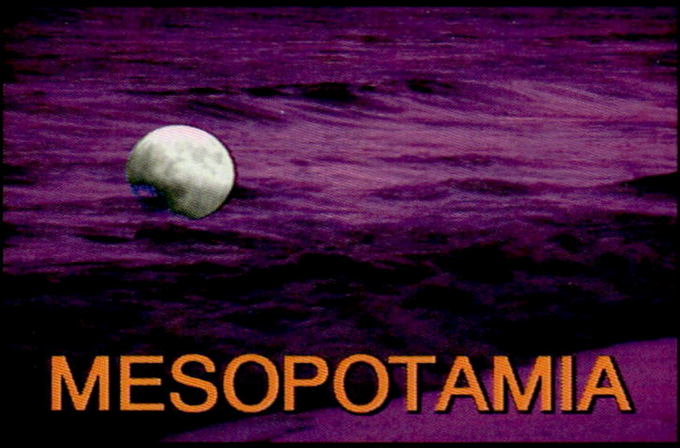

MESOPOTAMIA

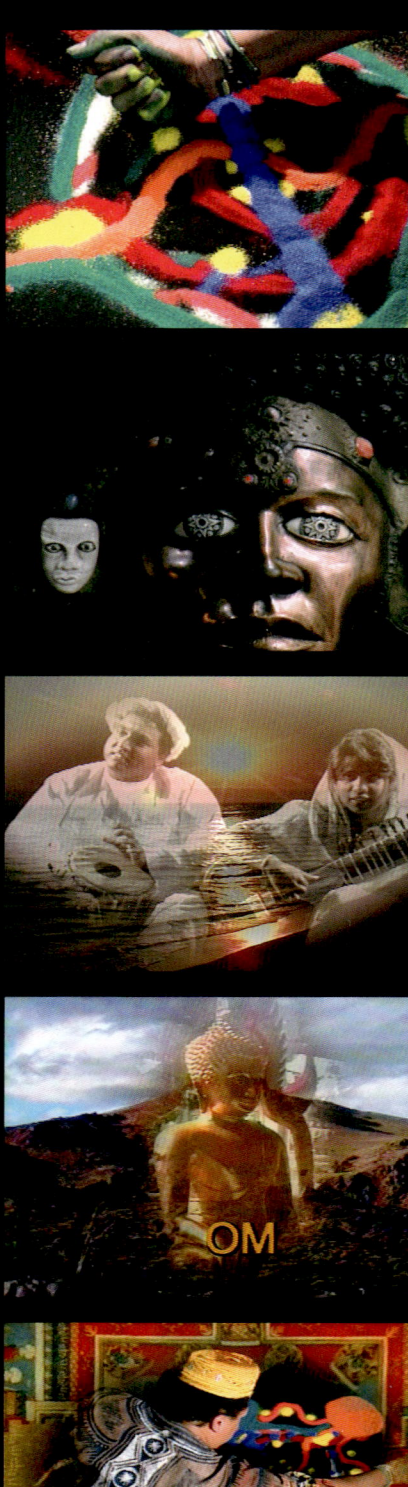

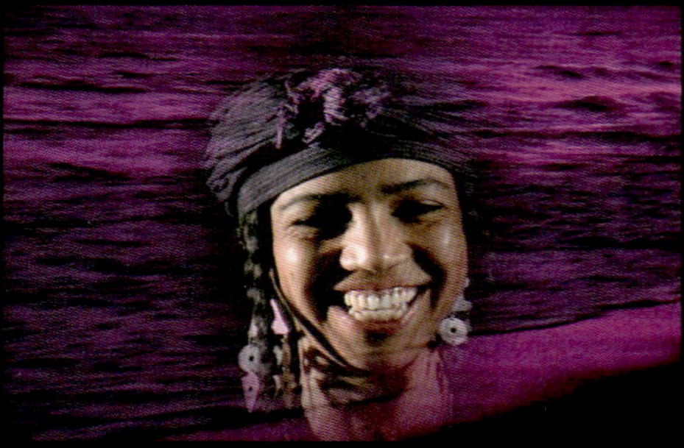

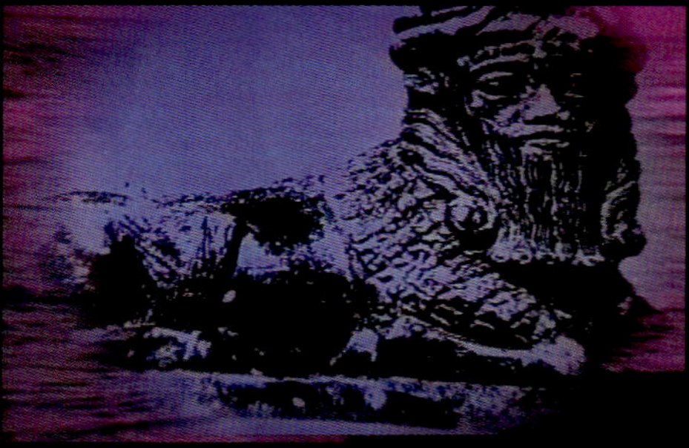

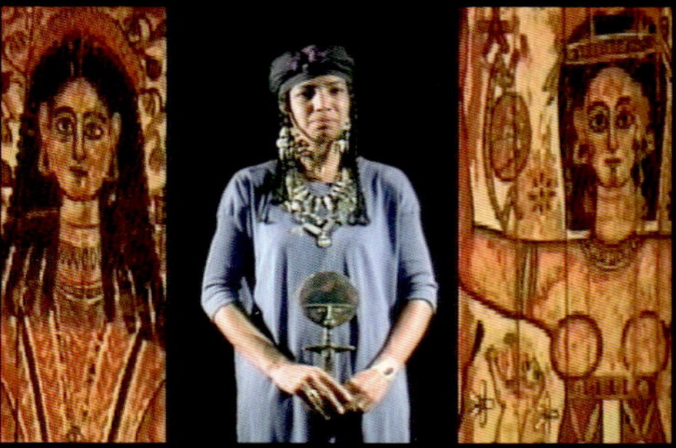

OM

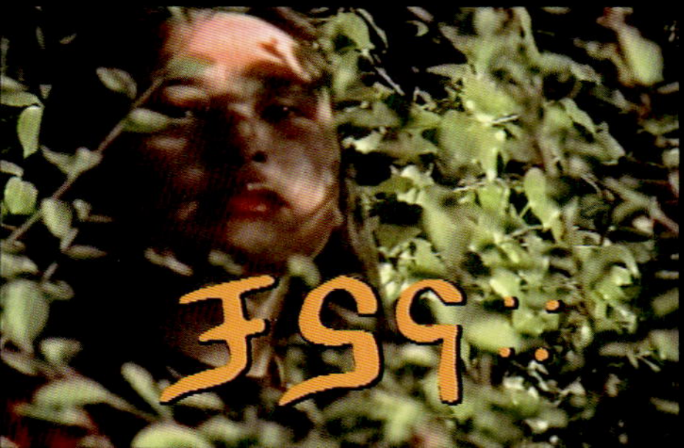

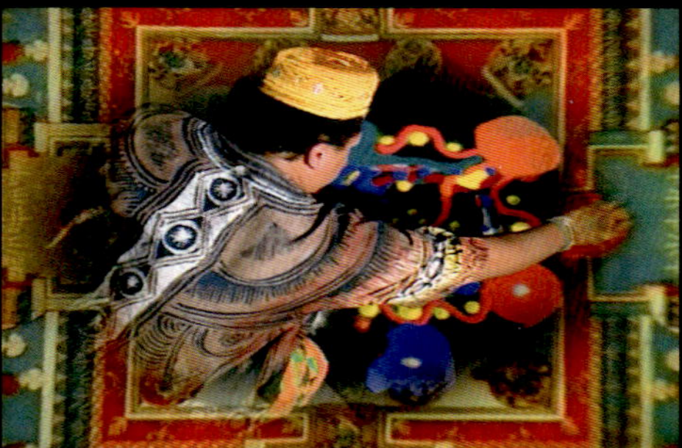

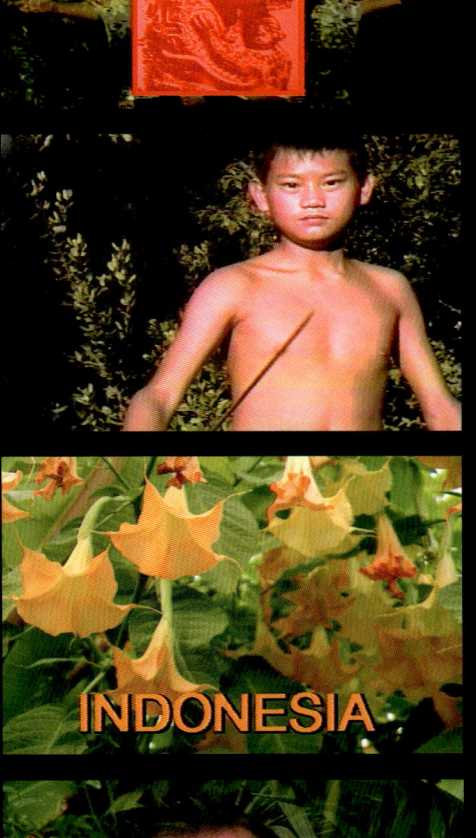

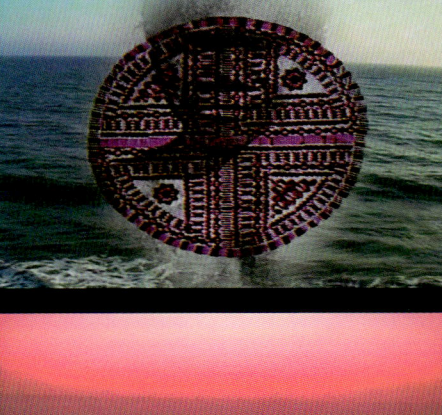

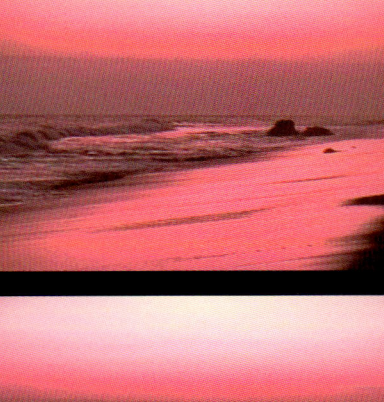

INDONESIA

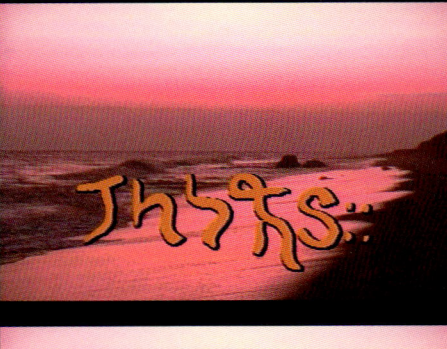

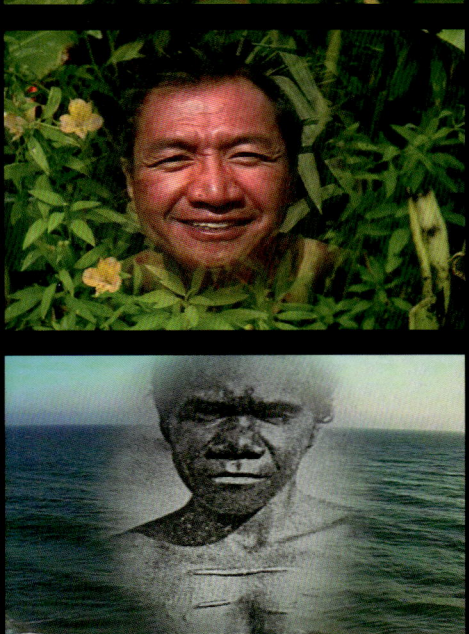

POLYNESIA

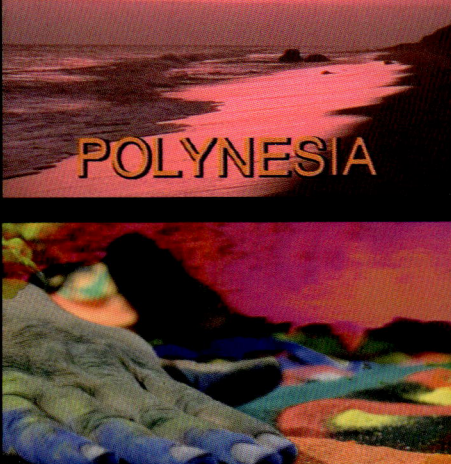

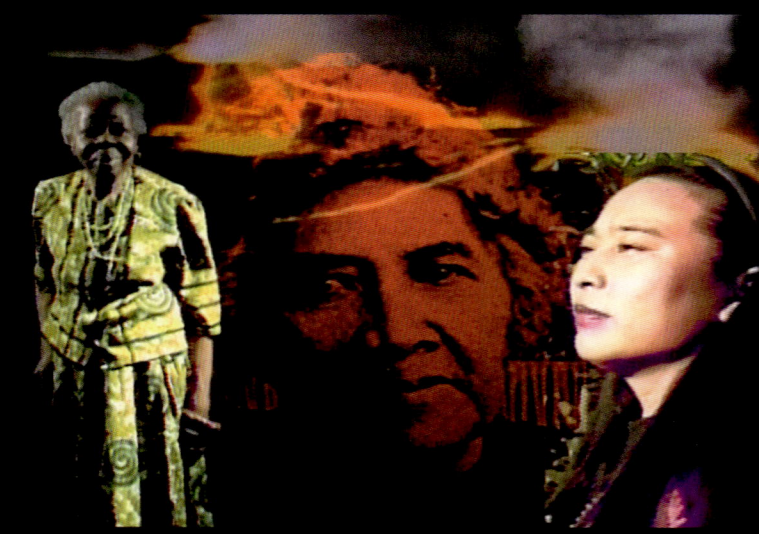

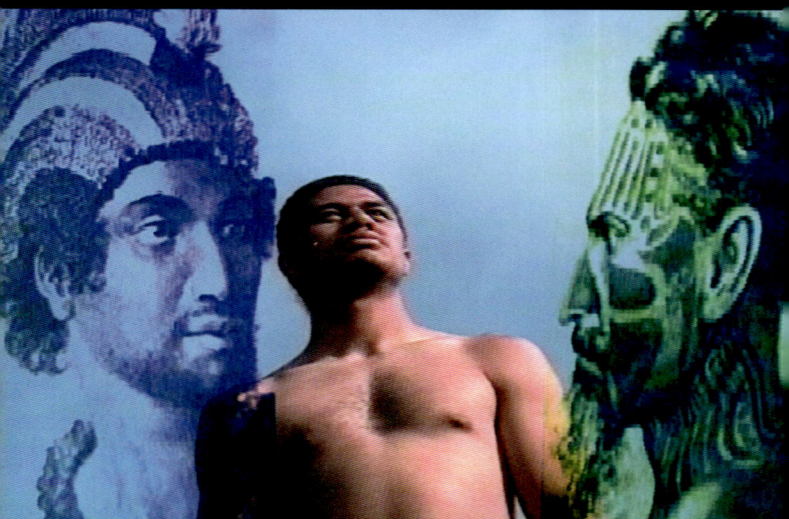

DOCUMENTA #9: Kassel, Germany
THE
FOLLOWING VIDEO RECORDINGS
REPRESENT DOCUMENTATION
FROM TELECOMMUNICTIONS
PERFORMANCE ART WORK
❋ A VIDEOPHONE EVENT: ❋

THE OTHERVISIONS ART BAND
at
THE ELECTRONIC CAFE INT'L.
Santa Monica, CA

1992, 11:29 min.

A video recording of a telecommunications performance
artwork of the Othervisions Art Band at the Electronic
Cafe International, Santa Monica, California, broadcast to
Kassel, Germany, for *Documenta 9*.

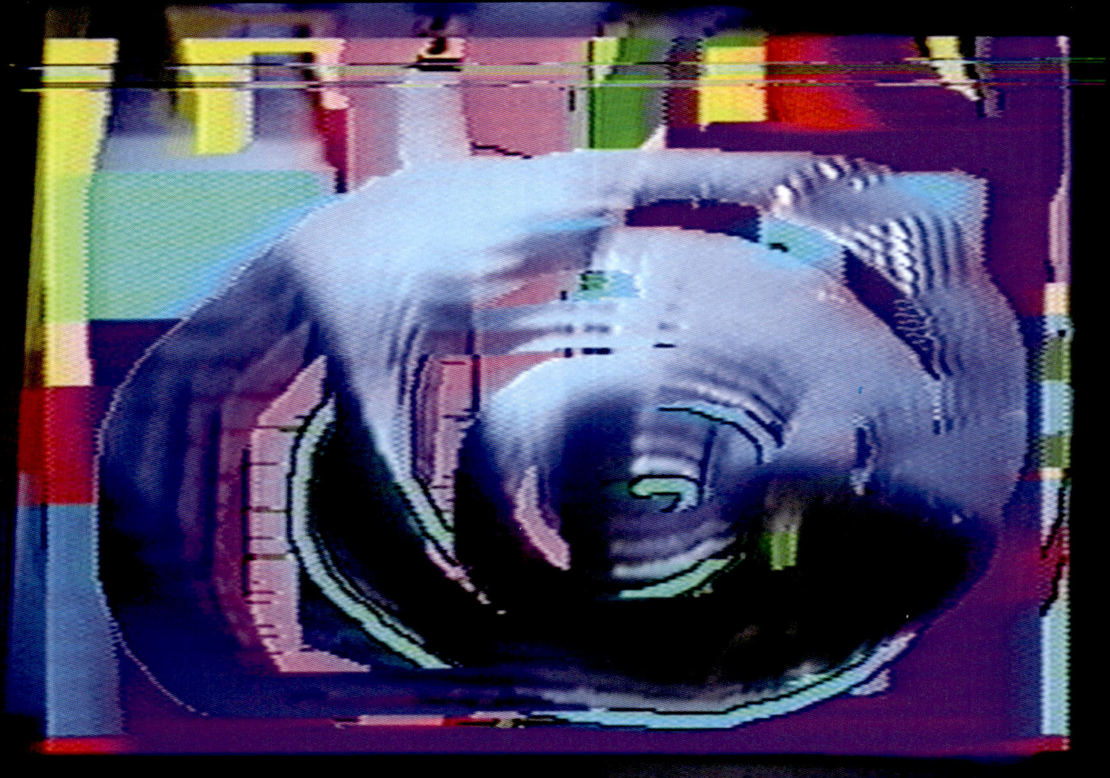

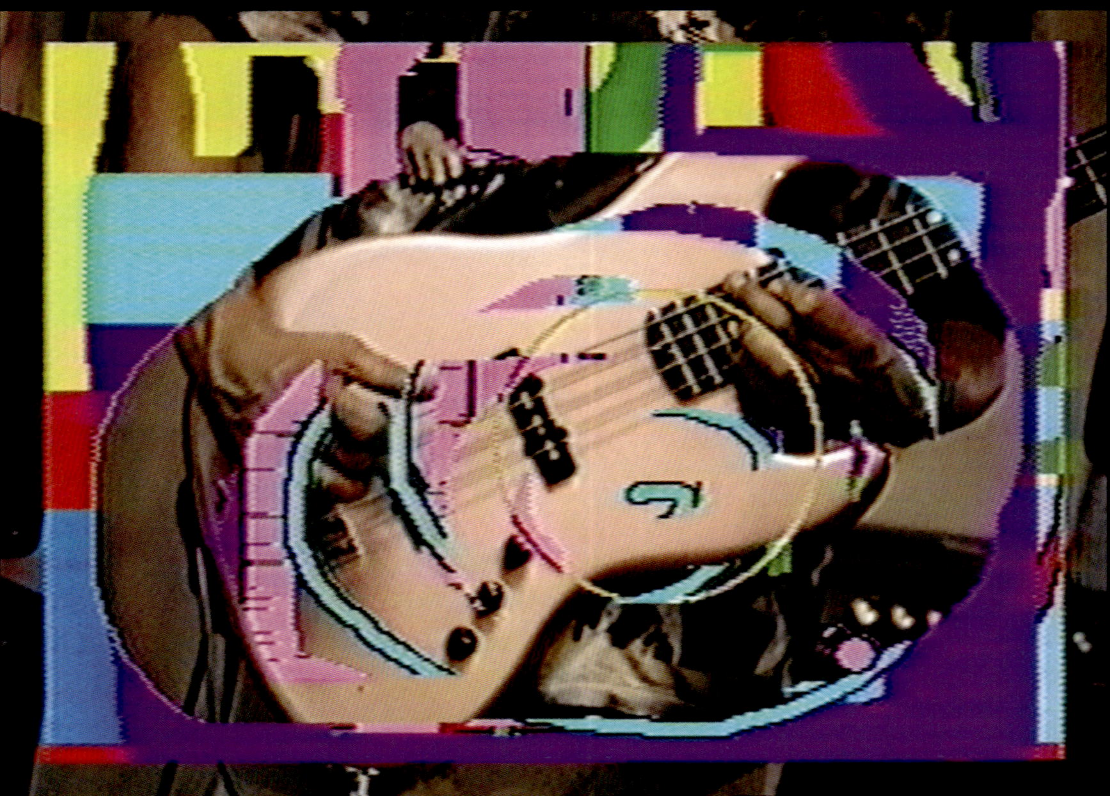

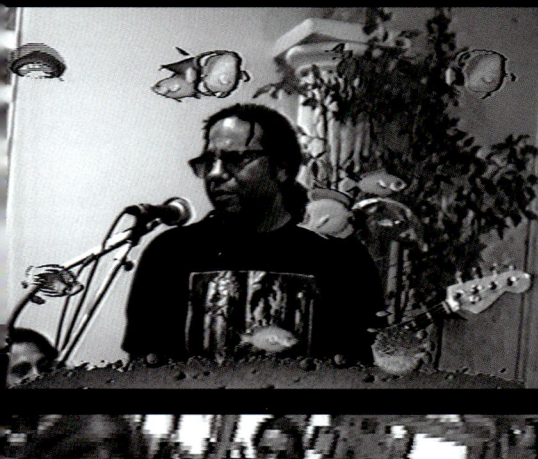

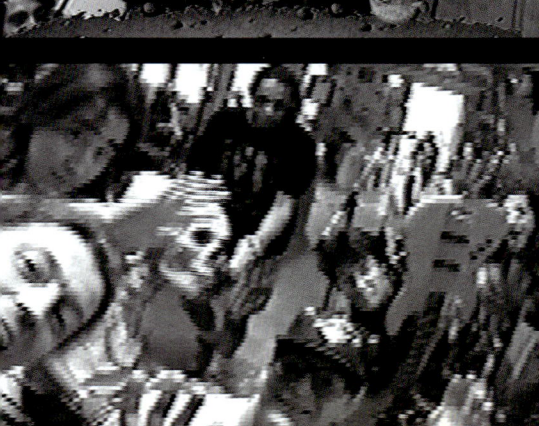

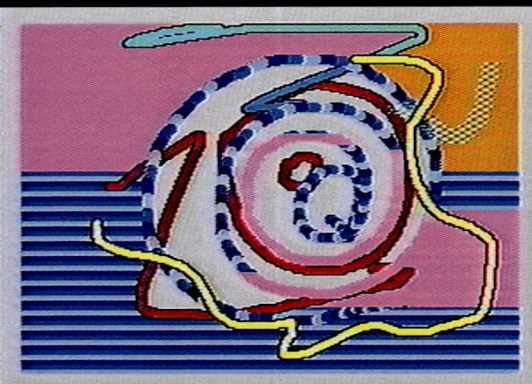

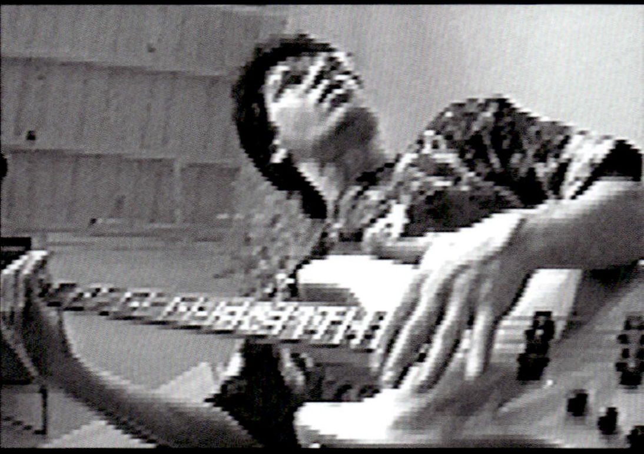

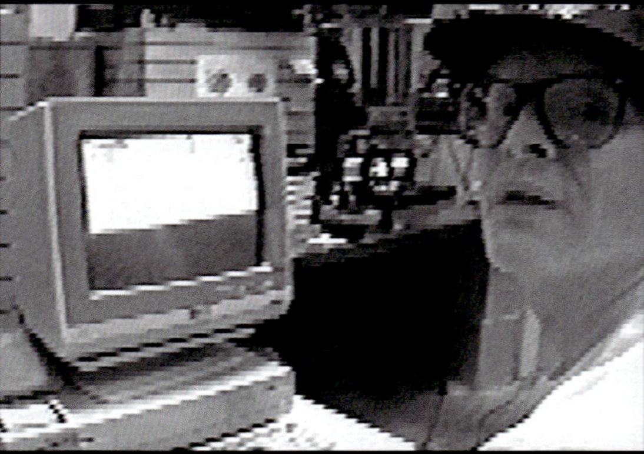

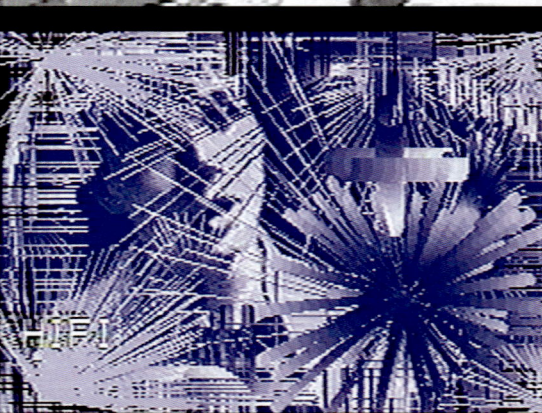

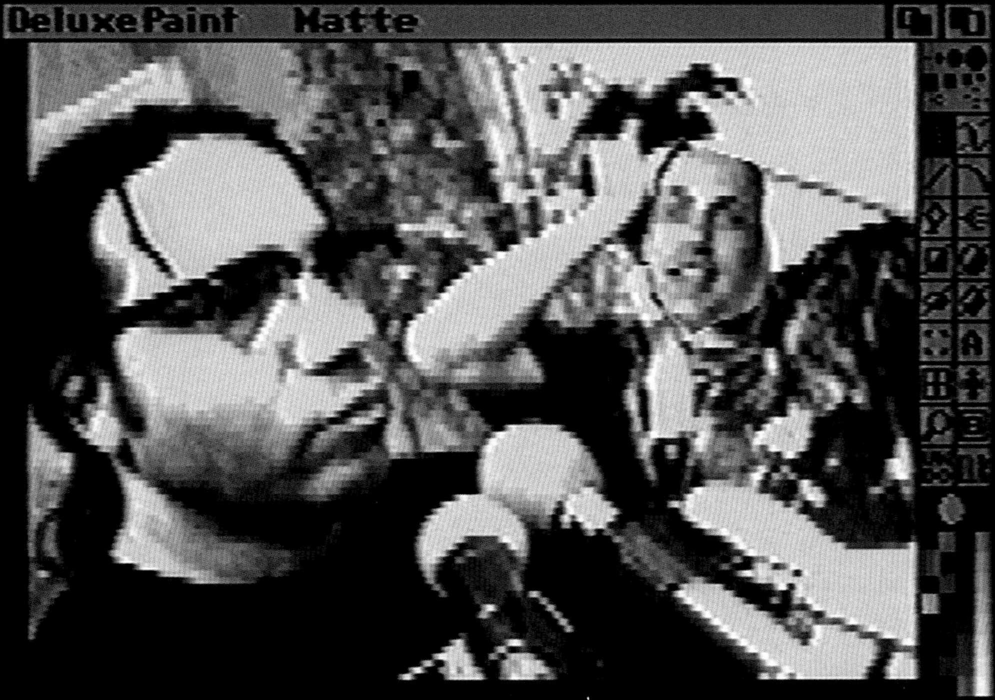
DeluxePaint Matte

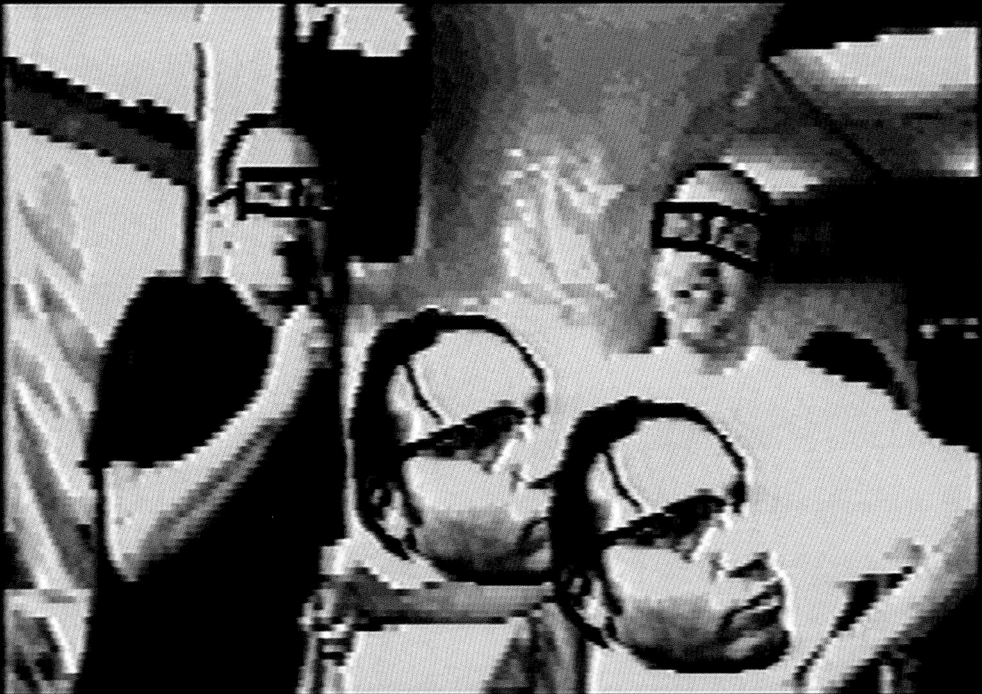

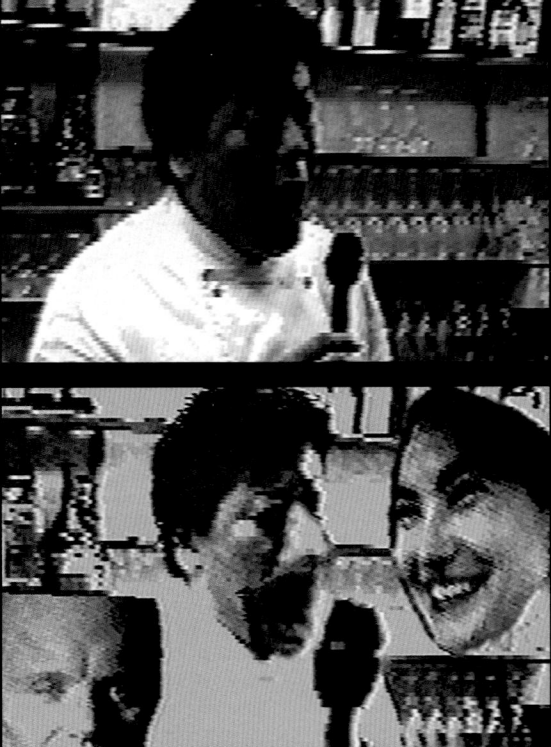

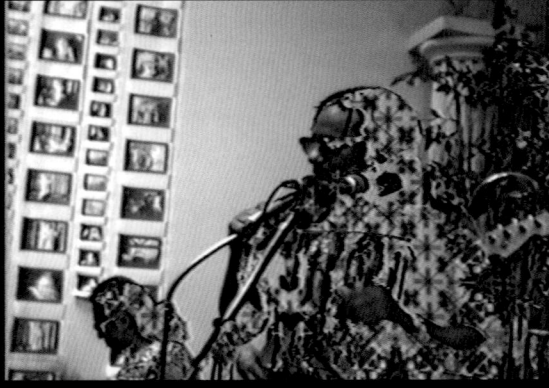

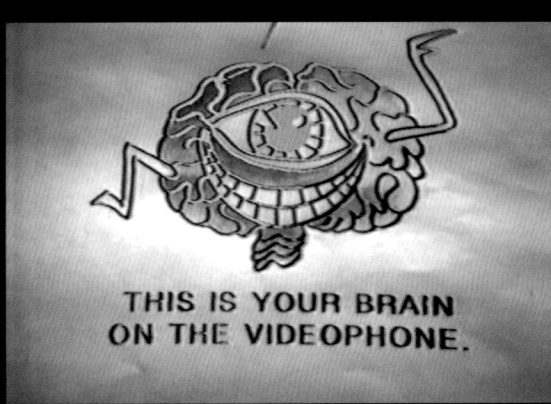

"VIDEOPHONE DAY"
FROM THE
SAN FANCISCO MUSEUM OF
MODERN ART / 3-3-92'

1992, 15:52 min.

Documentation of a demonstration of early
telecommunications art projects held at the San Francisco
Museum of Modern Art on March, 3, 1992.

THE FOLLOWING VIDEOTAPE IS AN EXAMPLE OF HOW THE VIDEO-TELEPHONE TECHNOLOGY IS UTILIZED AS A MULTIPLE TELECOMMUNICATION SYSTEM

(sound is included)
this is   the panasonic
visual telephone   unit

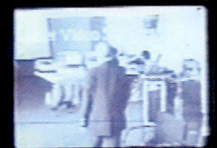

it sends/receives b/w
slow-scan still imges

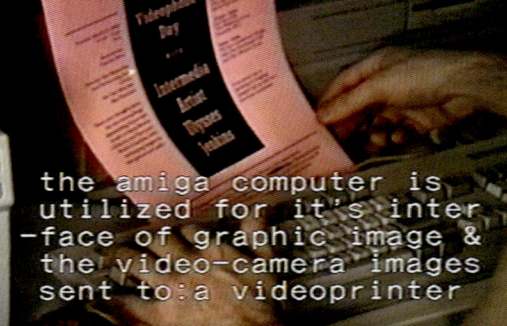

the amiga computer is
utilized for it's inter
-face of graphic image &
the video-camera images
sent to:a videoprinter

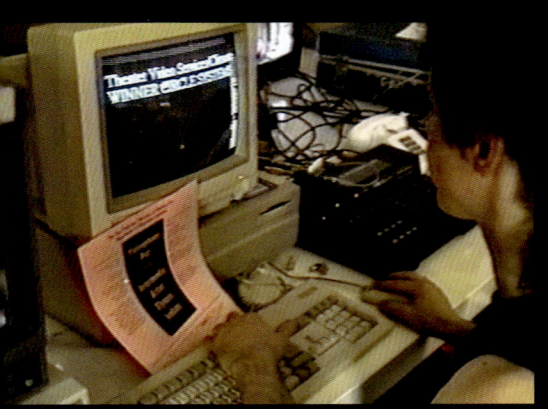

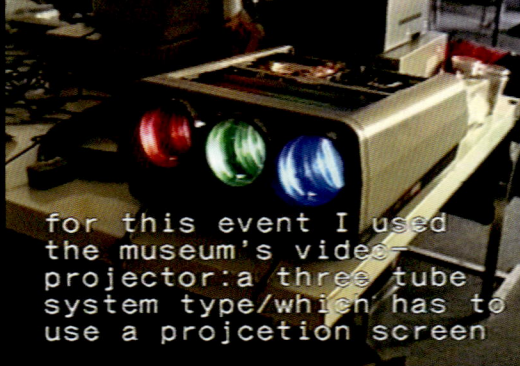

for this event I used
the museum's video-
projector:a three tube
system type/which has to
use a projcetion screen

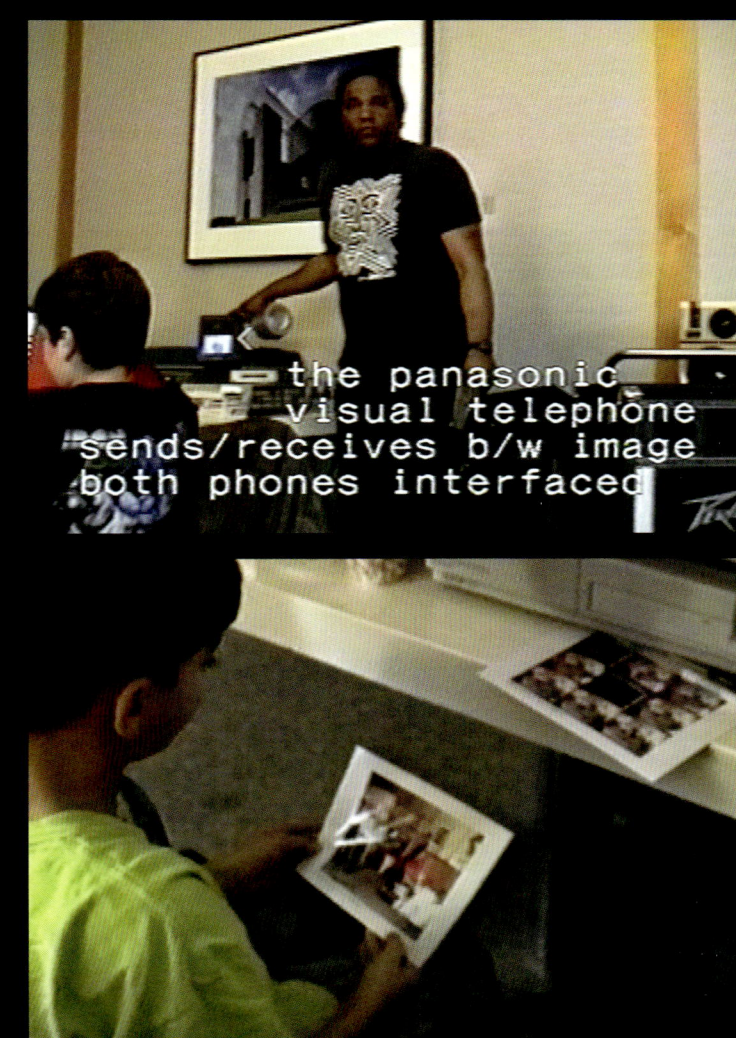

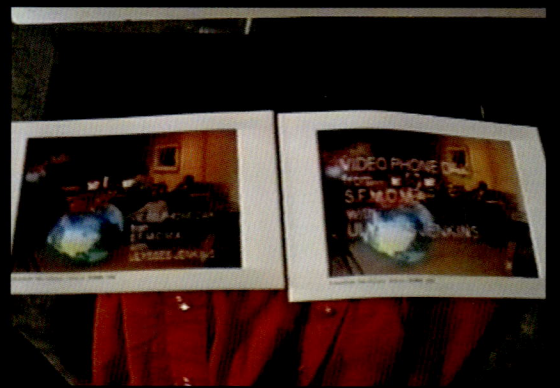
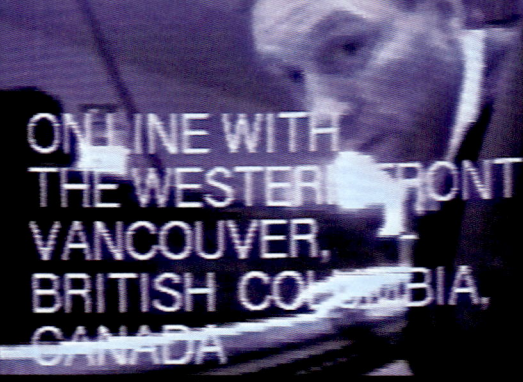

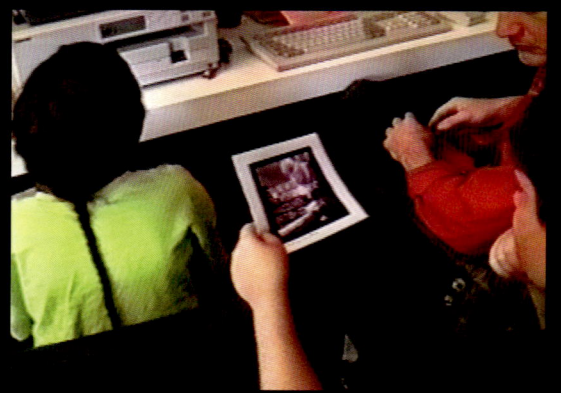
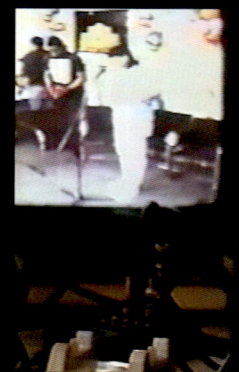
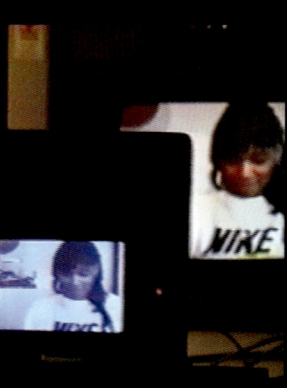

TALKING HUT

1994, 41:08 min.

This is video documentation of a telecommunications
artwork that embodies various contextual forms of
communications (experimental, virtual, ritual) based in
part on contemporary issues, utilizing the Panasonic
visual telecommunication system. Transmissions were
between Ulysses Jenkins at the Headlands Center for the
Arts, Sausalito, California, and visual artist
Daniel J. Martinez (outdoors) in Los Angeles.

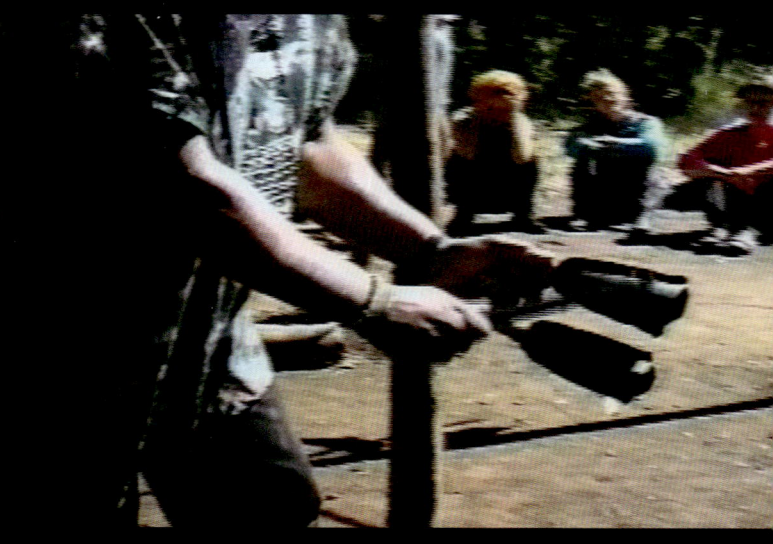

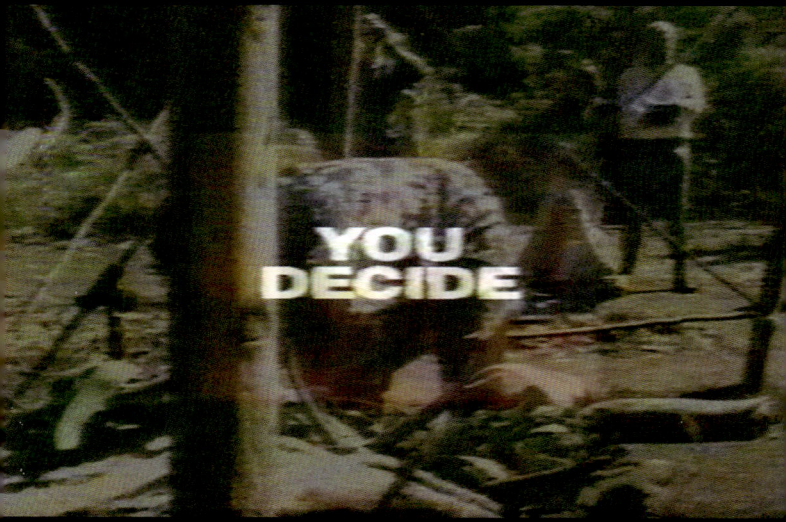

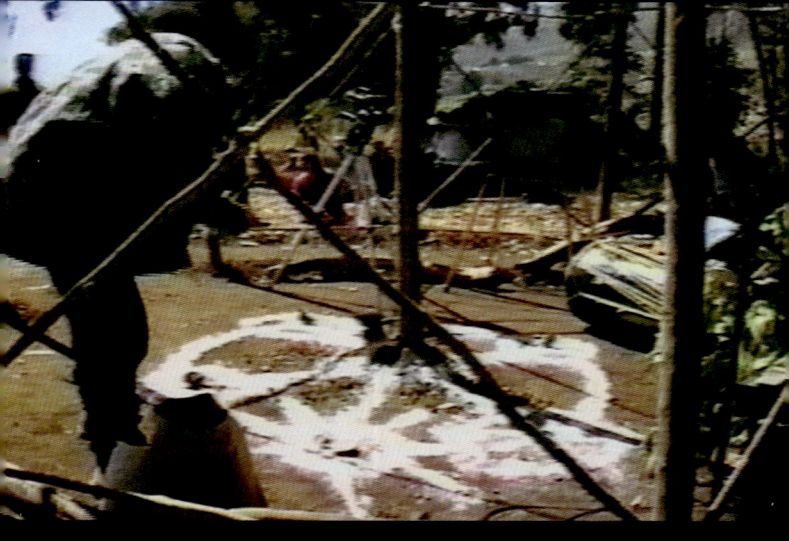

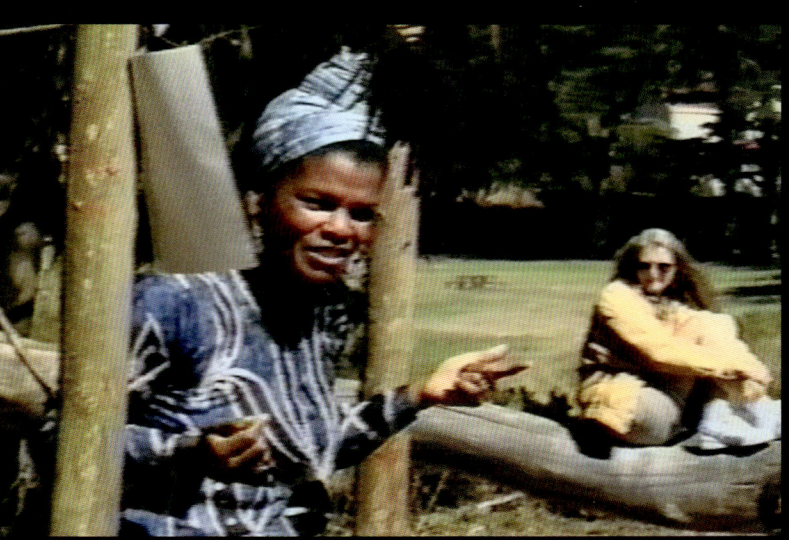

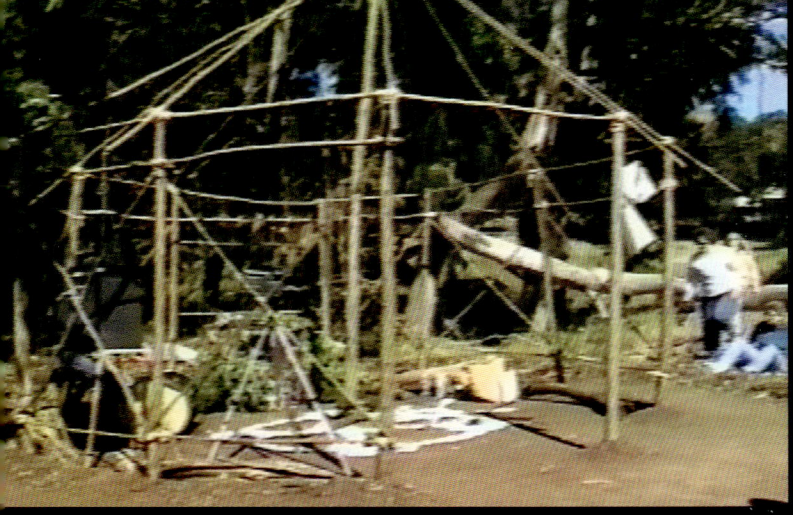

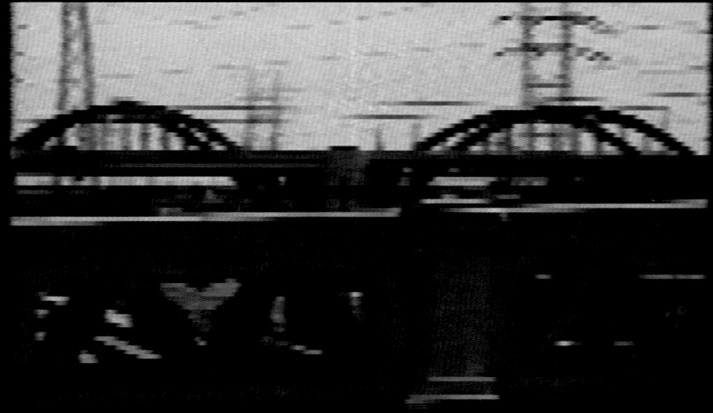

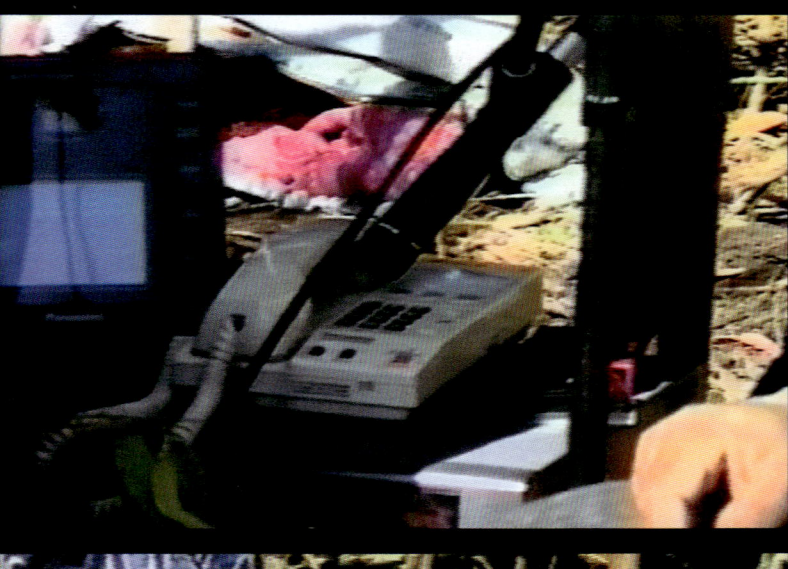

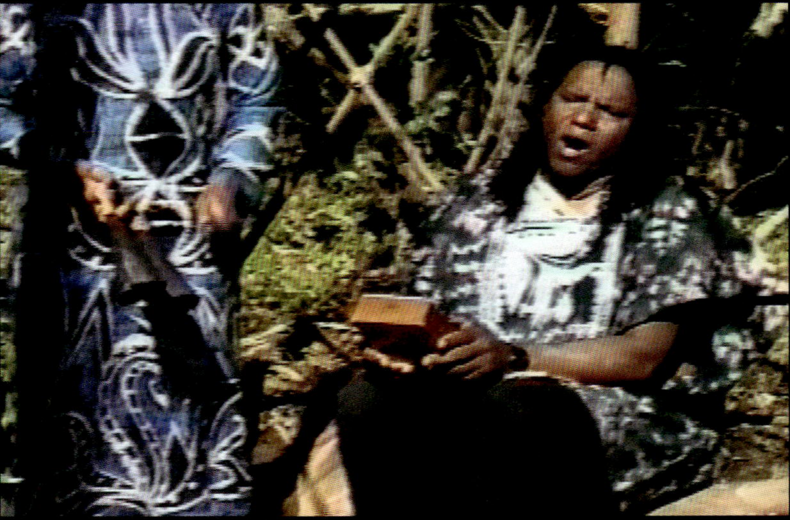

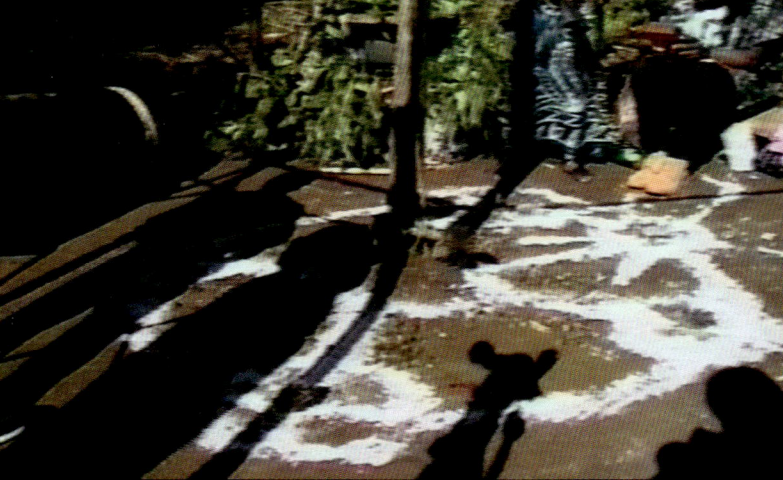

bequest

2002, 9:32 min.

A video art composition that presents a vision inspired by
the soundtrack narrative based on the song "Nature Boy"
by Eden Ahbez. *Bequest* acts as a ritual pertaining to the
washing out of negative images that have become prevalent
in the United States and the global community toward the
Arabic diaspora. —UJ

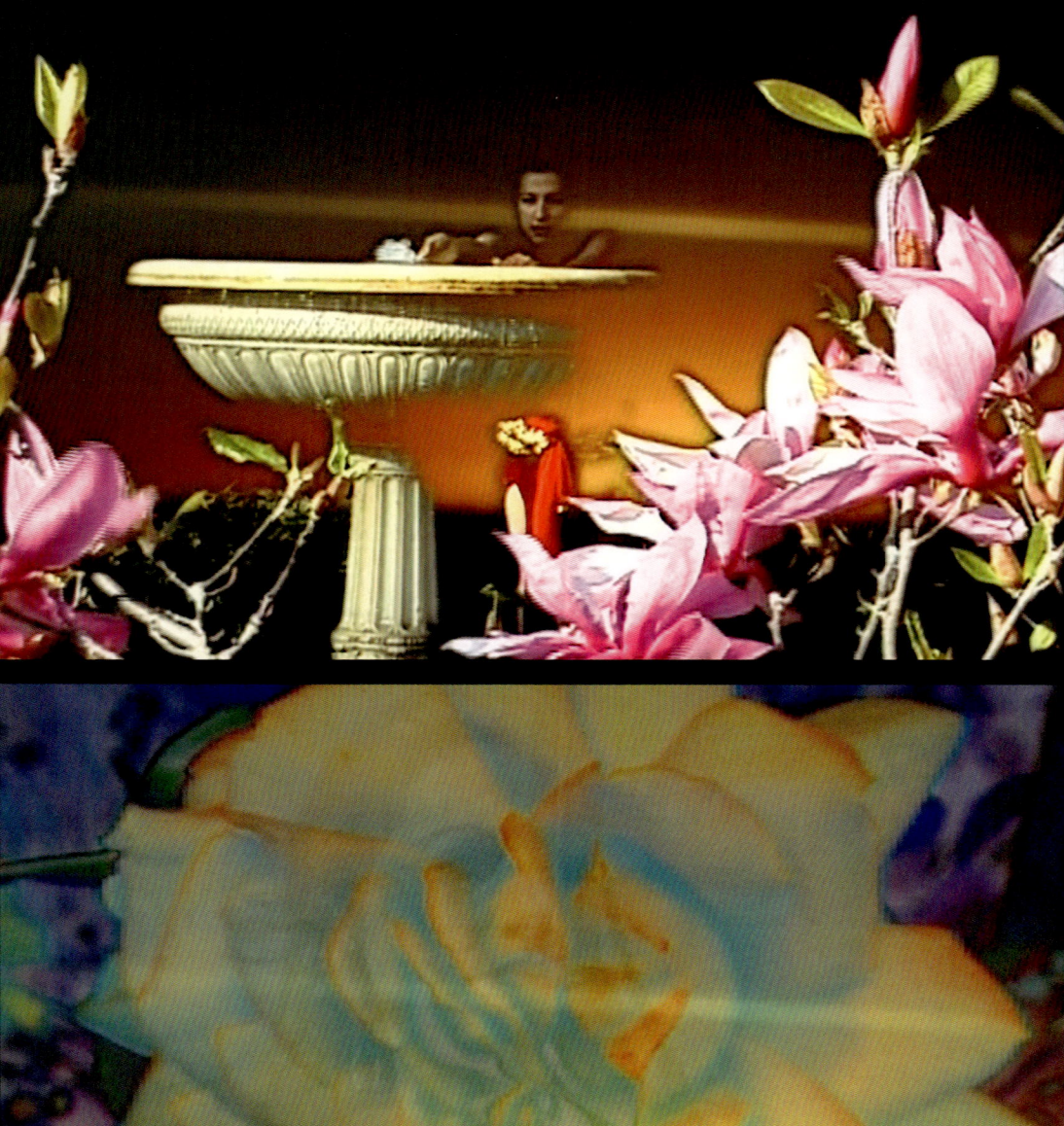

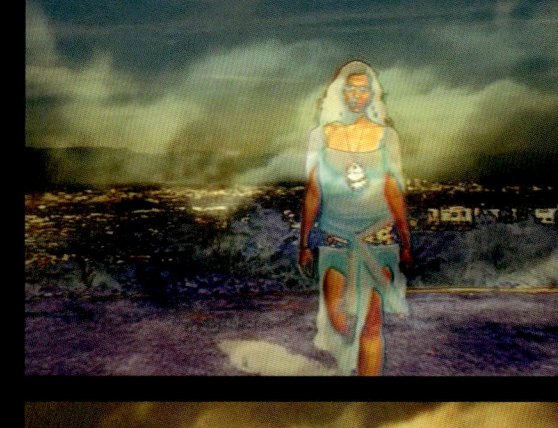

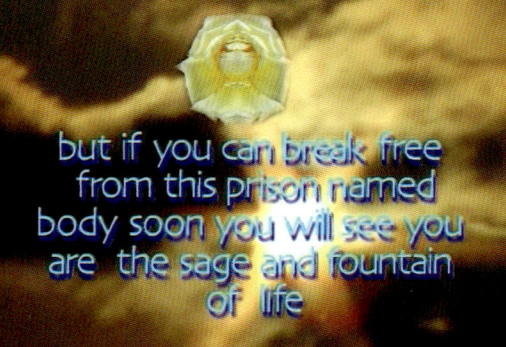

but if you can break free
from this prison named
body soon you will see you
are the sage and fountain
of life

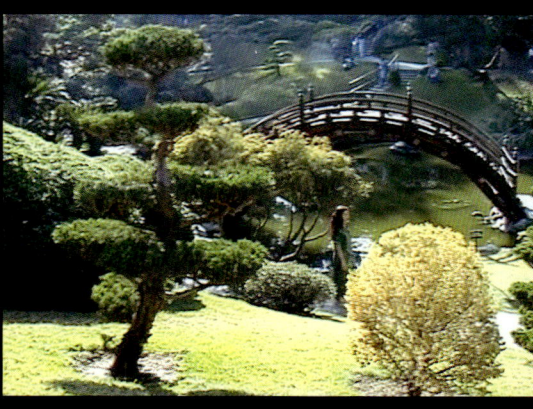

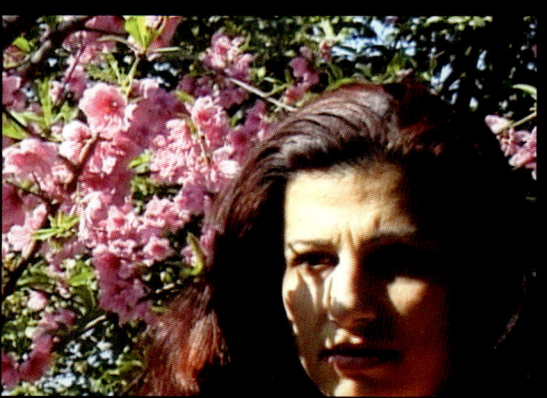

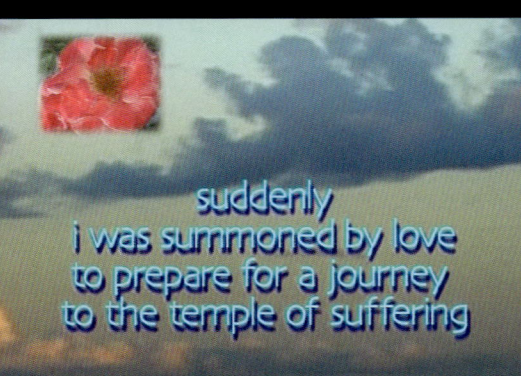

suddenly
i was summoned by love
to prepare for a journey
to the temple of suffering

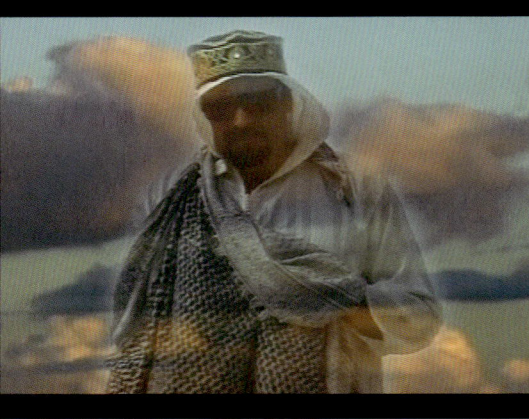

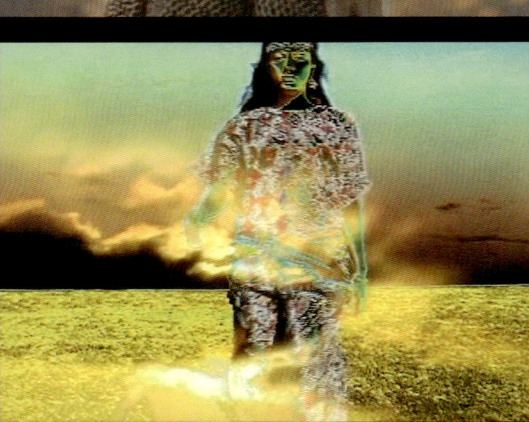

PLANET X

2006, 6:19 min.

This video takes the Planet X myth and interfaces it with
the Hurricane Katrina tragedy in New Orleans based on
their similar natural disaster principles. The avant-garde
jazz musician Sun Ra speaks a proclamation of prophecy
predicting a coming disaster for African Americans. —UJ

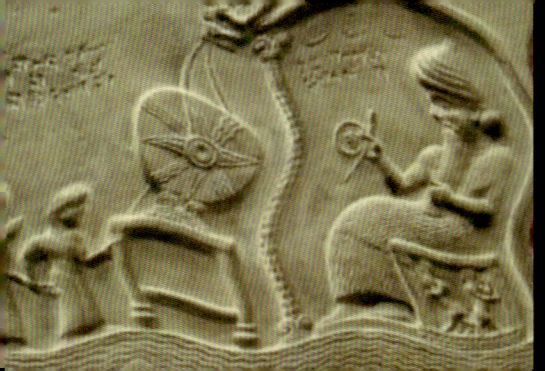

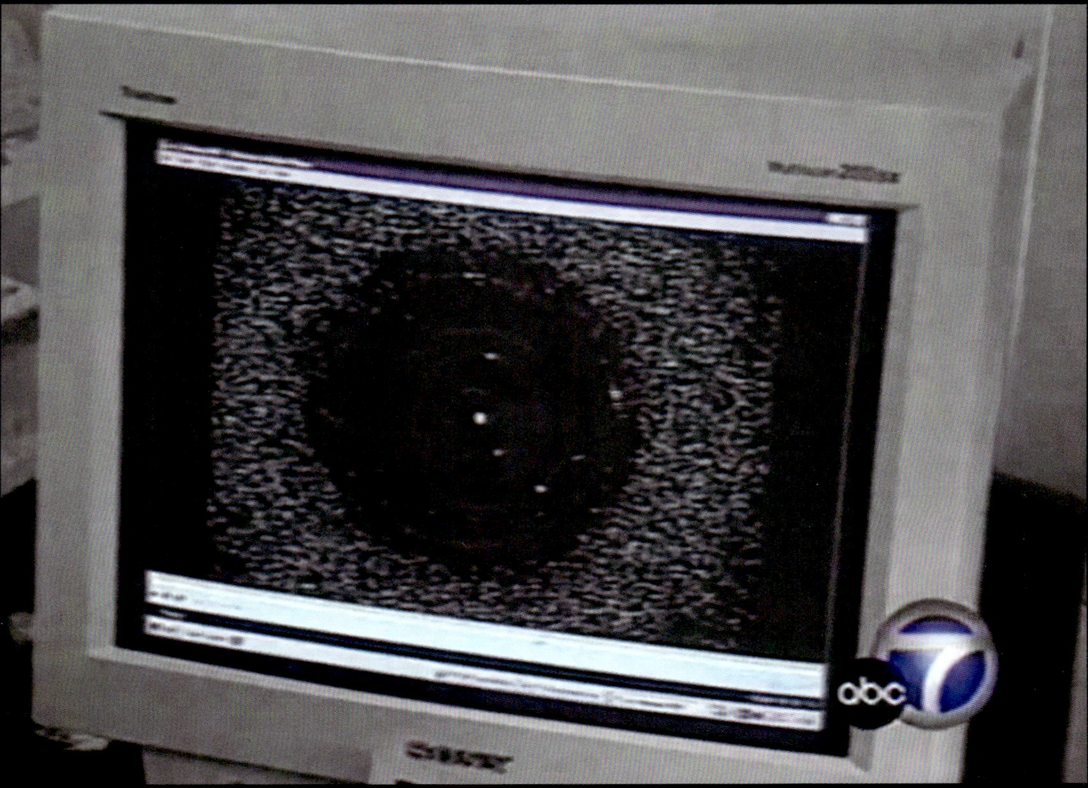

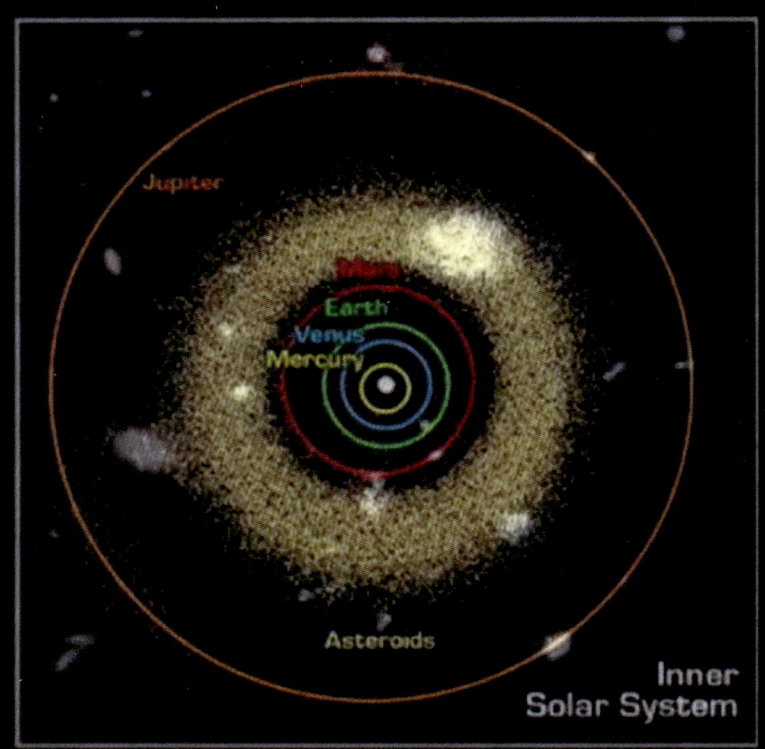

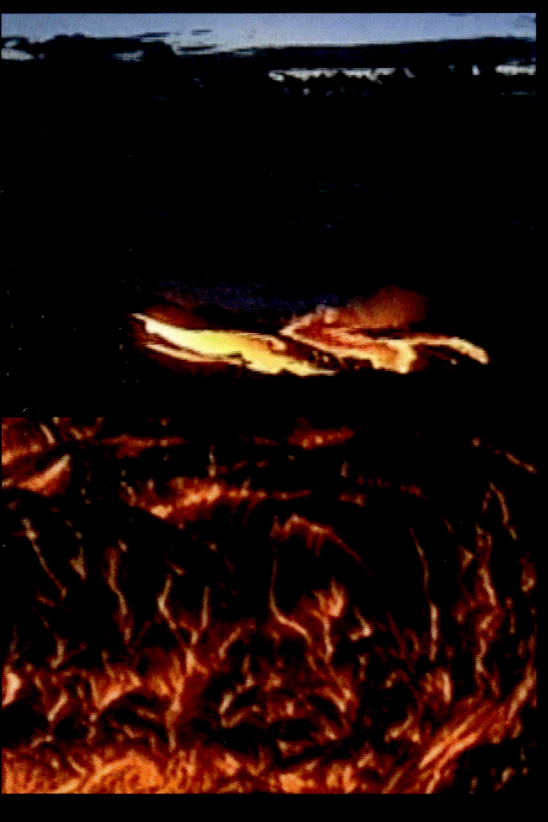

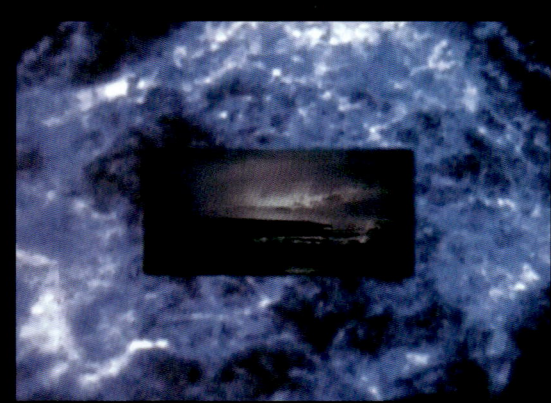

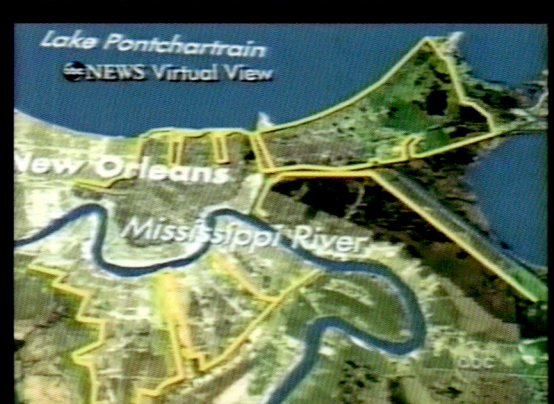

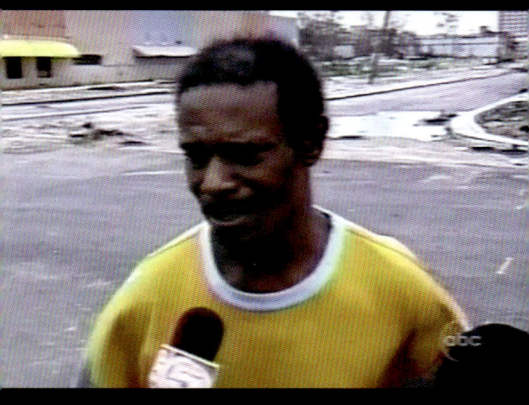

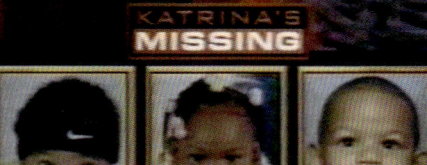

KATRINA'S
MISSING

1-800-THE-LOST
www. **missingkids.com**

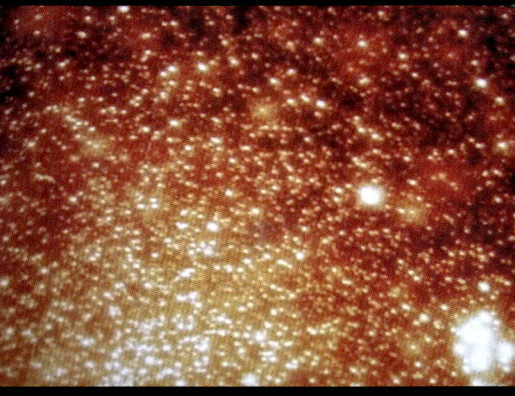

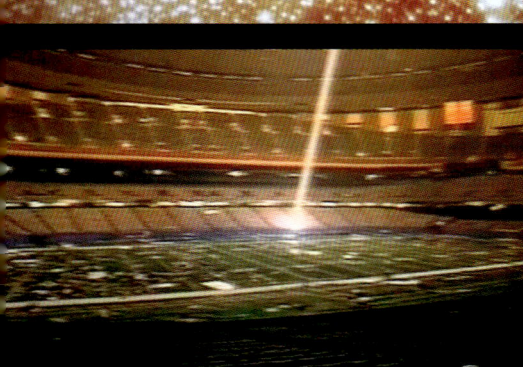

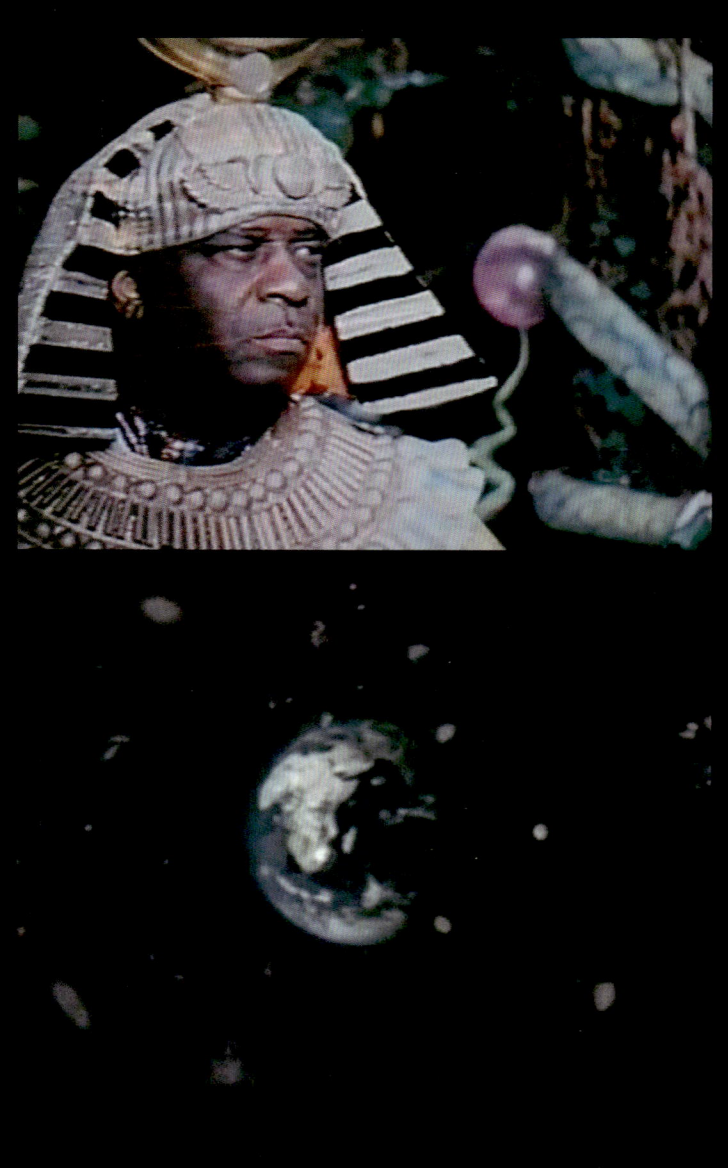

In The Midnight Hour

2009, 6:50 min.

A visit by David Hammons to John Outterbridge's studio.

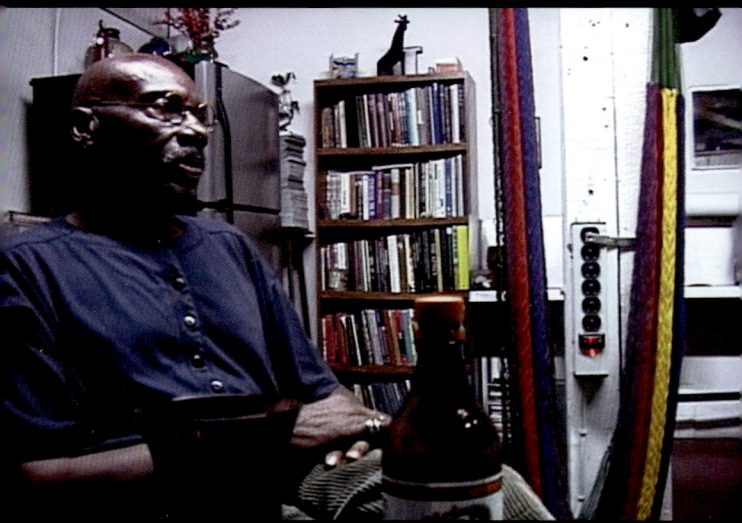

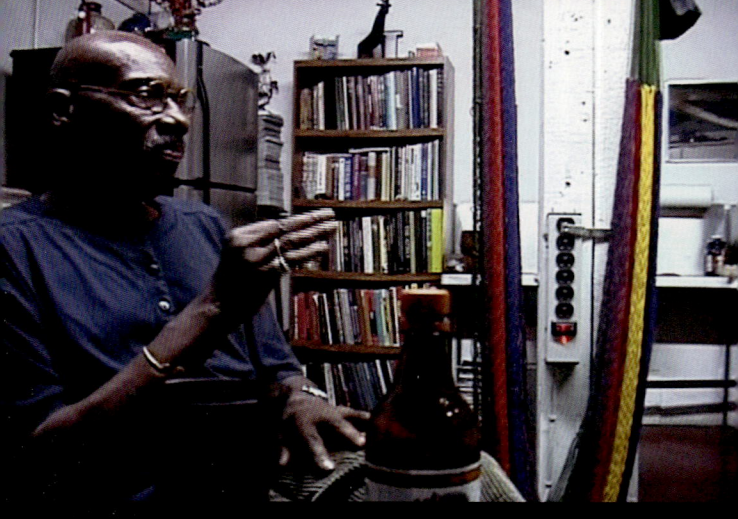

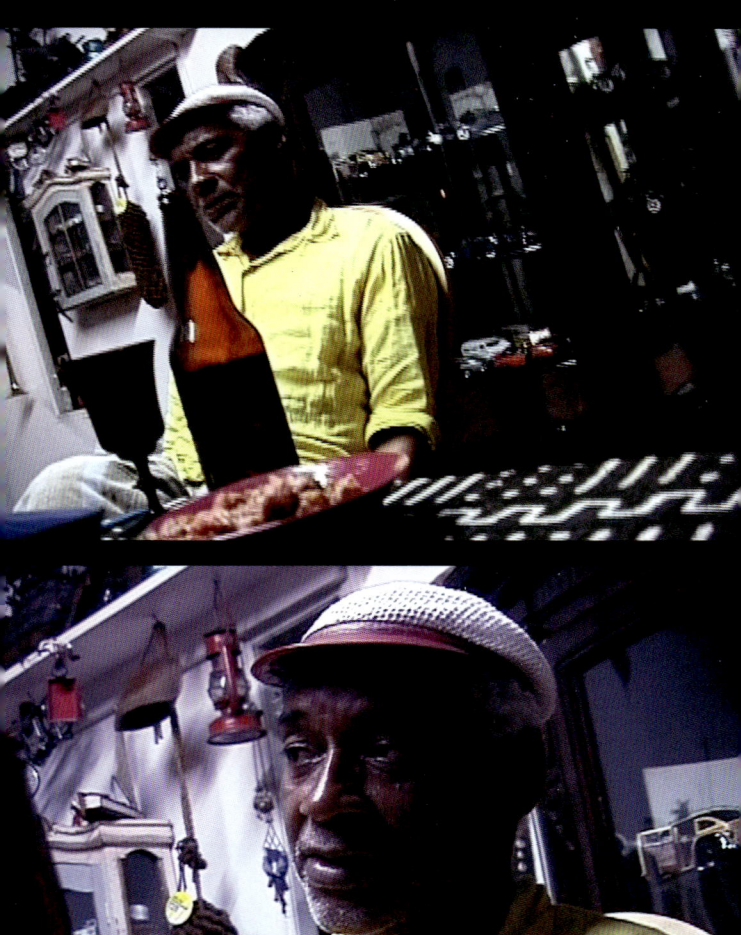

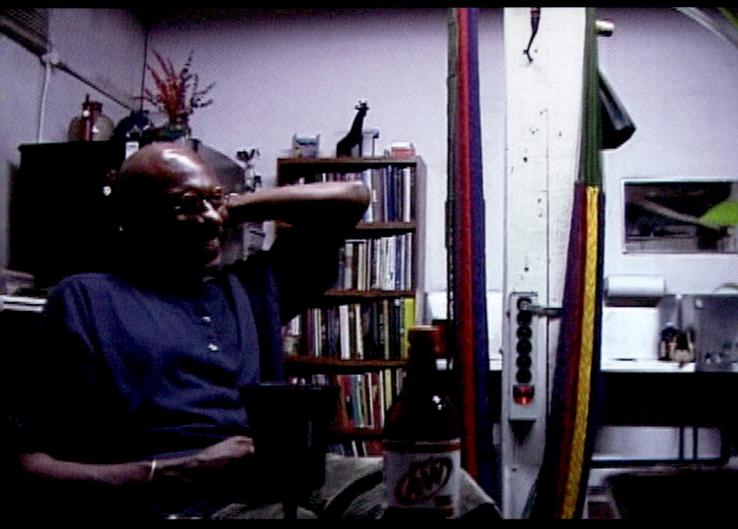

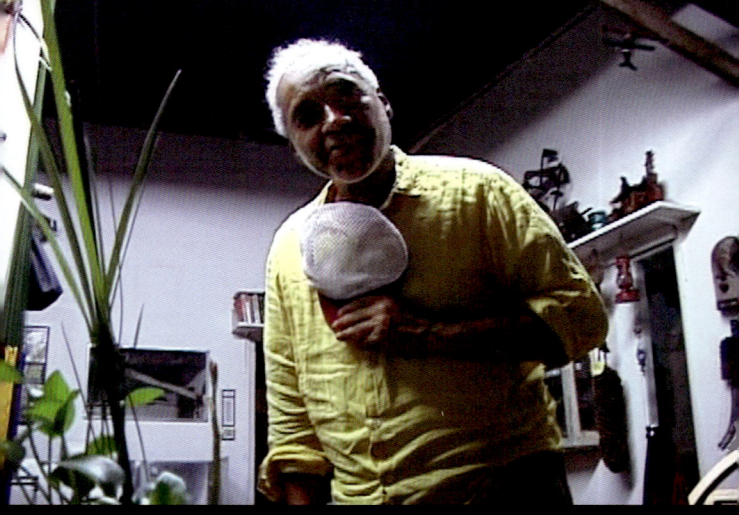

REFLECTIONS

MITOCHONDRIA
SENGA NENGUDI

It's a joy for me that Ulysses is getting his full due. Many of us have been fortunate recently to get a lot of play, so to speak, as artists. But Ulysses is in another category, because he was the only Black person doing video. Of course he did other things like the murals, but very specifically with video, he was a pioneer.

His birthday is September 19, and mine is September 18, and we always get in touch with each other during that time. In 1981 he created *Dream City* around our birthdays. There were a number of people involved in this twenty-four-hour performance, and people floated in and out, including Nobuko Miyamoto, who came through with dancing. But Maren Hassinger and I were there with Ulysses for the full duration. We were sort of like his side girls, with our costumes and all that. It was a special time, and it also signaled Ulysses's way of doing things, of incorporating diversity, providing a platform for this diverse group of artists. That was important for us because none of us—by which I mean, artists of color—were really acknowledged in the art mainstream. So it was important for us to see our value. That's one of the main things that came about through Ulysses's performances—all these people contributed their energy, their culture, their way of thinking to these projects.

Our histories are intertwined; it's hard to separate it because we were all in it together and all on the same rhythm. Maren and I and Franklin Parker worked a lot together as collaborators, in the beginning also with Houston Conwill. And when Houston left for New York, Ulysses took that spot. Each of us would have a concept, and then the others would chime in and be the performers for that concept. We often created performances to coincide with the openings of exhibitions that one or more of us participated in. *Flying* (1982), for example, was a truly collaborative piece we performed in Barnsdall Park for the opening of the exhibition *Afro-American Abstraction* at the Los Angeles Municipal Art Gallery, in which Maren, Houston, and I were included. We all had different ideas and were working together and bouncing off each other and growing from each other.

Ulysses was always gathering groups of people and had a flow of performers and energies going through. His Othervisions Studio was a magnet for artists—a space where one could try things out, work through ideas, and present installations and performances. We all danced together, and Ulysses was always up to the challenge. I would say, "Oh, Ulysses, can you stand on your head?" And he would reply, "Oh, sure." At the center of it all, we trusted each other. We still do. We trust each other so that whatever we get involved with, we're up to it because we know it's for the greater good. We didn't have any limitations, because we weren't part of the structure. We could do whatever we wanted to do, and there was no one to say no.

PARTNERS IN CRIME
MAREN HASSINGER

I believe I met Ulysses through Senga Nengudi, who was really good at finding "fellow travelers." There were so many other meetings, conversations, sharings, participations in performances of all sorts. We all worked together with our individual support systems, happily abandoning the past for the unknown and the possible.

Sometimes Ulysses's vivid articulations went right over my head, but I loved his ideas and his enthusiasm and would do most anything to support his practice. That practice, like mine and like Senga's, included collaboration. He liked to work with musicians. Senga liked to work with dancers. I liked working with both of them because *everything* was so open-ended. There were countless times we began a project sponsored by one or the other of us—improvised, rehearsed, performed. Then afterward, looking at the photographs and videos, we realized what a wonderful and enduring piece we had created.

Usually there was a leader we followed, and that person typically had secured the venue. In 1981 Ulysses decided to do a twenty-four-hour performance, called *Dream City*, at the studio of Rachel Rosenthal. Senga and I were the first performers as part of this twenty-four-hour investment. When we came in—it was about 7 am—Ulysses greeted us with something wrapped in plastic and then, as he gingerly peeled back the plastic holding his pinky fingers up, the smell began to invade the premises. It turned out he had found a dead cat that had been hit by a car and left in the street, and he picked it up and brought it in to begin the day of performance. We all nearly fainted.

That was the 1970s and early 1980s. Then Senga went to Colorado Springs, and I to New York City and other East Coast towns. We've both remained in those places while Ulysses continued to hold down the fort in Los Angeles. He prospered with video work and performance (without us). There was an enduring friendship with Rosenthal. And finally a plum teaching job at the University of California, Irvine.

The last time we collaborated was in San Francisco, at the Yerba Buena Center for the Arts in 2015. It was the final stop of the traveling exhibition *Radical Presence: Black Performance in Contemporary Art*, of which Ulysses, Senga, and I were a part. On opening day, both he and Senga participated in a performance piece I've done for a while called *Women's Work*. There was Ulysses, bravely supporting me, twisting and knotting strips of newspaper along with the others—all women.

Our friendship has endured because of Ulysses's brilliance, creativity, kindness, generosity, and sense of purpose in spite of the odds for success. Ulysses is family—in fact, coincidentally, my maiden name is Jenkins.

INTERMEDIAL DOGGEREL
KELLIE JONES

At an early point in his career Ulysses Jenkins took up the rude, crude, and burlesque qualities of the "doggerel" as a working concept. As he has written, "I saw 'doggerel,' an irregular, comic and trivial verse, 'only the lowly,' as an expression encouraging humble possibilities. This loose and poor style seemed adaptable as mocking adoration, a humorous adornment for a group of artists and their activities spurned by the mainstream 'avant-garde.'"[1] Jenkins's writing and practice elucidate the vibrant and increasingly visible Black, Latinx, and Asian American communities of artists and others who had been traditionally excluded from resources, visibility, and a sustainable livelihood in the art world, yet who continued to make things anyway.

"Doggerel" (or as he sometimes renders it, "doggereal") would also come to be associated with Jenkins's own creative style. Like the works of his California compatriots David Hammons, Maren Hassinger, and Senga Nengudi, the things Jenkins made had multimedia and transmedial lives, moving across genres from ephemeral actions to a more solidly object-based practice. Yet his basis in video raised the stakes, positioning the work as more resolutely intermedial, driven by the ever-present yet evanescent digital signal. For Jenkins, the transitive glitch, though inconsequential, was a compelling portal, opening onto the beating heart of the world, an approach that anticipates the work of the video artist and filmmaker Arthur Jafa. As with the contemporary artist Cauleen Smith, whose video projects move into and out of installation and performance, Jenkins's production would always be characterized by a decisively public-facing turn, from his earliest murals and parallel video activism with Video Venice News in the 1970s. Like the practice of his friends mentioned above, it constituted an avant-garde that never wanted to forget the vérité, the life of Blackness, its radical footprint. *Remnants of the Watts Festival* (1972) begins to encapsulate these ideas, with its mix of concert footage, photographs, interviews, and a camera traversing all aspects of the affair, at once commemorative and ebullient in its sketch of Black life, the whole forged from scraps, vestiges, and hints. Such aesthetics are seen in other projects such as *Televiews and Cable Radio* (1981) and the *Electronic Cafe Network* (1984) that concern transmission, communication—visual, poetic, mediated—and ultimately greater personal, if distanced, connection through the joining of electronic media with varied physical sites.

Some of Jenkins's renowned early collaborators constituted Studio Z, the informal collective that included Hassinger, Nengudi, and others who gathered in Hammons's capacious studio in the 1970s.[2] In the collaborative performance *Flying* (1982), Jenkins's digital work played a key role as part of a larger outdoor ensemble piece that staged an amelioration between nature and culture and contemplated African diasporic migrations. In 1983 Jenkins created an exquisite video of *Cake Walk*, a performance by Studio Z member Houston Conwill within his installation for New York's Just Above Midtown gallery, another site for Black visual experimentation. The mystical and ritual core of Conwill's projects in sculpture, live action, and painting found perhaps its greatest affinity in Jenkins's practice.

As the 1970s became the 1980s, those figures would eventually quit Los Angeles, and Jenkins's Othervisions Studio and Art Band expanded their experimental mantle, moving it toward a more resolutely cross-cultural and global future. *Without Your Interpretation* is emblematic of the evolving complexities and pleasures of Jenkins's process. It began as a live performance in 1983 with Life in the Park with Debris (part band, part performance collective) at the Art Dock and later at the music venue Lhasa Club. It continues its life as a video (1984), shot through with found and massaged moving-image fragments, offering a meditation on neoliberal power and its impact on a globally bound humanity. Along with Hassinger and Nengudi, the participation of Crono Childs, Todd Gray, Liz Rodriguez, and May Sun spoke to Jenkins's burgeoning coalitional universe. It is felt in the postmodern choreography of Rudy Perez and makeup by performance group Asco member Patssi Valdez, who both left their mark on *Without Your Interpretation*, and in collaborations with other Latinx artists, such as his longtime guitarist Michael Delgado and Daniel Joseph Martinez, whose atmospheric photograph of Jenkins outside Othervisions Studio that year reflects this era.

Jenkins's projects would always honor ritual as performative procession, his self-styling as a shaman and griot enlivened by poetry, music, and the Othervisions Art Band. Jenkins's intermedial doggerel also revealed diasporic Blackness, seen in *Lasisi: Ju Ju Funk* (1983), his homage to the musician Lasisi Amao, whose rocking Afro-pop made its way to Los Angeles from Nigeria by way of the UK, and in *The Nomadics* (1991), which plots Afro-Asian migrations along the Indian Ocean (or Swahili) Coast. In the latter video and in *Black Gold/Fever Performance at LACE* (2011), the continual creation of sand paintings by Matthew Thomas provides a crucial accompaniment. In this ancient and ephemeral practice, the shifting colored granules mark time, trace, and relation, constituting the fine print of the humble, interstitial, and omnipresent.

1   Ulysses Jenkins, *Doggerel Life: Stories of a Los Angeles Griot* (Los Angeles: Oreste, 2018), 6.
2   Their activities were documented in the 1977–78 exhibition *Studio Z: Individual Collective* at the Long Beach Museum of Art, which also supported video production for artists, including Jenkins.

HIGHER LEARNING
KERRY
JAMES MARSHALL

In 1978, Ronnie Nichols, Ulysses Jenkins, Greg Pitts and myself were the only black students at what was then called the Otis Art Institute of Los Angeles County. I started the year before, in January 1977; I was an undergrad and the rest of these guys were grad students. I knew of Ulysses because he was a mural painter before he went to art school. I used to see him painting on the Department of Motor Vehicles building off the Harbor Freeway. Greg was the first person I met on campus, in the parking lot after I dropped off my portfolio.

We *were* the Black Student Union! In '78 we were collaborating on an exhibition at the student gallery. Greg knew about a shoe-shine stand on Figueroa Street, and he suggested we go down there to take a picture for the announcement. I set up the camera and pushed the shutter button and jumped back into my seat before the timer ran out.

The show, "Two-Zone Transfer," was based on Ulysses's complicated feelings about identity. Whenever he started talking about things that were really important to him, people would start laughing. He was asking, "When I start to talk about myself and the issues that are relevant to my community, what's funny about that?" The performance piece was broken up into three dream sequences: a minstrel show, a sermon in a church and a version of James Brown's album *Live at the Apollo*. Ulysses was playing James Brown, of course; Ronnie, Greg and I were the Famous Flames. We made a video of the performance, which Ulysses used to apply for a $20,000 NEA grant; he was the first artist I knew personally to get one.

Aside from being in Ulysses's performance, I showed a series of drawings based on seeing something in your peripheral vision. The notion of visibility versus invisibility was starting to take shape in my work. I also made some sculptures using dolls to represent children who had been assaulted or sexually abused or murdered. There had been a rash of news stories in L.A. at the time. The work I made was somewhere between social realism and social activism.

It was a really dynamic time. What I miss is that there seemed to be a lot at stake in what we were doing at art school. Where you stood in terms of politics and representation mattered. The kind of work you made mattered. And people were less invested in their position in the market. We had no expectation that we'd participate in anything *like* an art market. So much was in flux.

Kerry James Marshall as told to Leigh Anne Miller / Courtesy of Art Media, LLC
Originally published in *Art in America* 104, no. 4 (2016): 47.

ULYSSES JENKINS, FRIEND/COLLABORATOR
MAY SUN

I met Ulysses in 1978, when we were both students at Otis Art Institute. I was a sculpture major creating multimedia installations, and he was a video-based artist creating avant-garde works addressing race and history and the African American community in Los Angeles. We studied with Gary Lloyd, who was making telecommunicative video works. Bruce and Norman Yonemoto were also part of our group, and Kerry James Marshall, who worked in the art library while a student, was a friend. I found Ulysses to be erudite, philosophical, generous, and community-minded.

In 1979 we went on a field trip with other students to Europe, led by the curator Germano Celant and the artist Wanda Westcoast. Ulysses had some surreal experiences abroad, including a racist encounter in a bar/restaurant in London. It was a whirlwind trip, visiting museums in London, Amsterdam, Cologne, Milan, Venice, Rome, Padua, and Paris, although I personally had to return home after Milan. We had about ten days in London and visited the British Museum, the Tate, the National Gallery, and other museums, and also went to see Stonehenge. After that, it was a fast and furious trip, hopping on trains from city to city. At all the museums along the way, Germano lectured on individual works. It was thrilling to see works by artists I admired—Joseph Beuys, Kazimir Malevich, Barnett Newman, Eva Hesse, Robert Rauschenberg, Walter De Maria, Mark Rothko, Richard Tuttle, Cy Twombly, Daniel Spoerri, and Yves Klein, among many others.

Ulysses and I kept up our friendship after Otis and we were in each other's performance art pieces. I was in his piece *Without Your Interpretation*, which was performed in 1983 at the Art Dock (the architect/artist Carleton Davis's loading dock turned performance art space in downtown Los Angeles) and at the Lhasa Club in Hollywood.

After Ulysses received an NEA fellowship grant in 1982, he started the art space Othervisions Studio, where he invited artists of color to experiment, collaborate, create, and exhibit work. It was a warm and welcoming place, and I attended a dance/movement workshop there taught by the renowned choreographer Rudy Perez. It was called "Art Moves" and was tailored for visual artists. Maren Hassinger and Senga Nengudi were in the class; we improvised with one another in collaborative pieces, and the three of us have remained lifelong friends. Another artist/dancer in the class was the late Crono, who was a key performer in my early performance art piece *Desperada in C Major* (1983) at the Lhasa Club.

Ulysses was a performer in two of my performance art pieces: *The Great Wall or How Red Is My China?* (1986, 1988) and *Running Dog/Paper Tiger* (1984). *The Great Wall or How Red Is My China?* developed out of a performance workshop led by Ruth Maleczech of Mabou Mines. It was produced by Los Angeles Contemporary Exhibitions (LACE) and Otis, and we performed it at LACE and later at New Langton Arts in San Francisco. The piece is about my visiting China and meeting my aunt who was a revolutionary leader. She told me she was good friends with Paul Robeson. Ulysses played the Robeson character. *Running Dog/Paper Tiger* addressed the condescending questions on the form immigrants had to fill out when applying for their US citizenship, and the perils of overt capitalism. It was shown at the Woman's Building Gallery in Los Angeles, on the same night as Maren Hassinger's performance piece *Voices*, which all of us were in.

When Ulysses moved to the Bay Area in the late 1980s, he came to see my 1991 installation *Fugitive Landing* at Capp Street Project in San Francisco. We kept up with each other's work and life, and I visited his Inglewood studio when he moved back to Los Angeles, and got to know the neighborhood. Later on, I rented a studio there for five years in a building owned by the artist Todd Gray, after Ulysses had alerted him that the building was for sale. Todd also performed in Ulysses's *Without Your Interpretation*.

There has always been a quality of caring in Ulysses's character, and he always looked out for his friends. I remember him telling me of the time his cat was ill and needed veterinary attention. He was rushing home from his teaching job, saying out loud, "please, please, make it before I get home." Today, whenever Senga and Maren are in town, we all get together for a reunion. Rudy Perez and I talk every week. All these friendships developed under the umbrella of Ulysses's far-reaching embrace, where he made room for all of us to meet and create together.

"LOOK AT WHAT I'M THINKING"
CAULEEN SMITH

I became aware of Ulysses Jenkins's work when I was a student in the Bay Area, through the Bay Area Video Coalition and at San Francisco State University, where we were shown a lot of video art. He and people like Philip Mallory Jones were stalwart figures; their presence was so vivid in the video world. I was studying experimental film, and these worlds—film and video—were pretty separate then. What I wasn't finding in the experimental film histories, I was finding in video art. This very plastic and relatively inexpensive medium lent itself to a high level of experimentation and refreshing ideas about representation that weren't codified into the standard narratives about what we were supposed to be making. Though I never had the privilege of studying with Ulysses, when I went to graduate school in Los Angeles, I met him through the artist Kira Lynn Harris, who was his partner at the time. He was unpretentious and curious about my work, treating me more like a peer than like the student I was.

His work has always been way ahead of the curve in terms of being rigorously, conceptually experimental. He was less concerned with representation than with ideas themselves—and with the medium and the material of video, which was fast, cheap, and accessible, being easy to dupe. The politics of making the work available was central to many people's practices back then. It's something that video can do, or at least could do at the time, that nothing else can.

The way Ulysses works in all these varied spaces, bringing a lot of different people together, has a California, or a West Coast, energy. It's like an absence of angst, an absence of concern for any kind of market for video art. And that allows for greater sociality in the work, which produces all this joy. At the same time, Ulysses is miraculous in his tenacity and productiveness. While others succumbed to a sort of calcification, he just kept creating and moving, maintaining an openness and generosity. His relationship to the technology and materiality of video is resistant to commercial commodification. His interest is in the material and what it will do, what it brings that you can't get any other way. I never tire of watching him perform in his videos because he's actually sending me somewhere. It's not coming from an idea of "look at me and what I represent," but rather "look at where I'm going and what I'm thinking about." He's thinking *through* video.

And then the Afrofuturism, of course, was a model for me and others who got permission from artists like Ulysses to follow through with our own ideas of what Afrofuturism could be. When I encountered Afrofuturism, I was already aware of his work and recognized right away that working with video was part of this exploration of the relationship between the body, technology, history, memory, reproduction. Those are things I inherited, or maybe appropriated, from him. I'm so happily and gratefully influenced by Ulysses Jenkins.

"One of a kind."

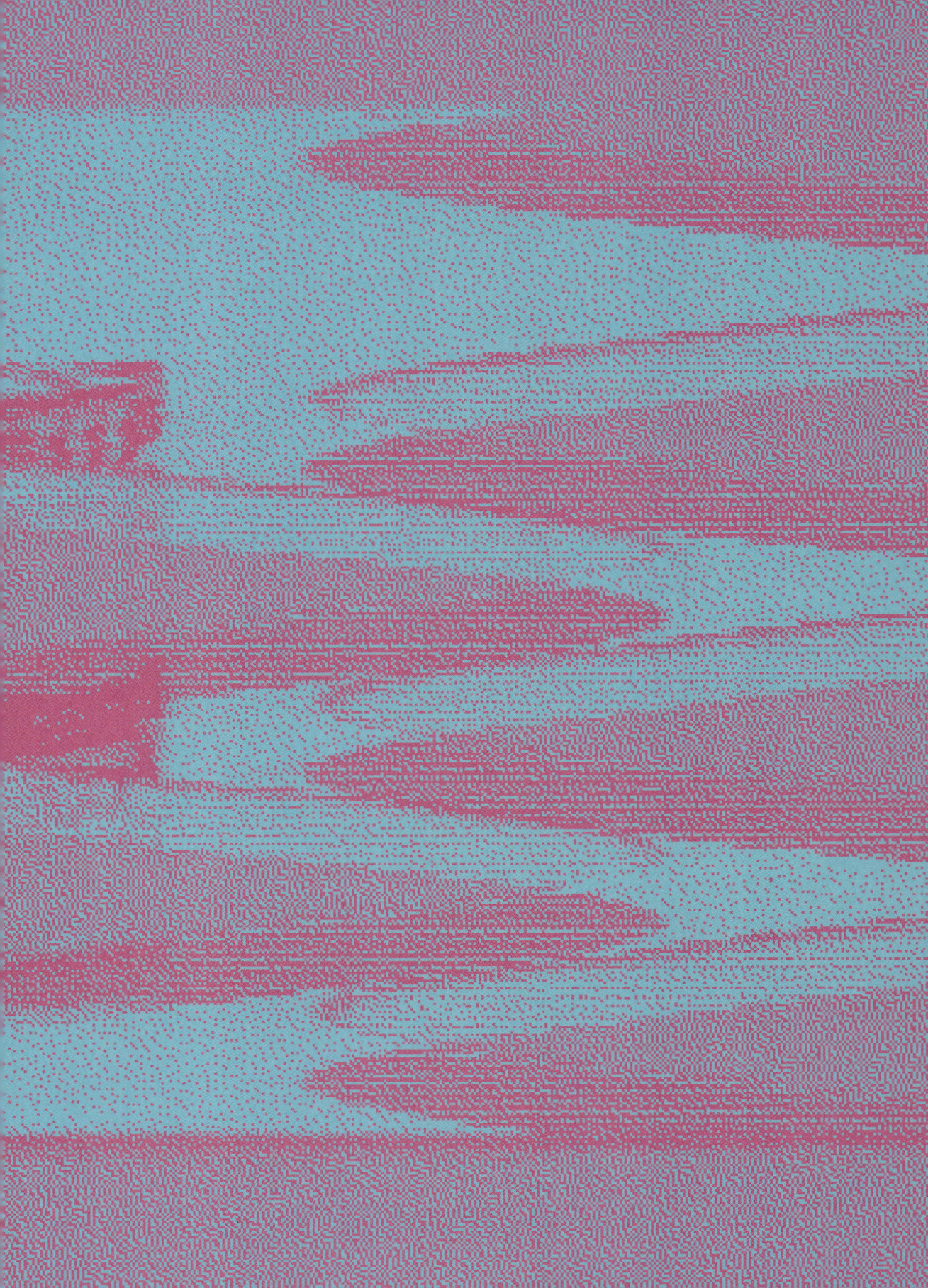

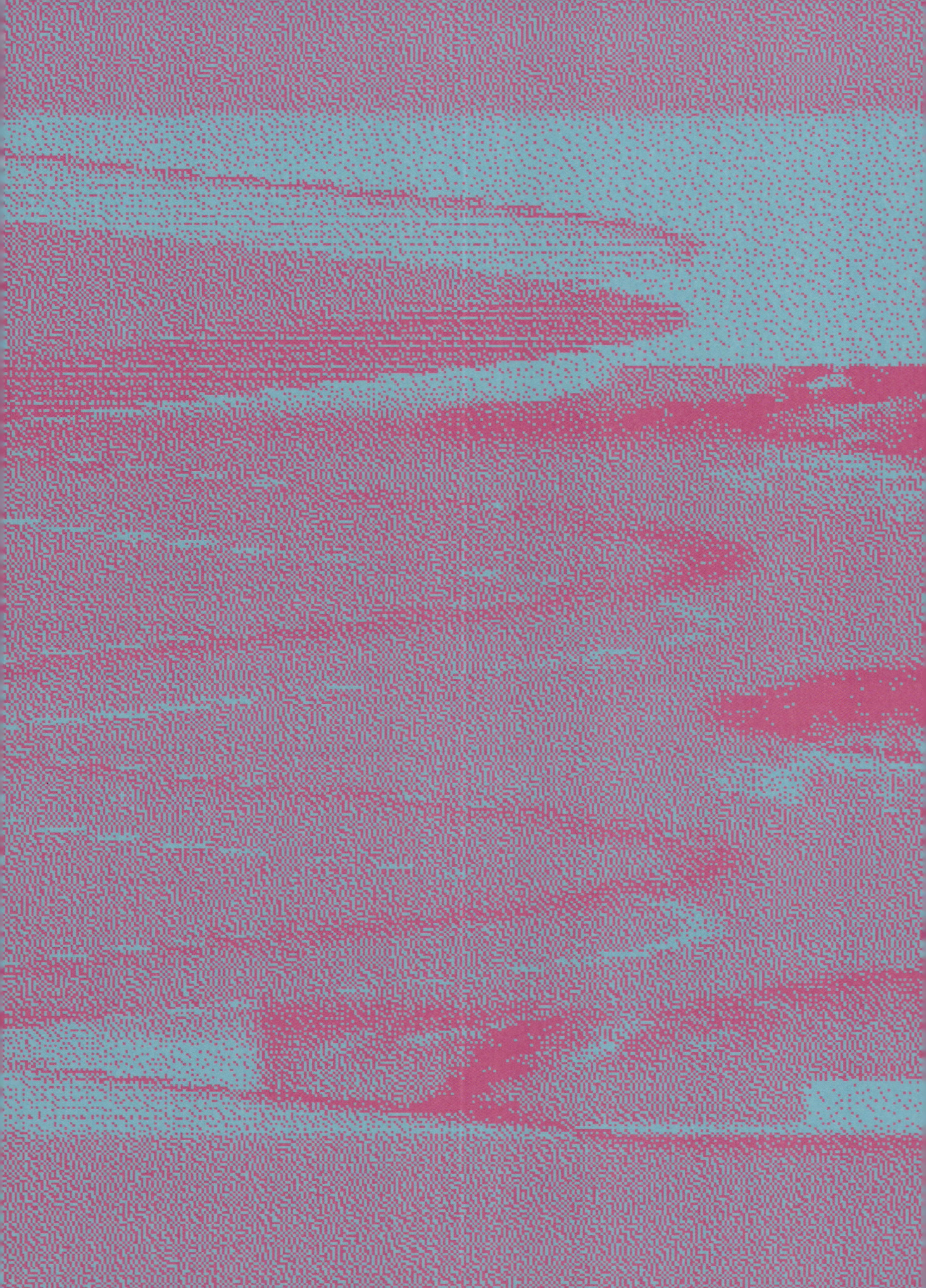

QUESTIONS BY
ERIN CHRISTOVALE AND MEG ONLI

TRANSMISSIONS: A ROUNDTABLE CONVERSATION

RESPONSES BY
GREG DE CUIR JR., MICHAEL BOYCE
GILLESPIE, CHRISSIE ILES, AND
ALESSANDRA RAENGO

QUESTION 1

Ulysses Jenkins's origins in video start during his time in Venice, California, when he was closing out his practice as a mural painter and cofounded a collective known as Video Venice News. He was in the field documenting several communities and cultural events throughout Los Angeles, including what is known to be his first video documentary, *Remnants of the Watts Festival* (1972–73, compiled 1980). Jenkins's foray into video synchs with the invention of the Portapak and a wider distribution and use of video as a format. How does the history of video art and its DIY sensibility align with Jenkins's overall practice? How does this format allow for a more democratized and inclusive space of production that ties into Jenkins's notion of multiculturalism and collectivity?

Greg de Cuir Jr.

"Back in the days when the myth of public access was being preached, I put down my paint brushes and grabbed a portapak." This is how Jenkins begins his early video documentary *Remnants of the Watts Festival*. It is not clear if the myth for him was seen in retrospect, upon the compilation of this piece in 1980, after a decade of early video art, which had two major stems: the public access documentary/journalism impulse, and the avant-garde experimental/performative impulse. Or maybe the myth was already hard-coded in the early 1970s. Either way, the idea of "access" or "action" is of interest here—the action of jettisoning traditional tools of artistic craft and picking up a new technological tool that promises a more direct, and perhaps more political, intervention into the world.

Jenkins's concern with the act of documenting can be seen in a number of his important early video works, which all deserve greater notoriety in histories of documentary. His first work, *Remnants of the Watts Festival*, is already a treasure as a document of Black culture and peoples in Los Angeles. Call it a missing link post–Watts uprisings and pre–*Killer of Sheep* (1977, dir. Charles Burnett). We might consider it a counter-history, given the more celebrated documentary film *Wattstax* (1973, dir. Mel Stuart). Jenkins deals with the interstices and the nonspectacle of shooting in Jordan Downs and Nickerson Gardens—that is, Watts proper. He documents the mundane organizational matters that engender the Watts Summer Festival and also what that festival really means as a cultural touch point for the residents of the area. As an artist, Jenkins is particularly interested in the arts and crafts exhibitions, as well as the stations for social action.

Alessandra Raengo

Jenkins's first commitment in taking up video as a medium was geared toward recording, documenting, and deploying video technology's ability to create alternative "channels," as a form of disruption of unidirectional broadcasting models. Embracing the camera as his "scalpel," as Greg suggests below, can be regarded in continuity with Jenkins's understanding of his previous painting practice, which, he said, attempted to replicate the radical interventions of Gordon Matta Clark's ana-architecture.[1]

His work embraces the aesthetic possibilities that derive from the very limitations of the medium, such as the need for in-camera editing, which, as Helen Westgeest describes, channeling Stephen Partridge's essay "Video: Incorporeal, Incorporated" (2006), "in the late 1960s drove artistic interest and experiment away from filmic conventions, such as montage, and toward the use of closed-circuit systems and instant playback." Like many other artists of his time, Jenkins embraced the new technology's intrinsic properties, including "immediacy, transmission, the 'live,' the closed-circuit, record-replay with time delay, feedback oddities, synthesizer manipulations, and synchronicity with sound."[2]

Ultimately, Jenkins adopted what Deidre Boyle has described as a "'process' video aesthetics."[3] Echoing many underground video groups in New York City that began to "explore the nature of television and portable video's potential as a medium for criticism and analysis,"[4] Jenkins said he was interested in "work in progress."[5] Although Jenkins's early documentary works (such as *Remnants of the Watts Festival*, *King David*, and *Momentous Occasions: The Spirit of Charles White*) display an interest in the brick-and-mortar definition of art, in a commitment to both identify and support spaces for Black artistic expression, he increasingly approaches video itself as one of such spaces.

As Jenkins recalled in 2008, "The work that we were doing was a school unto itself. We were putting on each other's shows."[6] Video offered both an instrument of documentation and a participant in these artists' ensembles, which at times, might include other totemic objects, such as the (rotting) dead cat, run over by a car, that Jenkins found and stored long enough to appear in the performance that opens *Dream City* (1983), to signify and reflect on the fear of "being run over by technology." Or the birthday cake Don Cherry brings onstage for Jenkins toward the end of the performative and largely improvised piece.

In *Dream City*, as Rebecca Peabody describes it, "Every two hours an artist or group took the stage for fifteen minutes; each performance was videotaped, and the recordings were then screened during the hour and forty-five minutes that elapsed before the next performance." She also notes how *Dream City* was "influenced visually and conceptually by Barbara McCullough's *Water Ritual #1* (1979)."[7] McCullough, in fact, had already documented many of the ephemeral and impromptu performances by Black artists in LA and is responsible for inspiring Jenkins's turn to ritual. *Water Ritual #1* was particularly influential, as was her 1981 video *Shopping Bag Spirits and Freeway Fetishes: Reflections on Ritual Space*, featuring David Hammons, Senga Nengudi, Maren Hassinger, and interviews with Betye Saar and Don Cherry.[8]

Michael Boyce Gillespie

Jenkins wrote in 1982: "I have composed an evolving sequence of rituals, which are in [a] constant state of metamorphosis. The rituals are concerned with social crisis and survival."[9] *Remnants of the Watts Festival* crucially documents the emergent sense of Black cultural production in the shadow of the Watts Rebellion and Jenkins's interest in the aesthetic practice of rituals. With jazz particularly in mind, there is a rich measure of jazz collectivity that resounds with the building of consciousness-raising institutions and practices devoted to enacting many of the principles of Black Power and its artistic wing, the Black Arts Movement. As Daniel Widener wrote, "The early 1960s saw increasing politicization among jazz musicians simultaneously inspired by the black freedom movement and pressed by declining sales, closing clubs, and the rise of rock and roll."[10] In this way, the documentary as an active remnant of the improvisatory conjuring embedded in these festival performances speaks to the inception of Jenkins's own practice with his Othervisions Art Band throughout his body of work. As Greg mentioned, I also began thinking a lot about Mel Stuart's *Wattstax* and the ways it does not operate strictly as a concert film. It becomes composed with a more dialogic structure with the addition of the rich contextual, more ethnographic/embedded observer sequences of the South Central communities coupled with the interstitial and abstracted chorale function of Richard Pryor. Importantly, the Wattstax concert at the LA Coliseum is a larger spin-off of the Watts Summer Festival. This spirit of a post–Watts Rebellion world making throughout Los Angeles communities of color is evident throughout much of Jenkins's early video documentaries. *District F* (1977) focuses on the attempts at desegregating public education through new redistricting initiatives. *King David* (1978) documents David Hammons's developing art practice before his pivotal move to New York City. *Momentous Occasions: The Spirit of Charles White* (1977/1982) is a stunning spotlight of White's art practice and mentorship of Black artists at Otis Art Institute (now Otis College of Art and Design). Focusing on the opening of a retrospective of his work in 1977 at Barnsdall Art Park's Los Angeles Municipal Art Gallery, the video features White and commentary from fellow artists and students past and present. This piece demonstrates the consequential role that White had in the Black arts communities of Los Angeles; as Kellie Jones notes, "White's cultural activism at the grassroots level was part of his profile; for him it was part of what constituted being an *artist*."[11] Jenkins's early documentaries offer an incredible detailing of social policy, art practices, and collectivities in part because of a technopolitics of access and circulation embedded in the video format. Also, the postproduction capacities of video informed the kind of alternative historiography concerns that would preoccupy Jenkins throughout his career.

GdC: The new myth making that he is angling toward is a narration of experience in Black Los Angeles. His early mid-length video *District F* investigates the situation at Santa Monica College and the inner-city high schools in Los Angeles that would, or should, feed the district's prospective student body. Here, for Jenkins, the act of documenting is the act of playing the role of investigative journalist. He talks to educators, administrators, parents, and others during this revealing study. One begins to understand his larger project here, even after making only two videos. Two key pieces made at this early stage of his career are *King David* and *Momentous Occasions: The Spirit of Charles White*. Both of these videos are studies of artists whose reputations tower over their cohort and also the subsequent generation of Black artists in the United States. The former is about David Hammons, and it offers long gazes at various pieces from his Spade series and body prints, while Hammons speaks on the soundtrack about his methods and beliefs. It seems that Jenkins shot this piece in the artist's studio, and as such the viewer is given an intimate visit and tour. Most likely this rare look at Hammons and his work, right at the moment when his career was rising, can be considered the first revelatory study of the artist. Charles White is likewise a rarely captured subject, and in fact was a professor and mentor to Hammons (Jenkins also studied with White at Otis). This video captures a celebrated solo exhibition for the artist, populated with other luminaries of the Black arts world, while crosscutting to White's artist talk and his lectures to a class of his students. Both of these works could be central to a meta-canon of Black artists studying the work of other Black artists. In the context of Jenkins's career, these videos were stepping-stones on the path to a full artistic expression that expanded and challenged the documentary form and tradition.

MBG: In his memoir *Doggerel Life*, Jenkins wrote, "I saw 'doggerel,' an irregular, comic and trivial verse, 'only the lowly,' as an expression encouraging humble possibilities. This loose and poor style seemed adaptable as mocking adoration, a humorous adornment for a group of artists and their activities spurned by the mainstream 'avant-garde.'"[12] In thinking about Jenkins's early practice, *Inconsequential Doggereal* (1981) is important for the ways it demonstrates an evolution and transition from his initial documentary impulse toward a more radical conception of "video-ritual" and transmission. If doggerel is a deliberately irregular poetic verse composed for comic effect, then the doggereal of Jenkins's *Inconsequential Doggereal* indeed enacts a comic tone but with deep attention to an accumulating quotidian trauma of "our repressed media unconscious."[13] The film scrutinizes the inconsequential terror that consequentially shadows and governs the everyday. The way the piece lingers and surges across trauma and the comedic reminds me of Lauren Berlant's definition of the "traumic" whereby "the beings under pressure and disturbed by what's happened around them are usually destined not to be defeated unto death but to live with the light and heavy effects of damage, still acting, being acted upon, and trying to keep things moving, which is to say, surviving."[14] At the start of *Inconsequential Doggereal* there is the artist at rest in the bath coupled with the absurdist mortality play of an artist in distress. Is the encroaching lawn mower approaching the prone Jenkins a comedic nod to Chris Burden's *Dead Man* performance (1972)? There's this frenetic attention to the mediascape, which intones rabid consumption and regulation, that keeps cycling back to Jenkins's nude repose in the bath. The film moves like a divining circuit with its ceaseless scanning and temporal interruptions of speed shifts, pauses, loops, fast forwards, and rewinds. I'm particularly struck by the extent to which it distills a 1980s Reaganomics structure of feelings as a mediatic channel of play across the galactic, the news reports on the economy, soft-core melodrama, "media indoctrination," elemental forms, and the ubiquitous escalations of the football carousing as amusement and terror. The figure of Jenkins undergoes a disarticulation bordering on a break across the film as the civility of his coffee in the bath gives way to fear and flashes of despondency. The final sequence, with Jenkins nude with the football alone in the fog, has a score that possesses the quality of a dystopian sonic trigger. After the montagic frenzy across the film, he is alone in a way that resonates as postapocalyptic. There is no progressive optimism of the dawn. There is only solitude and the mist.

Chrissie Iles

In Jenkins's hands, the Portapak camera—the latest model of the colonial technology through which the power relations of looking had been constructed since the nineteenth century—was transformed into a cosmological instrument of storytelling, world making, and self-empowerment. His transformation of the racialized social, economic, and scopic conditions of the new medium into a multicultural space of collective creativity occurred through his fusion of the electronic image with the already existing democratic technologies of music, sound, the body, and the voice. The implications of this relationality are profound, both for its expansion of the history and definition of video as a medium of fluidity and for the role of video and, more broadly, the moving image in shaping Black consciousness. In shifting the video camera away from its inscription within Western colonial concepts of technological "progress" and control to become one amongst other haptic instruments, Jenkins embedded it within a musical form, grounding the oral and visual storytelling of his early documentary projects in a collective structure of call-and-response between community members, musicians, and artists, including Jenkins himself. This dialogic exchange enacts the gathering, protecting, and storing of a collective history, memory, and identity embodied in the West African figure of the griot, at once poet, historian, singer, and musician. In his stated adoption of the griot's role across all his work, Jenkins resituates the documentary as part of a broader process of gathering and storing within and on behalf of a community. This emphasis on preserving (since Jenkins's tapes were not seen widely outside Los Angeles, the idea of their broadcast remained largely potential) both suggests a continuation of his mural painting in another form and engages the transcendental function of music and sound as memory, by which, as Servio Marín argues, the cultural seeds of a collective past, present, and future can be transported and dispersed.[15]

QUESTION 2

While attending Otis, Jenkins was in the Intermedia Department (now defunct) that bridged performance and video. One of his professors, who had a major impact on his practice, was the media arts scholar and theorist Gene Youngblood, whose seminal book *Expanded Cinema* (1970) was the first to argue

that video could be considered an art form and advocated for
new technologies at the time, such as computer art, special
effects, multimedia installations, and holography, as a way to
expand the cinematic field and consciousness. Are there ways
that you appreciate Youngblood's ideas of video as a significant influence on Jenkins's own practice?

AR: "If I am going to be part of this medium, I have to con-
textualize the black image," Jenkins has stated several times
over the years.[16] Although he acknowledged the formative
influence of Youngblood and his idea of "expanded cinema,"
he also said he did not have any models and was not in contact with the East Coast scene. His approach to the medium in
the attempt to redress overdetermined mass-media images of
Blackness charts a productive "third" way within what Greg
described as the documentary and the avant-garde impulses
in early video art, or what Andrew Uroskie has identified as
the Robert Morris/Rosalind Krauss lineage, which understood this expansion as a "post-medium" condition, insofar
as video's proximity to broadcasting threatens the modernist
tradition of understanding a medium by its "specificity," and,
on the other hand, Youngblood's idea of "expanded cinema"
as expressive of a Weltanschauung, the striving for an expansion of consciousness whose domain is life itself.[17] Jenkins
enters this lineage by originally elaborating an early mode
of "videographic criticism"—an immanent critique of mass
media's colonization of people's consciousness (the "mass"
in *Mass of Images* understood perhaps also as density and
volume), through the form that is closest to broadcast media,
i.e., video.

GdC: Youngblood first published his pioneering study
Expanded Cinema in 1970. Youngblood was Jenkins's professor (and would feature in his 1981 piece *Televiews and Cable
Radio*), and the book was likely an influence on Jenkins,
though he did not start "expanding" the form of his videos
until *Mass of Images* in 1978, which is structured in the form
of a media critique composed of a collage of images of Black
performers as Jenkins delivers a poetic-polemical monologue
about the harm caused by "years and years of TV shows" while
holding a sledgehammer and sitting in a wheelchair next to a
stack of television monitors. He wears a strange plastic shield
over his face in this short video, with his sunglasses perched
on top of it, creating almost a three-dimensional effect to his
visage. It might be that the shield represents the surface of
yet another television monitor, through which we interface
with Jenkins, and in which he is trapped in the painful representation that he claims not to relate with. This is in fact

the post-medium condition, in which you cannot extricate yourself from what Michel Foucault called the *dispositif* of the thing you would critique. Jenkins sutures himself into his subject. He is already afflicted, as evidenced by the use of a wheelchair. He is already a part of the machine. This critical notion can be seen as very much ahead of its time, either in relation to the development of video art or the expanded field of computer art and the internet, as the ultimate interface and (possibly?) the final point on the post-medium continuum.

MBG: In thinking about the possible influence of Young-blood's idea of expanded cinema on Jenkins's practice, two immediate points come to mind regarding the capacities of video: cosmic consciousness and the synesthetic. With *The Video Griots Trilogy*, composed of *Self Divination* (1989), *Mutual Native Duplex* (1990), and *The Nomadics* (1991), in particular, Jenkins enacts his own sense of these ideas in work centering on videographic rituals, the Black Atlantic, Indigeneity, visual historiography, ecomediatic critique, and speculative cartographies of culture. The sand mandala as cosmogram acts as the organizational principle of all the films in the trilogy by way of its critical meditation function, which in *The Video Griots Trilogy* context is meant to channel and incite affective and historical resonances.[18] If the griot is the embodied archive of the oral tradition, then Jenkins's video griot persona suggests the communicative capacities of the griot's role as videographic keeper of genealogies. *Self Divination* is the most historiographic-minded of the three with its focus on a man walking through Los Angeles and, by way of cross-fades to insert sequences of the American and Africanist past, across history. In *Mutual Native Duplex* there is the cross-cultural (Black and Native) animacy of historical reenactment coupled with the generatively steady score by Jenkins's Othervisions Art Band. The ancestral electronica free-jazz fusion of the band's work in all the films functions as more than mere accompaniment; it is, rather, a conduit for diasporic channeling that drives the sonic visuality and sociality inflection of the films.[19] With Tiffany Lethabo King's work in mind, *The Video Griots Trilogy* poses a richly sublime sense of Blackness and Indigeneity as a dialogic practice that might best be understood through the "intersectional frame" of the Black shoals. As King writes, "[T]he shoal functions as a site that introduces new formations, alternative grammar and vocabularies, and new analytical sites that reveal the ways that some aspects of Black and Indigenous life have always already been a site of co-constitution."[20] In this way, a significant part of Jenkins's work can be thought of as a distinctly adjacent iteration of the Black shoals ideal as a visual and expressive practice that signifies what he termed as an "indigenously Afro-American Universality."[21] Also, see Jenkins's *Bay Window* (1991) and *Being Witness: Haida* (1992). Finally, *The Nomadics* is the most Afrofuturist and/or Black speculative in its tone, with its Afro-Asiatic networking and world-making rapture. In total, the chronopoetics of the trilogy distills a perceptual and conceptual blending of one's sense of the world with the techno-orality of Jenkins as the video griot.

CI: The cinema to which Youngblood's book lends its name was perceived as a universal space rather than the racially segregated American experience that had only begun to be dismantled with the Civil Rights Act of 1964, just six years before the book was published. Whilst Jenkins was doubtless curious about Youngblood's broad metaphor of cinema as expanded consciousness, he would have been painfully aware of the troubling implications and stifling limitations of its whiteness. The presence of metaphysics, consciousness, synesthetic, nonverbal sensory perception, and cosmic technologies in his work is a manifestation of the collaborative influence, sharing, and exchange with his artist, filmmaker, and musician friends and peers, including Sun Ra and Don Cherry. Like Cherry, Jenkins's heritage is Indigenous as well as African American, and concepts such as Hopi threefold time would also have been familiar, articulated in what Michael has pointed out as the "indigenously Afro-American Universality" of his practice.

Where Jenkins's work touches on ideas explored by Youngblood, it articulates them in a deep and subtle way. Youngblood described the brain as being "like a major television studio-station" that makes videotapes of what it sees, and cites Stan VanDerBeek's "newsreel of dreams"—images creating a flow of information that permeates the unconscious.[22] Jenkins makes this cerebral communicative potential visceral and political, by what Julianna Donovan describes as composing through ritual. Jenkins's *Dream City* and *Without Your Interpretation* are empathic "ether gatherings . . . solvents of psychic and cultural sediment . . . decompositional poetics of plenum and ether, where organic, sourced, and recorded elements are fused together in dreamscapes eternally transforming in their metaphysical reverberations."[23] This open-ended fluctuation, its nonlinear pace calibrated to the gestures, breathing, speaking, and musical rhythms of the performers, deliberately enacts paramnesia, a distortion of memory that creates the illusion of remembering things experienced for the first time. This neural glitching demonstrates Arthur Jafa's observation that "despite the fact that we came with a full spectrum of incredibly rich traditions of expressivity (both material and immaterial), Black people came to be most strong in areas where we could carry out our cultural traditions in our nervous systems."[24] In this sense, one can argue that Jenkins is not manifesting Youngblood's Paleocybernetic process of universal becoming, but rather asserting what Bradford Young articulates as Black intentionality as a way of practicing new forms of Black sociality.[25]

QUESTION 3

There are some critical moments in Jenkins's early career that took place while he was studying at Santa Monica College (SMC) and at Otis. *Mass of Images* (1978) was made while he was in a class taught by John Sturgeon at SMC. *Two-Zone Transfer* (1979) was famously made with his classmates at Otis—Kerry James Marshall, Ronnie Nichols, Greg Pitts, and Roger Trammell—and was a work for which he received positive feedback from Nam June Paik, who was a visiting artist at the time. During these formative years, Jenkins continued to focus on video as a medium, but he also had access to the director of *Guess Who's Coming to Dinner* (1967), Stanley Kramer. In his manuscript *Doggerel Life*, Jenkins has cited a conversation with Kramer as influential to his understanding of the limitations that Black narratives can have in mainstream cinema.

At the same time that he was making these videos, the University of California, Los Angeles (UCLA) was having a surge of Black filmmakers entering their program in what has now been historicized as the LA Rebellion. Although not part of that filmic movement, Jenkins utilized the editing booths at UCLA to make his works and ended up becoming a close friend of the filmmaker Barbara McCullough. Does the LA Rebellion or the Hollywood film industry impact Jenkins's artwork in the 1970s and 1980s? Are there other institutions and practices that might offer an understanding of the community and/or allegiances that informed his practice?

GdC: It is hard not to read the early work of Jenkins in the context of the LA Rebellion filmmakers of the 1960s and 1970s. He was involved with the Black arts scene in Los Angeles, and likewise he did some postproduction work at UCLA and was affiliated with some of the filmmakers there. Jenkins did not come off as a cinephile, though, like the film students of this movement, and his frames of reference were drawn primarily from the visual arts world. The fact alone that he worked with half-inch video set him apart, as the filmmakers of UCLA were working with 8mm and 16mm, and probably would have looked down on the medium of video as beneath the art of cinema, or too close to broadcast television, or even too much aligned with the art world, which is probably not where those filmmakers wanted to be. Jenkins worked with his video camera in a very unassuming and unpretentious way, and this is not to say that the LA Rebellion filmmakers were superficial, but they were certainly hyperaware of the formal qualities of their work and the fact that they were making independent film art rather than mainstream commercial cinema. Of course their frames of reference were international forms of third cinema, politically engaged cinema, and they operated with the assumption that revolutionary content cannot be carried forth without revolutionary form. Jenkins on the other hand was not necessarily trying to foment revolution with his work, whether in the gallery or IRL. Ironically enough, he was using his video camera to peel back layers of Black society, to expose, rather than simply to record. In this sense Jenkins did not use his camera like a paintbrush—he did not decorate or beautify. Instead, he used his camera like a scalpel, to diagnose.

Jenkins did cite a conversation with Hollywood director Stanley Kramer that highlighted for him the limitations of Black narratives in mainstream cinema. When you come up in LA, you come up in the shadow of Hollywood, certainly if you are involved in any way with arts and culture, and for that reason alone Jenkins may not have wanted to play the suffocating industry game. Keeping context in mind, this was also the era of the pervasiveness of Blaxploitation films (in *Remnants* the festival organizer even states that the opening-night screening in their film festival was *Cleopatra Jones*). As an artist, Jenkins certainly took Hollywood and television as his targets, as seen in *Mass of Images*. The broadcast signal is what has the power to indoctrinate, according to Jenkins's work. And so the struggle for Jenkins is with the very tools of mass media, to turn them against their maker. Audre Lorde said that the master's tools will never dismantle the master's house. True indeed. But Stuart Hall proposed an oppositional position in reading dominant-hegemonic texts in television discourse (in 1973, right around the time Jenkins began his video work).[26] We might consider the act of picking up a video camera a radical position, a way not to oppose the encoding/decoding process but to jam the signal, or to hack the signal, or to emit a pirate signal. But we should also remember Jenkins's pragmatic recognition of the democratic myth of public access to media tools. It is only a side door, leading to a familiar courtyard.

AR: In keeping with Youngblood's approach to video as a means of communication, and as an essential tool within what he described as "the electronic revolution in the arts" (documented in his *Televiews and Cable Radio*), Jenkins's own work becomes increasingly focused on modes of interactive communication, beginning with his collaboration with Kit Galloway and Sherri Rabinowitz's Electronic Cafe Network, as part of the Summer Olympics Arts Festival in 1984, which connected diverse LA neighborhoods such as East LA, Little Tokyo, Korea Town, Venice, and Leimert Park, and continuing with his videophone series, from *Bay Window* (1991) to *University of California Irvine Video Performance* (1996).

In these experiments it is perhaps the concept of "art" that is being *expanded* insofar as Jenkins is interested in the specific cultural expressions coming from these diverse communities; but it is an expression that has to be stripped down—ready to be reencoded as a new, connecting signal. As he stated in 1984: "Everybody in every culture doodles."[27] In turn "doodling" might indeed be the art form most suited for these guerrilla "transmissions." In the process of attending to this "work," Jenkins makes a radical double-move: on the one hand, he is invested in demystifying and embracing technology, as a way to "be part of the future." In other words, he is attempting to install himself in the "signal." On the other hand, by leveraging communication technologies' capacity to support the sharing of art, what counts as "art" in his work becomes a very *expansive* concept: it includes performance art, spoken word, music . . . but also doodling. Indeed, the images that came through Jenkins's "transmissions" in 1984, when he participated in the Olympics Arts Festival project (which used one phone line for audio and one for video), were hung on the wall of the Electronic Cafe. This is a guerrilla/consumer version of the early "fax" technology AT&T had already introduced for commercial uses in 1965. Commercial, however, does not mean "accessible" and that's precisely the expansive politics of access that Jenkins is exploring.

Jenkins was a close friend of LA Rebellion filmmaker Barbara McCullough, who appeared in *Dream City*. He collaborated with Ben Caldwell, also studying at UCLA; he too was a close friend of McCullough's and the cinematographer for her *Water Ritual #1*. His work was highly experimental, and in *I & I: An African Allegory* (1979), he combines very different genres: experimental cinema, nonfiction reenactment, and a carefully crafted montage archival sequence. After graduating from UCLA, Caldwell also turned to alternative broadcast media from his "base" in Leimert Park. He was involved in

teleconferencing with Galloway and Rabinowitz at Electronic
Cafe in 1984, as "manager" of the Gumbo House in Leimert
Park, with Jenkins acting as "project artist."

It is certainly seductive to ponder the possibility that
this experience might have inspired Caldwell to establish
Video 333 (1985–88) in the same area and, in 1990, KAOS
network. Caldwell himself articulates his commitment to
these guerrilla broadcasting models when he writes, "Teleconferencing has the potential to bring new meaning to the
town-hall concept. . . . The possibility of generating an international network that can connect my studio in South Central
Los Angeles to other parts of the world suggests an expanded
approach to linking the ideas of community and the self-
determination of people."[28] If there is a zeitgeist Jenkins
shared with some of the LA Rebellion filmmakers, it is precisely the idea of building "lineages to come," by forging electronic signals for artists' ensembles of the future.[29]

Several of Jenkins's works appear to strive to provide
content for an unknown channel (one that has yet to be built),
by exploiting the interactive possibility of the medium. Legacy is a preoccupation only to the extent that it is a mode of
envisioning futural communities, and, in this sense, his sensibility is very similar to first-generation LA Rebellion filmmaker Larry Clark's dedication of *Passing Through* (1977) to
"musicians known and unknown."

MBG: Thinking about the relationship between Jenkins
and the LA Rebellion or his engagement with Hollywood, I
think the question of Black collectivity becomes significant.
As Huey Copeland and Naomi Beckwith write, "For cultural
practitioners of various stripes, collective practice has offered
an increasingly viable framework that defies art history's
usual emphases on the singular autonomous author and that
reframes the relationship between art's objects, makers, and
audiences."[30] For Jenkins, collectivity is evident by way of the
extensive collaborative nature of much of his work and, furthermore, his continued deliberation on the ideological con-
sequences of representation. In this way, *Two-Zone Transfer*
is especially important to consider. Engendered by the hagio-
graphic response to the death of Elvis Presley, the piece is a
1978 performance of renunciation of the erasure and rendering of Black cultural production. As Jenkins wrote, "The element of travel through time and space was used to transfer the
viewer's consciousness into a Black consciousness via a dream.
Thus the 'Two-Zones' of the title refer to the regional dichot-
omies in which we live."[31] Manifestly gesturing to phenom-
enologies, temporalities, a navigation of public transit, and
W. E. B. Du Bois's ideal of "double consciousness," the *two-*

zoneness of the piece is a restless dream about the "American Entertainment Institution" with Blackness as chronotopic state. Continuing in the same vein of *Mass of Images* with its dispute of antiblack visual culture, *Two-Zone Transfer* juxtaposes the revenant ceaselessness of blackface with the sacred and secular resistance of Black expressive culture as evidenced by a sermon and a semi-lip-synched dance to a live recording of James Brown. Greg Pitts, Kerry James Marshall, and Ronnie Nichols are the blackfaced minstrels donning blackened masks of Nixon and Ford that are the counterpoint to the holy grounding of the Black Church and the sermonic to the reverie of a James Brown reenactment. In total, the expressivity of the church and James Brown suggests an irrecuperable and nonfungible form that refuses the wholly commodifiable Blackness of minstrelsy. A part of this irrecuperable nature is a result of the interstitial nature of the reenactment as standing not in the place of James Brown but between the source and its sounding. The encounter between the deadness of the blackface and the liveness of Black performativity occurs as riveting psychohorror and a deeply intimate transmission of refusal. The video performance's thrilling unconscious (and subconscious) escapades end with its own call to WAKE UP: "You know all I've ever wanted was to be able to be myself and be good at what I do. But I've been confused and abused ... sidetracked by many things, but after a dream like that, I know I've got direction and I know what I'm up against."

CI: Jenkins's video and performance works of the early 1980s are inextricably linked to what came to be known as the LA Rebellion through two of its second-wave filmmakers, Barbara McCullough and Julie Dash, and their films *Shopping Bag Spirits and Freeway Fetishes: Reflections on Ritual Space* (1981) and *Praise House* (1991). Jenkins's videos *Dream City* and *Without Your Interpretation* are conjoined with these two films through a shared collective enactment of ritual, performed through improvisations of dance, poetry, music, song, gesture, storytelling, and ancestrally charged ceremonial actions.

"Solidified as divinations," as Julianna Donovan describes, these "assemblies of shrine, altar, love song, and hymn [that] are the physical byproducts of attuned acts" resonate as sites of healing.[32] Made in and around the rubble of rebellion in the still largely unrebuilt neighborhood of Watts, their textures and surfaces emanate an affect of its sacred detritus—"dirt, dust, ruin, water, sand, and smoke" that speaks of both decomposition and a fluid evolving.[33] As Donovan argues, in both Jenkins's and McCullough's works, the nuanced light, saturated colors, dissolves, and solarized

abstractions use blurriness and disorientation to induce a
kind of lucid dreaming in the viewer that attunes them to an
alternative world making that overwrites white readings of
Blackness as illegible, and reveals them to be illiterate. This
metaphysical poetics of the political also belies a psychic
exhaustion that the empathic togetherness and solidarity
between the artists, musicians, and performers in this group
of films seeks to heal.

QUESTION 4

In the early 1990s, shortly after Jenkins moved to the Bay
Area to continue to pursue video and performance work,
he noted in an artist statement that "the nature of my work
represents the premises of new-myth making, in regarding
the African-American experience as a universal component
to the world community. . . . I have utilized the storytelling
genre of the griot, which is the keeper of the cultural myths
and histories of a community, in African societies."[34] It is clear
from this statement that it is important for Jenkins to assert
the value of Black spectatorship as a way to capture cultur-
ally and socially diverse communities, lifestyles, and happenings. Is Jenkins's practice distinguished from and/or does it
intersect with the ongoing history of Black-owned and/or
Black-produced news media, public access programming, and
documentation?

AR: William Greaves, too, might have had a desire to
send "transmissions" but, differently from Jenkins, when he
arrived at *Black Journal*, he was already experienced in a wide
range of media forms—theater, film, television, radio, and,
importantly, the documentary genre—both as a performer
and behind the camera. Jenkins, on the other hand, developed his skills in a range of art forms, in response to what
he understood to be the needs of his video art practice: ini-
tially appearing as one of the main performers—mostly in the
nude, as a way to seize control of what he had experienced as
the default approach to images of Black subjects as inherently
comedic—he later contributed as musician, singer, and even
dancer.[35]
       Produced and broadcast by NET, *Black Journal* had to
abide by specific formats even when it was under Greaves's
editorial control. The program was concerned less with formal innovation than with allowing Black people to voice their
issues and bringing media attention to Black issues as seen

and understood by Black people. While their goals might have been similar, Jenkins's embracing of communication technologies as future-building tools appears stronger than Greaves's. At a formal level, Jenkins is also more concerned with an immanent videographic criticism of media images and the broadcasting communications model insofar as the sustainability of his "transmissions" hinges upon the creation of alternative channels.

One such channel might be coming from outer space, so to speak, as when, in *Planet X* (2006), Jenkins reads Hurricane Katrina as the outcome of what Sun Ra, on the radio show *Morning Becomes Eclectic* in the 1980s, had described as an event that was going to force Black people to recognize their circumstances and face the higher Being. Here again, Jenkins builds on what Michael has described as "cosmic consciousness" toward an even more pronounced Afrofuturist perspective than in the earlier work, one that he sees as entangled with forms of Black spirituality. Jenkins extends Sun Ra's humming at the end of the *Morning Becomes Eclectic* clip, places it on a loop, and deliberately renders it as a church hymn, while on the music track Jenkins's Othervisions Art Band strives to reproduce Sun Ra's speculative music.

CI: In 1971 Radical Software, a video activist magazine devoted to the cybernetic televisual environment, published a letter to the editors from Eldridge Cleaver, the Black Panther Party's minister of information, who wrote from Algeria:

> The International Section of the Black Panther Party has begun a video tape program to be directed to the United States and Europe on a regular basis to cover the spectrum of the international anti-imperialist revolutionary movement. We need much more equipment and material than we have accumulated so far, in order to make the best use of this revolutionary communications medium. Now we are in the process of building up a tape library for information, research, and distribution purposes. We would sincerely appreciate having some of the tapes you have announced in the RADICAL SOFTWARE paper. ... [W]e really need them and you can be certain that they will be put to fantastic use.... [W]e can then send you copies of our tapes in exchange. So far, we have produced all of six tapes here and we are already getting political repercussions. Time is of the essence, the faster we get them the faster we can make more powerful propaganda for the people's revolution around the world."[36]

Cleaver's letter reflects the fractured Black media landscape in America in the early 1970s, and the gap between radical left experiments with public access and broadcast TV. *Black Journal*, a television program born out of the second wave of uprisings following the death of Martin Luther King Jr., produced a rigorous reporting under the direction of Greaves, including extensive coverage of the Black Panthers and international, pan-African issues, but had lost its public and private funding and was in decline. WGBH's *Say Brother* (now *Basic Black*), the station's longest-running Black current affairs TV show, and other Black TV stations around the country (but not in Los Angeles) were more mainstream. Black video artists such as Jenkins were rare. Cleaver's request for videotapes by Videofreex and other white video activists reflects the lack of resources, access, and agency engendered by the Panthers' aggressive marginalization by the authorities.

Twenty-five years later, the myriad platforms made accessible by the internet, smartphones, and social media have enabled everyone, from artists to the government, to bypass television altogether, now reconfigured as a poisoned chalice of potentiality that both liberates and doubles down on normativity and algorhythmic state and corporate control. Within this fractious technological climate, Kahlil Joseph's *BLKNWS* takes on the mantle of Jenkins's utopian vision of Black media spectatorship and ownership, grounded in place. Based in South Los Angeles, it disperses its two-channel live feed globally, at an internet-paced consciousness but strictly off-line, rigorously avoiding all social media, to Black-owned businesses, medical centers, high schools, and other sites of community, as well as to museums and other art world spaces, including the Underground Museum. Its improvisational form demonstrates Joseph's observation that "Black people have never had a reliable news source; after Juneteenth, enslaved Black people didn't know they'd been freed. Black people get their news from music, behind closed doors, conversations, how people dress. There's an experimental nature to the Black being."[37]

QUESTION 5

In the mid-1980s Jenkins met Kit Galloway and Sherri Rabinowitz, who founded Electronic Cafe, a community-oriented art, technology, multimedia telecommunications, and cross-cultural communications network that introduced platforms such as videoconferencing and real-time collaborative telewriting and shared-screen drawing; he participated in their 1984 Summer Olympics Arts Festival project. Jenkins then went on to incorporate various forms of digital interventions and telecommunications in his work, including *Z-Grass* (1983) and his videophone performance for *Documenta 9* (1992). How does Jenkins's own idea of expanded cinema disrupt the infrastructure of broadcasting? How does his integration of early digital technology pave the way for or signal the work to come?

GdC: We might say that Jenkins is a pioneering Black video artist. There were not many like him on the scene in Los Angeles in the early 1970s, who had access to video equipment and the artistic pedigree to do something substantial with it. This was the era of activist video collectives, who used the medium to disrupt and comment on the commercial flow of broadcast content and produce studies of the status quo in art, culture, and society. Jenkins was involved in Electronic Cafe, and he was involved in group work through his music, but he operated more regularly as a solo artist. As he mentioned in one of his video interviews, when he was an arts student he was often asked by his peers why he was interested in making work about Black subjects and cultures. It was not considered to be either profitable or relevant or understandable then in the context of an arts education and its resulting professionalization. That might lend an understanding as to how far ahead of his time he was. As he has stated, there were no models to follow.

Jenkins has actually become the model. His influence can be felt in the video works of Marlon Riggs, who shared with him a deep engagement with and concern for Black communities, and who also used the medium of video to comment and critique, to create oppositional positions. Riggs, though, was situated more firmly in a televisual mode of discourse, even a public access field, much more than art world terrain. Jenkins himself moved very fluidly, from documentary modes to performative experiments to abstract expressions. It may be that his true legacy is his versatility, his cross-disciplinary nature. Probably the young artist that fits best in the lineage of Jenkins is Martine Syms. Not just because Syms is an LA artist straddling multiple disciplines, but because of the way she uses the medium of video as a critical tool to engage with mass-media representations. She carries the legacy of Jenkins into the contemporary moment.

What remains, other than to properly historicize Jenkins and his significance on the field of what was called "intermedia arts" when he himself was a student? That, and also to bring his legacy into the present moment, not to freeze it or to fix it in time, but to renew and extend its critical dispositions and formal innovations. Ulysses is of course a very mythical name, and the historical figure it derives from was known for his intellectual brilliance, his guile, and his versatility. That sounds about right for the modern-day iteration we are studying and celebrating here.

AR: On June 27 and 28, 2020, Arthur Jafa's *Love Is the Message, The Message Is Death* streamed live for forty-eight hours, courtesy of the thirteen institutions that had purchased it. The notorious and groundbreaking piece had not originally been made for the art world and was destined to be uploaded to YouTube had Kahlil Joseph not intervened to persuade Jafa that this was, indeed, an art object. Unknowingly, Jafa had perhaps put together a "transmission," i.e., he had made work for a "black channel to come." That channel, in Joseph's interpretation, might be *BLKNWS*.

If *Love Is the Message* and *BLKNWS* are instantiations of a "black channel to come," then Jenkins's oeuvre can be regarded as the prehistory of this moment. Perhaps, upon his shift from muralism to video art, that is what Jenkins had been trying to do all along: to send "transmissions." The medium of video also afforded him an opportunity to work on communication channels (the videophone videos) and, in a futural manner, to participate in alternative myth making (*The Video Griots Trilogy*) by proactively inventing new rituals and recording them for posterity. Yet in his work recording and transmitting coexist in a productive tension with the liveness and improvisatory qualities of performance art.

In the process of putting together "transmissions" for channels (and lineages) to come, Jenkins's productive confluence of performance art and recording technologies poses crucial questions for performance studies' grappling with the ontology of "performance," in the interplay between liveness, repetition, and recording.[38] His "black technopoetics" (as Louis Chude-Sokei might describe it), tethered between repetition (ritual's ontological ground) and improvisation (building on the liveness of performative gestures and of the medium itself), was particularly *expansive* and incorporated the "phatic" elements of oral mediated communication as part of his own art (the recurrence of "Can you hear me? Can you see me?" in the videophone works).[39]

So perhaps it is Joseph's *BLKNWS* that most powerfully resonates with what Jenkins's "transmissions" were trying to achieve, while maintaining a commitment to an ensemblic practice. Elsewhere, I have argued that under the ruse of the "news" genre, *BLKNWS* embraces the Blackness of social media platforms,[40] while indexing its commitment to the present-tense temporality of news media. Yet, on another level, in *BLKNWS* Black digitality is only channeling perhaps more explicit ways already "compressed, reproduced, ripped, remixed" Black modes of being and, especially for Joseph's and Jafa's recent work, a specific type of practice that foregrounds its own ensemblic process.[41] The recalcitrant "news anchors" who appear in *BLKNWS* are actors, artists, and curators from Joseph's circle of friends and interlocutors, or, more precisely, his "ensemble."[42] As a (structurally un)finished work, and similarly to Jenkins's own work, *BLKNWS* adopts the "process aesthetics" of early video art, offering itself up as a ritualized performance that is also a "happening," a creative gathering in the "now."

MBG: With the legacy of Jenkins's practice of and attention to mediatic channels, intermediality, performance, and the meaning making of visual culture in mind, I've been thinking about his work in relation to Terence Nance's *Random Acts of Flyness* (HBO, 2018). I'm especially thinking of Jenkins's *Secrecy: Help Me to Understand* (1995) and his statement that "the intent of the work is to examine how discrimination is ritualized in the media.[43] *Secrecy* distills this ritualization through a decoding of the media's conception of Blackness. The *Random Acts* series shares with Jenkins a spirited sense of this ritualization with an expansive focus on channel surfing, phantom programming, abrupt platform shifts, collaboration/collectivity as production practice, the image economy, and transmissions. Nance's staging of the variety/anthology show conceit is a consistently challenging and insightful enactment of Blackness as an exquisite refusal and recoding adjacent to Jenkins's own practice: "*Random Acts*, through its multidimensional depictions of blackness and disruptions of cinematic coherence, embodies a direct response to essentializing, taxonomical construal of Black visual culture."[44] Furthermore, work such as Sondra Perry's *IT'S IN THE GAME '17 or Mirror Gag for Vitrine and Projection* (2017), American Artist's *Blue Life Seminar* (2019), and Rosa-Uddoh Judoh's *Black Poirot* (2018) each has a rigorous essay film quality reminiscent of the fantastical devising of Jenkins's video work to center Blackness as a formal practice, cultural ideal, and historiographic principle. Each, as transmission, is emboldened and enlivened by a distinct measure of doggerel decomposition. Across Perry's examination of "the conditions of ownership, self-possession, and subjecthood" to American Artist's computer-animated dispute of "blue life" and the wages of police violence to Judoh's investigation of the mediatic narratives of nationhood through a disobedient modeling and manufacturing of a Hercule Poirot mystery, these works echo notes of dispossession and negotiations with power that are distilled through and by a mediatic circuit.[45]

CI: If broadcasting is interpreted through its pre-technological definition as the scattering of seeds, it could be considered an extended form of call-and-response. The disruptions, refusals, and transformations in Jenkins's early video and performance works can be traced in moving-image installations reverberating into the present as a form of echo-location. In Diamond Stingily's *How Did He Die?* (2016), the artist extracts a segment from Bess Lomax Hawes's black-and-white anthropological film *Pizza Pizza Daddy-O* (1967), documenting the singing games played by a group of fourth-grade Black girls in a school playground in Watts. Stingily disrupts the colonial camera's taxonomic observation by acting out the role of the griot, reclaiming its recording of community history as an act of reparative gathering and storing, projecting the reedited film large, behind a chain-link fence, slowed down and slightly out of focus, in a haptic blurring that signals repossession. Stingily's rescued segment addresses Black trauma in the present by invoking its past corporeal internalization in Watts by its children, who stand in a circle, calling back and forth: "My father died" / "How did he die?" / "He died like this." With each chorused response, the circle acts out their relatives' imagined fate, in a collectively intuited performance of bodily and social death, sung as doggerel.

Disrupting the infrastructure of broadcasting, a utopian idea in Youngblood's and Jenkins's time, becomes more tangible as a strategy manifested in what Legacy Russell terms the "glitch."[46] Works such as Devin Kenny's *Not This* (2018) use this refusal to address the media's role in amplifying an assumed criminality in Blackness. Images of police brutality toward young Black men are blurred into an abstract scrolling field of pink and purple light, enacting a form of sousveillance. Its fluid shape evokes the movement of an electronic recording signal, as though visualizing the video's musical soundtrack, composed by Kenny in collaboration with Betty Shelby, Brian Encinia, Jason Stockley, Jeronimo Yanez, and Peter Liang.

The political metaphysics of Jenkins's affective surfaces can also be traced in a section of Ja'Tovia Gary's video *An Ecstatic Experience* (2015), where blurred colors and hand-drawn patterns are overlaid onto archival footage of the playwright and civil rights activist Ruby Dee, bathing her in luminous light as she narrates the story of Fannie Moore's enslaved mother's ecstatic call for freedom. Gary's ritual space of invocation echoes the shared disruptive communality of Jenkins, McCullough, and Dash, extending it across time and space.

1   Ulysses Jenkins interviewed by Kellie Jones, "African American Avant-Gardes, 1965–1990," January 15–16, 2008, Getty Research Institute Oral History, https://primo.getty .edu/permalink/f/19q6gmb/GETTY_ROSETTAIE814441. Also see Mark Wigley, "Anarchitectures: The Forensics of Explanation," *Log* 15 (2009): 121–36; and Éric Alliez, "Gordon Matta-Clark: 'Somewhere Outside the Law,'" *Journal of Visual Culture* 15, no. 3 (2016): 317–33, translated by Robin Mackay.

2   Partridge paraphrased by Helen Westgeest, *Video Art Theory: A Comparative Approach* (Malden, MA: John Wiley & Sons, 2015), 20.

3   Deirdre Boyle, "A Brief History of American Documentary Video," in *Illuminating Video: An Essential Guide to Video Art*, ed. Doug Hall and Sally Jo Fifer (New York: Aperture, in association with Bay Area Video Coalition, 1990), 68.

4   Boyle, "A Brief History of American Documentary Video," 68.

5   Good examples of "process aesthetics" in Jenkins's work are *Inconsequential Doggereal* (1981) and *Dream City* (1983).

6   Jenkins interview, Getty Research Institute, 2008.

7   Rebecca Peabody, "African American Avant-Gardes, 1965–1990," *Getty Research Journal* 1 (2009): 214.

8   *Shopping Bag Spirits and Freeway Fetishes* was shot on video, which McCullough had learned more formally than Jenkins by taking classes with Shirley Clark at UCLA.

9   Ulysses Jenkins, "The Nature of Doggerel," 1985 (see page 18).

10   Daniel Widener, *Black Arts West: Culture and Struggle in Postwar Los Angeles* (Durham: Duke University Press, 2010), 128.

11   Kellie Jones, *South of Pico: African American Artists in Los Angeles in the 1960s and 1970s* (Durham: Duke University Press, 2017), 37.

12   Ulysses Jenkins, *Doggerel Life: Stories of a Los Angeles Griot* (Los Angeles: Oreste, 2018), 6.

13   Ulysses Jenkins, *Inconsequential Doggereal* treatment, June 21, 1982. Artist's archive, Los Angeles.

14   Lauren Berlant, "The Traumic: On BoJack Horseman's 'Good Damage,'" Post45, November 22, 2020, https://post45.org/2020/11/the-traumic-on-bojack -horsemans-good-damage/.

15   Servio Marín, "Spatial Narrative: Aural and Visual Construction in the Musical Narrative of Minority Discourse," *Studies in American Indian Literatures* 7, no.4 (Winter 1995): 11.

16   "Broadcasting: Transmission with Ulysses Jenkins and Sondra Perry," at ICA, University of Pennsylvania, Philadelphia, PhillyCam, uploaded April 2, 2018, https:// www.youtube.com/watch?v=6vZreV9FIXU.

17   Andrew V. Uroskie, *Between the Black Box and the White Cube: Expanded Cinema and Postwar Art* (Chicago: University of Chicago Press, 2014), 8–9.

18   The sand paintings in all three videos were done by Matthew Thomas.

19   I am thinking here of the improvisatory liturgy of the band as demonstrated in *Peace and Anwar Sadat* (1985).

20   Tiffany Lethabo King, *The Black Shoals: Offshore Formations of Black and Native Studies* (Durham: Duke University Press, 2019), 28

21   Ulysses Jenkins, "Statement of Genre," December 6, 1982. Artist's archive, Los Angeles.

22   Gene Youngblood, *Expanded Cinema: Fiftieth Anniversary Edition* (New York: Fordham University Press, 2020), 27–28, 387.

23   Julianna Donovan, "A Breathing Body in Ritual Ecology: The Aesthetics and Metaphysics of Black Experimental Film," *Film Studies Honors Papers* 8 (2020): 59, 64, https:// digitalcommons.conncoll.edu/filmhp/8.

24   Arthur Jafa and Tina M. Campt, "Love Is the Message, The Plan Is Death," *e-flux Journal*, no. 81 (April 2017), https://www.e-flux.com/journal/81/126451/love-is-the -message-the-plan-is-death/.

25   "Bradford Young," artist page, Liquid Blackness, https://liquidblackness.com/bradford-young.

26   Stuart Hall, "Encoding and Decoding in the Television Discourse," paper for the Centre for Cultural Studies, University of Birmingham, 1973.

27   Jenkins in a videotape about the Electronic Cafe Network Olympics Arts Festival project, 1984 (broadcaster unknown). Artist's archive, Los Angeles.

28   Ben Caldwell, "KAOS at Ground Zero: Video, Teleconferencing and Community Networks," *Leonardo* 26, no. 5 (1993): 422.

29   The idea of "lineages to come" is an operative concept within the work of the *liquid blackness* research group (Georgia State University, beginning in 2013), insofar as it offers a framework to retrace lineages of Black artists who were consciously making art for future generations to build upon. See Alessandra Raengo and Lauren McLeod Cramer, eds., "The Unruly Archives of Black Music Videos," *Journal of Cinema and Media Studies* 59, no. 2 (2020): 138–44.

30   Huey Copeland and Naomi Beckwith, "Black Collectivities: An Introduction," *Nka: Journal of Contemporary African Art* 34 (Spring 2014): 5.

31   Ulysses Jenkins, "*Two-Zone Transfer*: A Performance," n.d. Artist's archive, Los Angeles.

32   Donovan, "A Breathing Body in Ritual Ecology," 26.

33   Donovan, 18.

34   Ulysses Jenkins, "Artist Statement," n.d. Artist's archive, Los Angeles.

35   Jenkins's *Notions of Freedom* (2007), about the history of jazz, is dedicated to Miles Davis and uses motion-capture technology to render two dancing bodies—one had been a dancer for Sun Ra's ensemble and the other is Jenkins.

36   Eldrige Cleaver, letter to the editors, March 16, 1971, *Radical Software* 1, no. 4 (1971): 30, https://www.radical-software.org/volume1nr4/pdf/VOLUME1NR4_0032.pdf. The specific videotapes that Cleaver requested included recordings of Apollo 10, 11, and 13; the post–Kent State peace demonstration in Washington, DC; news coverage of the Kent State killings and Cambodia protest demonstrations; Nixon's State of the Union address; "the party the president threw for the astronauts"; a report on the new home computer; a video documenting the exhibition *Vision and Television* at the Rose Art Museum made by the video collective Videofreex, and the New York State Cable Access TV operators' convention.

37   Kahlil Joseph in conversation with Chrissie Iles, July 11, 2019.

38   Soyica Diggs Colbert, Douglas A. Jones Jr., and Shane Vogel, eds., *Race and Performance after Repetition* (Durham: Duke University Press, 2020).

39   Louis Chude-Sokei, *The Sound of Culture: Diaspora and Black Technopoetics* (Middletown, CT: Wesleyan University Press, 2015).

40   Alessandra Raengo, "The Heat Is On: Preliminary Reflections on Kahlil Joseph's *BLKNWS*," *Refract: An Open Access Journal of Visual Studies* 2, no. 1 (Fall 2019): 31–44. See also Aria Dean, "Poor Meme, Rich Meme," *Real Life*, July 25, 2016, https://reallifemag.com/poor-meme-rich-meme/.

41   As Aria Dean puts it, "We have long been digital, 'compressed, reproduced, ripped, remixed' across time and space. For blackness, the meme could be a way of further

figuring an existence that spills over the bounds of the body, a homecoming into our homelessness." Dean, "Poor Meme, Rich Meme."

42   Among those who appear are collector A. C. Hudgins, artist Henry Taylor, correspondent and comedian Alzo Slade, actress Amandla Stenberg, and curator Helen Molesworth. "Ensemble" is the way Fred Moten theorizes a relationship between the part and the whole, the soloist and the group, whose model is the cooperative and improvisational relationship between musicians in the jazz ensemble, which he sees as constantly experimenting with forms of sociality, as well as lawmaking and lawbreaking at the level of form. See Stefano Harney and Fred Moten, *The Undercommons: Fugitive Planning and Black Study* (Wivenhoe, UK: Minor Compositions, 2013). See also Moten's elaboration on the jurigenerativity of Blackness in Arthur Jafa's film *Dreams are colder than Death* (2013).

43   Ulysses Jenkins, "Video Statement: *Secrecy: Help Me to Understand*," 1994. Artist's archive, Los Angeles.

44   Jorge Cotte, "Radical Acts of Flyness," *Los Angeles Review of Books*, November 1, 2018, https://lareviewofbooks .org/article/radical-acts-flyness/.

45   See Shelleen Greene, "*IT'S IN THE GAME '17 or Mirror Gag for Vitrine and Projection*," in *Black One Shot 11.4*, ed. Lisa Uddin and Michael Boyce Gillespie, *ASAP/J*, July 6, 2020, https://asapjournal.com/b-o-s-11-4-its-in-the-game -17-or-mirror-gag-for-vitrine-and-projection-shelleen -greene/; and Nijah Cunninghan and Tiana Reid, "Blue Life," *New Inquiry*, September 24, 2018, https://thenewinquiry .com/blue-life/.

46   Legacy Russell's "glitch feminism" work will be of great use for the Ulysses Jenkins scholarship to come. See Russell, *Glitch Feminism: A Manifesto* (London: Verso Books, 2020).

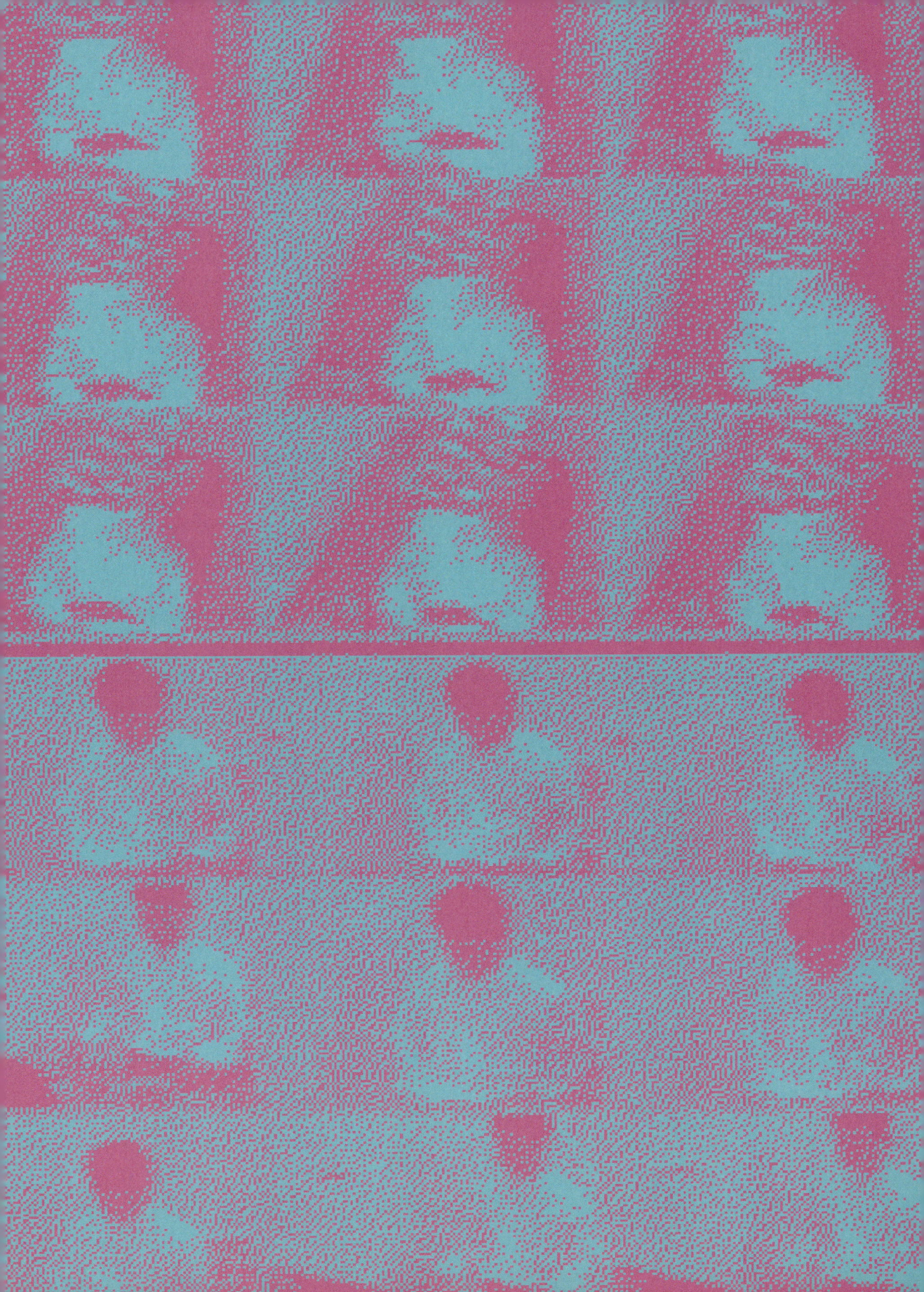

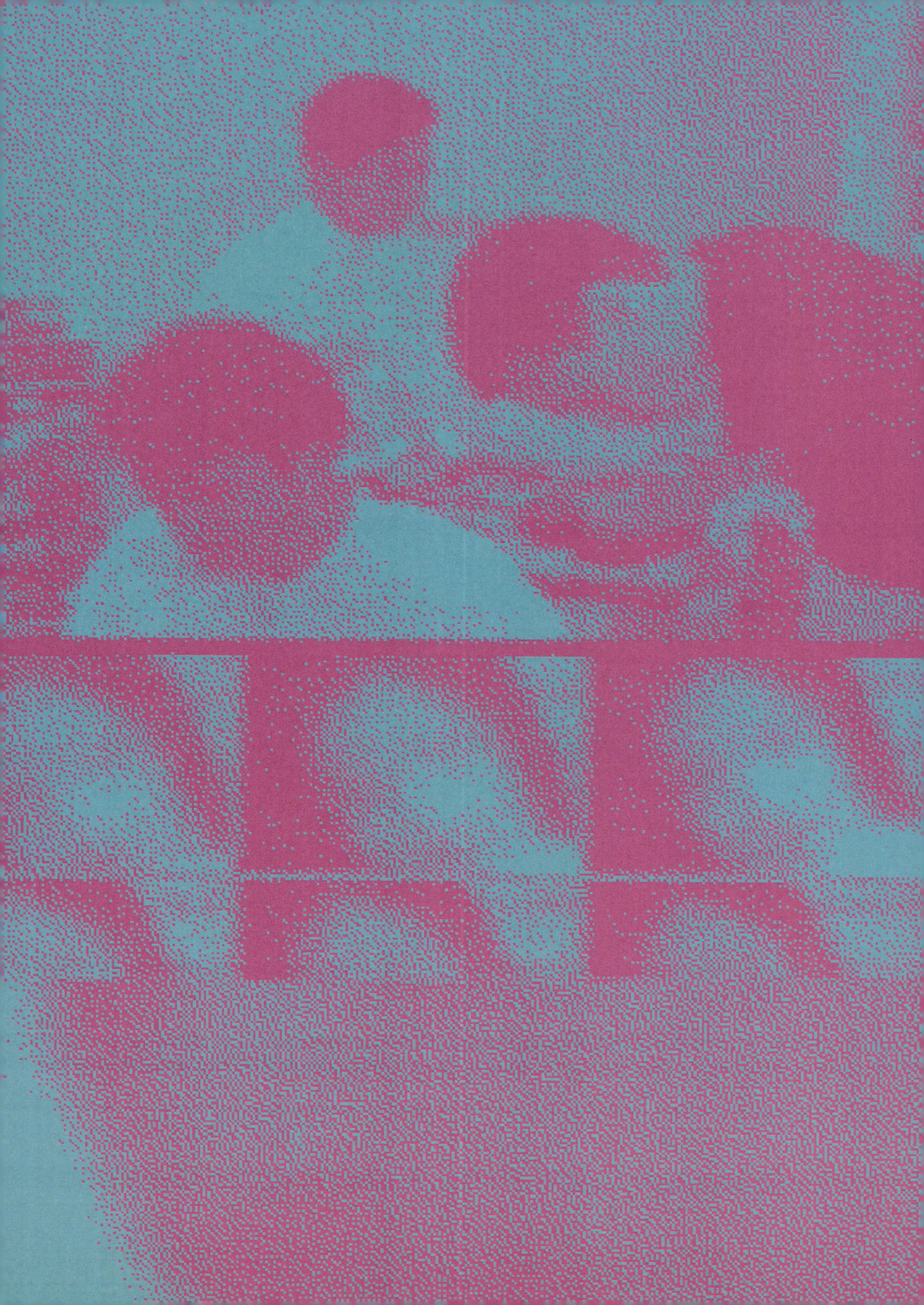

CHRONOLOGY

COMPILED BY LIV PORTE

EARLY 1940S

During WWII, Los Angeles is a central location for aircraft, ammunition, ships, and war supply production. The growth of this industry catalyzed an increase in the city's population, including African Americans migrating from rural Southern States.

1946

September 19: Ulysses Jenkins is born in Los Angeles.

1961

Jenkins begins to study art at Hamilton High School, in Westside Los Angeles.

1964

Jenkins leaves Los Angeles to pursue a painting and drawing degree at Southern University in Baton Rouge, Louisiana.

1965

August 11: In Watts, Marquette Frye, a twenty-one-year-old Black man, is pulled over and arrested for suspected drunk driving by a white California Highway Patrol Officer, Lee W. Minikus. Also arrested are Marquette's step-brother Ronald Riggs Frye, who was in the car, and his mother, Rena Price, who arrived on the scene. Both are arrested for attempting to break up the fight between Marquette Frye and arresting officers. A group of a few hundred concerned onlookers witness the confrontation and arrests. This altercation cements the crowd's anxieties and tensions based on years of police misconduct and discrimination against Black communities. The resulting uprisings would last six days and lead to thirty-four deaths and $40 million in property damage.

1966

The Watts Festival is founded by a coalition of antipoverty and Black nationalist groups to celebrate Black culture and heritage in the Watts neighborhood, and the diaspora at large. This festival is held each year on the anniversary of the Watts uprisings.

The brothers and artists Alonzo and Dale Davis open Brockman Gallery in South Central LA, one of the first Black-owned galleries in the city.

1967

Sony releases the first Portapak system, a self-contained battery-powered analog recording system, named the Sony DV-2400 Video Rover. The Portapak made it possible for an individual to shoot and record video without a large crew. Though a revolutionary piece of mobile recording equipment, it was limited in its ability to capture footage in uncontrollable light conditions and required the artist to walk to the camera to end the film, an aspect of production that became characteristic of 1970s video works.

August 13: Jenkins attends his first live concert, the James Brown Review at Cheetah in Santa Monica, California. Brown will be an influence on the artist throughout his career, with his music appearing in Jenkins's early performance and video *Two-Zone Transfer* (1979)

1969

Jenkins receives his BA from Southern University in Baton Rouge and returns to Los Angeles. He applies for a janitor position in a gallery on La Cienega Boulevard and exhibits a few paintings at Saint Paul's Catholic Church. He works as a display artist for the department store May Co.

1970

Jenkins works as a counselor for nondelinquent youth for the Los Angeles County Probation Department from 1970 to 1972, employing his art-making background as part of his approach to therapy.

1971

The nonprofit Electronic Arts Intermix (EAI) is founded in New York by the art dealer Howard Wise to support innovative artists working in video. These efforts include hosting festivals to exhibit contemporary videos and direct financial support for the development of advanced image-processing tools such as Eric Siegel's synthesizer and colorizer.

March 31: The director Melvin Van Peebles releases his landmark film *Sweet Sweetback's Baadasssss Song*. The work will have a significant influence on many creatives, including a young Jenkins.

1972

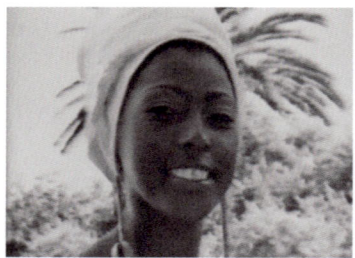

Remnants of the Watts Festival, 1972–73, compiled 1980, 55:44 min.

Jenkins paints *Rat Trap* along the side of a building in Venice, California. Of the mural, which is no longer standing, Jenkins has said, "The Rat Trap was my statement about how big money controls everything."

He attends a video production workshop held on Venice Beach, on the recommendation of the artist Michael Zingale.

Jenkins records *Remnants of the Watts Festival,* produced by the media collective that Jenkins cofounded, Video Venice News. The work is completed in 1980.

1973

Jenkins begins using public and cable access stations to disseminate videos recorded with Video Venice News, including *Remnants of the Watts Festival* and *Will Venice Survive.*

He applies and is accepted into Otis Art Institute's MFA program, but defers because of lack of financial support.

May 29: Tom Bradley is elected as the first Black mayor of Los Angeles.

1974

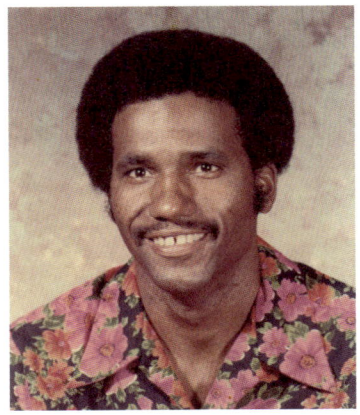

Ulysses Jenkins

September: Jenkins relocates to Hawaii with girlfriend Victoria "Pippi" Scott. Splitting his time between islands, he works as a substitute English teacher at Kelakeshe Elementary and manages the Kailua Bay Inn.

The Long Beach Museum of Art debuts a permanent video program under the vision of the former director of the museum Jan E. Adlmann. The curator David Ross is hired to steward the program.

1975

Jenkins returns to Los Angeles from Hawaii.

He is invited by the artist Judy Baca to work on *The Great Wall of Los Angeles,* a half-mile-long mural painted in the Tujunga Wash flood control channel. The mural, completed between 1974 and 1984, depicts key figures and events in the history of California related to diverse and traditionally marginalized communities.

Artists initiate the first Los Angeles jazz festival in and around the Watts community, among them Greg Bryant, Alonzo Davis, and John Outterbridge.

Artists Kit Galloway and Sherrie Rabinowitz initiate a project series titled "Aesthetic Research in Telecommunications" exploring the potential for collaborative performance opportunities in burgeoning virtual spaces such as internet cafés. This project series is considered the first "live immersive place" to share work with a captivated audience across multiple geographical borders.

1976

June: Jenkins paints the mural *The Azz Izz* on Crenshaw Boulevard between Forty-Eighth and Fifty-Eighth Streets for Brockman Gallery.

August 4–September 30: Jenkins is awarded a project grant with Brockman Gallery for the Centinela Valley Juvenile Diversion Mural Project, for which he oversees the undertaking of three murals in Lennox, Gardena, and Lawndale, respectively.

He paints the mural *Transportation Brought Art to the People* for the California Department of Motor Vehicles.

1977

Jenkins enrolls in Santa Monica College to prepare for graduate school.

While attending Santa Monica College, Jenkins works on the "sociological overview" *District F* for the college's administration in conjunction with their Equal Employment Opportunity Program. Jenkins co-creates this work with fellow students Robert Green, James Henry, Randy LeFall, and Leon Robinson.

Jenkins begins filming the painter Charles White for a video titled *Momentous Occasions: The Spirit of Charles White.* Jenkins will accumulate footage throughout their relationship, which flourishes while Jenkins studies with White at Otis Art Institute. Jenkins completes the film in 1982, after White's death in 1979.

1978

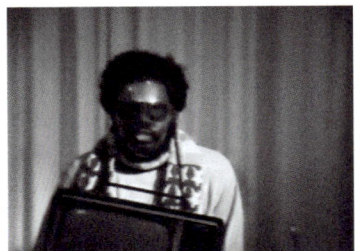

Mass of Images, 1978, 4:16 min.

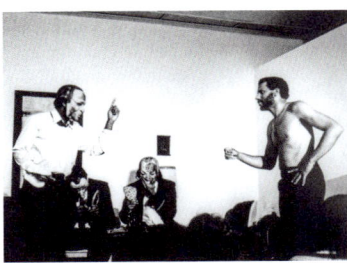

Two-Zone Transfer, 1979, 23:52 min. Performed on November 21, 1978

In the spring, Jenkins creates his first performance video, *Mass of Images.*

In the fall, Jenkins enrolls in the Intermedia Department at the Otis Art Institute.

November 21: Jenkins's *Two-Zone Transfer* is conceived and first performed in a student gallery at Otis with classmates Kerry James Marshall, Ronnie Nichols, and Greg Pitts.

Jenkins participates in the inauguration of artist Senga Nengudi's public art installation *Freeway Fets* with the performance *Ceremony for Freeway Fets* at an underpass in LA with members of the Black artist collective Studio Z, which included Houston Conwill, Kathy Cyrus, Ron Davis, Greg Edwards, David Hammons, Duval Lewis, Barbara McCullough, Franklin Parker, Joe Ray, RoHo, Roderick Kwaku Young, and occasionally Jenkins.

Otis merges with Parsons School of Design.

1979

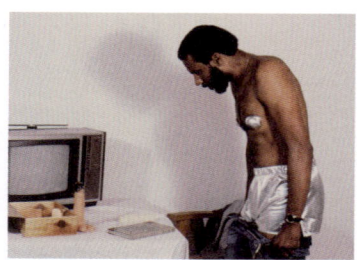

Just Another Rendering of the Same Old Problem, 1979. Performance.

Jenkins restages his performance *Two-Zone Transfer* with original performers Kerry James Marshall, Ronnie Nichols, and Greg Pitts. This video version receives an Alternative Gallery award from the Brockman Gallery.

May 8: Jenkins creates his final performance piece during his MFA program at Otis, titled *Just Another Rendering of the Same Old Problem.*

While attending Otis, Jenkins creates Alternative Media Program, a youth video program that aired on Group W Cable (formerly Theta Cable TV). He will produce a trilogy of videos—*Influence*, *Holiday Greetings*, and *Cableland*—addressing the influence of the media on young people.

After returning from a trip to England, Jenkins accepts a faculty position at the University of California, San Diego (UCSD), where he will teach for the next two years.

October 3: Charles White dies at the age of sixty-one.

1980

Jenkins receives his first National Endowment for the Arts (NEA) award, for *Two-Zone Transfer* (1979). He subsequently is able to complete *Remnants of the Watts Festival*, which he began working on in 1972.

October: Jenkins relocates to Los Angeles after feeling "weary of San Diego" because those surroundings did not give him "the opportunity to connect with the artists of color."

October 13: Jenkins's *Columbus Day: A Doggereal* is performed by Benny Duarte, Jesse Chuy Castro, Billie Harris, Jenkins, and Onaje Murray at Los Angeles Contemporary Exhibitions (LACE). The piece looks at the injustice inflicted on Native Americans and critiques the celebration of the national holiday Columbus Day.

During the fall and winter of 1980–81, Jenkins creates *Inconsequential Doggereal*. This is the first video in which Jenkins uses his "doggerel" editing technique.

HIV/AIDS spreads to North and South America, Europe, Africa, and Australia.

1981

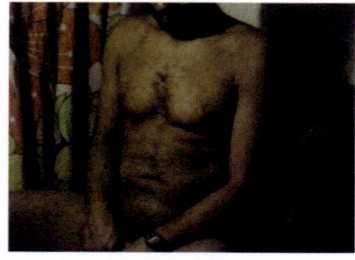

Inconsequential Doggereal, 1981, 15:19 min.

January 20: Ronald Reagan is inaugurated as the fortieth president of the United States and will serve two terms, until 1989.

March 13: In Jenkins's Los Angeles studio (passed down to him by Kerry James Marshall), which he was calling "Doggereal Space," he stages the performance *Adams Be Doggerreal*. The performance is Jenkins's first work to engage an audience with ideas of African rituals. Performers include Maren Hassinger and Senga Nengudi, and musicians Daoud, Calvin Keys, and Onaje Murray.

August 1: The American cable channel MTV is launched.

September 18: In celebration of his birthday, Jenkins performs *Dream City* in Rachel Rosenthal's studio in response to Reagan's election. The duration of the performance has been variously identified as eighteen, twenty-one, or twenty-four hours. Jenkins would use the video documentation to create two video versions of *Dream City* (1983): one five minutes long and the other thirty minutes.

October 6: The president of Egypt, Anwar Sadat, is assassinated by fundamentalist army officers.

In response to the assassination of the Egyptian president, Jenkins creates the performance *Peace and Anwar Sadat*, for longtime friend and collaborator Nancy Buchanan's performance series "Thanks but No Thanks" at the Church in Ocean Park.

Jenkins collaborates with Kit Galloway and Sherrie Rabinowitz on a project titled *Televiews and Cable Radio: A Two-Way Microwave Experiment* at UCSD.

He ends a lecturer position in video production at UCSD.

1982

Inconsequential Doggereal (1981) earns Jenkins his second NEA grant. He uses the award to establish Othervisions Studio. The studio will become the hub for Jenkins's collaborations with a wide range of artists, musicians, and performers.

He collaborates with Jacki Apple on *Garden Planet Revisited*, along with Bruce Fowler, Lin Hixson, Ann Homeler, and Martin Kersels.

Senga Nengudi performs *Flying* with Maren Hassinger, Jenkins, and Franklin Parker at Barnsdall Park for the opening of the exhibition *Afro-American Abstraction* at the Los Angeles Municipal Art Gallery.

Jenkins lectures in the Performance Department at California State University Dominguez Hills, in Carson.

July 30: Jenkins proposes a documentary on non-Western athletes for the 1984 Summer Olympics called *The Emergence of Excellence*. The proposal is not accepted.

1983

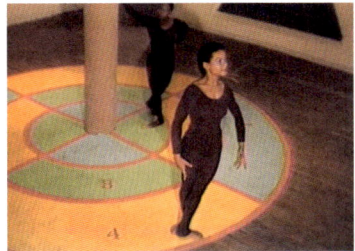

Cake Walk, 1983/1989, 26:26 min.

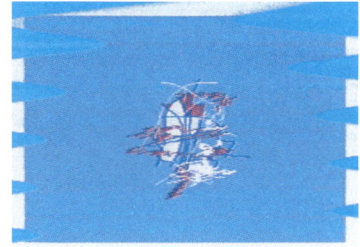

Z-Grass, 1983, 3:03 min.

November: Jenkins travels to New York City to record Houston Conwill's performances of *Cake Walk* at Just Above Midtown on November 12, 18, and 19. The documentation will not be completed until 1989.

Jenkins creates the video *Z-Grass* at the Long Beach Museum of Art, using a Data Max computer and the ZGrass paint program to construct a moving painting.

Without Your Interpretation is performed at the Art Dock. The work addresses ideas of ritual, crisis, and survival, and featured Jenkins's first performance with a live band, Life in the Park with Debris. It features performances from artists Crono, Bob Dale, Todd Gray, Maren Hassinger, Senga Nengudi, Franklin Parker, Reyes Rodriguez, and May Sun, among others. The performance is disbanded by the Los Angeles Police Department, but will be recorded and restaged in 1984 at the Lhasa Club with the addition of Barbara McMullough.

1984

Jenkins curates and is an exhibitor in the exhibition *Perspectives on Black Art: Afro-American Video Art* at California State University, Los Angeles.

March 5: Othervisions studio hosts Rudy Perez's "Art Moves," a movement workshop for artists.

Jenkins curates and produces an after-hours performance series, beginning at midnight, called "Out Night" at the Onyx Café.

July 28–August 12: Los Angeles hosts the Summer Olympics.

Jenkins participates in Galloway and Rabinowitz's Electronic Cafe Network for seven weeks during the Summer Olympics Arts Festival. The Electronic Cafe, funded by the Museum of Contemporary Art, is hosted at five restaurants across LA and allows the community to experiment with varied communication technologies to facilitate creative conversation among people who do not speak the same language.

1985

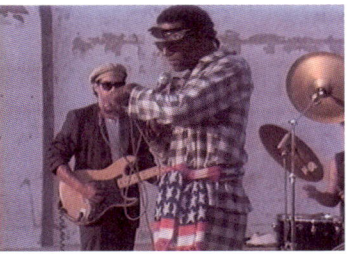

Without Your Interpretation, 1984, 13:53 min.

January 4–February 26: *Without Your Interpretation* is included in an exhibition on West Coast video art, *Video from Vancouver to San Diego*, at the Museum of Modern Art, New York.

Jenkins lectures in video production at the Otis-Parsons Art Institute, Los Angeles.

He returns to the subject of the assassination of Anwar Sadat and creates a video with his band Agents of Peace, featuring Jenkins, VinZula Kara, and Harry Demoss. Among Jenkins's works, this video has the most direct reference to contemporaneous music videos.

July: Commodore International puts their personal computer model called Amiga (later known as the Amiga 1000) on the market. It is distinguished from its competitor Apple Macintosh by its robust hardware, which particularly benefitted video production.

1986

Jenkins performs *Ever*4*Us* at Contemporary Arts Forum, Santa Barbara, with the Othervisions Art Band, whose members include Harry Demoss, VinZula Kara, Alan Nakagawa, Ochieng, and Walter Woods.

Jenkins works as the access coordinator and producer for Group W Cable (later named South Bay Cablevision), a public access station in Gardena.

1987

Jenkins is in residence for video production at the video annex of the Long Beach Museum of Art.

September 29: He presents the performance *Cats in the Catnip* at the Gallery Theater of the Municipal Art Gallery at Barnsdall Park, Los Angeles. The work addresses constructions of family and Jenkins's consistent themes of ritual and the figure of the griot. Performers include Lavina Jones, Senga Nengudi, and Franklin Parker.

1988

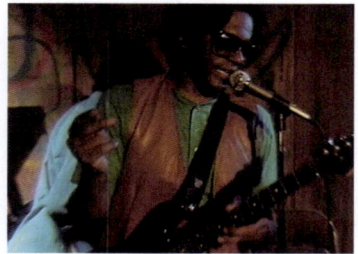

Stinji, 1988, 31:03 min.

Jenkins produces the video *Stinji* as a public-service announcement about the AIDS epidemic geared toward the African American community.

1989

Jenkins moves to Oakland to participate in a gang-intervention program that teaches the youth video production.

He produces *Self Divination*, the first part of his eventual *Video Griots Trilogy*, which also includes *Mutual Native Duplex* (1990) and *The Nomadics* (1991).

1990

Jenkins works briefly as the floor manager for the San Francisco television station KPIX-5.

He is an artist in residence from 1990 to 1992 with the California Arts Council.

Jenkins receives the Black Filmmakers' 1990 Experimental Video Award, for *Self Divination* (1989).

October 27–28: While in residence at the Exploratorium in San Francisco, Jenkins debuts his ritual performance *Bay Window*.

1991

March 3: Four Los Angeles police officers violently beat Rodney King following a high-speed chase. The beating is recorded and disseminated through the local television station KTLA. The four officers are charged with felony assault and other offenses.

1992

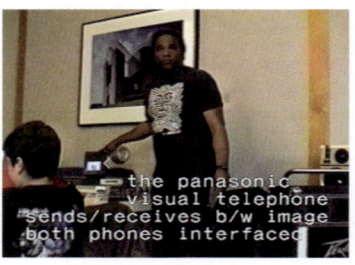

Videophone Day at SFMOMA, 1992, 15:52 min.

March 3: Jenkins presents a series of videophone performances at the San Francisco Museum of Modern Art.

April 29: In the trial for the beating of Rodney King, a jury acquits all four officers of assault and acquits three of the four of using excessive force. The LA Uprisings unfold over the course of six days in response to the acquittals. Three months later, the four officers are indicted on federal charges of violating King's civil rights, and in 1993 two of the officers are found guilty.

Jenkins is in residence at the Headlands Center for the Arts, where he will do several videophone performances, notably *Talking Hut*, the video of which will not be completed until 1994.

1993

Jenkins moves back to Los Angeles from the Bay Area. He begins teaching video and performance art as an assistant professor at the University of California, Irvine.

1994

April 20: Rodney King is awarded $3.8 million in compensation for damages in a civil lawsuit against the city of Los Angeles.

June 13: The bodies of Nicole Brown Simpson and Ron Goldman are found stabbed to death in

Brentwood, California. The murder trial of O. J. Simpson will
capture the city and nation.

In response to the media
surrounding Simpson's trial,
Jenkins creates the video
Secrecy: Help Me to Understand
addressing, he said, the "feed-
ing frenzy on African American
males in the global media."

The State of California
formally recognizes the
Gabrielino-Tongva Nation as the
indigenous community of Los
Angeles Basin.

1995

Jenkins receives a third
National Endowment for the
Arts award.

2000

Jenkins creates the video
Vulnerable, starring artists Kori Newkirk and Ransom
Rideout. The work explores
the weaponization of the Black
male body through a neo-noir
narrative.

2001

Z-Grass is included in *Race in
Digital Space* at the MIT List
Visual Arts Center in Cambridge,
Massachusetts, an exhibition
interrogating techno-culture's
influence on the social constructions of race and ethnicity.

September 11: Members of
the Islamic terrorist group
Al-Qaeda hijack four planes
to carry out suicide attacks
on major government-affiliated
institutions within the United
States. Two planes demolish
the twin towers of the World
Trade Center in New York City,
killing almost three thousand
people. A third plane hits the
Pentagon outside Washington,
DC, and the fourth crashes
in a field in Pennsylvania.

2002

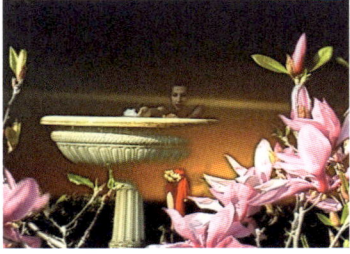

Bequest, 2002, 9:32 min.

Jenkins produces *Bequest* in
reaction to 9/11 and the subsequent war in Afghanistan.

He receives the State of the
Arts Award from the Claire
Trevor School of the Arts at
the University of California,
Irvine.

2005

August 23: Hurricane Katrina
(a category 5 hurricane)
touches down in the southeast-
ern United States with a con-
centration in New Orleans. The
hurricane's damage, including
the deaths of more than 1,800
people, will be amplified by the
federal government's failure to
adequately prepare the city
for a storm of this magnitude.

2006

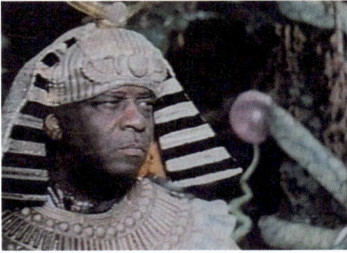

Planet X, 2006, 6:19 min.

In response to Hurricane
Katrina, Jenkins creates the
video *Planet X*, which looks at
the tragedy through the myth
of a cataclysmic event caused
by an asteroid. The video is
exhibited the same year in
the exhibition *Otis: Nine
Decades of Los Angeles Art* at

the Los Angeles Municipal Art
Gallery.

Jenkins contributes to *Side by
Side Part II*, a collaborative
performance by Maren Hassinger,
Senga Nengudi, David Hammons,
and Franklin Parker for the
exhibition *Les soirées nomades:
Nuits noires* at Fondation
Cartier pour l'art contemporain
in Paris.

2008

March 15–June 8: Jenkins is
included in the exhibition
California Video at the
J. Paul Getty Museum, Los
Angeles, curated by Glenn
Phillips.

2009

January 20: Barack Obama is
inaugurated as the forty-fourth
president of the United States
and the first Black president.

Jenkins installs the multimedia
piece *Notions of Freedom*
(2007) as part of the exhibition *Sound Migrationz in the
New Belgrade* at the Blok
Gallery in Serbia. *Notions of
Freedom* utilizes motion-capture
technology and video, and
features the soundtrack "Chief
Concern" by Kei Akagi.

2011

October 2: Jenkins's *Kiss*
performances are restaged at
the Hammer Museum as a part
of the exhibition *Now Dig
This! Art & Black Los Angeles,
1960–1980*, curated by Kellie
Jones. The exhibition, which
includes Jenkins's work, travels through 2013 to MoMA PS1,
Long Island City, New York; and
Williams College Museum of Art,
Williamstown, Massachusetts.

October 13: Jenkins performs
Black Gold/Fever at LACE as
part of the exhibition *Los
Angeles Goes Live: Performance
Art in Southern California,
1970–1983*, which opened in
September.

Jenkins participates in the exhibition *VideoStudio: Playback*, curated by Thomas Lax, at the Studio Museum in Harlem.

He exhibits a collection of videos in the citywide exhibition *Pacific Standard Time: Art in L.A. 1945–1980*, during which sixty cultural institutions across Southern California host programs to honor and engage with the history of the LA art scene.

2012

Jenkins participates in the exhibition *Radical Presence: Black Performance in Contemporary Art*, curated by Valerie Cassel Oliver at the Contemporary Arts Museum Houston, which travels through 2015 to Grey Art Gallery, New York University, New York; Studio Museum in Harlem, New York; Walker Art Center, Minneapolis; and Yerba Buena Center for the Arts, San Francisco.

2013

January 20: Barack Obama is inaugurated for his second term as president.

Alicia Garza, Patrisse Cullors, and Opal Tometi, three community organizers, create #BlackLivesMatter, a political, Black-centered movement, in response to the acquittal of George Zimmerman, tried for the 2012 killing of the unarmed seventeen-year-old Trayvon Martin in a residential neighborhood of Sanford, Florida. The organization has since grown to forty global chapters committed to hosting conversations that expose anti-Black racism within their communities on a cultural and institutional level.

2015

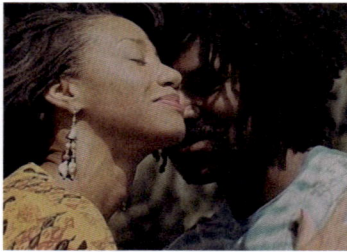

Self Divination, 1989 (Part I of *The Video Griots Trilogy*), 11:56 min.

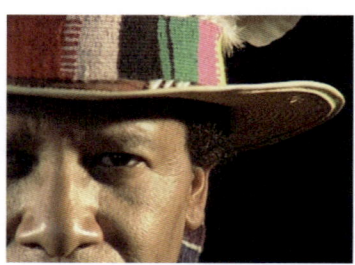

Mutual Native Duplex, 1990 (Part II of *The Video Griots Trilogy*), 11:53 min.

April 26: In conjunction with the Nicole Mitchell: Creative Music Summit at the Museum of Contemporary Art, Chicago, Jenkins participates in a panel discussion with jazz flutist Mitchell, musician Renée Baker, film scholar Jacqueline Stewart, and film producer Don DiNicola about the intersections of music and media as social practices. Jenkins closes the discussion by screening excerpts from his films *Two-Zone Transfer* (1979), *Cake Walk* (1983/1989), and *Secrecy: Help Me to Understand* (1994).

May 1: Jacqueline Stewart, curator at Black Cinema House, Chicago, hosts Jenkins for a screening of his *Video Griots Trilogy* comprising *Self Divination* (1989), *Mutual Native Duplex* (1990), and *The Nomadics* (1991).

May 2: Jenkins collaborates on Nicole Mitchell's performance of *Mandorla Awakening: Emerging Worlds* (2015) alongside her dynamic electro-acoustic chamber orchestra Black Earth Ensemble at the Museum of Contemporary Art, Chicago, as part of its tribute to the fiftieth anniversary of the Association for the Advancement of Creative Musicians (AACM).

2017

Jenkins's work is included in *Soul of a Nation: Art in the Age of Black Power* at Tate Modern, London; his work will also be shown when the exhibition travels to the Broad, Los Angeles (2019); and Museum of Fine Arts, Houston (2020).

2018

Jenkins produces the performance and video *Anachronism* as part of the exhibition *Ulysses Jenkins: Retrospective* presented by the Crafton Hills College Art Gallery, Yucaipa, California.

He is included in the group exhibition *Broadcasting: EAI at ICA*, a collaboration by Electronic Arts Intermix and the Institute of Contemporary Art, University of Pennsylvania, and curated by Alex Klein and Rebecca Cleman.

2019

December: The virus SARS-CoV-2 is first identified in Wuhan, China, and quickly becomes a global pandemic of the coronavirus disease known as COVID-19.

2020

Jenkins debuts, via Zoom, the virtual performance *Good Trouble* in honor of US Representative John Lewis at the 18th Street Art Center, Santa Monica.

EXHIBITIONS, SCREENINGS, PERFORMANCES, MURALS, AND COMMUNITY PROJECTS

SOLO EXHIBITIONS

2018

Ulysses Jenkins: Retrospective, Crafton Hills College Art Gallery, Yucaipa, CA

GROUP EXHIBITIONS

2019

Charles White: A Retrospective, Los Angeles County Museum of Art, Los Angeles, CA (*Two-Zone Transfer* [1979] shown at this venue of the touring exhibition organized by the Art Institute of Chicago)

Life Model: Charles White and His Students, Los Angeles County Museum of Art at Charles White Elementary School, Los Angeles, CA

2018

Broadcasting: EAI at ICA, Institute of Contemporary Art at the University of Pennsylvania, Philadelphia, PA

2017

Pursuing the Unpredictable: The New Museum, 1977–2017, New Museum of Contemporary Art, New York, NY

Soul of a Nation: Art in the Age of Black Power, Tate Modern, London, UK; Jenkins's work also included in the presentations at the Broad, Los Angeles, CA (2019); and Museum of Fine Arts, Houston, TX (2020)

2015

America Is Hard to See, Whitney Museum of American Art, New York, NY

Watch This! Revelations in Media Art, Renwick Gallery, Smithsonian American Art Museum, Washington, DC

2014

a/wake in the water: Meditations on Disaster, Museum of Contemporary African Diasporan Arts, Brooklyn, NY

2012

BAILA con Duende: A Group Art Exhibition, Watts Towers Art Center, Department of Cultural Affairs, Los Angeles, CA

Radical Presence: Black Performance in Contemporary Art, Contemporary Arts Museum Houston; traveled through 2015 to Grey Art Gallery, New York University, New York, NY; Studio Museum in Harlem, New York, NY; Walker Art Center, Minneapolis, MN; and Yerba Buena Center for the Arts, San Francisco, CA

2011

Civic Virtue: The Impact of the Los Angeles Municipal Art Gallery and the Watts Towers Arts Center, Los Angeles Municipal Art Gallery, Los Angeles, CA

Los Angeles Goes Live: Performance Art in Southern California, 1970–1983, Los Angeles Contemporary Exhibitions, Los Angeles, CA

Now Dig This! Art & Black Los Angeles, 1960–1980, Hammer Museum, Los Angeles, CA; traveled through 2013 to MoMA PS1, Long Island City, NY; and Williams College Museum of Art, Williamstown, MA

Sympathetic Magic: Video Myths and Rituals, Armory Center for the Arts, Pasadena, CA

VideoStudio: Playback, Studio Museum in Harlem, New York, NY

2009

Sound Migrationz in the New Belgrade, Blok Gallery, Belgrade, Serbia

2008

California Video, J. Paul Getty Museum, Los Angeles, CA

2007

Artifacts, Pieces, and Bits from the "Intersection 2007 Exhibition," Future Studio, Highland Park, CA

Backs In and Out of the Box, California African American Museum, Los Angeles, CA

Cross Sections, 18th Street Arts Center, Santa Monica, CA

2006

Les soirées nomades: Nuits noires, Fondation Cartier pour l'art contemporain, Paris, France

Otis: Nine Decades of Los Angeles Art, Los Angeles Municipal Art Gallery, Los Angeles, CA

2004

African American Artists in Los Angeles, a Survey Exhibition: Part One, Fade (1990–2003), Luckman Gallery, Ronald H. Silverman Fine Arts Gallery, California State University, Los Angeles, CA

2002

Rebirth Retoño, Trópico de Nopal, Los Angeles, CA

911: A Memorial for All, Boswell-Crowe Fine Arts Gallery, Los Angeles, CA

2001

Race in Digital Space, MIT List Visual Arts Center, Cambridge, MA; traveled to Studio Museum in Harlem, New York, NY, in 2002

1994

Panorama of the Audiovisual Poetry in the United States, 10th Videobrasil International Electronic Arts Festival, São Paulo, Brazil

Scratching the Belly of the Beast: Cutting-Edge Media in Los Angeles, 1922–94, Los Angeles Filmforum, Los Angeles, CA

When Worlds Collide, Museum of Modern Art, New York, NY

1992

Videophone Day, San Francisco Museum of Art, San Francisco, CA

1990

Oakland's Artists '90, Oakland Museum of California, Oakland, CA

1989

1960s Second Generation, South Gallery, California State University, Northridge, CA

1987

Newcomers '87, Los Angeles Municipal Art Gallery, Los Angeles, CA

1985

The Art of Memory/The Loss of History: Re-viewing History; Video-Documents, New Museum of Contemporary Art, New York, NY

Public Domain, Los Angeles Contemporary Exhibitions, Los Angeles, CA

Spaces: Looking In/Looking Out, Installation and Video Art by Seven California Artists, California African American Museum, Los Angeles, CA

Video from Vancouver to San Diego, Museum of Modern Art, New York, NY

1984

Perspectives on Black Art: Afro-American Video Art, California State University at Los Angeles, Los Angeles, CA

Shared Realities, Long Beach Museum of Art, Long Beach, CA

Video: A Retrospective, Long Beach Museum of Art, 1974–1984, Long Beach Museum of Art, Long Beach, CA

1983

Miles Above: Nineteen Return to Otis-Parsons, Otis Art Institute of Parsons School of Design, Los Angeles, CA

Video Lhasa, Lhasa Club, West Hollywood, CA

1982

The American Dream: Mediated, Los Angeles Contemporary Exhibitions, Los Angeles, CA

1980

Festival 80, Downtown Video Center, New York, NY

Los Angeles: The Ethnic Experience, Barnsdall Park Auditorium, Los Angeles Municipal Art Gallery, Los Angeles, CA

University of California, San Diego, Faculty Art Exhibition, Mandeville Art Gallery, University of California, San Diego, La Jolla, CA

SCREENINGS

2020

"Carl Craig Sessions: Screening II," *Dream City*, Dia Art Foundation, Beacon, NY

2018

"Cinema Room: Selected Videos by Ulysses Jenkins," ltd. los angeles, Los Angeles, CA

"Mass of Images: Black Power Era Experimenta," part of the series "Say It Loud: Cinema in the Age of Black Power, 1966–1981," Brooklyn Academy of Music, Brooklyn, NY

"Other Uses," Curtis R. Priem Experimental Media and Performing Arts Center at Rensselaer Polytechnic Institute, Troy, NY

2017

"Written and Bitten: Ulysses Jenkins and the Non-Ontology of Blackness," Human Resources LA, Los Angeles, CA

2016

"Black Cinema House Presents Ulysses Jenkins: This Is Your Future, What Do You Want to Say?," BING Art Books, Chicago, IL

"Los Angeles Filmforum and Metro Art Present *Passing Through* and *Notions of Freedom*," Union Station, Los Angeles, CA

2015

"MCA Screen: Creative Music Summit," Museum of Contemporary Art, Chicago, IL

2011

"Carousel Microcinema: Glossolalia 5.0," The Kitchen, New York, NY

1991

The Nomadics [*The Video Griots Trilogy*], American Film Institute Film and Video Festival, Hollywood, CA

1990

"Afrocentricity: Defining Our-selves," San Francisco Cinema-theque, San Francisco, CA

"Black Filmmakers Hall of Fame Awards," Oakland Museum of California, Oakland, CA

"Festival 2000," Kabuki Theater, San Francisco

1989

"Bytes and Pieces, LA Freewaves: A Celebration of Independent Video," American Film Institute, Los Angeles, CA

1988

"Night in Fullerton," Fullerton Community Arts Festival, Fullerton Public Library, Fullerton, CA

1987

*Ever*4*Us*, EZTV, Los Angeles, CA

1986

Peace and Anwar Sadat, Los Angeles Contemporary Exhibitions, Los Angeles, CA

1984

Televiews and Cable Radio, The Kitchen, New York, NY

1983

"Mr. Dead & Mrs. Free," Squat Theatre, New York, NY

"Shared Realities: A Cultural Arts Cable Series," Long Beach Museum of Art on Long Beach Cablevision Channel #3, Long Beach, CA

1982

"The American Dream: Mediated," Los Angeles Contemporary Exhibitions, Los Angeles, CA

1981

"Images of Dignity, Images of Degradation," Brockman Gallery, Los Angeles, CA

1980

Two-Zone Transfer, Mandeville Art Gallery, University of California, San Diego, La Jolla, CA

1979

"Ten Artists' Videotapes," Los Angeles Institute of Contemporary Art, Los Angeles, CA

"Video at LACE," Los Angeles Contemporary Exhibitions, Los Angeles, CA

PERFORMANCES

2020

Good Trouble, 18th Street Art Center, Santa Monica, CA

2018

Anachronism, Crafton Hills College Art Gallery, Yucaipa, CA (as part of the exhibition *Ulysses Jenkins: Retrospective*)

2015

Mandorla Awakening: Emerging Worlds, Museum of Contemporary Art, Chicago, IL (Nicole Mitchell in collaboration with Ulysses Jenkins)

2014

Improvisatore, Contemporary Art Center, Claire Trevor School of the Arts, University of California, Irvine, CA

2013

Kiss, MoMA PS1, Long Island City, New York, NY (in collaboration with Senga Nengudi and Maren Hassinger) (part of the exhibition *Now Dig This! Art & Black Los Angeles, 1960–1980*)

2011

Black Gold/Fever, Los Angeles Contemporary Exhibitions, Los Angeles (part of Pacific Standard Time)

Kiss, Hammer Museum, Los Angeles, CA (in collaboration with Senga Nengudi and Maren Hassinger) (part of the exhibition *Now Dig This! Art & Black Los Angeles, 1960–1980*)

2009

Quiet as Kept: Change, California African American Museum, Los Angeles, CA

2006

Side by Side Part II, Fondation Cartier pour l'art contemporain, Paris, France (in collaboration with Maren Hassinger, Senga Nengudi, David Hammons, and Franklin Parker) (part of the exhibition *Les soirées nomades: Nuits noires*)

2005

Becoming LA Culture, Electric Lodge, Venice, CA

2002

All-Stars of Performance Art Series, Barnsdall Art Park, Los Angeles, CA

Angeleno Bohemia Cafe, World Cafe Silverlake, Los Angeles, CA

2000

Drifting Next Century, Deep River, Los Angeles, CA

Earjam (eclectic aural resonances), Side Street Projects, Los Angeles, CA

Hot & Sticky: 12 Artists Whip up a FEAST of Performance Hybrids, Highways, Santa Monica, CA

Remembrance Words and Music, World Cafe, Los Angeles, CA

1999

An Evening of Performance Art and Execution Funk, Track 16 Gallery, Santa Monica, CA

1994

Help Me to Understand, videophone installation virtual ritual, Headlands Center for the Arts, San Francisco, CA

The Video Griots Trilogy, videophone events and screening, Banff Center for Arts and Creativity, Alberta, Canada

1993

Call & Response, videoconference calls between the Brand Library, Glendale, CA; KAOS Gallery Los Angeles, CA; and Electronic Cafe, Santa Monica, CA

1992

Talking Hut, videophone performance, Headlands Center for the Arts, San Francisco, CA, with Daniel Martinez on the Fourth Street Bridge, Los Angeles, CA

1990

Bay Window, Exploratorium, San Francisco, CA

1989

Beating the Bush, San Francisco Art Institute, San Francisco, CA (in collaboration with Othervisions Art Band)

1988

Inn Keeping: HOPE, Los Angeles Municipal Art Gallery, Los Angeles, CA

1987

Cats in the Catnip, Los Angeles Municipal Art Gallery, Los Angeles, CA (as part of the exhibition *Newcomers '87* in collaboration with Othervisions Art Band)

Cats in the Catnip, Japanese American Cultural & Community Center, Los Angeles, CA (as part of Fringe Festival in collaboration with Othervisions Art Band)

Cats in the Catnip, Lhasa Club, West Hollywood, CA (as part of the exhibition *Shredding Party* in collaboration with Othervisions Art Band)

1986

*Ever*4*Us*, Contemporary Arts Forum, Santa Barbara, CA

The Great Wall or How Red Is My China?, Los Angeles Contemporary Exhibitions, Los Angeles, CA (May Sun in collaboration with Jack Slater, Tom Recchion, Ulysses Jenkins)

1984

Without Your Interpretation n.2 with Life in the Park with Debris, Lhasa Club, West Hollywood, CA

1983

Without Your Interpretation with Life in the Park with Debris, Art Dock, curator Carl Davis, Los Angeles, CA

1982

Flying, Barnsdall Park, Los Angeles Municipal Art Gallery (in collaboration with Maren Hassinger, Senga Nengudi, and Franklin Parker, with Juana Nash, Lofty Amono, "Nastyee," and N'Dugu Jungles)

Garden Planet Revisited, Espace DbD, Los Angeles (Jacki Apple in collaboration with Bruce Fowler, Lin Hixson, Ann Homeler, Martin Kersels, and Ulysses Jenkins)

1981

Adams Be Doggereal, artist's studio, Los Angeles, CA

Dream City, Espace DdD, Los Angeles, CA

Peace and Anwar Sadat, The Church in Ocean Park, Santa Monica, CA (as part of performance event "Thanks but No Thanks")

1980

Columbus Day: A Doggereal, Los Angeles Contemporary Exhibitions, Los Angeles, CA

1979

Just Another Rendering of the Same Old Problem, Otis Art Institute of Parsons School of Design, Los Angeles, CA

"The Mexican Tape," collaboration (actor) with Jacki Apple, Vanguard Gallery, Los Angeles, CA

1978

Two-Zone Transfer, Otis Art Institute of Parsons School of Design, Los Angeles, CA (in collaboration with Kerry James Marshall, Ronnie Nichols, Greg Pitts, and Roger Trammell)

1977

"Confess," collaboration (actor) in performance by Sheila Orvis at the Woman's Building and the Los Angeles Municipal Art Gallery, Los Angeles, CA

MURALS

1978

The Great Wall of Los Angeles, conceived by Judith F. Baca with SPARC and located on the west wall of the Tujunga Wash flood control channel in the North Hollywood area of Los Angeles, CA

1976

The Azz Izz, Crenshaw Boulevard between 48th and 58th Streets, Los Angeles, CA 90043, commissioned by Brockman Gallery, Los Angeles, CA

Transportation Brought Art to the People, 3500 South Hope Street, Los Angeles, CA 90007, commissioned by California Department of Motor Vehicles, Los Angeles Citywide Mural Program

1974

Latter Rain, 413 Kawailoa Road, Kailua-Kona, HI 96734, Buzz's Original Steak House, commissioned by Komohana Artist Association

1973

Venice Pavilion: The History of Venice Murals, Windward Avenue and Ocean Front Walk, Venice, CA

1972

Rat Trap, Rose Avenue and Ocean Front Walk, Venice, CA

COMMUNITY PROJECTS

1993

Video Van Program, Mayor's Office Gang Prevention Program, San Francisco, CA

1992

Video Van Program, Mayor's Office Gang Prevention Program, San Francisco, CA

1990

Video Van Program, Mayor's Office Gang Prevention Program, San Francisco, CA

1973

KVST-TV, Viewer Sponsored Television Foundation, Hollywood, CA

Theta Cable TV Public Access Program, Santa Monica, CA

Watts Summer Festival and Parade, Los Angeles, CA

1972

Video Venice News Community Communications, Venice, CA

Watts Summer Festival and Parade, Los Angeles, CA

1971

Watts Summer Festival and Parade, Los Angeles, CA

DISCOGRAPHY
AND
VIDEOGRAPHY

DISCOGRAPHY

All recordings are by the Othervisions Art Band. Albums are listed in chronological order by release date.

Cats 'n' the Catnip
(Self-published, 1987)
Featuring: Michael Delgado, HASSAN, Ulysses Jenkins, VinZula Kara, Mark "STEW" Stewart, Walter Woods

find a hap.e.meal
(Self-published, 1997)
Featuring: Michael Delgado, Nancy Fasules, George Govender, Ulysses Jenkins, Oscar Del Pinal, Reyes Rodriguez

Serendipity
(Self-published, 1998–99)
Featuring: Michael Delgado, Ulysses Jenkins, Oscar del Pinal, Reyes Rodriguez, Brett Wrotten

Audio Files–Soundtracks of the Othervisions Art Band
(Self-published, 1999)
Featuring: Michael Delgado, Ulysses Jenkins, VinZula Kara, Nina Matthews, Tureeda Mikell, Alan Nakagawa, Oscar Del Pinal, Reyes Rodriguez

Through a Black Hole Unreluctantly: Othervisions (Volumes 1 & 2) (Double album, self-published, 2000)
Members not listed

Through a Black Hole Unreluctantly: Othervisions (Volumes 3 & 4) (Double album, self-published, 2000)
Featuring: Andre Burbridge, Crono, Michael Delgado, Harry Demoss, Marialice Jacob, Ulysses Jenkins, VinZula Kara, Alan Nakagawa, Oscar Del Pinal, Reyes Rodriguez, William "Bill" Roper, Mark "STEW" Stewart and Rashan, David Strathers, Walter Woods, Martina Young

Through a Black Hole Unreluctantly: Othervisions (Volumes 5 & 6) (Double album, self-published, 2000)
Members not listed

Through a Black Hole Unreluctantly: Othervisions (Volumes 7 & 8*) (Double album, self-published, 2000)
*Volume 8 has the subtitle *The Underground Culture of the Onyx Cafe by John Leech*
Featuring: Michael Bell, Crono, Bob Dale, The Dark Bob, Michael Delgado, Robert Hilton, Ulysses Jenkins, VinZula Kara, Calvin Keys, YaYa Maldonado, Jack Nathan, Gianni Neiviller, Charles Pagano, Oscar Del Pinal, Reyes Rodriguez, Fredric Santiago, Mark "STEW" Stewart, Matthew Thomas, Walter Woods, Brent Wrotten

Turquoise Blue
(Self-published, 2001)
Featuring: Michael Delgado, Ulysses Jenkins, Oscar del Pinal, Brent Wroten

Tudo Bem
(Self-published, 2008)
Featuring: Kurt Brundage, Michael Delgado, Ulysses Jenkins

Improvisatore Songs
(Self-published, 2008)
Featuring: Michael Delgado, Ulysses Jenkins, Oscar Del Pinal, Brent Wrotten

My Doggerelism
(Self-published, 2011)
Featuring: Andre Burbridge, Harold Hunter, Ulysses Jenkins, MaxAyn Lewis, Eugene Mingus, Eddie Washington

Othervisions
(Self-published, 2016)
Featuring: Michael "Ma" Bell, Kurt Brundage, Michael Delgado, Ulysses Jenkins, VinZula Kara, Oscar Del Pinal, Brent Wrotten

Performance-art soundtrack history of Othervisions Art Band, 1980–1994 (Box set of nine CDs, self-published, date unknown)

VIDEOGRAPHY

Remnants of the Watts Festival, 1972–73, compiled 1980
Black and white, sound
55:44 min.

District F, 1977
Black and white, sound
62 min.

King David, 1978
Black and white, sound
17:30 min.

Mass of Images, 1978
Black and white, sound
4:16 min.

Don't Ask Me About New York..., c. 1978 (missing)
Running time unknown

Cableland, 1979 (missing)
Running time unknown

Influence, 1979 (missing)
Running time unknown

Two-Zone Transfer, 1979
Color, sound
23:52 min.

Holiday Greetings, 1979–80
Black and white with color, sound
21:20 min.

Inconsequential Doggereal, 1981
Color, sound
15:19 min.

Televiews and Cable Radio, 1981
Color, sound
11:18 min.

Momentous Occasions: The Spirit of Charles White, 1977/1982
Black and white, sound
19:41 min.

Dream City, 1983
Color, sound
5:19 min.

Lasisi: Ju Ju Funk, 1983
Color, sound
12:50 min.

Z-Grass, 1983
Color, sound
3:03 min.

Art Moves, c. 1983
Color, sound
22:19 min.

Without Your Interpretation,
1984
Color, sound
13:53 min.

Up to Speed, c. 1984
Color, sound
11:02 min.

Peace and Anwar Sadat, 1985
Color, sound
21:32 min.

Cinco de Mayo, Gardena, 1986
Color, sound
10:58 min.

Ever*4*Us, 1987
Color, sound
17:19 min.

#9: Fat and Fucked Up, 1987
Color, sound
27:39 min.

#9: Primal Synthesis, 1987
Color, sound
31:26 min.

*#9: The Last Minstrel Show from
Below the Underground*, 1987
Color, sound
29:31 min.

*Theatré Twenty Two:
Harry Gamboa No Supper*, 1987
Color, sound
25:36 min.

*Theatré Twenty Two:
Juan Garza Royal Family*, 1987
Color, sound
28:24 min.

Stiṅji, 1988
Color, sound
31:03 min.

*Cake Walk: A Performance
by Houston Conwill*,
1983/1989
Color, sound
26:26 min.

Self Divination, 1989
(Part I of *The Video
Griots Trilogy*)
Color, sound
11:56 min.

Drawing to Conclusions, 1990
Color, sound
39:22 min.

Mutual Native Duplex, 1990
(Part II of *The Video Griots
Trilogy*)
Color, sound
11:53 min.

Bay Window, 1991
Color, sound
84 min.

The Nomadics, 1991
(Part III of *The Video Griots
Trilogy*)
Color, sound
12:36 min.

Videophone Poetry Event, 1991
Color, sound
82 min.

Being Witness: Haida, 1992
Color, sound
90 min.

*Documenta 9 Videophone
Performance*, 1992
Color, sound
11:29 min.

*Videophone Day at
SFMOMA*, 1992
Color, sound
15:52 min.

*Videophone Performance
Grand Rapids, MI*, 1992
Color, sound
118 min.

*Videophone Performance with
Kathy Georges*, 1992
Color, sound
114 min.

Headlands Open House, 1993
Color, sound
84 min.

Secrecy: Help Me to Understand,
1994
Color, sound
5:20 min.

Talking Hut, 1994
Color, sound
41:08 min.

Videophone Performance at Banff,
1994
Color, sound
61 min.

*New Year's Eve with Electronic
Cafe and Othervisions*, 1996
Color, sound
32:51 min.

*University of California
Irvine Video Performance*, 1996
Color, sound
102 min.

Vulnerable, 2000
Color, sound
5:59 min.

Bequest, 2002
Color, sound
9:32 min.

Planet X, 2006
Color, sound
6:19 min.

Notions of Freedom, 2007
Color, sound
15:41 min.

In the Midnight Hour, 2009
Color, sound
6:50 min.

Quiet as Kept, 2009
Color, sound
55:36 min.

*Tribute to Dona Zelita de
Saubara*, c. 2009
Color, sound
2:17 min.

*Black Gold/Fever Performance
at LACE*, 2011
Color, sound
6:17 min.

Primal Synthesis, 1980/2013
Color, sound
5:33 min.

*Tribute to Sherrie Rabinowitz
of Electronic Cafe*, 2014
Color, sound
6:59 min.

Anachronism, 2018
Color, sound
10:42 min.

*Across Back Below the Deep
Blue Sea*, 1995/2020
Color, sound
11:44 min.

Good Trouble, 2020
Color, sound
10:54 min.

SELECTED BIBLIOGRAPHY

Baker, Kenneth. "Oakland's Artists '90: The Oakland Museum through July 1." *San Francisco Chronicle*, May 13, 1990.

Blanc, Émilie. "Expanding Doggerelism: Ulysses Jenkins's Artistic and Teaching Experiences." Paper presented at the College Art Association Annual Conference 2015, New York, February 12, 2015.

Boyce, K. T. "*Art in Outerspace*: Gauging Public Response to High-Technology Art." *Leonardo* 24, no. 5 (1991): 553–56.

Buchanan, Nancy. "Ulysses Jenkins: *Cats in the Catnip—Rollin' Around in the Hay.*" *High Performance #40* (Winter 1987): 65–66.

Clemen, Rebecca, and Alex Klein, eds. *Broadcasting: EAI at ICA*. Philadelphia: Institute of Contemporary Art, University of Pennsylvania; New York: Electronic Arts Intermix, 2021.

Clothier, Peter. "*Spaces: Looking In Looking Out* at the Museum of African American Art." *LA Weekly*, October 18, 1985.

Crain, Mary Beth. "Drawing to Conclusions." *LA Weekly*, July 9, 1992.

Dean, Aria. "Written and Bitten: Ulysses Jenkins and the Non-Ontology of Blackness." *X-Tra* 19, no. 2 (Winter 2017), www.x-traonline.org/article/written-and-bitten-ulysses-jenkins-and-the-non-ontology-of-blackness.

Donovan, Julianna. "A Breathing Body in Ritual Ecology: The Aesthetics and Metaphysics of Black Experimental Film." Film Studies Honors Papers, Connecticut College, 2020, https://digitalcommons.conncoll.edu/filmhp/8.

Duplan, Anaïs. "Communication after Refusal: The Turn to Love and Polyvocality." In *Blackspace: On the Poetics of an Afrofuture*, 11–22. Boston: Black Ocean, 2020.

Epstein, Dan. "Between People's Heads." *LA Weekly*, August 29, 1997.

Farr, D. Francine. "Civilization and Nature." *Artweek* 13, no. 18 (September 4, 1982): 4.

Fifer, Sally Jo. "What Are You Going to Do after You Drink Up the Oceans? A Conversation with Ulysses Jenkins." *Video Networks (Bay Area Video Coalition)* 16, no. 4 (August 1992): 29.

Gaines, Malik. "City after Fifty Years' Living: L.A.'s Differences in Relation." *Art Journal* 71, no. 1 (Spring 2012): 88–105.

Jenkins, Ulysses. *Doggerel Life: Stories of a Los Angeles Griot.* Los Angeles: Oreste, 2018.

Johnson, Royal. "Coalition of Avant-Garde Artists Show Work Locally." *Los Angeles Sentinel*, September 12, 1985.

Jones, Kellie. "In Motion: The Performative Impulse." In *South of Pico: African American Artists in Los Angeles in the 1960s and 1970s*, 185–264. Durham: Duke University Press, 2017.

Kinney, Tulsa. "Is Art Dead?" *Coagula Art Journal*, no. 54 (November 1, 2001).

Lax, Thomas J., ed. *VideoStudio: Playback*. New York: Studio Museum in Harlem, 2011.

Lewis, Louise. "Video in Southern California." *Southern California Art Magazine*, no. 26 (February–March 1980).

Mouton, Regina. "Video and Performance: An Interview with Ulysses Jenkins." *Konceptualizations: Community Art Magazine* (1991).

Muhammad, Erika Dalya. "*Race in Digital Space*: Conceptualizing the Media Project." *Art Journal* 60, no. 3 (2001): 92–95.

Ngai, Sianne. "Animatedness." In *Ugly Feelings*, 89–125. Cambridge, MA: Harvard University Press, 2005.

Palmer, Verne. "Taking Art for Granted?" *Daily Breeze*, December 15, 1996.

"Pavilion Walls Graffiti Gives Way to Murals." *Los Angeles Times*, September 13, 1973.

Peabody, Rebecca. "African American Avant-Gardes, 1965–1990." *Getty Research Journal*, no. 1 (2009): 211–17.

Phillips, Glenn. "Ulysses Jenkins" (interview). In *California Video: Artists and Histories*, edited by Glenn Phillips, 110–13. Los Angeles: Getty Research Institute; J. Paul Getty Museum, 2008.

Snowden, Dan. "Maverick Visions: He Shares Village Tales via Videotech." *Los Angeles Times*, July 22, 1986.

Stayton, Richard. "West Coast Tries, 'Piecemeal,' to Create." *Los Angeles Herald Examiner*, March 21, 1986.

"Ulysses Jenkins." In *Now Dig This! Art & Black Los Angeles, 1960–1980*, edited by Kellie Jones, 292–97, 312–13. Los Angeles: Hammer Museum, University of California; New York: DelMonico Books/Prestel, 2011. Biography by Naima J. Keith.

"Ulysses Jenkins, *Dream City*: In the Time It Takes to Show Change, It's Happened; Espace DbD." *High Performance #17/18* (Spring/Summer 1982): 97, 182.

"Venice Murals." *Los Angeles Times*, September 13, 1973.

Von Blum, Paul. "Ulysses Jenkins: A Griot for the Electronic Age." *Journal of Pan African Studies* 3, no. 2 (September 2009): 135–52.

Woodard, Josef. "Aura of Audacity in Installations 'Blanket of Branches.'" *Santa Barbara (California) News-Press*, July 12, 1986.

Xanthoudakis, Rita. "Democratizing Technology: Getting There." *LA Weekly*, August 10, 1984.

CONTRIBUTORS

ERIN CHRISTOVALE

Erin Christovale is the Associate Curator at the Hammer
Museum in Los Angeles. She
is also the cofounder, with
Amir George, of Black Radical
Imagination, which has screened
nationally and internationally.

MEG ONLI

Meg Onli is the Andrea B.
Laporte Associate Curator
at the Institute of Contemporary Art, University of
Pennsylvania.

GREG DE CUIR JR.

Greg de Cuir Jr. has organized
programs at National Gallery
of Art, Washington, DC; ICA,
London; National Museum of
African American History and
Culture, Washington, DC; Palais
des Beaux-Arts, Brussels; Los
Angeles Filmforum; Locarno Film
Festival; Flaherty Film Seminar
in New York; Kurzfilmtage Ober-
hausen; Museum of Modern Art,
Warsaw; Museum of Contemporary
Art Vojvodina, Novi Sad; Alternative Film Video, Belgrade;
and other institutions. His
writing has been commissioned
by the Centre Pompidou, Paris,
and ICA, London, and featured
in *Cineaste*, *Jump Cut*, *Millen-
nium Film Journal*, *Art Margins*,
and other publications. De Cuir
lives and works in Belgrade as
an independent curator, writer,
and translator.

ARIA DEAN

Aria Dean is an artist and
writer based in New York. In
addition to a solo exhibition
at REDCAT, Los Angeles (2021,
traveling to Centre d'Art
Contemporain, Geneva, 2022),
recent solo and group exhibi-
tions and performances include
Greene Naftali, New York
(2021); *Made in L.A. 2020:
a version* (2021); Artists
Space, New York (2020); MIT
List Visual Arts Center,
Cambridge (2020); Institute for
Contemporary Art at Virginia
Commonwealth University,
Richmond (2019); Institute of
Contemporary Art, University

of Pennsylvania, Philadelphia
(2019); The MAC, Belfast
(2019); Tai Kwun, Hong Kong
(2019); Albright-Knox Art
Gallery, Buffalo (2018);
Schinkel Pavillon, Berlin
(2018); Swiss Institute, New
York (2018); and de Young
Museum, San Francisco (2017).
Her writing has appeared
in publications including
Artforum, *Art in America*,
e-flux, *New Inquiry*, *X-TRA
Contemporary Art Quarterly*,
Spike Quarterly, *Kaleidoscope
Magazine*, and *Texte zur Kunst*.

MICHAEL BOYCE GILLESPIE

Michael Boyce Gillespie is a
film professor at the City
College of New York and the
Graduate Center, City University of New York. His research
focuses on film theory, Black
visual and expressive culture,
popular music, and contemporary
art. He is author of *Film
Blackness: American Cinema and
the Idea of Black Film*
(Duke University Press, 2016);
coeditor with Lisa Uddin of
Black One Shot, an art criticism series devoted to the art
of Blackness on *ASAP/J*; and
editor of *Crisis Harmonies*,
a music criticism series on
ASAP/J. His recent work has
appeared in *Black Light: A
Retrospective of International
Black Cinema*, *Flash Art*,
Unwatchable, *Film Quarterly*,
and *Ends of Cinema*. His current
book project is entitled *The
Case of the Three-Sided Dream*.

MAREN HASSINGER

Maren Hassinger has built an
expansive practice that con-
nects humanity to nature
through a range of media.
Carefully choosing materials
for their innate character-
istics, she has explored the
subjects of movement, family,
love, nature, environment, con-
sumerism, identity, and race.
In each context, the artist
creates an eloquent response
to timely issues regarding
our relationship to the natural world and to each other.
Hassinger is the recipient of
numerous honors, including a
Lifetime Achievement Award

from the Women's Caucus for
the Arts. Her work is included
in the permanent collections
of the Art Institute of
Chicago; Baltimore Museum of
Art; Los Angeles County Museum
of Art; Guggenheim Museum;
Museum of Modern Art, New York;
and Whitney Museum of American
Art, among others.

CHRISSIE ILES

Chrissie Iles is the Anne and
Joel Ehrenkranz Curator at the
Whitney Museum of American Art.
Her curatorial focus is time-
based media art in America,
building inclusive intergenera-
tional counter-histories of the
moving image in American art
and researching the politics
of ephemerality and practices
of resistance. She has curated
several thematic exhibitions of
time-based media; recent exhibitions include *Cauleen Smith:
Mutualities* and *Alan Michelson:
Wolf Nation*. Iles is a member
of the Graduate Committee at
the Center for Curatorial Studies at Bard College, a visiting
critic at the Department of
Fine Art at Columbia University, and a faculty member of
the Curatorial Practice program
at the School of Visual Arts.
She was awarded an honorary
doctorate by the History of Art
Department at Bristol University, England.

DR. KELLIE JONES

Dr. Kellie Jones is Hans
Hofmann Professor of Modern Art
in Art History and Archaeol-
ogy and African American and
African Diaspora Studies at
Columbia University. A member
of the American Academy of Arts
and Sciences, she has received
awards for her work from the
Hutchins Center for African and
African American Research, Harvard University, and Creative
Capital | Warhol Foundation. In
2016 she was named a MacArthur
Foundation Fellow. Her writings
have appeared in a multitude
of exhibition catalogues and
journals. She is the author of
*EyeMinded: Living and Writing
Contemporary Art* (Duke University Press, 2011), and *South of
Pico: African American Artists*

in Los Angeles in the 1960s and 1970s (Duke University Press, 2017). As a curator, Jones has organized numerous major national and international exhibitions, including *Now Dig This! Art & Black Los Angeles, 1960–1980* at the Hammer Museum, Los Angeles (2011), and was co-curator of *Witness: Art and Civil Rights in the 1960s* at the Brooklyn Museum (2014).

KERRY JAMES MARSHALL

Kerry James Marshall is internationally renowned for his revolutionary portraits of Black subjects. His practice foregrounds painting but encompasses a range of media, from comics to sculpture, striving toward a literal and conceptual Black aesthetic. Often showcasing the daily lives of Black Americans, Marshall interrogates Western art history, challenging and recontextualizing the canon to include themes and depictions that have been historically omitted, helping to correct what he has called the "lack in the image bank" of Black subjects. Recently, his work has captured subjects as far ranging as the joy of Black love, historical activists, and traditions of abstraction via the Black Liberation Flag.

SENGA NENGUDI

Senga Nengudi's media-spanning oeuvre situates itself at the threshold of sculpture and object-related performance. Known for abstract-poetic work that uses ordinary materials such as nylon stockings, she casts new light on the relationship between work and viewer while critically exploring sociopolitical realities. The assemblage of material and body sits at the crux of Nengudi's work, and her kinetic sculptures become tactile, haptic sites for dance performances by long-time collaborator Maren Hassinger. Nengudi's nuanced practice continues to draw on influences ranging from Fluxus, the Gutai group and Happenings, to free jazz and spoken word, to Yoruba mythology, Japanese Noh theater, and

African ritual practices. The retrospective exhibition *Senga Nengudi: Topologies* (2019–21) was shown in Munich, São Paulo, Denver, and Philadelphia.

IKECHÚKWÚ ONYEWUENYI

Ikechúkwú Onyewuenyi is a Curatorial Assistant at the Hammer Museum in Los Angeles.

LIV PORTE

Liv Porte is the Curatorial and Public Programs Assistant at the Carpenter Center of Visual Arts, Harvard University.

ALESSANDRA RAENGO

Alessandra Raengo is professor of moving image studies at Georgia State University, the founding editor-in-chief of *liquid blackness: journal of aesthetics and black studies*, and the founder of the *liquid blackness* research group that initiated the journal in 2014. She is the author of *On the Sleeve of the Visual: Race as Face Value* (Dartmouth College Press, 2013) and of *Critical Race Theory and "Bamboozled"* (Bloomsbury Press, 2016). Her work has appeared in *Camera Obscura*, *Discourse*, *Adaptation*, *World Picture Journal*, *Black Camera*, *The Black Scholar*, *Flash Art*, *Refract*, *Journal of Cinema and Media Studies*, and several anthologies.

CAULEEN SMITH

Cauleen Smith is an interdisciplinary artist whose work reflects upon the everyday possibilities of the imagination. Operating in multiple materials and arenas, Smith roots her work firmly within the discourse of mid-twentieth-century experimental film. Drawing from structuralism, third world cinema, and science fiction, she makes things that deploy the tactics of these disciplines while offering a phenomenological experience for spectators and participants. Her films, objects, and installations have been featured in

numerous group exhibitions, and she has had solo exhibitions at, among others, MASS MoCA; Art Institute of Chicago; Institute of Contemporary Art, University of Pennsylvania; Museum of Contemporary, Chicago; Los Angeles County Museum of Art; Contemporary Art Museum, Houston; and, with Theaster Gates, at the San Francisco Museum of Modern Art.

MAY SUN

May Sun is a Los Angeles–based artist working in sculpture, multimedia installation, photography, drawing, and painting. She has exhibited nationally and internationally, including at MIT's List Visual Arts Center, Cambridge; Artpace, San Antonio; and the Asia Society Galleries, New York. Her numerous awards include two NEA Visual Artist Fellowships, a Getty Fellowship for the Visual Arts, an AIA Certificate of Recognition Award, and an Honor Award from the Los Angeles Westside Urban Forum. She received her BA in art from the University of California, Los Angeles, and attended the MFA program in sculpture at Otis Art Institute, Los Angeles. She has been a lecturer and visiting artist at art schools and universities nationally, and has taught at California Institute of the Arts and Otis College of Art and Design in Los Angeles. Sun was artist in residence at the Rinehart School of Sculpture at Maryland Institute College of Art in Baltimore in 2017 and 2018.

This book is published on the occasion of the exhibition *Ulysses Jenkins: Without Your Interpretation*, co-organized by the Institute of Contemporary Art, University of Pennsylvania, Philadelphia, and the Hammer Museum, Los Angeles.

The exhibition is organized by Meg Onli, Andrea B. Laporte Associate Curator, Institute of Contemporary Art, University of Pennsylvania, and Erin Christovale, Associate Curator, with Ikechúkwú Onyewuenyi, Curatorial Assistant, Hammer Museum.

Institute of Contemporary Art, University of Pennsylvania
September 17–December 30, 2021

Hammer Museum
February 6–May 15, 2022

Major support for *Ulysses Jenkins: Without Your Interpretation* has been provided by The Pew Center for Arts & Heritage, with additional support from Pamela J. Joyner and Alfred J. Giuffrida, and Lyndon J. Barrois and Janine Sherman Barrois. Support for curatorial research has been provided by The Andy Warhol Foundation for the Visual Arts and the Robert Rauschenberg Foundation. The republication of Ulysses Jenkins's *Doggerel Life: Stories of a Los Angeles Griot* is made possible with support from the J. Paul Getty Trust.

The views expressed are those of the authors and do not necessarily reflect the views of The Pew Center for Arts & Heritage or The Pew Charitable Trusts.

Editor: Michelle Piranio
Design: ELLA
Typefaces: Helvetica Now, Helvetica Monospaced, LL Bradford
Printed by Verona Libri, Italy

First Edition
Edition of 2000
ISBN: 978-0-88454-155-4

Institute of Contemporary Art
University of Pennsylvania
118 S. 36th Street
Philadelphia, PA 19104
www.icaphila.org

Hammer Museum
10899 Wilshire Blvd.
Los Angeles, CA 90024
https://hammer.ucla.edu

ICA is always Free. For All. Free admission is courtesy of Amanda and Glenn Fuhrman.

ICA acknowledges the generous sponsorship of Barbara B. & Theodore R. Aronson for exhibition publications. Programming at ICA has been made possible in part by the Emily and Jerry Spiegel Fund to Support Contemporary Culture and Visual Arts and the Lise Spiegel Wilks and Jeffrey Wilks Family Foundation, and by Hilarie L. & Mitchell Morgan. Marketing is supported by Brett & Daniel Sundheim. Public Engagement is supported by the Bernstein Public Engagement Fund. Exhibitions at ICA are supported by Laura Tisch Broumand & Stafford Broumand, Catherine O'Connor Carrafiell & John Carrafiell, Stacey Burke Frost & Benjamin Marc Frost, Jennifer Otto-Klein & John Klein, and by Stephanie & David Simon. Additional funding has been provided by The Horace W. Goldsmith Foundation, ICA's Board of Advisors, friends and members of ICA, and the University of Pennsylvania. ICA receives state arts funding support through a grant from the Pennsylvania Council on the Arts, a state agency funded by the Commonwealth of Pennsylvania and the National Endowment for the Arts, a federal agency.

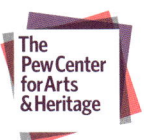

The Pew Center for Arts & Heritage

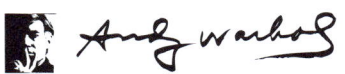

The Andy Warhol Foundation for the Visual Arts

Getty

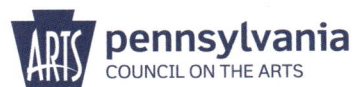

pennsylvania COUNCIL ON THE ARTS

WITHOUT YOUR INTERPRETATION

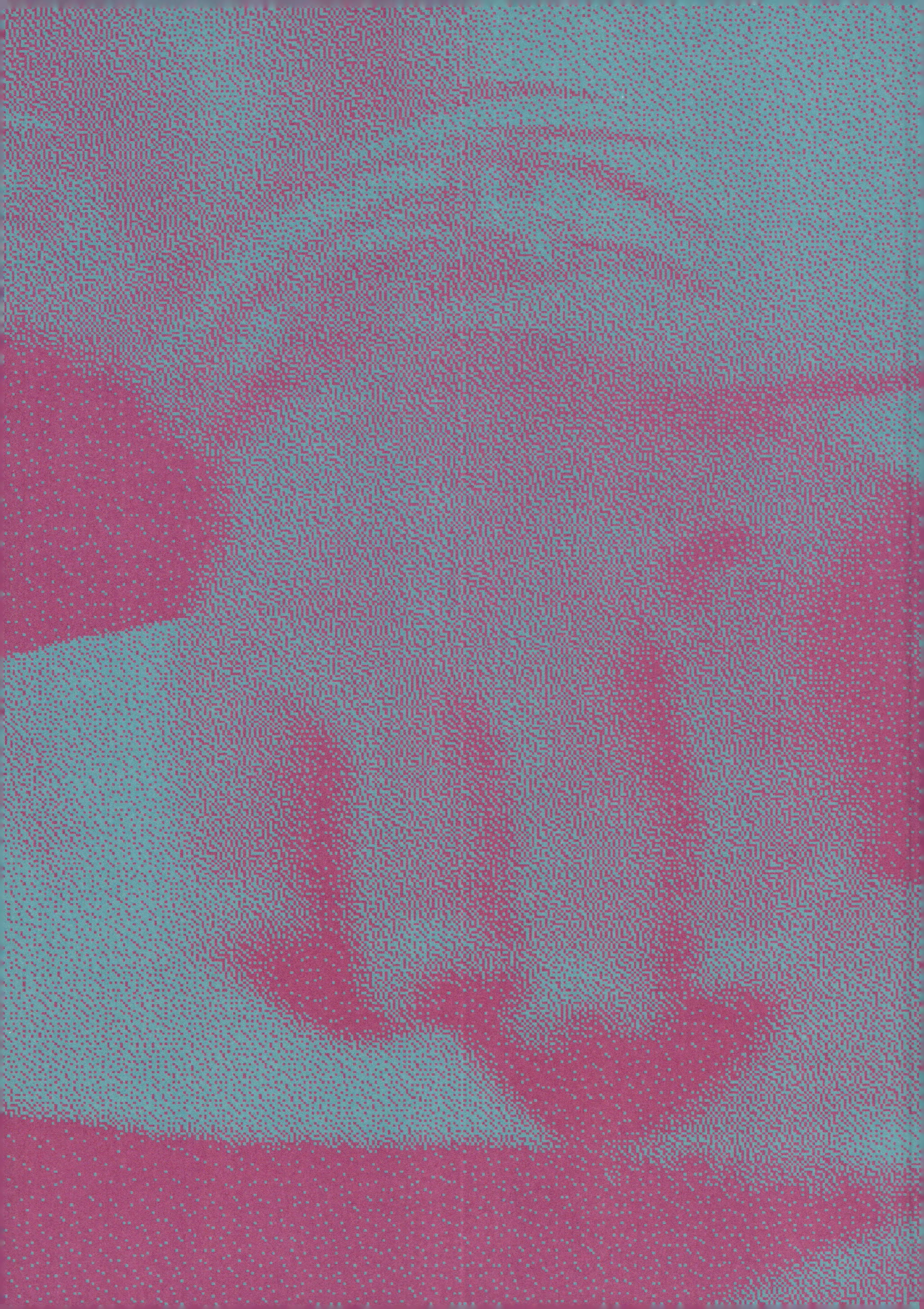